Justice Hugo Black and Modern America

Justice Hugo Black and Modern America

Edited by Tony Freyer

The University of Alabama Press

Tuscaloosa London

Manufactured in the United States of America
∞
The paper on which this book is printed meets the minimum requirements of American National Standard for Information Science-Permanence of Paper for Printed Library Materials, ANSI A39.48-1984.

Library of Congress Cataloging-in-Publication Data

Justice Hugo Black and modern America.

A reprint of 2 special issues of the Alabama law review, v. 36, no. 3 (spring 1985) and v. 38, no. 2 (winter 1987)
1. Black, Hugo LaFayette, 1886–1971—Congresses.
2. Judges—United States—Biography—Congresses.
I. Freyer, Tony Allan.
KF8745.B55J87 1990 347.73′2634 [B] 89–5059
ISBN 0–8173–0467–3 347.3073534 [B]
(alk. paper)

British Library Cataloguing-in-Publication Data available

To the memory of
Justice Hugo L. Black,
and to Francis N. Stites, Raymond G. Starr,
and Maurice G. Baxter,
teachers who made this memory
important.

Contents

Acknowledgments

The centennial of the birth of United States Supreme Court Justice Hugo L. Black was February 27, 1986. In commemoration of this date, the University of Alabama held a series of events during a three-year period, including two major conferences on April 12, 1985 and March 17 and 18, 1986. The first conference focused on Black's life prior to his appointment to the Supreme Court in 1937. The themes of this conference were Black's formative years in Clay County, Alabama; his early career in law and politics in Birmingham; his central role as a New Dealer in the United States Senate; and interpretations of him as an elected southern public official, representative of his times and region. The second conference examined Justice Black's long and distinguished service on the Supreme Court and its impact on American life.

Funding from the Hugo Black Centennial Fund, established in 1980 by several of Black's former law clerks; The University of Alabama School of Law Foundation; the American Bar Foundation; Harvard Law School; the Committee for the Humanities in Alabama, a state program of the National Endowment for the Humanities; and the Alabama State Bar made the Centennial Celebration possible. The Alabama Professional Chapter of the Society of Professional Journalists/Sigma Delta Chi and The Alabama State Bar were also cosponsors. Also contributing to the project were the Smithsonian Institution and The University of Alabama College of Arts and Sciences and Department of History, which provided release time from teaching during 1983 by designating me as a Bankhead Scholar.

I was privileged to serve as director of the Centennial Celebration. My debts are many: I wish to thank especially Elizabeth Black, Hugo L. Black, Jr., and Mrs. Mildred Black Faucett. Jerome A. Cooper and Justice Black's former law clerks also provided continuous support throughout the project, as did my Law School colleague Richard Thigpen. I am grateful, too, to the conference participants whose essays appear in this volume and to Congressman Claude Pepper. The support of Dean Charles Gamble, his executive assistant Gloria Purnell, and Dean Nat Hansford were indispensable, as was the budgetary expertise of the Law School's comptroller, Brenda Pope, and Dr. Robert L. Wells, Assistant Vice President for Research, Office for Sponsored Programs, University of Alabama. I also wish to thank Catherine D. Andreen of the office of University Relations. Dr. Joab Thomas, former President of the University, his executive assistant Harry J. Knopke, and Acting President Roger Sayers also made significant contributions.

The skillful work of the Law School's clerical staff, including Doreen S. Brogden, was invaluable, as was the aid of Assistant Dean Roy R. Wade and his fine staff. I also note with appreciation the interest of Malcolm MacDonald and The University of Alabama Press.

Finally, my own contribution to the Centennial Celebration would have been impossible without the love and support of my wife and son, Marjorie and Allan, my sister and brother, Joan and Jon Freyer, and my mother and father, Ida Marie Hadley and Robert A. Freyer.

Tony Freyer

Justice Hugo Black and Modern America

Introduction

Tony Freyer

The memory of a prominent public figure likely will not endure unless something about his or her life remains significant to succeeding generations. Few if any twentieth-century Americans struggled longer or more consistently to establish the balance between individual freedom and community welfare than Hugo L. Black. The success and failure he experienced as a public official were part of conflicts shaping the entire nation. This introduction offers one perspective on Black's life and times; other perspectives are developed in the essays that follow. First I discuss Black's contribution to American liberalism, particularly his struggle to resolve its internal conflicts. Next I explore the most famous dimension of this challenge, Black's approach to the First Amendment. In the final two sections I attempt to trace the source of Black's values in his ambiguous Southern heritage, focusing upon his involvement with Populism and Progressivism, and his law practice as a factor influencing membership in the Ku Klux Klan. I hope these thoughts and the insights of the accompanying essays will suggest to a new generation Black's contribution to the American nation—past, present, and future.[1]

Hugo Black and American Liberalism

Liberalism incorporated diverse strands, including distrust of special privilege and concentrated wealth and power, checked by a paternalistic government responsive to the plight of the common man and organized labor. But liberalism also embodied a profound

1. These comments are based extensively upon the material discussed in the following essays, though my interpretation of that material is often original. As a result, generally I will refer only to the particular essay or essays I draw from, except where additional citation is necessary to support my own point of view, or some additional evidence, particularly in those instances involving excerpts from letters in Justice Black's papers located in the Library of Congress. I thank the trustees of the Black estate for permission to use these papers, and the assistance of Dr. David Wigdore, of the LC's Twentieth Century Collection. Also, various passages in this introduction follow closely those in my book *Hugo L. Black and the Dilemma of American Liberalism* (Boston, 1989).

internal conflict. Many liberals rejected the traditional American fear of big government for a new reliance upon scientific management and bureaucracy. Other liberals, however, remained distrustful of increased government authority. They were convinced that continuing confrontation between the few and the many—the rich and the poor—prevented the scientific and disinterested operation of enlarged federal authority. Cold War tensions and McCarthyism did not prevent the consummation of Roosevelt's liberalism during the 1960s, when the Warren Court steadily expanded guarantees of individual rights. And yet, at the point of liberalism's fullest attainment, massive social disorder, assassinations of public leaders, and the Vietnam struggle seemed to justify the skeptics' concerns. Black's presumption that human nature did not change and that self-respect was essential to preserving the balance between majority rule and individual freedom shaped his response to the tensions within liberalism.[2]

Black's support of New Deal liberalism reflected these conflicts. New Dealers themselves were divided concerning big government: antitrust regulators resisted the bureaucratic planning represented by the National Recovery Administration, while southern defenders of segregation adamantly opposed federal protection of civil rights. The fight over Roosevelt's Court-packing plan facilitated the most pronounced split when southern Democrats joined Republicans in a conservative coalition to defeat the President. But although southern Democrats opposed the Fair Labor Standards Act (FLSA), they overwhelmingly voted with liberals to maintain increased federal responsibility for agriculture, the Tennessee Valley Authority, social security, and various other welfare programs. For his part, Black sided with the antitrust regulators against the NRA planners, was

2. The material in this section is discussed in virtually all of the essays in this volume. In addition, see: Mark Silverstein, *Constitutional Faiths: Felix Frankfurter, Hugo Black, and the Process of Judicial Decision Making* (Ithaca, N.Y., 1984); Gerald T. Dunne, *Hugo Black and the Judicial Revolution* (New York, 1977); Stephen Parks Strickland, ed., *Hugo Black and the Supreme Court: A Symposium*, (Indianapolis, Indiana, 1967); Bernard Schwartz, *Super Chief, Earl Warren and His Supreme Court—A Judicial Biography* (New York, 1983); James C. Cobb and Michael V. Namorato, eds., *The New Deal and the South* (Jackson, Mississippi, 1984); Stanley Vittoz, *New Deal Labor Policy and the American Industrial Economy* (Chapel Hill, N.C., 1987); Ellis Hawley, *The New Deal and the Problem of Monopoly* (Princeton, N.J., 1966); "Mr. Justice Black: A Symposium," 9 *Southwestern University Law Review* (1976–1977), 845–1155; Walter E. Murphy, *Congress and the Court, A Case Study in the American Political Process* (Chicago, 1962).

one of the small minority of Democrats defending Roosevelt in the Court fight, proposed the FLSA subsequently enacted in 1938, and favored virtually all federal social welfare measures. Unlike other southern Democrats, he voted with the liberals to establish the National Labor Relations Board. Yet, like Roosevelt himself, Black joined the conservatives, preventing passage of an Antilynch Bill.[3]

Roosevelt nominated Black to the Supreme Court primarily because of his effective defense of liberalism. As a Justice for over thirty-four years Black fulfilled Roosevelt's expectations, upholding federal economic regulation and social welfare programs. Beginning in 1937 he became part of the Court's new majority favoring the unprecedented peacetime delegation of authority to the President under the commerce, tax, and general welfare powers. At the same time, he joined in the eradication of the Fourteenth Amendment's economic due process doctrine, which before 1937 the Court had applied to limit or defeat altogether regulatory and social welfare policies. Throughout Black's judicial career he also led the fight to preserve the rights of workers. Ultimately, Black viewed Johnson's Great Society as the consummation of liberalism's expansion of big government, which the Court had encouraged for three decades.[4]

Meanwhile, the Court took the lead in making equal justice and civil liberties central to American liberalism. As Senator Black's and Roosevelt's opposition to the Antilynch Bill showed, the constitutional guarantee of individual rights received little if any support from the New Deal. To be sure, Black and other liberals resisted discrimination in the administration of various welfare policies. As a result, Black's Fair Labor Standards Act, the NLRB, Social Security Act, and related social welfare measures prohibited racial, ethnic, or religious discrimination. But this proscription had no direct bearing on racial segregation in the South, or on the restricted application of the Bill of Rights throughout the nation.[5] In addition, the unequal representation caused by legislative malapportionment—so familiar to Black in Alabama—was a problem for white and black voters in many of America's urban centers.

During Black's long tenure as a Justice, the Court eventually

---

3. On the Antilynch Bill see Dunne, *Black and the Judicial Revolution*, 49; and Roosevelt, as quoted in Harvard Sitkoff, "Impact of the New Deal on Black Southerners," Cobb and Namorato, eds., *New Deal and the South*, 118.

4. See Black to Lyndon B. Johnson, March 7, 1965, HLB Papers, Box #35, LC.

5. See, generally, Cobb and Namorato, eds., *New Deal and the South*.

overcame these inequities. Beginning in 1938, it slowly eroded racial segregation and black disenfranchisement, laying the foundation for the famous *Brown v. Board of Education* decision of 1954. The Court's gradual reinterpretation of the Fifteenth Amendment and the equal protection clause of the Fourteenth Amendment, moreover, fostered Martin Luther King's and the civil rights movement's defeat of massive southern resistance, culminating in the passage of the Civil Rights Act of 1964 and the Voting Rights Act of 1965. Similarly, the Court declared unconstitutional malapportionment, expanded the First Amendment's guarantees, and used the Fourteenth Amendment's due process clause to extend the Bill of Rights to the states.[6]

Black's role was central to this constitutional revolution.[7] He was among the Court's most vigorous supporters of the assault upon segregation, significantly influencing the unanimity of many pioneering desegregation decisions, including *Brown* itself. He also decided or concurred in leading opinions undermining black disfranchisement, and despite considerable opposition finally overturned legislative malapportionment, establishing the standard of "one man, one vote." Above all, Black developed fundamental First Amendment prescriptions enlarging the constitutional guarantees of free expression under the Bill of Rights. He also fashioned the controversial theory of total incorporation, which increased the protection of all citizens from arbitrary state action.

Yet Black also believed that the Constitution imposed limits upon individual rights. During World War II he wrote the Court's majority opinion upholding the tragic internment of Japanese Americans. He supported, too, the national interest over individual liberty where the rights of wartime enemies were at stake. Throughout his judicial career, Black also recognized some restriction of voting rights. In 1937 he joined a unanimous Court upholding the constitutionality of the poll tax; nearly thirty years later the Court reversed itself but Black defended the old precedent in dissent. He also sanctioned each provision of the Voting Rights Act of 1965 except the one requiring federal authorities to give prior approval before southern states could change legal or constitutional requirements involv-

6. The essays in Part II of this volume discuss these constitutional decisions; by far the fullest treatment is Schwartz, *Super Chief.*

7. For references to this and the following paragraph see especially, Dunne, *Black and the Judicial Revolution*; and Schwartz, *Super Chief.*

ing the franchise. Moreover, during the Vietnam struggle Black sought to curb the application of First Amendment guarantees to various protestors. Similarly, in cases involving sit-in demonstrations against segregated public accommodations, he favored circumscribing the rights protected under the due process and equal protection clauses of the Fourteenth Amendment.

Thus, Black believed that personal freedom was not an end in itself. Instead, individual liberty was essential because it facilitated democratic self-government upon which community welfare depended. Throughout Black's career as a Senator and Justice, the balance between the interests of the majority and minority was often disrupted. Thus, Black's endorsement of big goverment's control of economic and social policy-making during the Great Depression and of the Japanese internment and wartime enemies decisions during the War were consistent with Americans' fears that community security was threatened during the 1930s and 1940s. Paradoxically, the rise of Hitler's racist authoritarianism also encouraged a heightened concern for the rights of blacks and other minorities beginning in the late 1930s. As a result, Black also supported the Court's gradual expansion of constitutional guarantees of individual freedom. Indeed, during the Cold War and McCarthy era he went beyond most Americans, advocating a greater degree of individual liberty. By the 1960s the civil rights and Vietnam struggles culminated in a triumph of individual freedom which seemed to vindicate Black's defense of the First Amendment. Yet as Black grappled with the shifting balance between majoritarian democracy and broad guarantees of individual liberty during the post-war years, it was the interdependency of each rather than the primacy of either that he sought to preserve.[8]

The assumption that human nature remained the same throughout all time shaped Black's search for balance. From childhood until death at eighty-five, he studied deeply the Greek and Roman classics and English and American history. This examination convinced him of the truth of a passage he underlined in his copy of Edith Hamilton's *The Greek Way*. According to Thucydides, Hamilton wrote, "since the nature of the human mind does not change any more than the nature of the human body, circumstances swayed by

8. I am indebted to Harry T. Edward, "Justice Black and Labor Law, " in this collection for the interpretive framework I use throughout this Introduction.

human nature are bound to repeat themselves, and in the same situation men are bound to act in the same way unless it is shown to them that such a course in other days ended disastrously." This reasoning also meant, Black often told those closest to him, that the evils of Hitler, racial segregation, the McCarthy era, or the disorder of the 1960s grew out of human anxieties which "had been the problem since the time of Tacitus." But Black was also sure that the constancy of human character demonstrated the correctness of Tacitus' observation that a people could "choose to maintain their greatness by justice rather than violence." The primary responsibility of public officials, then, was to encourage the higher rather than the lower sentiments of the people.[9]

These assumptions were the foundation of Black's personal code. Accordingly, he wrote his son Sterling during World War II that, viewing "history closely enough," there was "much evidence that while human progress is slow, it is nevertheless sure. While we may have a relapse at any time, I think that this country has during my lifetime moved in the direction of a better distribution of justice, in the large sense of the word, to the advantage of the people of the nation." Moreover, he observed, "from long experience in many governmental affairs, I have long since decided that [government] works about as well as anybody could expect, despite the petty political mistakes which crop up in the activities of those engaged in public service. Furthermore, I think we have a much better government than we had in 1789, and will have a still better one in 1989." Consequently one should not become "a member of the Edgar Allan Poe Melancholia Club."[10]

In addition, the blending of Black's experience and study of the classics and history taught the value of personal self-respect. "So long as you do your duty" and "live so as to keep your own self-respect, and keep your head in the midst of temporary disappointments," he wrote his other son, Hugo, Jr., during the war, "I shall be just as proud of you as though you occupied the shoes of General Eisenhower, himself." At the same time, he urged, nothing was "really disgraceful except that which is dishonorable and it is never dishonorable to fail to achieve something if the person does the best he

---

9. Daniel J. Meador, *Mr. Justice Black and His Books* (Charlottesville, Va., 1974). The quotations from Hamilton and Tacitus are at pages 14 and 30.

10. Black to Sterling Black, April 11, 1944, HLB Papers, Box #3, LC.

can." It was essential also to appreciate the "many kind and gentle persons who try to make other people happy. So the knowledge you have acquired concerning the badness of some human beings should enable you to appreciate more the qualities of the others." Meanwhile, he stressed, "be philosophical about what you see and hear, enter into no controversies for the single purpose of being controversial, and be as nice to everybody on all occasions (even those whose conduct you detest) as you would like for people to be to you." Black also told Sterling that, because "individual human beings have many weaknesses, both physical and mental," it "cannot be expected that societies composed of such individual units will somehow achieve perfection over night."[11]

Respectability, moreover, was vital to preserving the interdependency between individual rights and community welfare. To a "self-respecting man" such as Einstein, Black wrote in a memorial to the great thinker, "life without liberty" was not "worth living." History and the classics "proved" that the death of Socrates, the crucifixion of Jesus the "Great Dissenter," the conflicts culminating in Magna Carta, the persecution of seventeenth-century Puritan dissenter John Lilburne, and Madison's and the Founding Fathers' struggle resulting in Independence and the Constitution were fundamentally no different from the human travails which forced Einstein to flee Hitler's tyranny. Yet this same unchanging human condition also meant that the "desire of people to be free from government oppression" was the "same all over the world," throughout all time. The Constitution, he said, "with its absolute guarantees of individual rights," was the "best hope for the aspirations of freedom which men share everywhere." As a result, the government's McCarthy-inspired persecutions during the 1950s challenged "basic assumptions" of the First Amendment, that "our government should not, even for the best of motives, suppress criticism of the way public affairs are conducted," and that the nation's "security depends upon freedom of expression rather than upon suppression of expression."[12]

Black also shared the traditional American distrust of concentrated government power. Thus, he fought to reconcile the costs of

---

11. Black to Hugo L. Black, Jr., January 18, 1945, HLB Papers, Box #3, LC. For a fuller discussion of *respectability* see Bertram Wyatt-Brown's "Ethical Background of Hugo Black's Career," in this collection.

12. *Address Delivered by Hugo L. Black . . . Einstein Memorial Meeting–Town Hall (N.Y.C.), May 15, 1955* (printed privately, copy in possession of School of Law, University of Alabama).

big government—resulting from taxation and the potential for abuse—to the benefits gained from using it to preserve social security and to protect individual rights. As a result, personal liberty was never an end in itself. Instead, the organic unity of the community and the rights of the individual should reinforce one another in harmonious balance. Respectability was integral to this balance because an individual possessing it was liberated from material and social dependency. Rejection of discrimination in the administration of the Fair Labor Standards Act and opposition to the Antilynch Bill represented *Senator* Black's attempted adjustment of majority and minority interests. Appointment to life-tenure on the Court freed Black from the political exigencies compelling this particular trade-off. From the late 1930s on he was one of the nation's foremost champions of racial justice and civil liberties. And yet, during World War II and the civil rights and Vietnam eras, he did not hesitate to subordinate individual freedom to community welfare in cases where he felt the balance was threatened. This was his answer to the conflicts within liberalism.

The First Amendment

The tensions inherent in Black's liberalism were perhaps most apparent in his defense of the First Amendment. Increasingly during the early Cold War years, Black argued for the guarantee of free speech as an absolute right. In the *Douds* case of 1950 he set forth the constitutional reasoning supporting this fundamental principle. Nearly twenty years later during the Vietnam struggle, however, he seemed to retreat, arguing in the *Tinker* case of 1969 that certain forms of expression were not worthy of absolute protection under the First Amendment.[13] Although critics attacked Black, charging inconsistency, he claimed that his constitutional views had not changed. Considered in light of the life-long effort to balance individual rights and majority rule, this contention was correct.[14] And yet Black did not explore the deeper conflicts motivating the search for balance.

---

13. *American Communication Association v. Douds*, 339 U.S. 382 (1950); *Tinker v. Des Moines Community School District*, 393 U.S. 503 (1969).

14. Hugo L. and Elizabeth Black, *Mr. Justice and Mrs. Black: The Memoirs of Hugo L. Black and Elizabeth Black* (New York, 1986), 217–18; Dunne, *Black and the Judicial Revolution*, 418–19.

American Communication Association v. Douds (1950) arose out of the union's refusal to comply with the anticommunist-oath provisions of the Taft-Hartley Act of 1947, the first major legislative setback for organized labor since the establishment of the NLRB. The union argued that the oath violated freedom of speech and conscience guaranteed by the First Amendment. The federal government claimed, however, that the law's requirements represented a valid exercise of the commerce power, which was the constitutional basis of the Taft-Hartley Act. Chief Justice Vinson sustained the law. Black dissented. Vinson's decision undermined the "freedom to think" as an "absolute" right, Black said. "Centuries of experience testify that laws aimed at one political or religious group" generated "hatreds and prejudices which rapidly spread beyond control." He recognized that, like anyone else, communists committing "overt acts" in violation of valid laws can and should be punished. But the possibility that some communists might commit such acts did not justify assigning "guilt" by "association or affiliation." The foundation of the First Amendment was, Black stressed, that "our free institutions can be maintained without proscribing or penalizing political belief, speech, press, assembly, or party affiliation." He concluded that this was "a far bolder philosophy than despotic rulers can afford." It was, however, the "heart of the system on which our freedom depends."[15]

Black believed that the experience of his family members and friends demonstrated how such fears created guilt by association, undermining individual freedom and respectability upon which community welfare depended.[16] Thus, though the Court sought to safeguard Americans by deferring to the government's suppression of unpopular beliefs, Black distinguished the advocacy of controversial doctrines from overt conduct. He was confident that the best way to defend American democracy was to allow communists to compete in the marketplace of ideas.[17]

Yet this powerful defense of free speech did not prevent Black from dissenting in the *Tinker* case of 1969. Late in 1965, three teenagers decided to express their disagreement with the government's policy

---

15. 339 U.S. 382, 448–49, 452.

16. Virginia Foster Durr, *Outside the Magic Circle: The Autobiography of Virginia Foster Durr* (Tuscaloosa, Ala., 1986) 195–233, 307–308.

17. See especially Anthony Lewis, "Justice Black and the First Amendment," in this collection.

in Vietnam by wearing black armbands to school. The principals of the Des Moines, Iowa, schools the young people attended were aware of the planned action and instituted a policy prohibiting it. The three youths attended classes: no significant interference with school activities resulted. Yet the schools' officials enforced the new policy, suspending the three until they returned to class without their armbands. Through their fathers the teenagers petitioned the federal district court, praying for an injunction restraining the school authorities from instituting the disciplinary procedure and seeking nominal damages. In due course the court dismissed the complaint, upholding the constitutionality of the officials' action on the ground that it was reasonable in order to prevent disturbance of school discipline. On appeal, a divided federal circuit court sustained the district court's holding. The United States Supreme Court then granted certiorari.[18]

A majority of the Supreme Court reversed the lower court's decision. For his seven Brethren, Justice Abe Fortas noted that the youths' conduct resulted in no disorder or disturbance in school activities nor interference with the right of other students to be left alone. Thus, precedents concerning speech or action that intruded upon the work of schools or the rights of fellow students were not controlling. Under the Constitution, he went on, "free speech is not a right that is given only to be so circumscribed that it exists in principle but not in fact. Freedom of expression would not truly exist if the right could be exercised only in an area that a benevolent government has provided as a safe haven for crackpots." The First (and by incorporation, the Fourteenth) Amendment said that neither Congress nor the states may "abridge the right to free speech." Fortas concluded that "[t]his provision means what it says."[19]

These were the views to which Black dissented. He conceded that although he had "always believed" that under the First and Fourteenth Amendments neither the federal nor state government had "any authority to regulate or censor the content of speech, [he had] never believed that any person has a right to give speeches or engage in demonstrations where he pleases and when he pleases." Black be-

18. This paragraph and those following are taken more or less in toto from Tony Freyer "The First Amendment and the Conference Commemorating the Centennial of Justice Hugo L. Black: An Introduction," 38 *Alabama Law Review* (Winter 1987), 215–21. For full citation see that article; here generally I provide references for direct quotes only.

19. 393 U.S. 503, 513.

lieved the Court's majority opinion pushed free expression beyond proper limits for two reasons. First, the decision undercut traditional sources of order. "School discipline, like parental discipline, is an integral and important part of training our children to be good citizens—to be better citizens." Following the Court's holding, he predicted that "some students . . . in all schools will be ready, able, and willing to defy their teachers on practically all orders. This is the more unfortunate for the schools since groups of students all over the land are already running loose, conducting break-ins, sit-ins, lie-ins, and smash-ins."[20]

Black also objected to the Court's rationale for its decision. The majority opinion suggested that because the students' wearing of the armbands had not brought about significant disruption or disorder, the school policy was an unreasonable interference with freedom of expression. It was to this use of reasonableness as the standard governing the case that Black objected. Indeed, since his appointment to the Court in 1937, Black had been among those principally responsible for convincing the Court to repudiate that "old test." And what standard should have governed the case, according to Black? One that was consistent with his conviction "that taxpayers send children to school on the premise that [the school is] . . . operated to give students an opportunity to learn, not to talk politics by actual speech, or by 'symbolic' speech."[21]

To understand why the *Tinker* dissent was consistent with Black's well-known defense of free expression asserted in the *Douds* dissent, we must know more about his constitutional thought. Black believed of course that human nature did not change. As a result, the rules governing conduct established during one period could provide guidance during another, and people living today could learn useful lessons from history, classical literature, and philosophy. This logic meant that the Constitution, even though written two centuries ago, was an appropriate guide for the behavior of contemporary Americans. Through provisions like the First Amendment, moreover, the Constitution placed limitations upon the power of state and federal government. Judges were bound to adhere to these limitations with-

---

20. *Id.*, 517, 524, 524–25.

21. *Id.*, 522–24. For Black's views on the standard of "reasonableness" see John P. Frank, "Hugo L. Black: Free Speech and the Declaration of Independence," in Ronald D. Rotunda, ed., *Six Justices on Civil Rights* (New York, 1983), 45–48.

out altering them, and as faithful servants of the document, judicial authority extended beyond all other lawmaking branches. Essentially, Black agreed with the famous aphorism that the Supreme Court was bound by the Constitution, but the Constitution is what the justices say it is.[22]

These philosophical presumptions compelled a thoroughgoing, "absolutist" view of the Bill of Rights. Yet, a serious analytical problem arose because the Bill of Rights applied to the federal, not state, government, and this restriction significantly limited its scope. In an eloquent dissent in *Adamson v. California*, Black, at least to his own satisfaction, resolved the problem by announcing that the due process clause of the Fourteenth Amendment incorporated the Bill of Rights' guarantees. According to this reasoning, the first eight amendments were binding upon the states.[23] He denied that his theory was inconsistent with historical evidence. Historians disagreed, however, pointing out that the actual intent of the framers of both the Bill of Rights and the Fourteenth Amendment was problematic. Thus, Black confronted a conflict between particular values he desired to defend and the overriding belief in judicial subservience to a literal interpretation of the Constitution.[24]

A vital instance of this difficulty was Black's distinction between speech and conduct. Read literally, he said, the First Amendment guaranteed "[t]he right to think, speak, and write freely without governmental censorship or interference." This was "the most precious privilege of citizens vested with the power to select public policies and public officials." Where there was more action than speech, however, Black believed that the democratic system of government made possible by free debate could be subverted. "[I] have always been careful to draw a line between speech and conduct," he wrote in 1968, the year *Tinker* came to the Court. "I am vigorously opposed to efforts to extend the First Amendment's freedom of speech beyond speech. . . . [The Constitution does] not immunize other conduct in addition to these . . . particularized freedoms."[25] Social order, no less than vigorous written and spoken expression, then, was essential to democracy. Unrestrained conduct too easily disintegrated

---

22. Frank, "Black: Free Speech," 14–23; see also G. Edward White, *The American Judicial Tradition, Profiles of Leading American Judges* (New York, 1976), 332–33.
23. 332 U.S. 46, 71–72 (1948).
24. See note 22.
25. Hugo L. Black, *A Constitutional Faith* (New York, 1968), 43, 44–45, 53.

into disorder, and, Black emphasized, "the crowds that press in the streets for noble goals today can be supplanted tomorrow by street mobs pressuring . . . for precisely opposite ends."[26]

But what about cases like *Tinker* where there was no significant disturbance? This was a hard question because it pointed out the conflict between the exercise of judicial discretion and a deference to the plain words of the Constitution. The question arose, given the literalist principle, what was it that under the First Amendment was absolutely prohibited? More particularly, at precisely what point does free expression become conduct not protected by the First Amendment? To be sure, it is for the Court to decide, but it must do so according to some standard, and the very act of fashioning that standard requires judicial interpretation. In order to defend the school policy, Black, in *Tinker*, subordinated the students' right to symbolic expression to the need to preserve institutional authority. He essentially used a balancing test to sustain one value over another. The underlying principle controlling this test was none other than reasonableness, the very rule Black claimed Fortas had applied in the majority opinion.[27]

In cases involving conduct Black admitted that some balancing was inescapable, but he thought its use should be narrowly circumscribed. "[B]alancing should be used only where a law is aimed at conduct and indirectly affects speech," he said in 1968. "[A] law directly aimed at curtailing speech and political persuasion can, in my opinion, never be saved through a balancing process."[28] By making this concession and distinction, Black thus acknowledged the limits of his absolute defense of free expression.

This reconciliation of constitutional principle was central to Black's larger struggle to preserve the interdependency between individual freedom and majority rule. The federal government's McCarthy-era prosecutions excluded controversial ideas from the intellectual marketplace. The resulting fear, ignorance, and guilt by association undermined democracy and faith in constitutional rights, threatening the freedom of all Americans. Black's understanding of human nature and history convinced him that Americans would have rejected the communists' ideas if given the

26. *Cox v. Louisiana*, 379 U.S. 559, 584 (1965).
27. Frank, "Black: Free Speech," 49, 51.
28. Black, *Constitutional Faith*, 61.

opportunity to consider them objectively. Such evaluation, in turn, would have strengthened both the public's faith in democracy and respect for individual rights.

The symbolic protest in *Tinker* aroused the same concerns but with opposite results. Black's presumption about the constancy of human nature convinced him that, despite evidence to the contrary, the protestors' armbands disrupted the objective discussion of ideas in the classroom. According to Black, the students were not presenting arguments which others would objectively refute. Instead, the protestors relied upon silent though controversial conduct, inviting an emotional rather than reasoned response. Given the massive social unrest which characterized the period, this sort of behavior, Black believed, ultimately undermined free debate in public education which was so vital to maintaining the balance between democracy and personal liberty.

Even so, Black's two dissents suggested just how intractable was the conflict within American liberalism. Americans generally supported the expansion of big government to preserve social welfare. But there was considerable disagreement over how far to extend this authority in defense of freedom of expression. Thus a Court dominated by liberals upheld the Truman Administration's repudiation of free speech in *Douds*, but sustained symbolic conduct in *Tinker*. Although Black also reached opposing outcomes in the two cases, central to his decisions was the persistent struggle to balance individual and community interests. Ultimately, neither the Court nor one of its most liberal members successfully resolved the tension within liberalism. Black's enduring contribution was, however, that his constitutional theory of the First Amendment enabled others to reach a result with which he himself disagreed.

The Ambiguity of Black's Southern Heritage

The influence of the South upon Black was ambiguous. He lived in or near the small north Alabama town of Ashland in Clay County for about twenty years before eventually settling in Birmingham, where he stayed until elected to the U.S. Senate nearly twenty years later. During his tenure in the Senate, Black traveled to Alabama regularly, living in Birmingham each summer. As a Justice, Black repeatedly visited that city and the community of his birth until public criticism of the Court's civil rights decisions compelled his absence between the eary 1950s and mid-1960s. Thus, it was not surprising that throughout his long life Black consciously described himself as a Southerner. Yet the degree to which this heritage shaped his public career remained a matter of dispute because the values and interests constituting southern culture were often conflicting and diverse. These tensions were particularly apparent in Black's experience with Clay County's Populist revolt and his subsequent defense of Progressive causes as a Birmingham police judge and county prosecutor before World War I.[29]

Although Black always considered himself a Southerner, he often disagreed with the popular beliefs dominating the region. "Our affection for the South is probably very much the same," he wrote his Georgia cousin amidst the tumultuous civil rights unrest of the early 1960s, "but our belief about what would be good for the South, its people and the Nation, may differ some." Just as southern leaders "failed to give the South the proper kind of informtion," before the tragic Civil War, he warned, "ignorant, emotional or prejudicial people" were trying to convince contemporary Southerners that they could "devise ways to defy and defeat the will of the Nation," as proclaimed in the Thirteenth, Fourteenth, and Fifteenth Amendments, which "declared that there must be no discrimination in this country on account of race or color."[30] Similarly, he wrote Lyndon and Ladybird Johnson that "All of us have a Southern heritage and both of you Southerners have been favorites of mine for a long time." Yet unlike many southerners who opposed federal support of the nation's economic and social welfare, Black said he admired Johnson's "equal devotion to every part of our country and your determination to work towards the national goal of equal justice to all our people, regardless of place, race, religion, or belief."[31]

Black's origins and family background in part explained this ambiguity. He was born near and grew up in Ashland, an isolated rural community located in the Appalachian foothills. Like many residents of the upland, northern part of Alabama, Black's parents accepted racial separation as a matter of custom but resisted its imposition by law. By contrast, the whites in Alabama's black belt, where a majority of blacks lived, demanded the rigorous legal en-

29. For differing views of Black's "southernness," compare the essays by Howard Ball, Sheldon Hackney, Bertram Wyatt-Brown, and Abigail M. Thernstrom–Timothy G. O'Rourke in this collection.

30. Black to Edna Street Barnes, November 14, 1962, HLB Papers Box #1, LC.

31. See note 4.

forcement of racial segregation. It was not surprising, then, that Black's recollection of occasions when his mother and father defied racial mores shaped his own views toward race relations throughout his life. During the civil rights struggle Black revealed how deeply rooted these views were: "I do not recall ever having heard anything contrary to them in my home," he said in a letter to a relative, "and I am sure that my Sunday School teachers in the little churches at Ashland, Alabama came very near to expressing this same philosophy when they talked to me about the Sermon on the Mount and repeated the story of the Good Samaritan."[32]

Black's defense of strong government to protect the public welfare from corporate abuse was also longstanding. In 1962 he provided background about family members to Irving Dilliard, who was preparing to publish a collection of Black's opinions. Orlando Toland, his mother's brother was a "very prominent lawyer in the State of California, and a member of the first Board of Public Utility Commissioners that state ever had," Black recalled. "He started the fight against the Southern Pacific Railroad Company's dominance in politics and was a democratic nominee for Lieutenant Governor in that State when [Progressive] Hiram Johnson took that plank of the Democratic Platform and was elected."[33] Indeed, the political and legal success of his uncle encouraged Black to become a lawyer. Also, Toland's stand for the public control of corporations occurred not long after Black studied the initial legislation establishing federal regulation—the Interstate Commerce Act of 1887 and the Sherman Antitrust Act of 1890—in law school. Thus, the emergence of state and federal economic regulation affiliated with the rise of Progressivism and its relationship to the professional success of his relative shaped Black's view of the need to keep private enterprise accountable to the public interest.

In other ways Black's Clay County past influenced his perception of government. The population of Ashland during Black's childhood and youth was about 350. In late nineteenth- and early twentieth-century America, this sort of small rural community experienced profound economic dislocation. Rural population steadily decreased as expanding urban population created a vast market for manufactured goods, stimulating the growth of huge corporations. Popula-

---

32. See note 30.
33. Black to Irving Dilliard, July 25, 1962, HLB Papers, Box #25, LC.

tion decline, economic adversity, and the emergence of corporate big business converged, threatening the nation's agricultural way of life. Through his father's mercantile business, young Black and his family felt these pressures. Because the merchants provided farmers and their tenants the credit they needed to survive, the Black family and the local farming community were bound together. In bad times everyone suffered together, though not equally. Although the merchant depended on large urban wholesalers for the credit he provided his neighbors and upon the railroads to transport the goods he purchased to sell, he was better able to protect himself by charging rates of interest as high as 50 to 75 percent. Merchant Black further reduced risk by acquiring a mortgage on the farmer's land or a lien on his crop. Hugo Black understood the need to control big business, then, in terms of its ramifications for individuals within this broader social order.[34]

The influence of Black's small-town, north-Alabama heritage was also evident in the ambiguous influence of Populism. After Reconstruction, bosses emerged as the leaders of Alabama's conservative Democrats, including black-belt planters and the state's powerful business group known as the Big Mules. The Populists, however, drew support from farmers who had already lost or were about to lose their status as independent landowners. To meet the threat Populists throughout Clay County and the rest of north Alabama, attempted to join forces with black tenants and farmers. The Populists also espoused both Jefferson's distrust of public authority and the need for stronger government to remedy economic ills and to check corporate power and special privilege. Yet the paradoxical advocacy of limited and enlarged government posed a dilemma the Populists were never able to resolve. The bosses countered with appeals to the Jeffersonian distrust of big government, attachment to states' rights, and to memory of Republican-led federal intervention during Reconstruction. Fundamentally, though, the conservative Democrats proclaimed themselves the party of white supremacy. The resulting racial tensions led to the lynching of forty-eight blacks during 1891 and 1892 alone. Ultimately, the Populists were no match for such tactics, and they gradually declined in influence after William Jennings Bryan's famous defeat in 1896.[35]

34. Virginia Van der Veer Hamilton, *Hugo Black: The Alabama Years* (Tuscaloosa, Ala., 1982), 3–46.

35. *Id.* See also the essays in this collection by Sheldon Hackney, Bertram Wyatt-Brown, Jr., and J. Mills Thornton.

Black's view of Populism was ambiguous. His father was "about as far" from "being classified as a Populist," Black wrote in 1962, "as anyone I knew in Clay County." Indeed the usually loyal Democrat was "so much against the Populists that he would not support the Bryan ticket in 1896 because he felt that Bryan was too near to being a Populist."[36] From an early age Black embraced his father's loyalty to the Democratic Party. "I have taken part in many elections since, in some of which I was a candidate," he wrote in 1968, "but even now, seventy-six years later, the sweetness and satisfaction of that 1892 Cleveland victory has never been surpassed. Which reminds me, as have many other apparently natural characteristics, that I am my father's son." In 1892 Black was just six years old.[37]

But if he accepted the Democrats as an organization, he, like his parents, did not condone the bosses' racial demagoguery. Similarly, neither the senior nor junior Black could accept the party's use of such political devices as the white primary and malapportionment which established the Black Belt's domination over Clay County and north Alabama. Thus, from the Populists Black learned how to challenge the conservatives' primacy within the Democratic Party, for the Populists helped Black to understand the value of a constituency-oriented, face-to-face political style. Their defeat also revealed, however, that in the future only Democratic candidates were likely to get elected using such a style.[38]

The ambiguities of Black's southernness were compounded when he started a public career in Birmingham. By the time Black arrived in 1907, the city was still a boom town. After less than forty years Birmingham's mills and mines had attracted nearly 133,000 residents, creating Alabama's largest urban center. At the same time, nicknames such as "Bad Birmingham" and the "Murder Capital of the World" characterized a community troubled by persistent crime, periodic labor unrest, repeated racial and ethnic conflicts, and innumerable industrial accidents. In order to meet the challenge the city's respectable citizens supported Progressivism's increased government intrusion into the private lives of Birmingham's citizens. In this environment Black thrived. Within a decade he established one of the city's most successful law practices. At age twenty-five he

---

36. Black to Irving Dilliard, July 13, 1962, HLB Papers, Box #25, LC.

37. Black and Black, *Mr. Justice and Mrs. Black*, 8.

38. The conclusions in this paragraph follow the views developed in the Hackney, Wyatt-Brown, and Thornton essays considered in conjunction with Hamilton's, *Alabama Years*, 3–46.

was appointed local criminal court judge and three years later was elected Jefferson County prosecutor.[39]

Black's law practice and political rise aligned him with Progressivism in Birmingham. But the city's and the state's Progressives represented an alliance of disparate groups, including urban businessmen, humanitarians, and rural agricultural interests. Prior to the nation's entry into World War I, Birmingham's Progressives won support for the city's annexation of the suburbs, established a commission government, overcame the exploitive convict lease and fee system, advocated at least some amelioration of racial tensions, and attempted to accommodate the Prohibition crusade. Black's clients and his political constituency were as diverse as the Progressives themselves, including individuals and groups who generally opposed one another, particularly downtown and suburban ethnic and religious groups. As a lawyer, police judge, and county prosecutor he attacked the convict-lease and fee systems and defended injured plaintiffs or criminal defendants despite pervasive racial and ethnic prejudice. But Black's enforcement of prohibition and the preference for the new suburban, evangelical Protestant majority it represented as a result of annexation and commission government eventually undercut his political base. Opposed by both Birmingham's social elite and bosses, he joined the Army during World War I, and following the Armistice practiced law until 1926.[40]

During his tenure as a public official Black recognized and enforced the community's conviction that individual accountability and social welfare were interdependent. As a police court judge he defended popular sentiments regarding personal conduct and community solidarity. In so doing he pursued one of the Progressives' leading causes—the attack upon the fee system. A muckraking Progressive journal revealed that a Jefferson County sheriff's taking of fees that properly were designated for the prisoners' meals reputedly earned him $80,000 annually. At the same time Progressives advocated greater government efficiency in the enforcement of vagrancy laws. Those hurt most by the fee system and the vagrancy laws were blacks. Judge Black's conduct as police judge reflected these values

39. *Id.*; and especially Carl V. Harris, *Political Power in Birmingham, 1871–1921* (Knoxville, Tenn., 1977).

40. *Id.*; see also Paul Murphy, "The Early Social and Political Philosophy of Hugo Black: Liquor as a Test Case, " in this collection. For the disparate character of the Progressives see Sheldon Hackney, *Populism to Progressivism in Alabama* (Princeton, N.J., 1969).

and interests: he attacked the fee system but he also faithfully enforced the vagrancy laws.[41]

At the same time many of Birmingham's respectable citizens opposed the convict-lease system. It was common for counties to lease convicts to private businesses, particularly corporations. Lacking an adequate tax base for prisoner support, local governments shifted food, shelter, and discipline costs to private enterprise which in return received cheap labor. The system was also characterized by considerable brutality. Yet since most prisoners were poor blacks, and the populace resisted raising taxes to support a race unfairly stigmatized as criminal by nature, the system persisted. The abuse inherent in the system, however, undermined respect for law and order upon which white business leaders depended to preserve peace within the black community. In addition, white labor groups resisted convict-leasing because it created unfair competition with free workers, threatening their livelihood and independence. The system thus embodied the tensions inherent in the interplay between race relations and the community's commitment to respectability. Although many whites regarded blacks as inferior, orderly free black employees nonetheless were essential to Birmingham's general welfare. And Black supported the ambiguous Progressive cause as the President of the Alabama Anti–Convict Lease Association.[42]

Black's rural Alabama roots and involvement in Birmingham Progressivism prepared him for the conflicts within liberalism. Like other southerners who supported Roosevelt's New Deal, he favored expanded government to check the growth of big business. In addition, he shared with many southern progressives another belief which subsequently influenced the New Deal: that the preservation of social welfare was an appropriate responsibility of government, though the scope of such a duty was much disputed. This reliance upon more expansive public authority, however, did not extend to the defense of racial justice or minority rights per se. And yet, Black's Clay County family heritage, and the Progressives' support for at least some equality under law as shown in the battle against the fee and convict-lease system, was consistent with his support for the repudiation of discrimination in the administration of various New

---

41. See note 39.
42. Harris, *Political Power in Birmingham*, 210.

Deal social programs.

Underlying the continuity of these values was Black's belief in unchanging human nature and the absolute conviction that maintaining the balance between stable community relations and personal liberty depended upon preserving self respect. Yet enlarged government not only increased the means of encouraging respectability but also threatened it because of the potential for abuse. Not surprisingly, Black's attempt to resolve this conflict drew upon the same ambiguous southern heritage which had shaped his support for liberalism in the first place.

Lawyer and Klansman

Undoubtedly the most famous symbol of the ambiguous character of Black's southern heritage was his short-lived membership in the Ku Klux Klan. Clearly, this affiliation arose in part out of political exigencies involving Prohibition and the ethnic and racial conflicts unleashed throughout the South and the nation following World War I. Black himself acknowledged that his Senate victory would have been virtually impossible without the Klan's support.[43] Yet in and of itself such an explanation was incomplete, for Black provided another rationale for his action which also rings true. During the late 1950s he told an interviewer that "I was trying a lot of cases against corporations, jury cases, and I found out that all the corporation lawyers were in the Klan. A lot of jurors were, too, so I figured I'd better be even up. . . . I wanted that even chance with the juries."[44] Thus, whatever the impact of narrow political considerations, Black's law practice also shaped his decision to join the Invisible Empire.

In letters to his son, Hugo, Jr., Black explained how he eventually succeeded as a lawyer. "As you know, my first year or two in Birmingham did not net me enough to support me but for my extra compensation derived from making insurance reports."[45] He learned quickly that he made more money by "representing individual" union members rather than "the unions themselves." Moreover, the

---

43. For a thorough discussion of the Ku Klux Klan membership issue see references cited in notes 34, 35, and 40.

44. *N.Y. Times*, Sept. 26, 1971, at 76, col. 1 (interview with Justice Black), as quoted in Ball, "Justice Hugo L. Black," note 21 in this collection.

45. Black to Hugo Black, Jr., April 27, 1950, HLB Papers, Box #3, LC.

"prestige" he increasingly acquired in the "community frequently drew business of non-union members and even business enterprises, " he said. Finally, the lessons of his experience showed that a "too highly specialized" practice, "sometimes causes a lawyer to adopt highly specialized or narrow views. This you can readily understand with reference to 'corporation lawyers' but it is wise to remember that 'labor lawyers' can be similarly moulded."[46] Even so, Black's clients were hardly ever corporations. Instead, they included the whites and blacks of all social classes who suffered injuries because of Birmingham's industrial hazards. By 1926 the representation of clients in personal injury and other cases annually earned Black $40,000, perhaps more than any other lawyer practicing in Birmingham.[47]

Unlike the plaintiff's lawyers serving the needs of many different clients one case at a time, corporate attorneys became expert in those areas of law relating to large, incorporated enterprise. A very common litigation involved personal injury in which a maimed plaintiff sued the corporation for damages, arguing that the harm occurred because of the company's negligence. The jury decided whether the facts warranted recovery and, if so, what amount. These realities of practice meant that plaintiffs and corporate lawyers generally occupied distinct professional roles, so that one rarely represented the clients of the other.[48]

Black virtually never defended corporations in accident cases. Shortly after he established himself as a winning plaintiff's lawyer, an attorney from one of the city's leading corporate firms offered Black a partnership. "When I came to Birmingham in September 1907, " he wrote, "I felt no hope or chance whatever of even getting a salaried legal job with any kind of law firm. Now, seven years later, I was offered a partnership in what I rated as one of the best." Yet, Black recalled watching the same lawyer "argue cases for the street car company and other companies defending serious personal injury and death cases. . . . [and] I expressed some doubt as to whether I could enjoy a practice limited to that kind of work."[49] Finally, even

---

46. Black to Hugo Black, Jr., November 29, 1949, HLB Papers, Box #3, LC.

47. Black Legal Papers, HLB Papers, Box #51, LC.

48. These observations are based in part upon my own interviews with various lawyers, several of whom knew Black first hand. Also suggestive is Black and Black, *Mr. Justice and Mrs. Black*, 27–47.

49. Black and Black, *Mr. Justice and Mrs. Black*, 39–40.

though acceptance would have placed him in the city's most influential and prominent social group, he declined. The decision in effect meant that he counted on achieving his political and legal ambitions by representing middling and lower class clients, rather than those from the economic and social elite.

The jury and contingent-fee systems contributed most to success in general practice. The numerous trials Black witnessed in the Clay County court house taught him that the jury was the depository of community sentiments. Particularly in accident cases, a lawyer won by tapping these values; and success resulted in a contingent fee, a percentage of the amount the jury awarded the injured plaintiff. If, however, the jury decided against the plaintiff the lawyer received nothing. An effective personal-injury attorney, then, was one who was able regularly to convince juries that his client should receive damages. Yet in Birmingham, as elsewhere, the law restricted those eligible for jury service to the generally respectable, tax-paying, property-holding citizens of the community. Women, blacks, and the poor usually were excluded, whereas the litigants appearing in the city's courts came from all walks of life. Consequently, the successful trial lawyer had to know just what emotions to touch amidst the tangle of hopes, fears, prejudices, sympathies, and interests "respectable" jurors shared regarding ethnic, racial, religious, worker, and business groups.[50]

Black's sensitivity to the ambiguity inherent in the popular attachment to community respectability and individual independence, learned in Ashland, equipped him for success before Birmingham's juries. On one level this awareness taught simply, he wrote his son Hugo, Jr., to avoid "saying things that may leave lasting scars." When "a young lawyer in Birmingham made a personal attack on me . . . I killed him with kindness. The result was a jury verdict for every cent of the damages that I claimed. What I am suggesting as to the trial of lawsuits is the hard way," he concluded. "The easy way is to attack your opponent with vigor."[51] At a deeper level, however, Black's intense concern for his family's community standing and moralistic education in religion and the classics enabled him to touch jurors' conflicting emotions regarding personal accountability, independence, and dependency. A lawyer, "whose career

50. See note 48; and the references cited in notes 51 and 52.
51. Black to Hugo Black, Jr., February 2, 1950, HLB Papers, Box #3, LC.

depends to a very large extent on his capacity to persuade," should, he wrote Hugo, Jr., referring to the ancient Roman teachings of Cicero and Tacitus, "possess internal wisdom and goodness" if he seeks to "appeal to exalted ideals of . . . [his] hearers."[52]

The case of *Mary Miniard v. Illinois Central Railroad* suggested why "wisdom" and the appeal to "ideals" could win. Miniard, a passenger on the railroad, claimed that the company was guilty of "willful and wanton negligence in allowing a negro woman [who apparently was insane] to abuse her and insult her, and humiliate her." Representing Miniard as plaintiff, Black asked the jury to award damages commensurate with the "humiliation and indignity" she had suffered because of the railroad's alleged negligence. Black thus evoked the vague but potent sentiments absorbed in the community's attachment to respectability. Birmingham's people, at least the sort who possessed some property and sat on juries, feared that industrialization threatened the code of responsible individual behavior upon which the citizen's independence and community stability depended. Accordingly, Black pitted the railroad—the symbol of impersonal, irresponsible power—against a lone, free, and innocent white woman. That is, he suggested, the alleged indignities harmed Mary Miniard's reputation. Admittedly, since a black woman was the supposed instigator, Black's argument also touched the jury's racial presumptions. But since she was insane, insofar as race was an issue it was almost certainly secondary to the more compelling demand that the railroad be held accountable to the community's standard of conduct. What made this particularly true was the fact that a railroad corporation, much more than an insane black woman, had the means to pay damages.[53] Black won the case.

A case involving black plaintiff Willie Morton suggested how complex were the community's attitudes concerning race. Morton was a convict held twenty-two days beyond his prison sentence as a worker for a Birmingham steel company. He turned to Black to win release from the corporation which in fact held him unlawfully, but the case touched the larger issue of the convict lease system. More particularly, the failure to hold corporations and public officials accountable for clear violations of the law—such as keeping Willie Morton three

52. *Id.*, November 29, 1949.

53. *Mary Miniard v. Walker D. Hines as Director General of Railroads, Transcript of Record*, HLB Legal Papers, Box #3, LC.

weeks beyond his lawful term of imprisonment—encouraged community instability associated with race and class conflict. The jury decided in Morton's favor, awarding $137.50 in damages, and Black and his partner received half.[54]

The *Miniard* and *Morton* cases were typical of hundreds that Black won. Ironically, his willingness to represent all groups resulted in defending the cause of the Ku Klux Klan. As long as Black practiced law before Birmingham juries he consistently won cases involving Jews, Catholics, and blacks. He triumphed even though the city's jurors came from the same white, Protestant, middle- and upper-class citizenry who shared the klan's values. When, moreover, Black defended whites possessing those same values the jury also favored his side. The most famous instance of this was Black's successful defense of Edwin R. Stephenson, a Protestant pastor of uncertain official standing, who shot and killed Father James E. Coyle in broad daylight on the front porch of the Catholic priest's rectory, not far from the Birmingham courthouse. After shooting the unarmed Coyle, Stephenson turned himself in and confessed to the city's police chief. The attack followed Coyle's conduct of a marriage ceremony between Stephenson's daughter and a Puerto Rican. Coinciding with the klan's mounting terrorist campaign against ethnic and racial minorities, the trial and Black's defense aroused emotions in Birmingham and throughout the state. Black was also undoubtedly aware that members of the jury were klansmen, and Black won Stephenson's acquittal.[55]

Black's involvement with the Klan was not insignificant. In response to the social tensions pervading Alabama and the rest of the nation the Klan's influence had steadily increased during the early 1920s. In Alabama, moreover, the klan and Prohibition became virtually synonymous; according to newspaper reports it was "hard to tell where the [Anti-Saloon] League ends and the Klan begins." Meanwhile the organization's clandestine whippings, burnings, and attacks upon the innocent mounted. Publicly, however, its spokesmen disclaimed the violence in order to recruit new members not only from the white Protestant laboring classes, but also among respectable professionals. Gradually, Black realized that since he was the candidate of neither the Democratic party's bosses nor the political

54. Hamilton, *Alabama Years*, 32–33; Black and Black *Mr. Justice and Mrs. Black*, 35–36.
55. Hamilton, *Alabama Years*, 85–87, 89–90, 92–94.

elite, his election to statewide office was impossible without klan affiliation. As a result, in 1923, while condemning violence, he nonetheless took the eternal oath of loyalty to the Invisible Empire.[56] At a public klan gathering after his election in 1926 Black admitted that without his fairly extensive klan activity over the intervening years he "would not have been called, " even by his "enemies, " a U.S. Senator from Alabama. Yet Black had secretly resigned from the organization the year before, and once he took his Senate seat, he increasingly repudiated the Invisible Empire.[57]

Thus, simple political expediency alone did not explain Black's association with the Ku Klux Klan. His livelihood and remarkable success as a plaintiff's lawyer depended upon the understanding of and appeal to the values shared by Birmingham's juries. Meanwhile, during the immediate post-war years the causes of Prohibition and the Invisible Empire became linked. Respectable white Protestants made up the rank and file of both movements, and they were also the same people sitting in the community's courts as jurors. It was a tribute to Black's lawyerly skill that he was able consistently to win favorable verdicts from these very citizens even for clients such as Willie Morton. But this was possible essentially because he persuaded jurors to subordinate their ethnic and racial prejudices to the broader attachment to respectability. When, however, individual and community self-respect reinforced prejudice itself, as in the Stephenson case, Black's response was predictable. Since Black had the support of neither the established political bosses nor the social elite, in a bid for high office he had little choice but to cultivate the same mainstream Protestant majority upon whom his law practice depended and which increasingly favored Prohibition and the klan.

Even so, the same values shaped Black's repudiation of the klan. The Invisible Empire's influence faded once respectable citizens realized that its violence undermined the very social stability and self respect it purported to defend. In addition, as it became apparent that the economic dislocation of the Great Depression posed a greater danger to community and individual welfare than did the consumption of alcohol, the Prohibition crusade also declined. Black had always supported individual rights as essential, primarily be-

---

56. The quote is from J. Mills Thornton III, "Hugo Black and the Golden Age, " 36 *Alabama Law Review* (Spring 1985), note 13, at 905. Thornton's article and that by Murphy, "Liquor on a Test Case, " in this collection explore the Prohibition-KKK nexus.

57. Hamilton, *Alabama Years*, 137, as quoted.

cause of their relationship to the wider social order. Once the public felt threatened by that which it formerly had trusted, Black sought to reassert the balance between personal liberty and majority rule.

Conclusion

Black's public career reflected the tensions of modern America. From the late nineteenth century on, the nation's industrial preeminence existed amidst social inequities, racial injustice, and the loss of personal independence. Populists, Progressives, and New Deal liberals supported greater federal authority to meet this challenge. But despite the political triumph of Roosevelt's liberalism, Americans disagreed over the extent to which big government's protection of social welfare and increased defense of individual rights were reconcilable. The ambiguities of Black's southern heritage, and legal and political experience, shaped Black's approach to liberalism. Unlike those who emphasized the primacy of either majority rule or individual freedom, Black struggled to maintain the interdependency of both. The certainty that human nature remained constant throughout time sustained the conviction that he could establish the appropriate balance. As a lawyer, elected official, and Justice of the Supreme Court Black often failed to gain enough popular support to fulfill his vision. What endured from a life devoted to this struggle, however, were constitutional principles and personal values which provided the means to achieve the goal in the future.

I.
The Alabama Years, 1886-1937

JUSTICE HUGO L. BLACK: A MAGNIFICENT PRODUCT OF THE SOUTH

*Howard Ball**

I. Black's Southern Heritage

Hugo Black was a magnificent product of the South. He was born on February 27, 1886, in a log cabin in rural Clay County, Alabama. Named after two well-known Frenchmen, Victor Hugo and the fabled Marquis de La Fayette, Black was the eighth and last child of Martha and William Black. His family, Black later recalled, arrived from Georgia in the early nineteenth century. He noted proudly: "My relatives, my ancestors were all, without exception, on the Southern side [in the Civil War] . . . . [M]y father himself, at fifteen years of age, ran away from home to join the Confederate Army."[1] Fifty-one years later, in 1937, Black was appointed to the United States Supreme Court, where he served for thirty-four years. In September 1971, at the age of 85, he was hospitalized because of an incapacitating stroke, and he sadly resigned his seat.[2] A few days later, September 25, 1971, this gentle, yet steely, southerner was dead, and an elemental force in American jurisprudence was gone from the High Bench.

Black's roots were sunk deeply in the red clay of the Alabama

---

* Dean and Professor of Political Science, College of Social and Behavioral Science, University of Utah. B.A. 1960, CUNY-Hunter College; Ph. D. 1970, Rutgers University. The author originally prepared this Article for delivery at the Annual Southern Political Science Association meeting, November 1984, Savannah, Georgia. The author delivered excerpts from this Article and other remarks during this symposium.

1. Black, *There Is a South of Union and Freedom*, 2 GA. L. REV. 10, 15 (1967).

2. For a comprehensive view of Black's Alabama period, see V. HAMILTON, HUGO BLACK: THE ALABAMA YEARS (1972). The authors of a 1979 book on the Burger Court noted that Black "kept on his desk a small card bearing the exact lengths of service of John Marshall and Stephen J. Field. Both had served thirty-four terms and [Black] would surpass both in a few months." B. WOODWARD & S. ARMSTRONG, THE BRETHREN: INSIDE THE SUPREME COURT 139 (1979). "He had resisted Warren's and then Douglas's hints that he resign, and he had done his best to ignore Harlan's remarks that perhaps they both had stayed on too long." *Id.*

hill country of the "other South"—the newly emergent industrial South of Birmingham, Alabama. Black's "Southern heritage . . . left him with vivid memories of what hard-core poverty is really like, and his ears still [rang] with the heady prescriptions of Populist orators as to what needed to be done."[3] He was born into poverty and was surrounded by racism, frontier individualism, and Populism. The grim poverty he saw as a child was the paradoxical heritage of the South. Richest in natural resources, yet poorest in venture capital, this region had the most blight and poverty in America, and Black reflected the paradox.[4]

Populism emerged in the South largely because of this economic dilemma. Clay County, Alabama, was a stronghold of the movement, and, as a resident of the area and as a bright, sensitive person, Black was imbued with the ideas of Populism.[5] Because of his vigorous opposition to monopoly and his fierce commitment to economic competition and the economic rights of the southern poor, black or white, some of his in-laws disparagingly called him "a young Bolshevik."[6]

His economic views, especially his life-long attitudes about corporate power and monopoly, reflected his commitment to the ideals of Populism. When he began practicing law in Birmingham, he refused an offer to join a prominent, corporate law firm and chose instead to serve as police court judge and prosecutor in the city. "He saw in Birmingham the drama of helpless people confronting the power of the big absentee corporations that dominated their lives."[7] Regarding these absentee, corporate monopolies that so cruelly treated their workers, Black stated simply: " '[I'd] bust 'em up into little firms.' "[8] As prosecutor for Jefferson County, Alabama, Black's "name became anathema"[9] to these corporations. He prosecuted coal companies for shortweighting their employees, and insurance companies saw their less than fair settlements with injured workers set aside by prosecutor Black.[10] As a

3. Berman, *The Racial Issue and Mr. Justice Black*, 16 Am. U.L. Rev. 386, 386 (1967).

4. Durr, *Hugo Black, Southerner*, 10 Am. U.L. Rev. 27, 28 (1961).

5. *See id.* at 31.

6. Berman, *Hugo L. Black: The Early Years*, 8 Cath. U.L. Rev. 103, 111 (1959).

7. Durr, *supra* note 4, at 30.

8. Ball, *Hugo L. Black: A Twentieth Century Jeffersonian*, 9 Sw. U.L. Rev. 1049, 1054 (1977) (quoting Justice Black).

9. Berman, *supra* note 6, at 110.

10. *Id.*

United States Senator, in 1930 he sharply spoke out against monopoly:

> Monopoly should be discouraged . . . . Chain groceries, chain dry goods stores, chain drugstores, chain clothing stores, here today and merge tomorrow, grow in size and power. Railroad mergers, giant power monopolies, bank mergers, steel mergers, all kinds of mergers, concentrate more and more power in the hands of the few. In the name of efficiency, monopoly is the order of the day . . . . We are rapidly becoming a Nation of a few business masters and many clerks and servants. The local business man and merchant is passing, and his community loses his contribution to local affairs as an independent thinker and executive.[11]

Black's economic radicalism was his direct response to the environment he found in Birmingham, Alabama. The city, at the turn of the twentieth century, was a rowdy, lawless steel town. "[G]rowing to maturity in the Alabama outback and beginning the practice of law admidst the raw and still new industrialization of Birmingham,"[12] Black's impressions of life were his Birmingham impressions. Profoundly impacting on his political, economic, and social/racial views, it was the place where Black practiced law, served as a police court judge and prosecutor, married, taught Baptist Sunday School, raised his children, joined many fraternal organizations (including the Ku Klux Klan), developed his political base, and ran his senatorial campaigns.

In the newly born, smokestack South, Birmingham was "the industrial system at its rawest and most brutal and Black's sympathies were with the little people."[13] The existence of a large black minority (about 40%) living in the Birmingham-Bessemer area forced Black to confront the pervasive racism of the era. As an attorney in Birmingham in 1909, he represented coal miners in their first strike in the State of Alabama[14] and defended blacks who were kept in the city jail longer than their sentences required.[15]

A frontier-type lawlessness was present in Birmingham and its environs. Black, as police court judge, county prosecutor, and prac-

---

11. Ball, *supra* note 8, at 1055.
12. Meador, *Mr. Justice Black: A Tribute*, 57 VA. L. REV. 1109, 1111 (1971).
13. Durr, *supra* note 4, at 31.
14. Berman, *supra* note 6, at 108.
15. *Id.*

ticing attorney dove into the sordidness with great intensity and purposefulness.

Appointed to the Birmingham Police Court in 1912, he was a tough judge, yet treated fairly everyone in his court, including blacks.[16] In 1914 he ran successfully for prosecutor of Jefferson County, Alabama. Working against the illegal activities of the local police and the "immoral" fee system, Black believed that "the people were tired of having hundreds of Negroes arrested for shooting craps on pay day and crowding the jails with these petty offenders."[17] Elected in December 1914, his first action as prosecutor was to release 500 prisoners who had been mistreated under the fee system. Soon afterwards, Black uncovered the "incredibly brutal," third-degree police measures used by the police to gain confessions from blacks. Although the Bessemer district was out of his county's jurisdiction, Black presented the information to the grand jury, which adopted his report and ended the horrors taking place in Bessemer.[18]

Black left the prosecutor's office in 1917, served in the Army for a year, married Josephine Foster, a beautiful Birmingham socialite, and joined a great many fraternal organizations. Black "was an incorrigible joiner;"[19] he affiliated with the American Legion, the Knights of Pythias, the Masonic Lodge, Civitans, Odd Fellows, Pretorians, and in September 1923 Black joined the Robert E. Lee Ku Klux Klan, Chapter Number 1, in Birmingham, Alabama.

The Klan episode always was discussed whenever Black's political jurisprudence was examined. Evidently, Black was a member of the Klan for less than 2 years—September 1923 to July 1925. One explanation behind his Klan membership was that a Jewish friend in Birmingham, Herman Beck, asked Black to join to "coun-

---

16. *See id.* In a 1967 address to University of Georgia Law School graduates, Justice Black revealed to the graduates his view of the importance of the local lawyer and drew, again, upon his experiences as a young attorney in Birmingham 50 years earlier. The task of the lawyer, he said, was "to see that the rule of law prevails throughout this Nation. [Black was not] talking about some majestic and intangible principle of justice. Rather, . . . about the lawyer's responsibility to give of himself and his talents in those very ordinary, day-today situations where his counsel is often so badly needed." Black, *supra* note 1, at 13.

17. Berman, *supra* note 6, at 109. The fee system was an integral element of local justice systems in the South for many years. Essentially, officers of the court, including the police, would receive a salary generated from the fines paid by those arrested and convicted by these law enforcement personnel. *Id.*

18. *See id.* at 110.

19. *Id.* at 111.

terbalance the troublemakers who were beginning to dominate it."[20] Black's explanation sounded more plausible: "I was trying a lot of cases against corporations, jury cases, and I found out that all the corporation lawyers were in the Klan. A lot of jurors were too, so I figured I'd better be even up . . . . I wanted that even chance with the juries."[21] (For example, at the time that Black joined the Klan, the Grand Dragon of the Alabama KKK was the Assistant Attorney General of the State of Alabama.)[22]

Birmingham was also the seedbed for Black's politics. He was the inveterate politician; he remained so after he went on the High Bench. After Black was on the Supreme Court, Justice Stanley Reed noted privately: "[Y]ou can't change people. Black was always a politician and he didn't and can't cease to be one by becoming a judge."[23] Reed's conversationalist colleague, Felix Frankfurter, disliked Black for the same reasons and felt that Black was a rural, country bumpkin in judicial robes who delivered "flapdoodle" in the name of democracy.[24] What Reed and Frankfurter never understood was that, in Black's view, politics provided the poor people of Alabama with their only powerful and legitimate response in their battle against inequity and injustice.

After he left the Klan, Black ran for the United States Senate in 1926 as the "poor man's" candidate. His campaign slogan typified that stance: "I am not now, and have never been a railroad, power company, or a corporation lawyer."[25] Elected to the Senate, Black quickly became a champion of New Deal policies. In 1928 he supported the Democratic Party's Presidential candidate, Al Smith, a Catholic, and opposed Tom Heflin's efforts to enter the Senate. Black also fought to safeguard Negro rights in the wages-hours legislation that became law during the New Deal. These actions did not endear him to the Klansmen in his home State.

In short order, Black became "one of the most liberal of the New Deal Senators [and the Klan in Alabama] "was deteriorating into a band of racist terrorists."[26] In the Senate, Black developed a

---

20. Berman, *Hugo Black and the Negro*, 10 AM. U.L. REV. 35, 40 (1961).

21. N.Y. Times, Sept. 26, 1971, at 76, col. 1 (interview with Justice Black).

22. Berman, *supra* note 6, at 112.

23. Noonan, Book Review, 9 SW. U.L. REV. 1127, 1131 (1977) (reviewing G. DUNNE, HUGO BLACK AND THE JUDICIAL REVOLUTION (1977) (quoting Justice Stanley Reed)).

24. Noonan, *supra* note 23, at 1131.

25. Ball, *supra* note 8, at 1054.

26. Berman, *supra* note 20, at 40.

reputation as a congressional investigator with a "bulldog tenacity."[27] Although he later decried as false the reputation he had earned as a relentless challenger of shipowners and commercial airline officials,[28] Black always went for the "jugular"[29] in his role as legislative investigator. His determination to get to the essence of the matter, combined with the congressional investigation phase of his Senate career, created part of Hugo Black's "seamless web of life at the law."[30] As a United States Supreme Court Justice, Black exhibited the same tenacious characteristics he flashed as an Alabama official and as a United States Senator.

Ironically, when his name was sent to the Senate by President Roosevelt in 1937, the angry Klan leadership in Alabama was the group that turned over to a conservative newspaper, the *Pittsburgh Post-Gazette*, the information about Black's Klan membership.[31] When the story broke, Justice Black already had been confirmed by the Senate, and he was on a European vacation with his wife prior to taking his seat on the High Bench.

The story exploded across the nation. The *American Mercury* called him "a vulgar dog"; *Time* magazine uttered that "Hugo [wouldn't] have to buy a robe, he could dye his white one black."[32] When Black returned to America, he went on national radio for about 11 minutes and said: "I did join the Klan. I never rejoined."[33] Claiming that he had many Catholic, Jewish, and black friends, he concluded: "[M]y discussion of this question is closed."[34]

President Roosevelt, on September 14, 1937, told his press conference "that he had not known of any Klan link when he appointed Black to the Court. [Roosevelt declared:] "I only know what I have read in the newspaper.' "[35] Justice Black, however, had a different memory. In 1968, in a private note appended to a letter

27. Gregory & Strickland, *Hugo Black Congressional Investigation and Public Utilities*, 29 OKLA. L. REV. 543, 544 (1976).

28. *See generally* V. HAMILTON, *supra* note 2, at 221-34.

29. Woodward and Armstrong wrote that "Black had always advised both the other Justices and his own clerks to 'go for the jugular.' " B. WOODWARD & S. ARMSTRONG, *supra* note 2, at 38.

30. *See* Gregory & Strickland, *supra* note 27, at 543-45.

31. Berman, *supra* note 3, at 390.

32. Berman, *supra* note 6, at 103.

33. V. HAMILTON, *supra* note 2, at 295-96.

34. *Id.*

35. Berman, *supra* note 6, at 104.

he had sent to one of his biographers, Black wrote:

> President Roosevelt, when I went up to lunch with him, told me that there was no reason for my worrying about my having been a member of the Ku Klux Klan. He said that some of his best friends and supporters he had in the state of Georgia were strong members of that organization. He never, in any way, by word or attitude, indicated any doubt about my having been in the Klan nor did he indicate any criticism of me for having been a member of that organization. The rumors and the statements to the contrary are wrong.[36]

Certainly, his actions on the High Bench, beginning with Negro rights cases such as *Chambers v. Florida*,[37] quickly indicated to his critics that Black was not a Klansman in a black robe. By the time that a unanimous Court handed down the watershed school integration decision of *Brown v. Board of Education*,[38] Black was having difficulty with his Birmingham crowd. After 1954 he found it increasingly painful to return to the South, and his only son, Hugo L. Black, Jr., was forced to relinquish his law practice in Birmingham and to move to Miami, Florida, because of the adverse impact of his father's civil rights and liberties activities on the High Bench.[39]

This ostracism, for Black and his family, was extremely difficult for the southern Jurist. Toward the end of his life, Black's greatest happiness was being invited back to the South, a place that strongly influenced him. He loved the South, and, as a lawyer, legislator, and Jurist, he "tried to help free it from the obsession (racism) which has stunted its development."[40] Black was an optimist: he saw a new South slowly emerging, phoenix-like, from the ashes of Jim Crowism. Black was fond of a nineteenth-century, Georgian politician and statesman, Benjamin H. Hill. Hill had fought hard to bring the South back to full partnership in the Union after the Civil War. Black often quoted Hill's remarks:

---

36. Statement appended in the file (Apr. 8, 1968), to a letter from Hugo L. Black to Virginia Van der Veer Hamilton (Apr. 10, 1968), Hugo L. Black Papers, Manuscript Division, Library of Congress, Washington, D.C., Box 31 [The Hugo L. Black Papers hereinafter are cited as Black Papers.]. Black hoped that appended statement to Dr. Hamilton's letter would "correct for posterity any idea about President Roosevelt's having been fooled about [his] membership in the Klan." *Id.*

37. 309 U.S. 227 (1940).

38. 347 U.S. 483 (1954).

39. Berman, *supra* note 3, at 394.

40. Berman, *supra* note 20, at 42.

" 'There was a South of slavery and secession—that South is dead. There is a South of union and freedom—that South, thank God, is living, breathing, growing every hour.' "[41]

Black believed that a new South was emerging but that this evolution had to be nurtured by a patient national government. As a Senator, he was concerned about the forceful, heavy hand of the federal government trying to quicken this development in his South.[42] As a Supreme Court Justice, he was concerned equally about the heavy-handedness of federal legislation. For example, he dissented in the 1965 Voting Rights litigation that came to the Court in *South Carolina v. Katzenbach*.[43] Section 5 of the Voting Rights Act called for southern jurisdictions to come to Washington, D.C., to have all voting changes approved by the Department of Justice. Black's slashing dissent predicted that his southern states would be compelled

> to *beg* federal authorities to approve their policies . . . . [He asserted:] I cannot help but believe that the inevitable effect of any such law which forces any one of the states to *entreat* federal authorities in far away places for approval of local laws before they can become effective is to create the impression that the state or states treated in this way are little more than *conquered provinces*.[44]

These legal and jurisprudential attitudes of Black were manifestations of his basic view of how change would come about in the South. At a war bond rally on June 19, 1945, Black had the following to say about human nature and changing attitudes: "The drive toward realization of human ideals cannot be forced upon the people from above. It must grow out of the people themselves. For example, neither courts nor legislatures could require tolerance if there were in the hearts of the people themselves no desire for fairness and justice."[45]

Black the southerner was forever Black the educator. His southern background provided him with what one of his law clerks

---

41. Black, *supra* note 1, at 15 (quoting Benjamin H. Hill).

42. *See* Berman, *supra* note 20, at 41 (discussing Senator Black's reasons for opposing federal anti-lynching legislation, the Wagner-Costigan Bill, in 1935).

43. 383 U.S. 301 (1966).

44. *Id.* at 358-59 (emphasis added). For an extended discussion of section 5 of the 1965 Voting Rights Act, see generally H. Ball, D. Krane & T. Lauth, Compromised Compliance: Implementation of the 1965 Voting Rights Act (1982).

45. Berman, *supra* note 20, at 36 n.5.

called a "touch of Protestant Pessimism."[46] While people committed errors and behaved with great passion and prejudice, Black "never really lost his strong belief that the people could judge, think, and . . . act as a responsible political body if their leaders appealed to their noble side."[47] Black's entire life was dedicated to achieving this kind of noble response from people, especially from his kinfolk in the Deep South.

II. Hugo Black: A Tough, Steely Southerner on the Bench

Hugo Black's actions on the High Bench "combined the wisdom and breadth of vision of a learned student of history with the disingenuous certitude of a backwoods politician."[48] The Justice from Alabama was a "combination of the steel-hard and the soft."[49] Gracious and unpretentious, Black was an indomitable jurist when he made up his mind on an issue of law.

Black was not "a 'court politician,' and did not seek to impose or push his views in any face-to-face kind of way."[50] Constantly engaged in conversations with his brethren, Black was "willing to discuss points but did not seek to impose on them."[51] However, Black's determination often led him to engage in actions that were labeled "blackmail" by some of his brethren.

During conference sessions, he communicated with his colleagues by way of written memos and oral arguments. If suggestions flew, he was a tough negotiator, and one of his memos would find its way into the Court opinion; if not, he would use that memo as the basis of a statement of concurrence or dissent. For example, in the 1969 Supreme Court decision *Alexander v. Holmes County Board of Education*[52] Chief Justice Burger supported the State and Justice Department requests for a delay in the desegregation of school districts in thirty-three Mississippi counties. Black wrote

---

46. Ball, *supra* note 8, at 1051 (quoting Howard & Freeman, *Perspectives: Hugo L. Black*, Virginia Times Dispatch, Dec. 12, 1971 (Both Howard and Freeman are former law clerks of Justice Black.)).

47. Ball, *supra* note 8, at 1051 (quoting Justice Black's son, Hugo L. Black, Jr.).

48. THE BURGER COURT 240 (V. Blasi ed. 1982).

49. Meador, *supra* note 12, at 1113.

50. Letter from former law clerk of Justice Black during 1961 term to Howard Ball (May, 1969) (remarking at one point that Black did not "lobby").

51. *Id.*

52. 396 U.S. 19 (1969).

and circulated to his fellow Jurists a scathing dissent that attacked Burger's actions, and, after the completion of oral arguments during the initial conference session, Black clearly revealed his position on the desegregation matter: integration must begin without delay—the time for all deliberate speed (the 1955 *Brown* standard) had to come to an end.

For Black, that 1955 standard was a serious judicial error that allowed the southern communities to avoid or delay implementation of integration plans. " 'I never should have let Felix get that into the opinion,' Black often said to his clerks"[53] after 1955. He felt that the Court should issue a simple, direct order to the Mississippi school districts to desegregate immediately. "If anybody writes," Black threatened, "I dissent."[54]

His colleagues knew that Black would put his belief into action; a dissent was written and circulated after Burger wrote a draft opinion calling for delay in the implementation of the Mississippi desegregation plans. "Too much writing and not enough action," Black wrote in a memorandum to the other Justices after he read the Burger draft.[55] After 6 days of intense negotiations, the other Justices went along with Black to avoid breaking the unanimity of the Court on the question of school desegregation.

Burger, assisted by Harlan and Stewart, attempted to create another draft, but then decided to accept Brennan's compromise draft, developed with the aid of Justices Douglas and Marshall, as Black had encouraged earlier. The Brennan draft was a short, two-page per curiam that ended the era of "with all deliberate speed" ("it is no longer constitutionally permissible") and clearly indicated that " '[t]he obligation of every school district is to terminate dual school systems at once and to operate now and hereafter only unitary schools.' "[56]

One of Black's basic tendencies was his resistance to what he believed were the incorrect constitutional positions of his colleagues. A law clerk wrote: "He is concerned only with his work. Indeed there is no Justice more committed to the business of the Court than he."[57] During his 34-year tenure as Associate Justice,

53. B. Woodward & S. Armstrong, *supra* note 2, at 38.
54. *Id.* at 44.
55. *Id.* at 52.
56. *Id.* at 55 (quoting *Alexander*, 396 U.S. at 20).
57. Meador, *Justice Black and His Law Clerks*, 15 Ala. L. Rev. 57, 61 (1962).

Black repeatedly bombarded his colleagues with legal messages about points of law that they might have overlooked in reviewing litigation.

The correspondence between the Brethren revealed that other Justices often responded to these written queries by changing their minds and voting differently. As one example, Justice Tom Clark wrote Black: "I'm sorry about the FHA case—I never studied the claim frankly—From what I've read of the brief since you called my attention to it, I believe you are right—I may change my vote tomorrow."[58]

Clarity and simplicity of expression were hallmarks of the many statements Black produced during his 34 years as Supreme Court Justice. He was extremely critical of his Brethren when they misused the legal language, whether the error involved constitutional roaming in search of the meaning of due process or a seemingly simple letter to a colleague who had retired. His criticism left a bad taste in the mouths of some of his colleagues.

When, for example, Justice Owen Roberts left the Court in 1945, Chief Justice Stone asked the members of the Court to sign the "customary letter."[59] Black, however, strongly objected to one of Stone's sentences in that draft and so informed Stone. Black was unwilling to sign anything that he believed was incorrect or imprecise. Black essentially had objected to the sentence: "You have made fidelity to principle your guide to decision."[60]

Frankfurter reacted angrily, a response reflecting the personal feelings he had about Black. He wrote to his Brethren:

> I could never be a party to the denial, under challenge, of what I believe to be a fundamental truth about Roberts, the Justice—that he "made fidelity to principle" his guide to decision. I *know* that was Justice Brandeis's view of Roberts, whose character he held in highest esteem.[61]

---

58. Letter from Tom Clark, Associate Justice of the Supreme Court, to Hugo L. Black (n.d.), Black Papers, *supra* note 36, Box 58.

59. Black Papers, *supra* note 36, Box 62.

60. *Id.*

61. *Id.* According to Frankfurter, Brandeis did not hold the same high esteem for the character of Justice Black and once told Frankfurter that " ' "Black hasn't the faintest notion of what tolerance means, and while he talks a lot about democracy, he is totally devoid of its underlying demand which is tolerance in his own behavior." ' " Noonan, *supra* note 23, at 1131 (quoting diary of F. Frankfurter, in turn quoting L. Brandeis).

Stone enlarged the discussion by showing Black's correspondence to all the Justices. Black responded by refusing to add his signature to any letter unless the matter were settled as he had argued. Black knew that Stone would not send Justice Roberts a letter unless all the Justices had signed it. Stone capitulated to Black's blackmail, and the revised letter was sent to Roberts in accordance with Black's wishes.[62] As might be expected, Frankfurter and Stone became embittered toward Black.

While Black was forceful and cunning in fighting for his ideas, he was also compassionate. Despite their mutual professional clashes, Black was Frankfurter's patient and compassionate friend after Frankfurter retired in 1962 because of ill health. In May 1963 and in subsequent months, Frankfurter wrote lengthy letters to Black about pending state action, sit-in cases.

After stating that "one of the most tenacious of [his] life-long habits [was] not to inhibit expression of an idea [he had] a strong conviction to make utterance," Frankfurter's "impulse" was to write about how Black should vote on a legal question, with the hope that Black "would not resent the motive of [Frankfurter's] writing nor what [he had] written."[63] He suggested:

> I am dead sure that if you could write a separate little piece setting forth the essentials of what you told all of us twice at Conference—that you would never consent to any decision which held that the Constitution of the United States compelled you to do business with whom you did not want to do business—you would be speaking moderately, and even a few words of moderation along the lines I have tried to recall would have a powerful educative effect not only on the Negroes but also on whites. You could, of course, include an expression of your credo on the subject of racism, but were you to add a moderating note it would be one of the greatest services you could render the Nation and the Court.[64]

Black was extremely courteous and gracious to Frankfurter; he sent gentle letters (and fresh grapefruit) to his erstwhile opponent. After reading Black's dissenting opinion in the sit-in case *Bell v. Maryland*,[65] Frankfurter again wrote Black:

---

62. Black Papers, *supra* note 36, Box 62.
63. *Id.* Box 60.
64. *Id.*
65. 378 U.S. 226 (1964). Black wrote, in dissent, that the fourteenth amendment "does not of itself, standing alone, in the absence of some cooperative state action or compulsion,

> I was brought up to believe that it is not proper to congratulate a judge on the views he expresses in an opinion, because presumably a judge's views are the compulsions of his conscience, [this letter] is, I believe, the first time I have departed from my deep conviction on this subject to tell you of my pride in you for your dissent.[66]

Black's response was typical of the Jurist's graciousness:

> Our differences, which have been many, have rarely been over the ultimate end desired, but rather have related to the means that were the most likely to achieve the end we both envisioned. Our years together, and these differences, have but added to the respect and admiration that I had for *Professor* Frankfurter even before I knew him—his love of country, steadfast devotion to what he believed to be right, and to his wisdom.[67]

Black's correspondence with Sherman Minton and others embraced a similar feeling of compassion for fellow Jurists who struggled on the same path. Black knew Minton from their days together in the Senate. During Minton's final illness, Black continuously called and wrote Minton letters that kept him abreast on the comings and goings in the Court and in Washington, D.C.[68]

Many people sought his advice, on and off the federal bench. Over time, Justices came to Black in the hope that Black would handle personal and legal problems involving them and the Court. For example, in August 1965 Douglas wrote to Black asking whether Black could speak with the wife of a new Justice to the Supreme Court: "Abe Fortas's wife is very upset over Abe's appointment. It is apparently a very serious crisis. I thought maybe you could think of something to do."[69] Despite his own occasional anger over Black's actions, Justice Murphy wrote memos to Black and asked him to listen to Murphy's personal "troubles."[70] Earl Warren, a few years before his retirement as Chief Justice, also wrote to Black thanking him for his help and stated: "[N]othing in

---

forbid property holders, including restaurant owners, to ban people from entering or remaining upon their premises, even if the owners act out of racial prejudice." *Id.* at 326 (footnote omitted).

66. Black Papers, *supra* note 36, Box 60.
67. *Id.* (emphasis in original).
68. *Id.* Box 61.
69. *Id.* Box 59.
70. *Id.* Box 61.

the past thirteen years has given me more pleasure and satisfaction than my association with you. That association has really made them rewarding years for me."[71]

Black also was respected for his practical wisdom pertaining to matters beyond the scope of the Court's docket. Black always responded to these requests, even requests from Colleagues such as Frankfurter who earlier had worked to deprive Black of the Chief Justiceship. For example, in a letter to Black in 1941, Douglas was insistent when he stressed to the Alabamian: "Felix has done it again to you . . . . [T]here is no question in my mind that he was responsible for your [not getting the Chief Justiceship in 1941.]"[72]

Other men came to Black for counsel in their efforts to gain a seat on the federal bench. While Sherman Minton was serving on the Seventh Circuit Court of Appeals in Chicago, he wrote Black about that "god awful town (Chicago)," and how he "missed [them] all in Washington."[73] In January 1943 Wiley Rutledge wrote Black to thank him for his help while Rutledge was in Washington, D.C., testifying before the Senate Judiciary Committee prior to his elevation to the Court:

> Without making any assumption whatever as to what action the Senate may take, I want you to know how very much I treasure your kindness. Believe me, it means a great deal to me. I am sorry that you went to so much trouble to get the message through.[74]

In addition, Black labored many hours and months to help Jerome Frank (a well-known, New Deal Democrat who was Chairman of the Securities and Exchange Commission) obtain a position on the Second Circuit Court of Appeals. Frank frequently was recommended for a post on either the Supreme Court or the court of appeals, but, because he was Jewish, he constantly was disregarded for these positions. From 1938 until his appointment to the court of appeals in 1942, the two men communicated regularly. In January 1939 Frank wrote to Black: "I learned this morning that, because of Frankfurter's appointment [Frankfurter was also Jewish], the President feels hesitant about appointing me. Perhaps you'd be

71. *Id.* Box 64.
72. *Id.* Box 61.
73. *Id.* Box 62.
74. *Id.* Box 28.

willing to say something."[75]

Black, who respected Frank's capability as an attorney and his loyalty to New Deal concepts, worked on this appointment. When a vacancy opened up on the Second Circuit, Black wrote to Roosevelt in support of Frank: "In my judgment he fully measures up to the requirements of the position. In addition, I happen to know that he has served most faithfully in other positions upon the expectation that certain rather definite commitments would give him an opportunity for judicial service."[76] Shortly thereafter, Roosevelt nominated Frank to fill the vacancy on the federal bench.

Black never was concerned about this type of political intervention. He strongly supported people whom he believed were ideologically in line with Roosevelt and the New Deal. This "political" tactic of Black annoyed a number of his Colleagues, but did not phase the Alabamian. Justice Reed had said to Frankfurter: "You can't change people. Black always was a politician and he didn't and can't cease to be one by becoming a judge."

As an ideologue, a fervent New Dealer, and a lover of Jefferson's democracy,[77] Hugo Black was committed to the supremacy of the actions of the elected representatives. When Warren E. Burger began his tenure as Chief Justice of the United States in October 1969, Hugo Black already had developed a fairly comprehensive political theory of government in a representative democracy. Having written almost 1,000 opinions over the preceding 33 years,[78] he had handcrafted a well-developed set of beliefs about the nature of governmental power, the relationship between the states and the federal government, the role and functions of the federal judges in our governmental system, and the fundamental constraints upon governmental and judicial powers in a democracy.

Black was committed to a dream of an ongoing and vigorous democracy[79] and, in his effort to realize these ideals, overlooked the fallibility of his fragile Colleagues. He was a classic true be-

---

75. *Id.*

76. *Id.*

77. *See* Ball, *supra* note 8, at 1049.

78. *See* Haigh, *The Judicial Opinions of Mr. Justice Hugo L. Black*, 9 Sw. U.L. Rev. 1069 (1977).

79. *See generally* H. Ball, The Vision and the Dream of Justice Hugo L. Black (1975).

liever, unshakeable in his beliefs about government powers and limits on power. While the "overriding personal impression of the Judge was one of great humanity, love, warmth, and youth,"[80] Black had an unremitting, "intense moral commitment, concentrated through the focus of an unwavering vision, and brought to bear with an immense prowess."[81] He "would not compromise his principles,"[82] even if that decision meant classification as judicial blackmailer and flapdoodler.

III. Hugo Black's Political Jurisprudence in 1969

A. Legal Positivism

A scholarly admirer of Justice Black wrote that

> [f]ew jurists have had the impact on law and society of Mr. Justice Hugo Lafayette Black. A constitutional literalist to whom every word in the document represented a command, he nonetheless used the language of the Constitution to propound a jurisprudence that has had a lasting effect on the development of American constitutional law. His contributions were towering. They stand as jurisprudential and intellectual landmarks in the evolving history of the land he loved so well.[83]

When Chief Justice Burger took over the Court leadership in 1969, Hugo Black had served for 32 years as an Associate Justice, during which time he crafted a complete political jurisprudence. Before examining Black's activities as a member of the Burger Court, renewing Black's judicial philosophy as it had developed by 1969 is important.

In a letter to a Mississippi citizen who complained to his fellow southerner about the Supreme Court's school desegregation policy, Black wrote:

> [Y]ou worry about citizens being denied their "Freedom of choice." Government is bound to deny citizens freedom of choice at some time to some extent and on certain subjects. That is one of the great objects of government so that we have a country of law and order

---

80. Letter from former law clerk of Justice Black during 1969 term to Howard Ball (1969).

81. Lewis, *Hugo Black—An Elemental Force*, N.Y. Times, Sept. 26, 1971, at 1, col. 2.

82. Letter from former law clerk, *supra* note 80.

83. H. Abraham, Justices and Presidents 202 (1974) (footnote omitted).

> instead of one of anarchy and riot, and I believe in having the former kind of country as I always did back in the days when you were in my Sunday School class in Birmingham.[84]

This response captured the essence of his political jurisprudence: the need for the creation of a government strong enough to provide for orderliness and security but not strong enough to deprive persons of their inalienable rights as free citizens in a representative democracy.

While he has been labeled with many, often contradictory titles—liberal, activist, nationalist, states' righter, literalist, conservative, to name a few—Black's political jurisprudence, as it unfolded, consisted of legal positivism. He was, first and foremost, a twentieth-century Jeremy Bentham:

> There [was] a touch of Jeremy Bentham in Justice Black, a Bentham with an unmistakably American accent. The intense energies of both [were] engaged by zeal to reform the laws, to cleanse away its excrescences, to look upon law as a clean instrument of popular will, not as the patina of the judges' gloss. For Bentham the enemy was the common law, fastening itself on the statutes; for Justice Black it [was] judge-made law as an encrustation on the Constitution.[85]

Justice Black's philosophies on governmental powers and the federal judges' role in our constitutional system clearly revealed his positivism. He was an eighteenth-century thinker who functioned in the twentieth century.[86] His political jurisprudence rejected the idea of natural law and the view that judges ought to be social engineers. Black believed that "the only relevant law . . . is 'positive' law, which consists of commands made and enforced by a sovereign."[87] Lawmaking in a democracy is a legislative, not a judicial function. Legislators, freely elected by the people in a democracy, have the constitutional responsibility for legislating for the com-

---

84. Black Papers, *supra* note 36, Box 53. One historian has indicated that Black, after leaving Birmingham for the Senate in 1927, did not attend formal worship services, and one of Black's law clerks, Jerome Cooper, described him as a "reverent agnostic." *See* Mauney, *Religion and First Amendment Protections: An Analysis of Justice Black's Constitutional Interpretations*, 10 PEPPERDINE L. REV. 377, 379 (1983).

85. Freund, *Mr. Justice Black and the Judicial Function*, 14 UCLA L. REV. 467, 473 (1967), *quoted in* Yarbrough, *Mr. Justice Black and Legal Positivism*, 57 VA. L. REV. 375, 387 (1971).

86. *See* Ball, *supra* note 8, at 1050.

87. Yarbrough, *supra* note 85, at 378.

mon good, as determined by the legislature.

In Black's view, judges are responsible for interpreting the law, when cases are properly before the courts, by going to the intent of the founders and the legislators and, if necessary, to the literal meaning of the words of the statutes in question. Furthermore, a law may be unwise or asinine, but, unless it runs afoul of a specific prohibition of another "positive law of superior status," that is, the clear prohibitions of the Bill of Rights and, to a lesser extent, the generalities in the fourteenth amendment, it is a valid law. Judges must not put their gloss on the law of the legislature nor must they substitute their values for those of the legislators when the jurists disagree with the political and social values of the elected officials.[88]

This view of the role and responsibility of the representatives elected by the people, who are themselves the key to a functioning democracy,[89] was the bedrock of Black's legal positivism. The 1787 constitutional system established a pattern of representative government that had, at its heart, the concept of legislative supremacy. Governmental action, including the powers of the legislature and other elected politicians, was restricted and enumerated in the Bill of Rights. The "human evils" addressed in these amendments were perennial ones. Black did not consider the Bill of Rights to be an outmoded, eighteenth-century "strait jacket";[90] he believed that the problems present in 1787 still exist today and that free speech and press, freedom of religion, and the right to a jury trial, to name a few, are necessary for the continuation of democracy.

The constitutional system gave federal courts the primary role of ensuring that these freedoms of expression and thought, vital to the continuance of a democracy, rigorously were enforced, and the system monitored the efforts of elected political leaders who occasionally tried to restrict these rights. But these federal courts had to restrain themselves from interfering with governmental activities that specifically were not prohibited by the supreme positive law of the system: the United States Constitution.

---

88. *See id.*

89. *See* H. Ball, *supra* note 79, at 2-5.

90. Adamson v. California, 332 U.S. 46, 89 (1947) (Black, J., dissenting).

B. Powers of Government

Quoting with favor Justice Holmes' dissent in *Tyson & Brother v. Banton*, Black clearly stated his position on governmental powers that

> "a State legislature can do whatever it sees fit to do unless it is restrained by some express prohibition in the Constitution . . . and that Courts should be careful not to extend such prohibitions beyond their obvious meaning by reading into them conceptions of public policy that the particular Court may happen to entertain."[91]

The fundamental responsibility of political leaders in a democracy is to "develop definite and precise laws under the authority of a written constitution."[92] As he reminisced in 1965, he had been taught that "legislators, not judges, should make the laws."[93] Furthermore, Black held the opinion that the Constitution enabled the elected representatives "to do virtually anything [the legislature] wishes in controlling the economy"[94] and indicated in a letter to one of his students that government at all levels "was fully clothed with the power to govern and to maintain order."[95]

The Japanese exclusion cases[96] best exemplify Black's commitment to the principle of legislative-executive supremacy and its responsibility to provide law and order for society at large. One critic commented that Black's *Korematsu v. United States*[97] opinion for the Court majority was "the most Klanlike of his decisions."[98] A review of the events of the period clearly shows that Justice Department and War Department lawyers deliberately kept the truth from the federal courts—that citizens of Japanese ancestry posed no threat to national security—and that, during this period of time, a form of basic xenophobic racism existed.[99]

---

91. H. Black, A Constitutional Faith 28 (1968) (footnote omitted) (quoting Tyson & Bro. v. Banton, 273 U.S. 418, 446 (1927) (Holmes, J., dissenting)).

92. Black, *Foreward* to Confronting Injustice: The Edmund Cahn Reader xi (L. Cahn ed. 1966).

93. Black, *Reminiscences*, 18 Ala. L. Rev. 3, 10 (1965).

94. Berman, *Hugo Black at 75*, 10 Am. U.L. Rev. 43, 50 (1961).

95. Black Papers, *supra* note 36, Box 28.

96. Korematsu v. United States, 323 U.S. 214 (1944); *Ex parte* Mitsuye Endo, 323 U.S. 283 (1944); Hirabayashi v. United States, 320 U.S. 81 (1943).

97. 323 U.S. 214 (1944).

98. Noonan, *supra* note 23, at 1130.

99. *See generally* P. Irons, Justice at War (1982) (a complete account of this episode in American political, military, and legal history).

However, examination of internal memos and conference notes of the Supreme Court Justices who heard these case arguments reveals that Black, Frankfurter, and Stone were committed to legislative and executive supremacy in this area of political action, even if it resulted in applying racially discriminatory policies to a small group of American citizens. For Black, an acquaintance of General DeWitt,[100] "military orders called for the 'exercise of military, not judicial judgment'; he stated, 'it is unnecessary for us to appraise the possible reasons which might have prompted the order to be used in the form it was.' "[101]

Black believed that his friend Douglas acted inappropriately when he argued for individual rights while the nation was at war. Justice Black wanted the President and Congress to assume their constitutional responsibilities and believed that the loss of freedom was a small cost for the maintenance of a democratic system. He never recanted from his harsh position in *Korematsu* that "[p]ressing public necessity may sometimes justify the existence of such restrictions."[102]

Indeed, in his correspondence to his friend Harold Ickes, Secretary of the Interior before and during the war, Black indicated his concern about the presence of potential saboteurs in America and received from Ickes information about the activities of the Italian- and German-Americans living in the United States.

In February 1941, before America's entry into the war, Ickes sent Black a lengthy report entitled *Research Project on the Influence of Nationality Groups on Election Returns*. This report examined the electoral impact of the millions of Italian- and German-Americans living in America and described the propaganda activities of the Nazi movement in America. The author of this report believed that America "faced the danger of nationality groups as factors in American politics."[103]

The report's ominous conclusion was obvious to the Justice from Alabama:

> The danger arising from such nationality groups united as *Volksgruppen* and using their political power as American voters in the

---

100. *See* Ball, *Politics over Law in Wartime: The Japanese Exclusion Cases*, 19 Harv. C.R.-C.L. L. Rev. 560, 568 n.10 (1984) (citing Black Papers, *supra* note 36, Box 59).

101. *Korematsu*, 323 U.S. at 215.

102. *Id.* at 216.

103. Black Papers, *supra* note 36, Box 34.

> interests of their homeland instead of the interests of the United States, cannot be overestimated. To decide what is to be done about it will be up to the people and the Government of the United States, once the facts have been clearly put before them.[104]

Black was concerned sufficiently about this issue that he met with Ickes to continue discussion on the dilemma.[105]

In the context of pre-war xenophobia, which involved the highest circles of government, Black's views of forceful governmental responsibility and judicial self-restraint in evaluating harsh governmental measures were understandable. Throughout his career as Jurist, he felt compelled to support strong law-and-order actions of the political policymakers absent clear constitutional proscriptions on the use of governmental power.

C. Restricting Governmental Powers

With no federal court intervention, legislators and executives were given almost unlimited freedom in economic and social policymaking. Justice Black believed, however, that the United States Constitution prohibited legislative efforts which would deprive persons of their basic civil liberties. "Justice Hugo Black believed, and evangelically so, that [this theme] recurs again and again throughout human history."[106]

Justice Black detected a pattern in an historical recurrence involving the relative ease with which people lost their liberties. Black concluded from his readings of historical events that a democracy could survive only through the maintenance of the basic freedoms of speech, press, assembly, and religion, as well as the right to an open and fair public trial. Federal courts, therefore, were responsible for protecting these fundamental freedoms. The most prominent feature in his landscape was his being "convinced that in this 'absolute' [of the First Amendment] lies the only security for the maintenance of a democratic society under law."[107]

1. The "firstness" of the first amendment.—The Bill of Rights, especially the first amendment, the Civil War amendments, and the civil rights statutes, formed the basis of the fundamental

104. *Id.*
105. *Id.*
106. Gregory & Strickland, *supra* note 27, at 543.
107. Meador, *supra* note 12, at 1109.

positive law that restricted legislators from infringing upon the inalienable rights of individuals. Black "took [the] Declaration of Independence seriously when it referred to 'unalienable rights.' [He] thought of the Bill of Rights as the necessary corollary to those inalienable rights . . . ."[108]

For Black, "[t]he right to think, speak, and write freely without governmental censorship or interference is the most precious privilege of citizens vested with power to select public policies and public officials."[109] Justice Black believed that absolute freedom from governmental control over speech and thought provided the community with hope for an open and just society. Throughout his career, he was an ardent advocate of the unfettered right of free speech, free press, freedom of assembly, and freedom of religion. He rejected all judicially created tests (such as clear and present danger, bad tendency, and, especially, the balancing formula employed by Frankfurter and Harlan) used by Justices as they attempted to resolve first amendment litigation before the Court.

He never deviated from his absolute commitment to the "firstness" of the first amendment. In 1947 Black expressed his belief that the first amendment was

> the supreme law of the land, [and] has thus fixed its own value on freedom of speech and press by putting these freedoms wholly "beyond the reach" of *federal* power to abridge. No other provision of the Constitution purports to dilute the scope of these unequivocal commands of the First Amendment. Consequently, [he did] not believe that any federal agencies, including Congress and [the Supreme] Court, have power or authority to subordinate speech and press to what they think are "more important interests."[110]

The senior Justice believed it was fitting that his last opinion on the Court also dealt with a first amendment controversy—the "Pentagon Papers" litigation.[111] He again maintained his absolutist position regarding these freedoms in the case and wrote that the first amendment was "offered to *curtail* and *restrict* the general

---

108. Frank, *Hugo L. Black: Free Speech and the Declaration of Independence*, 1977 U. ILL. L.F. 577, 582 (1977).

109. H. BLACK, *supra* note 91, at 43.

110. Smith v. California, 361 U.S. 147, 157-59 (1959) (Black, J., concurring) (emphasis in original) (footnote omitted).

111. *See* New York Times Co. v. United States, 403 U.S. 713 (1971). Justice Black authored a concurring opinion in the case. *Id.* at 714 (Black, J., concurring).

powers granted to the Executive, Legislative, and Judicial branches."[112] Black consistently defended the basic constitutional freedoms, even when they were involved in controversial issues such as obscenity, loyalty oaths, antisubversive legislation, and congressional investigations. For the Alabamian and the majority of the Court, these were the lifeblood of any representative democracy.[113]

While Justice Black was certain about the absoluteness of the first amendment freedoms, he always distinguished between cases involving speech and those involving speech plus conduct. "I draw the line between speech and conduct,"[114] wrote Black in 1968. "I am vigorously opposed to efforts to extend the First Amendment's freedom of speech beyond speech, [the Constitution does] not immunize other conduct in addition to these . . . particularized freedoms."[115] Black felt that a vast difference existed between conduct, especially the actions of street protestors, and the printing and distributing of a pamphlet by a radical organization. "Reading history, Black believed that tramping, singing, marching, demonstrating, picketing people with the most worthy of motives but acting outside the boundary of the law to achieve their goals would lead to counter-demonstrations, marches, tramping by their opponents."[116] These passionate actions carried the possibility of breakdown in law and order and the rejection of reasoned, rational discussion on public issues.

For the Justice, the loss of societal orderliness had to be prevented to maintain the fragile fabric of a representative democracy. "[T]he crowds that press in the streets for noble goals today can be supplanted tomorrow by street mobs pressing the courts for precisely opposite ends,"[117] Black wrote in a partial dissent in 1965. Congress and the states, in Black's view, were responsible for the prevention of lawlessness.

Cox v. Louisiana[118] is one example of Black's perspective of the first amendment-conduct issue. Cox and other blacks had been

---

112. *Id.* at 716 (Black, J., concurring) (emphasis in original).
113. *See id.* at 720.
114. H. Black, *supra* note 91, at 53.
115. *Id.* at 44-45.
116. H. Ball, *supra* note 79, at 197.
117. Cox v. Louisiana, 379 U.S. 559, 584 (1965) (Black, J., dissenting).
118. 379 U.S. 559 (1965).

arrested and charged with breaching the peace, obstructing public passage, and picketing a courthouse. While the Court majority invalidated all charges, Black dissented in part because he felt strongly that the courthouse picketing charge should have been upheld:

> A state statute . . . regulating *conduct*—patrolling and marching—as distinguished from *speech*, would, in my judgment be constitutional. [The first and fourteenth amendments do not] grant a constitutional right to engage in the conduct of picketing or patrolling, whether on publicly owned ground or on privately owned property. . . . Picketing, though it may be utilized to communicate ideas, is not speech, and therefore is not of itself protected by the First Amendment.[119]

2. *Civil rights in the fourteenth amendment.*—The first amendment was absolutely clear for Black, but the due process and equal protection clauses in the fifth and fourteenth amendments were less so. For Black, the due process clause was troublesome. " 'No one,' " he said, " 'ever has marked its boundaries,' " and consequently, he believed that " '[i]t is as elastic as rubber.' "[120] This elasticity led some of the Supreme Court Justices on a subjective search for the meaning of due process.

Black went to the historical antecedent, the Magna Carta, for his conception of the essential meaning of due process. "Due process of law," for Black, meant that persons were to be tried in accordance with the procedural guarantees (fourth, fifth, sixth, and eighth amendments) in the Bill of Rights, and in accordance with "laws passed pursuant to constitutional power, guaranteeing to all alike a trial under the general law of the land."[121] All persons must be given equal treatment according to "the law of the land that already existed at the time the alleged offense was committed."[122]

Black's understanding of history and his concern about substantive judicial interpretations of due process (such as Frankfurter's "shock the conscience" standard[123]) led him to develop a

---

119. *Id.* at 575-78 (Black, J., dissenting) (emphasis in original).

120. Yarbrough, *Justice Black, The Fourteenth Amendment, and Incorporation*, 30 U. MIAMI L. REV. 231, 233 (1976) (quoting 81 CONG. REC. 1294 (1937) (statement of Senator Hugo Black)). Black's view of the judicial role will be examined in the next segment of this Article. *See infra* notes 145-57 and accompanying text.

121. H. BLACK, *supra* note 91, at 34.

122. *Id.* at 33.

123. Gideon v. Wainwright, 372 U.S. 335, 339 (1963) (quoting Betts v. Brady, 316 U.S. 455, 462 (1942)), overruling Betts v. Brady, 316 U.S. 455 (1942).

procedural due process concept that emphasized equal treatment in the legal process for all persons, regardless of wealth,[124] age,[125] or race.[126] Justice Black hoped that this concept ultimately would gain implementation by the Supreme Court majority.

Some scholars perceived a "darker side" to Black's civil libertarianism, which focused on his interpretation of the fourth amendment's prosecution against "unreasonable" search and seizures.[127] Black translated the fourth amendment in very restrictive terms and emphasized the language of the amendment rather than its historical roots. In reviewing fourth amendment cases during Black's tenure on the Supreme Court from *Wolf v. Colorado*[128] through *Mapp v. Ohio*[129] and from *Berger v. New York*[130] and *Katz v. United States*[131] to *Coolidge v. New Hampshire*,[132] Black was reluctant to extend the meaning of the search and seizure protection.[133] He had misgivings about the "exclusionary rule" that the Court created in the 1961 *Mapp* decision,[134] and he argued against its use in light of the protection against self-incrimination already present in the fifth amendment.[135]

Some have speculated that Black, as a southern police court judge and, later, as the crusading prosecuting attorney in Birmingham, Alabama, strongly believed that " 'the method of catching a thief [is not] very important, provided he got a fair trial afterwards.' "[136] As the fourth amendment most directly affected police work in the investigatory and accusatory stages of criminal prosecution, he may have empathized with law enforcement agents and

---

124. *See Gideon*, 372 U.S. at 344 (opinion by Black, J.).

125. *See In re* Gault, 387 U.S. 1, 59 (1967) (Black, J., concurring).

126. *See* Powell v. Alabama, 287 U.S. 45 (1932).

127. *See* Landynski, *In Search of Justice Black's Fourth Amendment*, 45 FORDHAM L. REV. 453, 453 (1976) (citing L. LEVY, JEFFERSON & CIVIL LIBERTIES: THE DARKER SIDE (1963)).

128. 338 U.S. 25 (1949) (in which Justice Black concurred), *rev'd*, Mapp v. Ohio, 367 U.S. 643, 654-55 (1961).

129. 367 U.S. 643 (1961) (in which Justice Black concurred).

130. 388 U.S. 41 (1967) (in which Justice Black dissented).

131. 389 U.S. 347 (1967) (in which Justice Black dissented).

132. 403 U.S. 443 (1971) (in which Justice Black concurred and dissented). *Coolidge* was heard during the last term that Black served on the Court.

133. *See* Landynski, *supra* note 127, *passim.*

134. *See generally id.* at 463-79.

135. *See id.* at 475-79 (quoting *Coolidge*, 403 U.S. at 497 (Black, J., concurring and dissenting)).

136. Landynski, *supra* note 127, at 495 (quoting interview with Justice Black, in Washington, D.C. (Dec. 5, 1961)).

consequently may have restricted his perception of unreasonable searches and seizures.

As seen in the Warren Court's majority opinions in *Berger*, *Katz*, and *Griswold v. Connecticut*,[137] the Court was moving specifically toward a new definition of the concept of privacy. The Court majority found this concept not in the Constitution itself but in its "penumbras."[138] Black vehemently dissented from this substantive interpretation of due process in these and other cases. His overriding concern was that the Court majority used the clauses of the Bill of Rights, including the fourth and fourteenth amendments, to paint broadly new, *judicially created* rights.

The "equal protection of the laws" language in the fourteenth amendment presented Black with an even more problematic constitutional expression. To compensate for the "nebulous, open-ended character"[139] of equal protection, Justice Black returned to the historical context for some sense of the clause's original intent.

In time, Black came to believe that the equal protection clause was the constitutional prohibition on all state actions that invidiously discriminated on the basis of race. For Black, race and the related characteristics of alienage and national origin were the only major "suspect" categories in equal protection cases.[140] The Supreme Court, as well as other federal courts, were obligated to *scrutinize strictly* those cases, such as school segregation, that involved official state discrimination based on race.

Aside from civil rights litigation involving state action and racial discrimination, the use of equal protection had fundamental limits.[141] Black did not believe in a broad, substantive interpretation of the equal protection clause. Most state action litigation that came to the federal courts for review had to be examined by those courts using the "reasonableness" test.

---

137. 381 U.S. 479 (1965).

138. *See, e.g*, *id.* at 482-86. In dissent Black observed that "[t]he Court talks about a constitutional 'right of privacy' as though there is some constitutional provision or provisions forbidding any law ever to be passed which might abridge the 'privacy' of individuals. But there is not." *Id.* at 508 (Black, J., dissenting). "I think it belittles [the Fourth] Amendment to talk about it as though it protects nothing but 'privacy.' " *Id.* at 509.

139. Yarbrough, *Justice Black and Equal Protection*, 9 Sw. U.L. Rev. 859, 899 (1977).

140. *See generally id.* at 903-08 (citations omitted). Yarbrough points out that Black's thoughts about the equal protection clause were his "least satisfying of his constitutional positions [and that Black never could] develop a clear, precise, internally consistent conception of equal protection." *Id.* at 900.

141. *Id.* at 899.

Justice William O. Douglas' majority opinion in *Harper v. Virginia State Board of Elections*,[142] in which the Court majority struck down the Virginia poll tax law as being invidious, was an example of substantive interpretation. Black, dissenting, criticized the majority for giving "equal protection a new meaning."[143] Black stated:

> I have heretofore had many occasions to express my strong belief that there is no constitutional support whatever for this Court to use the Due Process Clause as though it provided a blank check to alter the meaning of the Constitution as written so as to add to it substantive constitutional changes which a majority of the Court at any given time believes are needed to meet present-day problems. Nor is there in my opinion any more constitutional support for this Court to use the Equal Protection Clause, as it has today, to write into the Constitution its notions of what it thinks is good government policy.[144]

Congress, rather than the Supreme Court, has the constitutional power to change the meaning of the equal protection clause by changing, through constitutional amendment, the words of the document. Short of a massive display of arbitrary and repugnant racial discrimination, ill-advised or distasteful public policies of state legislatures cannot be overturned by federal courts simply because they find these state laws to be unwise. The judges' perceptions about constitutional power and limits on that power turn inexorably to Black's view of the role of the federal courts in our constitutional democracy.

D. *The Role of Federal Judges in Our Constitutional Democracy*

Hugo Black insisted, throughout his career in politics and on the Court itself, that courts must be tied to the words of the Constitution: " 'A judge untethered by a text is a dangerous instrument.' "[145] Black had been taught that legislators made the laws, and he saw that the lower federal courts and the Supreme Court had the ability to block legitimate social engineering of the national Congress and President Roosevelt throughout most of the

142. 383 U.S. 663 (1966).
143. *Id.* at 672 (Black, J., dissenting).
144. *Id.* at 675-76 (footnote omitted).
145. Black, *supra* note 92, at xii (quoting Edmond Cohn).

decade of the 1930's. Consequently, Black utterly rejected the concept of a federal judiciary that would "leave them completely free to decide constitutional questions on the basis of their own policy judgments."[146] He decided that courts had no constitutional right to tell a community what social policy was good (or bad) for them.

Justice John M. Harlan wrote that Black

> reject[ed] the open-ended notion that the Court sits to do good in every circumstance where good is needed, and insists that . . . federal judges are contained by the terms of the Constitution, no less than all other branches of government authority. He consider[ed] himself to be a judge of cases, not of 'causes,' and unhesitatingly [set] himself against federal judicial intervention whenever he [was] unable to find in the Constitution or valid legislative authority the basis for such action.[147]

Justice Black criticized judicial forays into the natural law wonderland of substantive due process or equal protection accompanied by the Justices' subjective judicial standards ("fundamental fairness" or "shock the conscience") and insisted that the federal courts follow the *plain meaning* of the laws rather than substitute their views for those of the elected representatives of the people.

Because of his life-long effort to constrain the legislative proclivities of federal courts, Black perceived that due process of law "encompassed all of the specific prohibitions of the Bill of Rights and the Constitution. It did not encompass anything else."[148]

Justice Black's dissent in *Adamson v. California*[149] reflected his strong feelings about judicial meddling. In an interview given shortly before his death in 1971, this 1947 opinion was, for Black, "his most significant opinion written."[150] *Adamson* involved the constitutionality of a California trial practice that permitted the trial court and lawyers to comment on and juries to consider as evidence of guilt a defendant's refusal to testify on his behalf during the trial. Adamson, on trial for murder had not testified, and

---

146. H. BLACK, *supra* note 91, at 24.

147. Harlan, *Mr. Justice Black—Remarks of a Colleague*, 81 HARV. L. REV. 1, 1-2 (1967).

148. Letter from former law clerk, *supra* note 80.

149. 332 U.S. 46 (1947).

150. Yarbrough, *supra* note 120, at 231 (citing interview with Justice Black, in Washington, D.C. (July 6, 1971)).

the prosecuting attorney argued that Adamson's silence was an admission of guilt. He was convicted, but he appealed his conviction, Adamson argued that the state practice violated due process of law.

The Court split, 5 to 4, on the question. The majority opinion, written by Justice Stanley Reed, rejected Adamson's contention and upheld the conviction. The Court stated that "the due process clause of the Fourteenth Amendment does not draw all the rights of the federal Bill of Rights under its protection."[151] Although most of the states did not allow the California practice, the Court "s[aw] no reason why comment should not be made upon his silence. It seem[ed] quite natural"[152] to the Court.

Justice Black dissented because, in his opinion, the Reed decision, especially the Frankfurter concurrence, "reassert[ed] a constitutional theory . . . that [the Supreme] Court is endowed by the Constitution with boundless power under 'natural law' periodically to expand and contract constitutional standards to conform to the Court's conception of what at a particular time constitutes 'civilized decency' and 'fundamental principles of liberty and justice.' "[153]

Reviewing the legislative history of the fourteenth amendment led Black to the following conclusion:

> [O]ne of the chief objects [of the Amendment] was to make the Bill of Rights applicable to the states . . . . And I further contend that the "natural law" formula which the Court uses to reach its conclusion in this case should be abandoned as an incongruous excrescence on our Constitution. I believe that formula to be itself a violation of our Constitution, in that it subtly conveys to courts, at the expense of legislatures, ultimate power over public policies in fields where no specific provision of the Constitution limits legislative power.[154]

For Black, the Bill of Rights was a set of relevant protections against governmental mischief. He explained:

> I cannot consider the Bill of Rights to be an outworn 18th Century 'strait jacket' . . . . Its provisions may be thought outdated abstractions by some. And it is true that they were designed to meet an-

---

151. *Adamson*, 332 U.S. at 53.
152. *Id.* at 56.
153. *Id.* at 60 (Black, J., dissenting).
154. *Id.* at 74-75.

> cient evils. But they are the same kind of human evils that have emerged from century to century wherever excessive power is sought by the few at the expense of the many. In my judgment the people of no nation can lose their liberty so long as a Bill of Rights like ours survives and its basic purposes are conscientiously interpreted, enforced, and respected so as to afford continuous protection against old, as well as new, devices and practices which might thwart those purposes. . . . I would follow what I believe was the original purpose of the Fourteenth Amendment—to extend to all the people of the nation the complete protection of the Bill of Rights. To hold that this Court can determine what, if any, provisions of the Bill of Rights will be enforced, and if so to what degree, is to frustrate the great design of a written Constitution.[155]

Legislatures, said Black, have the fundamental "right to invade [an individual's privacy] unless prohibited by some specific constitutional prohibition."[156] Judges must be prevented, he believed, from using their powers to review cases " 'to substitute their wisdom for that of the people's representatives.' "[157] In his 34-year tenure as a Supreme Court Justice, Black was steadfast in this general concern about federal courts having the freedom to rewrite the fundamental law and about how the freedom to do so would impact negatively on a democracy.

IV. Justice Black on the Burger Court: 1969 and 1970 Terms

In 1969, "[s]till driven by a burning evangelical need to persuade his colleagues of his views, Black worked intensely at his job."[158] This year marked Warren E. Burger's initial term on the Supreme Court, as the new Chief Justice. Justice Hugo Black served with Chief Justice Burger for two terms, 1969 and 1970. A review of the major opinions of the Court during this time revealed Black as a tough Jurist who continued to joust with his Brethren on the perennial questions of governmental power and the restraints on that power. During these two terms, Justice Black wrote a total of twenty-four majority opinions, seven concurring opinions, twenty-nine dissenting opinions, and eight other separate

---

155. *Id.* at 89.
156. H. Black, *supra* note 91, at 9.
157. Yarbrough, *supra* note 85, at 935 (quoting Justice Black).
158. B. Woodward & S. Armstrong, *supra* note 2, at 62.

opinions.[159]

The specific policy disputes during the 1969-70 time period differed from past disputes involving domestic and foreign crises (black activist activities, urban rioting, civil rights disturbances, war, anti-Vietnam War protests, riotous protests on public school and university campuses, sensational public trials such as the trial of the "Chicago Eight," political and social changes, political assassinations, and the impact of reapportionment, for example). For Justice Black, these problems illuminated anew the perennial dilemmas of governmental power, liberties of the people, and the role of the federal courts in these controversies.

A. Powers of the Government

In the sixty-eight opinions that Black wrote over the course of his last two terms on the Court, he maintained that governing agencies were chiefly responsible for establishing public policies unless specifically prohibited by a clear, constitutionally imposed restraint.

Black dealt with a number of cases involving the scope of administrative agency powers in adjudicating disputes. Primarily in dissent, he continued to argue that the federal courts should allow administrative agencies to make final rulings on the issues before the federal courts and that the Supreme Court should review the issues and should make substantive judgments.[160] In *Evans v. Abney*[161] and *Palmer v. Thompson*,[162] two controversial racial segregation cases, Black's majority opinions concluded that state actions in Georgia and Mississippi reckoning with the return of public lands to private trustees and the closing of public swimming pools did not run afoul of the equal protection clause of the fourteenth amendment. Local governments, with no clear showing of discrimi-

---

159. Haigh, *supra* note 78, app. at 1123-24.

160. *See, e.g.*, Citizens to Preserve Overton Park, Inc. v. Volpe, 401 U.S. 402, 421-22 (1971) (Black, J., concurring in part, dissenting in part); Wyman v. Rothstein, 398 U.S. 275, 277 (1970) (Black, J., dissenting); Lewis v. Martin, 397 U.S. 552, 560-63 (1970) (Black, J., dissenting); Dandridge v. Williams, 397 U.S. 471, 489 (1970) (Black, J., concurring); Rosado v. Wyman, 397 U.S. 397, 430-35 (1970) (Black, J., dissenting); Wheeler v. Montgomery, 397 U.S. 280, 282 (1970) (Black, J., dissenting); Goldberg v. Kelly, 397 U.S. 254, 271-79 (1970) (Black, J., dissenting); Zuber v. Allen, 396 U.S. 168, 197-211 (1969) (Black, J., dissenting).

161. 396 U.S. 435 (1970).

162. 403 U.S. 217 (1971).

natory purpose, were not in violation of the Constitution simply because people disagreed with them.[163]

In *Evans*, Black let stand a Georgia court decision invalidating a trust that created a public park in Macon, Georgia, rather than integrating the public facility and thereby violating the terms of the original trust. Writing for the Court, Black reasoned that

> any harshness that may have resulted from the state court's decision can be attributed solely to its intention to effectuate as nearly as possible the explicit terms of [the] will. . . .
>
> . . . [T]he effect of the Georgia decision eliminated all discrimination against Negroes in the park by eliminating the park itself, and the termination of the park was a loss shared equally by the white and Negro citizens of Macon, Georgia.[164]

In *Palmer*, Black upheld a decision of the local government in Jackson, Mississippi, to close all public swimming pools rather than to integrate them. Black wrote that

> no case in this Court has held that a legislative act may violate equal protection solely because of the motivations of the men who voted for it. . . . Furthermore, there is an element of futility in a judicial attempt to invalidate a law because of the bad motives of its supporters.[165]

For Black, the record showed "no state action affecting blacks differently from whites."[166]

Chief Justice Burger, who considered himself a moderate in racial matters, felt uncomfortable with the *Evans* opinion. He believed that the Court could rectify the matter even though no state action existed. " 'We are the Supreme Court and we can do what we want,' "[167] he told a perplexed Justice Harlan. Finally, Burger wrote Black a memorandum: " 'Dear Hugo, This is a difficult case with a result I do not relish, but the question is one for the states (states, unlike federal agencies and this Court, are not infallible). Seeing it as a state question, I join your opinion.' "[168]

---

163. *See Palmer*, 403 U.S. at 227; *Evans*, 396 U.S. at 445.

164. *Evans*, 396 U.S. at 444-45.

165. *Palmer*, 403 U.S. at 224-25.

166. *Id.* at 225.

167. B. Woodward & S. Armstrong, *supra* note 2, at 61 (quoting Chief Justice Burger).

168. B. Woodward & S. Armstrong, *supra* note 2, at 61-62 (quoting memorandum from Chief Justice Burger to Justice Black).

In other dissenting opinions, Black would have supported state determinations of the nature of juvenile statutes. In *In re Winship,*[169] for example, he maintained that the State could use the "preponderance of evidence" standard in juvenile proceedings. "Nowhere in [the Constitution] is there any statement that conviction of crime requires proof of guilt beyond a reasonable doubt."[170] Contrary to the Court majority, Black argued that the Constitution did not require this type of proof and that the majority's " 'natural law due process' notion" violated the principle of a government of limited powers.[171]

Winship was the last occasion Black had to debate this position with his philosophical opponent, Justice John M. Harlan, Jr. Black considered the Court majority's response yet another example of judicial tampering with the words of the Constitution, a judicial practice Black fought against throughout his tenure on the Court.

In a number of other opinions decided in these two Court terms, regarding comity,[172] illegitimate children,[173] hair-length regulations in public schools,[174] and state referendums,[175] the senior Justice strongly supported the states' right to develop and implement social policy without federal judicial interposition.

Given the domestic turbulence of the period, the case of *Illinois v. Allen*[176] took on unusual importance for Justice Black during the 1969 Court term. Black believed in the primacy of order and respect for law, and he was troubled grievously to see the spectacles taking place in the courtrooms toward the end of the 1960's decade. Thus, when *Allen* came to the Court, Black quickly pushed it through in an attempt to respond to the courtroom travesties that he had been reading about in the press.

During *Allen,* the trial judge had expelled a noisy defendant from the courtroom, and Burger asked Black to write the opinion for the Court majority. Black enthusiastically attacked the case because it provided him the "opportunity to tell trial judges how

---

169. 397 U.S. 358 (1970).
170. *Id.* at 377 (Black, J., dissenting).
171. *Id.* at 381-82.
172. *See* Wisconsin v. Constantineau, 400 U.S. 433, 443-45 (1971).
173. *See* Labine v. Vincent, 401 U.S. 532, 538 (1971).
174. *See* Karr v. Schmidt, 401 U.S. 1201, 1202 (1971).
175. *See* James v. Valtierra, 402 U.S. 137, 142-43 (1971).
176. 397 U.S. 337 (1970).

they could deal with disorderly courtroom behavior without violating the rights of the accused."[177] In his opinion, Black extolled the virtues of the courtroom ("palladiums of liberty"[178] and "citadels of justice"[179]) and concluded that, to maintain decorum in the court, a trial court constitutionally could bind and gag the defendant, could cite him for contempt, or could expel him from the courtroom until the defendant's behavior changed.[180]

In these last 2 years of his tenure on the Court, Black also continued to support the application of broad congressional powers. In *Boys Markets, Inc. v. Retail Clerks Union, Local 770*,[181] he dissented from the majority's decision allowing a federal district court, despite a federal statute to the contrary,[182] to enjoin workers from striking.[183] In his dissent, Black wrote that he "believe[d] that the making and the changing of the laws which affect the substantial rights of the people are primarily for the Congress, not [the Supreme] Court."[184] In *United States v. Vuitch*,[185] Black reversed and remanded a federal district court's dismissal of an indictment against a licensed physician on the ground that a congressional abortion statute was unconstitutionally vague.

After reviewing his opinions on the general question of power of local, state, and national governments, Black maintained his original jurisprudential position during his service with Chief Justice Burger. The full responsibility for developing and implementing social and economic policy rested with the elected officials. In a 1965 dissent, Black wrote: "[M]any good and able men have eloquently spoken and written, sometimes in rhapsodical strains, about the duty of this Court to keep the Constitution in tune with the times. . . . For myself, I must with all deference reject that philosophy."[186] Black believed that judges must not use "subjective

---

177. B. Woodward & S. Armstrong, *supra* note 2, at 62.

178. *Allen*, 397 U.S. at 346.

179. *Id.* at 347.

180. B. Woodward & S. Armstrong, *supra* note 2, at 62-63. While the *Allen* case did not involve a political defendant or an anti-war protestor, Douglas dissented because he felt the precedent set in *Allen* was a harsh one when applied in these political trials. *Id.* at 63.

181. 398 U.S. 235 (1970).

182. *Id.* at 237 n.1.

183. *Id.* at 253. The decision overruled an earlier Supreme Court opinion, Sinclair Ref. Co. v. Atkinson, 370 U.S. 195 (1962).

184. *Boys Markets*, 398 U.S. at 256.

185. 402 U.S. 62 (1971).

186. Griswold v. Connecticut, 381 U.S. 479, 522 (1965) (Black, J., dissenting).

considerations"[187] to invalidate legislation that they do not like. In 1969 and in 1970 Black continued to urge judicial self-restraint with the same mixed results he had realized in his previous 32 years on the High Bench.

B. Restrictions on Governmental Power

In the troublesome decade of the 1960's, many highly controversial issues confronted the Burger Court. Selective service and conscientious objectors, obscenity, national security, the Vietnam War, freedom of the press, voting rights, and the cruel and unusual punishment cases were some of the controversies that found their way into the Supreme Court. Black's responses to these issues and their underlying principled foundations were characteristic of his general response over the decades to litigation involving fundamental freedoms and governmental intrusions.

In litigation dealing with governmental censorship of the press,[188] press libel and slander of public officials,[189] the right of association and admission to the bar,[190] obscenity,[191] and freedom of expression, Black insisted that first amendment freedoms provide persons with an unfettered freedom to speak, write, associate, and express themselves in traditional ways.

New York Times Co. v. United States,[192] the most controversial of these first amendment cases, came to the Court at the very

---

187. *Id.*

188. *See* New York Times Co. v. United States, 403 U.S. 713, 717 (1971) (Black, J. concurring).

189. Rosenbloom v. Metromedia, 403 U.S. 29, 57 (1971) (Black, J., concurring in the judgment); Ocala Star-Banner Co. v. Damron, 401 U.S. 295, *ante* 277 (1971) (Black, J., concurring in the judgment (included with dissent in Monitor Patriot Co. v. Roy, 401 U.S. 265, 277 (1971) (Black, J., concurring in part, dissenting in part))); Time, Inc. v. Pape, 401 U.S. 279, *ante* 277 (1971) (Black, J., dissenting (included with dissent in Monitor Patriot Co. v. Roy, 401 U.S. 265, 277 (1971) (Black, J., concurring in part, dissenting in part))); Monitor Patriot Co. v. Roy, 401 U.S. 265, 277 (1971) (Black, J., dissenting); Ginzburg v. Goldwater, 396 U.S. 1049, 1049 (1970) (Black, J., dissenting).

190. *See, e.g.*, Law Students Civil Rights Research Council v. Wadmond, 401 U.S. 154, 175 (1971) (Black, J., dissenting); *In re* Stolar, 401 U.S. 23 (1971); Baird v. State Bar, 401 U.S. 1 (1971).

191. United States v. Thirty-Seven (37) Photographs, 402 U.S. 363, 379 (1971) (Black, J., dissenting); United States v. Reidel, 402 U.S. 351, *post* 379 (1971) (Black, J., dissenting) (included with dissent in United States v. Thirty-Seven (37) Photographs, 402 U.S. 363, 379 (Black, J., dissenting)).

192. 403 U.S. 713 (1971) (per curiam).

end of Black's tenure as Associate Justice. On June 13, 1971, the *New York Times* began publishing a top secret government report documenting the history of American involvement in the Vietnam War. On Tuesday, June 15, 1971, United States Attorney General John Mitchell obtained an order from a federal district court enjoining future publication of the report by the *Times*. The action astounded Black, and he expressed his incredulity to his clerks.[193]

This serious attempt by the national government to prevent the free press from publishing an important story was, in Black's opinion, an egregious form of prior restraint. But the use of the judiciary as the instrument of suppression of first amendment liberties was even worse, according to the Justice.

The controversy came to the Court because the Justices granted certiorari on June 25, 1971. In a brief per curiam note, the Court set aside the injunctions: The national government " 'carries a heavy burden of showing justification for the enforcement of such a restraint.' [Lower federal courts] held that the Government had not met that burden. We agree."[194] All the Court Justices wrote or joined in concurring or dissenting opinions. This concurrence was Justice Black's last written opinion, and it contained a strong statement on behalf of the absoluteness of the first amendment's freedom of the press:

> The press was protected so that it could bare the secrets of government and inform the people. Only a free and unrestrained press can effectively expose deception in government. And paramount among the responsibilities of a free press is the duty to prevent any part of the government from deceiving the people and sending them off to distant lands to die of foreign fevers and foreign shot and shell. In my opinion, far from deserving condemnation for their courageous reporting, [the newspapers] should be commended for serving the purpose that the Founding Fathers saw so clearly.[195]

The Justices were involved in a difficult set of negotiations to resolve the dilemma. While four Justices—Black, Douglas, Brennan, and Marshall—favored granting certiorari, one additional vote was needed to hear the case as an emergency appeal from the court of appeals. Four other Justices—Burger, Harlan, White, and

---

193. B. WOODWARD & S. ARMSTRONG, *supra* note 2, at 139.

194. *New York Times*, 403 U.S. at 714 (quoting Organization for a Better Austin v. Keefe, 402 U.S. 415, 419 (1971)).

195. *New York Times*, 403 U.S. at 714-20 (Black, J., concurring).

Blackmun—wanted to hear oral arguments in October and to continue the injunctions until then. The critical, deciding vote belonged to Justice Potter Stewart, a Jurist whom many thought Nixon would name as Warren's replacement in 1969. Stewart finally decided to vote for certiorari, and " '[r]eluctantly Harlan joined the others in voting to grant cert.' "[196]

After hearing oral arguments on June 26, 1971, the Justices attempted to resolve the quandry by reviewing the secret documents. Only Black, Douglas, and Brennan believed that the press had an absolute right to publish. For the others, the contents of the documents would play a major role in the judgment of the Supreme Court.[197] The Justices met again in disagreement: Burger wanted more argument, and only Black, Douglas, and Brennan were clearly on the side of the press. Stewart, the key vote, concluded that the government had not shown a danger, and he voted to lift the injunctions. The logjam was broken with a final vote of 6 to 3 with Burger, Blackmun, and Harlan in the minority.

"For Black, this decision represented the most important First Amendment opinion of his career—a final accomplishment in his efforts to gain acceptance for First Amendment values."[198] Telling his clerks that the government had "deceived us all this time,"[199] he went about the task of putting down, for a final time, his thought on the "firstness" of the first amendment.

Black also asserted first amendment freedoms in the various selective service cases that came to the Court during this time.[200] He sided with young persons who intentionally were mistreated by government.[201] In *Astrup v. Immigration & Naturalization Service*,[202] Black persuaded the Court unanimously to rule that the government had committed a wrong. Chief Justice Burger, in a note to Black, explained his belief that the young person had worked out a bad bargain, but stressed that he felt compelled by Black's argument to join in the majority opinion.

---

196. B. Woodward & S. Armstrong, *supra* note 2, at 142 (quoting memorandum from Justice Hugo L. Black to Chief Justice Warren Burger).

197. B. Woodward & S. Armstrong, *supra* note 2, at 139-40.

198. *Id.* at 147.

199. *Id.*

200. *See, e.g.*, Welsh v. United States, 398 U.S. 333 (1970); Toussie v. United States, 397 U.S. 112 (1970); Breen v. Selected Serv. Local Bd. No. 16, 396 U.S. 460 (1970).

201. Astrup v. Immigration & Naturalization Serv., 402 U.S. 509 (1971).

202. 402 U.S. 509 (1971).

While Black generally defended the rights of young persons to hold unorthodox views, nevertheless, he felt compelled to dissent in *Cohen v. California*.[203] In *Cohen*, a young man had been convicted for "offensive conduct" for wearing, in a Los Angeles, California, county courthouse a jacket with the words "Fuck the Draft" emblazoned on its back. At first Black voted to dismiss summarily the conviction, but, as the case dragged on and he heard oral arguments, he had a change of heart. " 'What if Elizabeth [his wife] were in that corridor,' he asked [his clerks]. 'Why should she have to see that word?' "[204] In the end, he decided to join the dissenting opinion written by Justice Blackmun and joined, also, by Burger. For Blackmun and Black, "Cohen's absurd and immature antic . . . was mainly conduct and little speech."[205]

Many controversial criminal procedure cases came to the Court during the last terms of Black's service. Black's judgments were a continuing reflection of his views on both due process and the federal courts' role in this area of constitutional law.[206] Three cases, *Coolidge v. New Hampshire*,[207] *Coleman v. Alabama*,[208] and *Ashe v. Swenson*,[209] reflected Black's continuity of jurisprudence in due process litigation before the Court.

In the sixth amendment *Coleman* case, an example of a Court turnaround on the results of an important constitutional issue, Black wrote a concurring opinion. In conference, the justices had voted 7 to 1 that a person charged with a crime had no right to an attorney at a preliminary hearing before a magistrate to determine whether sufficient evidence existed to continue the proceedings to the trial stage of the process. The Justices' initial reaction was that the sixth amendment right to the assistance of counsel did not ex-

---

203. 403 U.S. 15 (1971).

204. B. Woodward & S. Armstrong, *supra* note 2, at 131 (quoting Justice Black) (brackets in B. Woodward & S. Armstrong).

205. *Cohen*, 403 U.S. at 27 (Blackmun, J., dissenting).

206. *See, e.g.*, Coolidge v. New Hampshire, 403 U.S. 443, 443 (1971); United States v. White, 401 U.S. 745, 754 (1971) (Black, J., concurring); Williams v. United States, 401 U.S. 646, 660 (1971) (Black, J., concurring in the result); Mayberry v. Pennsylvania, 400 U.S. 455, 466 (1971) (Black, J., concurring in judgment); Baldwin v. New York, 399 U.S. 66, 74 (1970) (Black, J., concurring in the judgment); Coleman v. Alabama, 399 U.S. 1, 11 (1970) (Black, J., concurring); Ashe v. Swenson, 397 U.S. 436, 447 (1970) (Black, J., concurring); Turner v. United States, 396 U.S. 398, 425 (1970) (Black, J., dissenting).

207. 403 U.S. 443 (1971).

208. 399 U.S. 1 (1970).

209. 397 U.S. 436 (1970).

tend to this pretrial action. The sole dissenter was Harlan, who "thought that the preliminary hearing was part of the prosecutorial process."[210]

Brennan was given the task of writing the opinion for the majority. After reading the Brennan draft, however, Black "announced that he had reconsidered and would join Harlan in dissent."[211] Reconsidering one's conference vote evidently was not unusual. In a letter to the author, Black wrote:

> [M]y votes at conference are never final. They are tentative and I am always ready to change the vote if I reach the conclusion that my vote was wrong . . . . Nor is there anything altogether extraordinary in the fact that a Justice to whom an opinion is assigned to write one way may write it another way.[212]

Burger wrote to Black asking the senior Justice to explain his turnabout. Black responded tartly:

> "Dear Chief, Amendment VI. . . .
>
> Although the Sixth Amendment doesn't go into detail on when [a person's right to the assistance of counsel begins], it would disregard reality to say that a preliminary trial is not an important part of a prosecution under which a state is preparing to punish a man . . . .
>
> Where is there anything in the Constitution that says although a man has the right at the time of prosecution, he cannot claim that help the first time he needs counsel?"[213]

The next occurrence illuminated Black's words on turnabouts on the Court. After Harlan circulated his dissenting opinion, supported by Black, Brennan began to worry that he would lose his majority. He vowed to a law clerk: " 'I'm not going to lose another one,' "[214] and Brennan revised his opinion to defend Coleman's right to have an attorney at a preliminary hearing. With that change accomplished, most of the other Justices stayed with Brennan, much to Burger's chagrin. In this surprising development, the Chief found himself on the losing side of the controversy. When Black's concurring opinion was announced in *Coleman*, it empha-

---

210. B. WOODWARD & S. ARMSTRONG, *supra* note 2, at 69.
211. *Id.*
212. Letter from Hugo Black to the author (Jan. 21, 1969).
213. B. WOODWARD & S. ARMSTRONG, *supra* note 2, at 70.
214. *Id.* at 71 (quoting Justice Black).

sized that "the explicit commands of the Constitution provide a full description of the kind of 'fair trial' the Constitution guarantees, and in [Black's] judgment that document leaves no room for judges either to add or to *detract* from these commands."[215]

Ashe, another case decided during the 1969 term of the Court, involved a man charged with robbing six men at a poker game. The State found Ashe not guilty of the charge of robbing one of the six and tried him for robbing another poker player. This time the jury found him guilty. With the exception of the Chief Justice, all the Justices believed that the defendant should be set free. Black assigned Stewart to write the opinion for the majority. Stewart's opinion focused on the meaning of double jeopardy and collateral estoppel.[216] Black, still concerned about judicial creativity, wrote a separate concurring opinion that focused on his now familiar theme of judicial self-restraint: "In my view, it is a wholly fallacious idea that a judge's sense of what is fundamentally 'fair' or 'unfair' should ever serve as a substitute for the explicit, written provisions of our Bill of Rights."[217]

Coolidge was a controversial case heard during the 1970 Court term. It involved the search and seizure protections of the fourth amendment in a particularly heinous crime allegedly committed by Edward Coolidge.[218] Primarily on evidence seized without a search warrant by the police through the cooperation of Coolidge's wife, he was convicted of murdering a teenager. Coolidge appealed the conviction on grounds that the police searches were unreasonable ones and that the evidence uncovered was inadmissible in light of *Mapp*.

Black felt that all the evidence should be allowed and that the conviction should stand, although he evidently did not want to overturn *Mapp*.[219] The Court again was divided evenly. Justices Burger, Blackmun, White, Marshall, and Stewart wanted to exclude the evidence. Harlan appeared to be the swing Justice and tentatively opted for excluding the evidence in light of *Mapp*. After heated discussions among the Justices and their clerks, Harlan agreed to join the Stewart opinion, which reversed the conviction

---

215. *Coleman*, 399 U.S. at 12-13 (Black, J., concurring) (emphasis added).
216. *Ashe*, 397 U.S. at 436.
217. *Id.* at 447 (Black, J., concurring).
218. *Coolidge*, 403 U.S. at 443.
219. B. Woodward & S. Armstrong, *supra* note 2, at 116.

and remanded the case back to the state court, and all the Justices agreed to hold off a full-blown discussion of the continued viability of *Mapp* for a better, cleaner case.[220]

The five-man majority opinion had reversed and remanded because the search warrant enabling the police to search Coolidge's automobile was issued by the State's Attorney General, who was actively in charge of the investigation and later was the key prosecutor at the trial, instead of a neutral and detached magistrate. Black's dissent in *Coolidge* was a bitter one. Laying into the judicial creativity of the five-man majority, Black argued that the exclusionary rule was "judicially created" and that "the Fourth Amendment properly construed contains no such exclusionary rule."[221] "The Fourth Amendment prohibits unreasonable searches and seizures. The Amendment says nothing about consequences. It certainly nowhere provides for the exclusion of evidence as the remedy for violation."[222]

The Court majority, Black concluded, believed it had a fourth amendment "rulemaking capacity" to modify the words of the Constitution when, in fact, they do not have this power. For Black, the search was a reasonable one, the warrant was issued properly, and the conviction should have been upheld by the Court. He remarked: "It is difficult for me to believe the Framers of the Bill of Rights intended that the police be required to prove a defendant's guilt in a 'little trial' before the issuance of a search warrant."[223] Black continued to dissent in other criminal justice cases because he felt that the majority unconstitutionally was tampering with the words of the Constitution.[224]

C. *The Role of the Federal Judge*

Justice Black sharply dissented twenty-nine times during his last two terms on the Court because, for the most part, the Court majority placed an arbitrary gloss on the words of the Constitution and on the plain meaning of legislation.[225] In *Mills v. Electric*

220. *Id.* at 117-19.
221. *Coolidge*, 403 U.S. at 493 (Black, J., concurring in part, dissenting in part).
222. *Id.* at 496.
223. *Id.* at 499.
224. *See* notes 225-36 and accompanying text.
225. See, for example, Justice Black's dissent in Coleman v. Alabama, 399 U.S. 1, 11 (1970) (Black, J., dissenting); Boys Markets, Inc. v. Retail Clerks Union, Local 770, 398 U.S.

Auto-Lite Co.,[226] Black dissented from the Court opinion that vacated a court of appeals ruling involving the Securities and Exchange Act of 1934 and thereby prevented the plaintiffs' from collecting attorney's fees in the absence of statutory provisions for such fees. "The courts are interpreters, not creators, of legal rights to recover," Black wrote, "and if there is a need for recovery of attorney's fees to effectuate the policies of the Act here involved, that need should, in my judgment, be met by Congress, not by this Court."[227]

In *Bivens v. Six Unknown Named Agents of Federal Bureau of Narcotics*,[228] Black dissented because the Court majority created a federal cause of action for damages for an unreasonable search by federal agents. This task was for the Congress, not the courts, Black maintained.[229] In *Boddie v. Connecticut*,[230] another 1970 term dissent, Black criticized the Court majority for reversing a lower federal court decision against a party who claimed that the Connecticut divorce statute, requiring nominal court fees, was unconstitutional. Black believed that, absent specific constitutional or statutory provision, marriage and divorce are controlled by state policy. Criminal and civil actions are different. The Bill of Rights safeguards against obtrusive and illegal governmental action against criminal defendants only. Black stated that, in civil suits, government is neutral; there is no punishment depriving anyone of life, liberty, or property.[231] Black added that natural law concepts lack any constitutional precision. He observed:

> These concepts mark no constitutional boundaries and cannot possibly depend on anything but the belief of particular judges, at particular times, concerning particular interests which those judges have divined to be of 'basic importance.'
>
> . . . I believe that the only way to steer this country toward its great destiny is to follow what our Constitution says, not what judges think it should have said.[232]

235, 255 (1970) (Black, J., dissenting); *In re* Winship, 397 U.S. 358, 377 (1970) (Black, J., dissenting).

226. 396 U.S. 375 (1970).
227. *Id.* at 397 (Black, J., dissenting in part).
228. 403 U.S. 388 (1971).
229. *Id.* at 429 (Black, J., dissenting).
230. 401 U.S. 371 (1971).
231. *Id.* at 391 (Black, J., dissenting).
232. *Id.* at 393.

Justice Black also dissented in a number of cases involving civil rights, the powers of Congress to remedy voting rights discrimination, and a broadening interpretation of the fourteenth amendment's equal protection clause.[233]

To summarize his tenure on the Burger Court, Justice Black was insistent that ours is a government of laws. Federal judges are obligated to validate these laws in controversial litigation that came to the Court. "Even though I like my privacy as well as the next person," said Black in 1968, "government can invade it under many circumstances."[234] For the Justice, "government at all levels was fully clothed with the power to govern and to maintain order."[235]

The Black refrain was a clear one: when judging the constitutionality of legislation, federal courts must go to the literal words and the historical chronicles of the Constitution and its framers. If changes were needed in these fundamental, positive laws, they had to be made by the people's representatives in constitutionally prescribed ways. "This approach can easily be seen as naive, but is in fact extremely complex, with deep philosophical and jurisprudential roots."[236]

V. Conclusion

Because he had witnessed mischievous acts of federal courts,[237] Justice Black fully and deeply was committed to a political jurisprudence of judicial self-restraint with regard to the making and unmaking of social and economic public policies. At the same time, he was committed equally to an aggressive federal judiciary that would protect the people's fundamental freedoms to participate as free men and women in the civil culture and the polity.

A determined, gritty, yet gracious Jurist, Black continually was working, from 1937 until his final days on the Court in 1971, to educate his Brethren about these solemn judicial responsibilities and obligations. For Black, dividing the line between judicial self-

---

233. See generally H. Ball, D. Krane & T. Lauth, *supra* note 44, for an examination of Justice Black's views of the 1965 Voting Rights Act, especially section 5 of the Act.

234. H. Black, *supra* note 91, at 9.

235. Meador, *supra* note 12, at 1110.

236. Letter from former law clerk, *supra* note 50.

237. "To people who have faith in our nine Justices, I say I have known a different court from the one today." H. Black, *supra* note 91, at 11.

restraint and judicial activism was easier if the federal courts would disabuse themselves of subjective values such as "shock the conscience," "fundamental sense of civilized justice," "offend the community," "sporting sense of fair play," and other such natural law standards.

In his correspondence with Frankfurter, Black often spoke of their mutual differences. But these differences related to the means most likely to achieve the end both envisioned. Black's ultimate goal, only partially achieved while he sat on the High Bench, was to minimize judicial discretion and to "leave basic policy changes to the democratic processes."[238]

This democratic ideal was Hugo Black's intimate nexus to the political thought of another great southerner, Thomas Jefferson. Both Black and Jefferson, loyal sons of a New South, believed that only an enlightened citizenry could maintain the very fragile fabric of democratic processes in a free society.[239] His striving for this principle of representative democracy has become the enduring legacy of Justice Hugo L. Black.

---

238. W. Mendelson, Justices Black and Frankfurter: Conflict in the Court 73 (1961).

239. Ball, *supra* note 8, at 1049-50.

THE CLAY COUNTY ORIGINS OF MR. JUSTICE BLACK: THE POPULIST AS INSIDER

*Sheldon Hackney**

An uncomplicated view of Hugo Black exists, a view that connects his role as a powerful dissenter on the Supreme Court, the champion of individual liberty and free speech, with his origins in the Populist stronghold of Clay County, Alabama. According to this view, Black was a natural-born tort lawyer, a consistent defender of "the little man" against members of the social or economic elite and especially against concentrations of power and privilege.

Arriving as a complete outsider in Birmingham, Alabama, in 1907 to begin his legal career, Black received no invitation into an establishment firm, but began to scratch out a living as a personal injury attorney representing the working man and sympathizing with unions. From those humble beginnings, he became a reform-minded police court judge, antiestablishment solicitor (prosecutor) of Jefferson County, winner of a Populist-style race for the United States Senate, staunch proponent of the New Deal and attacker of the malefactors of great wealth as a tough Senate investigator, and finally, Franklin Roosevelt's first appointee to the Supreme Court. As Supreme Court Justice, Black fashioned an influential philosophy of the Constitution based on a Madisonian antipathy toward concentrations of power and on a fervent belief in individual freedom as clearly defined in various parts of the Bill of Rights, especially the first and fifth amendments.[1]

---

* President and Professor of History, University of Pennsylvania. B.A. 1955, Vanderbilt University; M.A. 1963, Ph. D. 1966, Yale University.

1. The author leaned heavily on V. HAMILTON, HUGO BLACK: THE ALABAMA YEARS (1972). The other standard biographical source is G. DUNNE, HUGO BLACK AND THE JUDICIAL REVOLUTION (1977). For convenient sources of Black's opinions, see generally I. DILLIARD, ONE MAN'S STAND FOR FREEDOM: MR. JUSTICE BLACK AND THE BILL OF RIGHTS (1963); Durr,

Assuming this neo-Populist framework, the task of the biographer is fairly straightforward. The vignettes fall neatly into place with the exception of a few recalcitrant facts, and they can be explained as acts of political expediency—not laudable but certainly understandable in an aspiring politician in Alabama in the first third of the twentieth century.

When Hugo Black joined the Ku Klux Klan in 1923, it was a major force in Alabama politics. The Klan was antiblack, anti-Catholic, anti-Jewish, and antiforeigner, and it used violence and intimidation to force wayward individuals of any description to conform to the code of personal morality of the white, protestant, rural majority. The Klan was intolerant and extralegal and was the pathological form of the common white people's attempt to control the forces of change threatening their world. In addition, Hugo Black showed nativistic sympathies by favoring immigration restriction during his Senate campaign, exploited racial prejudice in defending Edwin R. Stephenson for killing a Catholic priest, suppressed, as solicitor, newspapers carrying illegal liquor ads, defended the handling of *The Scottsboro Boys* case with anti-Yankee rhetoric, and opposed the antilynching bill during his second term as Senator.

On the other hand, even more numerous examples demonstrated Black's enlightened Populism. For example, the case that established his legal practice in Birmingham was his successful recovery of damages on behalf of a black man who illegally had been kept at work in the mines beyond his prison term under the convict lease system. Many other instances of unusually fair treatment for blacks and poor whites under Hugo Black's regime as police court judge and county solicitor followed. Black's major legislative effort as a Senator was the Black-Connery Bill, which would have provided for a 30-hour week. Though never enacted, portions of the Black-Connery Bill found their way into the Fair Labor Standard Act of 1938.

Unless one made unusual demands for purity and enlightenment in the context of Alabama politics before, for example, the Voting Rights Act of 1965, Hugo Black's public career appears unproblematic; it is the story of the rise of an unusually talented and

---

Hugo Black, Southerner, 10 Am. U.L. Rev. 27 (1961); Haigh, *Mr. Justice Black and the Written Constitution*, 24 Ala. L. Rev. 15 (1971).

energetic proponent of "the common man." The biographer might want to grapple with the psychological problem posed by Black's personality: our foremost twentieth-century champion of individual liberty and free speech was himself a strict disciplinarian at home, domineering everywhere, and conventional in most matters of personal behavior.[2] Then again, this characterization would serve a good, general description of Black's idol, Thomas Jefferson.

Such were my assumptions on the only occasion that I was ever in Black's presence, a lengthy afternoon visit in 1964 arranged by my wife, Lucy Durr, the daughter of his first wife's sister. Having married Black's adoring niece, I also had absorbed the Durr family view of "Uncle Hugo," a view that combined unqualified admiration of the public man and love of the charming, devoted, and involved family man with a muted realism about Uncle Hugo's stubbornness, his strong-willed, competitive, and, to some extent, stern personality.

I was still, on that occasion, a graduate student at Yale University at work on a study of Alabama in the Populist and Progressive era, but I had met and talked with several of Justice Black's former law clerks. Through their eyes, Justice Black appeared as an unusually hard-working Justice and a demanding task master, but he was also an exceedingly charming and thoughtful boss who took a deep personal interest in each of his clerks, just as he did with each member of his extensive family and hundreds of friends. Characteristically, they reported that Justice Black tolerated their arguing points of law with him, even encouraged it, but he never gave into their point of view. They might notice that he subsequently would change his position on a topic about which they had been arguing, but he never would acknowledge that his clerks had caused him to change his mind.

All of these family perspectives were confirmed for me during that memorable afternoon of conversation in the comfortable upstairs study of his house in Alexandria. I was properly awestruck, so I remember few of the details of our conversation. I do recall making a mental note, in my worst graduate student style of one-upmanship, that Justice Black's view of reconstruction was not up to date, nor did his ample shelves contain the most recent aca-

---

2. *See* H. Black, My Father, A Remembrance 92-93 (1975); G. Dunne, *supra* note 1, at 43; Durr, *Hugo L. Black: A Personal Appraisal*, 6 Ga. L. Rev. 1, 7-9 (1971).

demic histories. Then, when cocktails were served, Justice Black made a point of explaining that his doctor had prescribed a drink before dinner; otherwise, as I knew, he never drank and had been a prohibitionist in state politics.

The only passage of discussion that afternoon that has stuck in my mind, because it was so striking then, arose as the three of us together watched the evening news on television. As was frequently the case then, a civil rights demonstration dominated the broadcast. Lucy's and my sympathies were clear and unqualified, so I was surprised when Justice Black turned and asked whether we had noticed the looks on the faces of the demonstrators, looks of hatred and fanaticism. An animated discussion followed about the motives of demonstrators and the dynamics of protest movements that, accurately or not, is the principal residue in my mind from that occasion.

As I recall that vivid moment, Justice Black was not expressing his view, developed in later civil rights cases, that officials have a right to impose reasonable limits on the public use of governmental buildings—a view that accommodates itself to the fundamentalist version of the first amendment by drawing a sharp distinction between speech and action.[3] He was noticing, however, the authoritarian and anarchistic elements at work in the civil rights movement, elements that eventually led to the fragmentation of the movement. His observation upset me then because he detected a protofascist tint in a movement that I tended to see in Manichaean terms as the forces of light battling the forces of darkness. Clearly, his sense of public order had been disturbed by what he saw, and I went away to puzzle periodically about the apparent contradiction this revealed in his personality. How could the champion of the "little guy," the public servant whose principles stemmed from Populist protest against the established order, have such a strong commitment to public order and express such clear reservations about the most prominent "little guys" on the current scene?

Had I been better informed about recent constitutional history, I would have recognized in Black's attitude on that day the nub of his running argument with Felix Frankfurter about judicial

---

3. *Justice Black and the Bill of Rights*, 9 Sw. U.L. Rev. 937, 943-45 (1977) (reprint of CBS News Special, Dec. 3, 1968).

restraint in the face of legislative will. Black so much distrusted power that he distrusted it in the hands of the people as well as in the branches of government, or, at least in his view, the Constitution prescribes certain fundamental freedoms that even the people cannot abridge through their democratic representatives. In a system of rules, the rules had to be applied fairly, and even the majority ought not to be able to alter certain basic rules or rights.

The more I have thought and read about Hugo Black over the subsequent years, the more I have found inadequate the uncomplicated view of him as a great man who merely worked out different ways of applying the Populist principles of his boyhood as he found himself in larger and larger public arenas. In a region that likes its prophets and rebels to have a bit more of the maverick in them, Hugo Black climbed to the top with the principles of an outsider and the behavior of an insider.

There is, I discover, a way to read his life that stresses the conforming side of his nature. To begin with, he was raised in modestly privileged circumstances in Ashland, the county seat of Clay County, Alabama. The Clay County of his boyhood was a hotbed of Populism, to be sure, but his own family were not Populists. They were too prosperous and too much a part of the social fabric of the town to have joined such a political rebellion. Populism in Alabama was for those who lived on the economic margin or whose ties to the social order had been loosened by geographic mobility, downward social mobility, or some other alienating force.[4]

Also of note, Jeffersonian ideals, expressed in rhetoric about the worth of the common man as opposed to men of power and special privilege, was political orthodoxy in Alabama. The historian cannot distinguish Populist newspapers from Democratic newspapers by the slogans on their mastheads or the rhetoric in their editorials. "Equal rights to all; special privilege to none" was a commonplace motto on both sides of the political divide. Hugo Black as a boy would have absorbed equalitarian principles and a reverence for Thomas Jefferson without having to feel like a rebel, a dissenter, a marginal man, or an outsider. On the contrary, as the bright and energetic son of the town's leading merchant, Hugo undoubtedly grew up in relatively comfortable surroundings with a secure sense of his place and his family's place in the upper

---

4. *See* S. Hackney, Populism to Progressivism in Alabama 23-31 (1969).

reaches of local society. Given this background, he was a natural "insider."

Nothing he ever did was very far away from the mainstream. At The University of Alabama Law School, he was an officer in his small class of twenty-three students. When he went to the rough, industrial, frontier town of Birmingham to practice law, he started from scratch, but he soon came to the attention of an older, more established lawyer who maneuvered Black into position as police court judge. He made that system work efficiently, yet fairly, with a combination of toughness and compassion. He may have offended the sheriff and the police on occasion, but he accomplished what the legal establishment and the general public wanted him to accomplish. Furthermore, he joined every organization in sight and became a popular teacher in the Baptist Sunday School, not an unusual way to build a legal practice and a natural thing for a gregarious, unmarried young man to do.

Later, after winning election as Jefferson County Solicitor, he repeated his reformist performance. He released petty offenders from jail and, thus, angered the officials who were the beneficiaries of the fee system, prosecuted people without regard to their social position or influence, and cleared the docket in a whirlwind 30 months in office.

After a patriotic stint in the army, Black returned to Birmingham and pursued his very successful and highly lucrative practice as a plaintiff's attorney. At the same time, he built his political base to run for the United States Senate through activities that included joining the Ku Klux Klan and lining up allies in every county of the State. While becoming known as the young "bolshevik" attorney in Birmingham, Black lived on the fashionable southside, belonged to the country club, and courted and married Josephine Foster whose family was about as close as Alabama then could come to landed aristocracy, though the current generation had left the land and had moved to town. Both Josephine and her sister, Virginia, served terms as officers of the Junior League in Birmingham, a charitable organization that allowed young women of the most socially acceptable families, while displaying their social status, to do good works. Ironically, the Junior League helped awaken the political sensibilities of Josephine and Virginia by bringing them into contact with the grim realities of poverty and racial injustice. This well may have played a part in Senator

Black's broadening notion of justice and fair play.

Black waged another Populist-style campaign in 1926 to win a peculiar, five-sided race for the United States Senate over John H. Bankhead, Jr., of Jasper, a corporate lawyer and coal mine operator whose father had died in office in the United States Senate in 1920 and whose brother William Bankhead was already an influential member of the House of Representatives. Once in the Senate, Black tried to avoid prominence in the election campaign of 1928 that split the South, and he remained a Democratic Party loyalist. He gradually became an influential member of the Senate, his wife became the president of the Senate wives club, and he acted as a political ally of the Bankhead brothers.

Soon after the election of Franklin Roosevelt in 1932, Black emerged as a leading New Deal loyalist in the Senate and made a national reputation as an advocate of the 30-hour work week and as an investigator of the ocean mail subsidy program, airmail contracts, and utility lobbyists. For such services, including his backing of the court-packing bill, President Roosevelt made Hugo Black his first nominee for appointment to the Supreme Court in August 1937.

On the Court, Hugo Black was also a loyalist; he developed and maintained a deep regard for the Court as an institution, so much so that he became privately critical of William O. Douglas' personal life because it threatened to bring discredit to the Court. Conversely, he was able to maintain warm personal friendships with colleagues on the Court with whom he frequently disagreed.[5] One might also note that his, and the Court's, greatest mistake was its rule that upheld the arbitrary internment of Japanese-Americans during World War II, an act that can be explained by the patriotic loyalties of Black and his colleagues on the Court.

Hugo Black also remained loyal to Alabama even through the period following the *Brown* decision when he widely and publicly was reviled at home and when some of the animosity toward Justice Black was taken out on Hugo Black, Jr., and his family, then living in Birmingham. Through those dark days when the Justice could not visit the State with any pleasure, he continued to favor Alabamians for his clerkships and to stay in touch with family and

5. Cooper, *Mr. Justice Hugo L. Black: Footnotes to a Great Case*, 24 ALA. L. REV. 1, 6 (1971).

friends at home.[6]

How then might we reconcile these two differing views of Hugo Black, the Populist dissenter and champion of the ordinary individual against the power of entrenched economic interests, and Hugo Black, the institutional loyalist and patriot with an aversion to unseemly personal conduct and disorderly behavior? How could the same man be such a natural "insider" that he put institutional loyalty high on his list of values and became a superb organization politician, but be "outsider" enough that he allowed his Democratic sympathies to guide him throughout his career as a public servant, politician, and federal judge?

I believe the answer is to be found in Clay County, in his secure upbringing that made him a natural "insider," in the Jeffersonian social values that were the common coin of politics, and in the morality of personal responsibility that was the civic side of rural Protestantism.

Hugo Black, in one of his rare interviews in later years, remarked that most of his ideas came from the Old Testament.[7] I believe that was true. As the historian of ethics and behavior in the Old South has written about southerners of a slightly earlier period, "[t]hey had a sense of oneness with ancient values—both Old Testament and classical—concepts that still had pertinence in lives of hardship and inequity."[8] Black's remarkable self-education in the classics and in the history of the Revolutionary era merely confirmed the moral code that he had absorbed as a boy from his family and community, a code that owed as much to Old Testament concepts of duty as to Jeffersonian concepts of rights.

Whether one has in mind the laws or the prophets, the Old Testament is full of stories having to do with duty, with what an individual owes God and his fellow human beings. The thread that ties together the view of Black as an uncomplicated Populist and the view of Black as an institutional loyalist is the strong sense of responsibility that Black had and thought everyone else also should have. He especially thought that people in positions of power should be punctilious in their observance of the rules. His

---

6. *See generally* Meador, *Justice Black and His Law Clerks*, 15 Ala. L. Rev. 57 (1962).

7. *See* Note, *Justice Black and First Amendment "Absolutes": A Public Interview*, 37 N.Y.U. L. Rev. 549, 562 (1962).

8. B. Wyatt-Brown, Southern Honor: Ethics and Behavior in the Old South 25 (1982).

devotion to this notion of fair play, rather than any personal identification with the oppressed classes, governed Black's strong sense of justice. He was much more concerned with the fair functioning of the system and with the proper execution of responsibilities than he was with transferring power to the working class.

For Hugo Black, liberty and responsibility were not separate values, but necessarily were linked as the defining dimension of his public philosophy. His public philosophy mixed Old Testament requirements and Jeffersonian ideals in a way that could have been accomplished only by a great man who came naturally by both sources of wisdom in his native Clay County, Alabama.

LISTER HILL, HUGO BLACK, AND THE ALBATROSS OF RACE

*Virginia Van der Veer Hamilton**

Lister Hill and Hugo Black held public office during epidemics of bigotry in their home state of Alabama, during the 1920's directed against Catholics, Jews, and blacks, but, beginning in the late 1940's, aimed principally toward blacks. Both men made fundamental concessions to gain and, in Hill's case, continued to hold political office. Following Black's nomination to the United States Supreme Court, the revelation that he had joined the Ku Klux Klan and had accepted its support in his first campaign for the United States Senate aroused a nationwide furor. Hill's less dramatic compromises attracted no such widespread attention. Keenly aware of the prejudices of his white constituency, Hill deemed it expedient never to acknowledge publicly that he had been reared a Catholic and that some of his ancestors had been Jews. To retain elective office in Alabama for 45 years, he campaigned, voted, and filibustered against every civil rights measure to come before Congress. Despite all Hill's precautions, his political opponents relied chiefly upon the emotional issue of race in their continuing efforts to defeat him and others who followed his leadership. But paradoxically, because of their concessions to the prejudices of Alabama voters, Black and Hill attained and retained the power to contribute more toward enriching the lives of average citizens than any public servants in the history of this State.

Hill and Black shared a dedication to what Hill always spoke of as "the cause." Its issues varied, but the main thrust of "the cause" remained constant: to improve the economic, political, and,

---

*Professor of History and University Scholar Emerita, The University of Alabama at Birmingham. B.A. 1941, M.A. 1961, Birmingham-Southern College; Ph.D. 1968, The University of Alabama. This essay is based upon research for a biography of Lister Hill. For the most part, the following footnotes are confined to citations for the sources of direct quotations.

when feasible, the social status of the less privileged. Their study of Thomas Jefferson, their association with Franklin Roosevelt, their own progressive inclinations, and, in Black's case, the lingering influence of Populism, had attracted Hill and Black to "the cause."[1]

White Alabama voters, often inaccurately portrayed as abiding and monolithic regressives, twice elected Hugo Black their Senator and elected Lister Hill eight times to the House and five times to the Senate. Initially, both men courted political support from the ranks of prohibitionists, small farmers, newly enfranchised women, Methodists, Baptists, union members, and veterans, all seeking a larger share in political leadership after the First World War. To members of that informal coalition, Black and Hill were to add during the 1930's the overwhelming majority of voters in north Alabama, grateful to backers of the Tennessee Valley Authority that had rescued their region from poverty, as well as thousands of other white Alabamians who looked to Franklin Roosevelt to forestall further economic disaster, to restore the nation's equilibrium, and to improve their lot in life. After Black left politics, Hill attracted the backing of most of Alabama's public schoolteachers; numerous employees of military installations and other federal and state agencies; the majority of probate judges and municipal officials; the *Birmingham News* and *Age-Herald*, Alabama's most widely circulated, progressive newspapers in the 1940's and early 1950's; thousands of poorer whites, many of them women, newly enfranchised in the 1950's by virtual abolition of the cumulative poll tax; and a slowly growing number of black voters.

By espousing federal programs that intruded into and profoundly altered Alabama's economy, Hill and Black also attracted the same enemies: leaders of big business, major industries, the Alabama Power Company, the Farm Bureau, and the Extension Service; owners of valuable agricultural, mineral, and timber lands; and those who guarded the interests of these groups as corporation lawyers, state legislators, and members of the Alabama State Democratic Executive Committee. Governor Bibb Graves, adopting the

1. Interview with Judge Clarence Allgood, former campaign aide to Senator Lister Hill, in Birmingham, Alabama (Nov. 20, 1978); interview with Gould Beech, former administrative assistant to Senator Lister Hill in Magnolia Springs, Alabama (Mar. 24, 1978); interview with Robert Frazer, Senator Lister Hill's first congressional secretary in Arlington, Virginia (Mar. 16-17, 1985).

vernacular of most of his constituents, fastened the enduring label of "big mules" on these elements in his State.

Alabama's political landscape altered dramatically between the onset of World War II and the end of Hill's career more than a quarter of a century later. But the nature of his adversaries remained essentially unchanged although, in the process of mutation, many of Hill's opponents appeared in the guises of Democratic regulars, members of the States' Rights Party, supporters of the Citizens' Council, Alabama Democrats, "Eisenhower Democrats," and "Rebels for Martin" before eventually emerging openly as Republicans.

The identity of those who consistently supported and opposed Hill and Black emphasizes that, despite the trappings of bigotry adopted by both sides, the protracted struggle between advocates and antagonists of "the cause" was fundamentally economic in nature. Their immediate conflict revolved around control of the politics and economy of Alabama. But in a broader sense and over the longer run, this contest was between those who *knew* they had benefited and those who *thought* they had been deprived unfairly of property or control because of federal activism in economic and societal matters.

Lister Hill's great-grandfather, a self-educated preacher, had moved to Alabama from North Carolina in 1829, in hopes of improving his economic status and democratizing his church, and had been fortunate enough to secure land in the fecund Black Belt. When the Civil War put an end to dreams of attaining wealth through cotton and slaves, men in the Hill family chose the traditional, middle-class route of education for professions in medicine, dentistry, the law, and the church. Lister's father, trained at prestigious schools in the East and England, achieved international prominence as a pioneer in heart surgery. Following his marriage to a member of a wealthy Mobile family, Dr. Hill began to acquire valuable real estate holdings in and around Montgomery.

Forebears such as the Hills typified Alabama's ambitious, white majority. But some of Hill's maternal ancestors represented tiny minorities in a region populated overwhelmingly by Protestant Christians. These antecedents, Jews by birth, had adopted the Catholic faith after living for a number of years in the South. Reared a Catholic, Lister had been sensitized by his mother to the plight of those who found themselves members of two often-threatened minorities. Preparing for a political career, he renounced Catholicism and adopted the Methodist faith of his father's ancestors. But word that he had once been a Catholic and that some of his forebears had been Jews followed Hill throughout his long public career and provided opponents with fuel occasionally for newspaper accounts and more often for anonymous leaflets and ugly gossip. When thus attacked, Hill sought to ignore or to equivocate.

Largely because of Dr. Hill's money and influence, his son had been elected Democratic nominee for a seat in Congress in 1923 from Alabama's impoverished and, except for Montgomery, sparsely settled second congressional district. Fewer than 18,000 people, making up less than 6% of the district's total population, qualified or bothered to take part in this primary. Hill's victory had been a prime example of V.O. Key's thesis that a candidate's friends, neighbors, and, in this instance, relatives could make a crucial contribution to an Alabama political career during the first half of the twentieth century. Not yet 29 years of age, Hill created a small stir as the "baby" of the 68th Congress. With no opponent in seven subsequent Democratic primaries, he held the second district seat as a virtual sinecure.

His early start, his base in politically symbolic Montgomery, his energy and ambition boded well for Hill. He appeared certain to move quickly to the United States Senate, perhaps to succeed the respected Oscar Underwood or to replace what many Alabamians considered a political embarrassment, that folksy raconteur J. Thomas Heflin. One Senate seat from Alabama seemed destined for another member of the "royal" Bankhead family from the mining country of northwest Alabama. Traditionally, the second seat also had been occupied for the most part by other men of economic substance, well-connected within the intimate bounds of the Alabama gentry, such as John Tyler Morgan, Edmund Pettus, Joseph F. Johnston, and Underwood. This being the case, who was to block this ambitious congressman from south Alabama when he aspired to the Senate?

Hill and his supporters received a quick answer to this question. In 1926 drys, war veterans, small farmers, and the highly organized Klan dispatched another ambitious neophyte as Underwood's successor. The unexpected victory of Hugo Black, who had risen from small farmer and country storekeeper origins, presented a new obstacle to Hill's aspirations. In 1930 and 1936 Hill considered, but dropped, the idea of opposing John Bankhead, Jr. In 1932 he chose not to run against Black and explained privately: "[Black] and I represent too much the same people and agree too well. . . . I really do not know an issue I could raise with him."[2]

During the 1930's, Hill and Black almost wholeheartedly involved themselves in the ferment led by Franklin Roosevelt. Although both had been open and outspoken foes of the Alabama Power Company, they were slow to grasp the potential of George Norris's sweeping scheme for development of the Tennessee River Valley. But Black and Hill came to admire the stubborn Nebraska Senator and, being practical politicians, to realize the futility as well as the danger of damaging their standing with the new administration in opposing a program enthusiastically endorsed by FDR and, thus, almost certain to be put into effect.

Although Hill had taken 7 years to come around to the Norris approach, he laid aside his earlier doubts about putting the federal government in the power business and emerged in 1933 as House sponsor of the future Tennessee Valley Authority (TVA). From his post on the House Military Affairs Committee, and as chairman in 1937, Hill helped to fend off attacks on TVA by private power interests. As a Senator, he kept careful watch on Wendell Wilkie, Dwight Eisenhower, the promoters of the Dixon-Yates plan, and others he considered real or potential enemies of TVA.

Hill and Black were to reap enormous political benefit from their decision to give enthusiastic backing to Norris's grand scheme. Citizens of the Tennessee River Valley, barely aware of the role played by a Senator from faraway Nebraska, would give these two Alabamians much of the credit for their new prosperity. As their lives were enriched by industries, barge traffic, jobs, fertilizer, cheap electricity, and improved soil, the hitherto isolated and predominantly rural people of north Alabama would constitute their State's major base of support for Hill and Black, dispatch other progressives to represent them in Washington, like John Sparkman, Robert E. ("Bob") Jones, Carl Elliott, Albert Rains, and Kenneth Roberts, help James E. Folsom twice attain the governorship, and play a decisive role during the early 1950's in keep-

2. Letter from Lister Hill to William W. Hill (Mar. 2, 1930) (available in Lister Hill Papers, Special Collections, Gorgas Library, The University of Alabama).

ing Alabama loyal to the national Democratic Party.

Although Norris had succeeded in wooing Roosevelt to the unprecedented concept of TVA, Black fared less well in seeking White House support for his revolutionary proposal that the work week in American industry be limited to 30 hours in hopes of creating more jobs. To discuss Black's role in laying groundwork for and seeking passage of a wages and hours law is outside the province of this Article.[3] But it fell to Lister Hill and Claude Pepper, running for the Senate in 1937 as champions of federal wage and hour standards, to register victories that demonstrated widespread southern support for this principle, broke the congressional logjam, and led to passage of the Fair Labor Standards Act of 1938, destined to have far-reaching impact upon the South. Although Hill supported most measures of Roosevelt's first two administrations and took special interest in helping rural Americans to electrify their homes and assisting tenants and sharecroppers to become landowners, his leadership in behalf of TVA and the Fair Labor Standards Act comprised the most substantive contributions of his House career.

In personal style, Hill and Black differed sharply: Hill, cautious, a behind-the-scenes persuader, a public glad-hander, very much the gentleman in politics, an insider who worked within the system; Black, more daring, more of an innovative thinker, a fierce adversary and fearless investigator, a loner in the clubby atmosphere of the Senate. During the 1930's, both were leading spirits among an informal Washington group that often met socially to discuss the exciting events of their times. The group included fellow Southerners like Clifford and Virginia Durr, Aubrey Williams, and Jonathan Daniels, as well as administration figures such as Henry Wallace, Thomas Corcoran, and Thurman Arnold. No two members of this circle of friends had closer ties, based upon the friendship between their wives, their backgrounds and their careers in the same State, mutual admiration, and shared dedication to "the cause," than Black and Hill. Nonetheless, as 1938 approached, Hill seriously pondered whether or not to seek his friend's seat in the Senate.

Leaders of Alabama's business, industrial, and timber inter-

---

3. *But see generally* Shannon, *Hugo La Fayette Black as United States Senator*, 36 Ala. L. Rev. 881 (1985).

ests, infuriated that their senior Senator was leading the fight for a floor under wages and a limit on work hours, had been gearing up to oppose Black's reelection. But Roosevelt, eager to avenge himself upon opponents in the Senate and the High Court, made this fight unnecessary. As suddenly and unexpectedly as he had emerged, Black disappeared from the Alabama political scene.

Fourteen years after Hill had entered the House, the road to the Senate finally seemed clear. His only remaining obstacle was aging Tom Heflin, whose political career was haunted by still fresh memories that he had been a Catholic baiter and, in 1928, a Democratic renegade. In a campaign focused upon the wage-hour law, Hill, supported by organized labor, north Alabama, and, implicitly, Franklin Roosevelt, won almost two-thirds of the total vote and all but twelve of sixty-seven counties. Less than 150,000 voters, barely over 10% of Alabama's heavily disfranchised voting-age population and almost all of them whites, participated in the selection of their new Senator.

In 1944 the same economic interests that had mobilized to fight Black in 1938 turned in full force against Hill. With Bibb Graves dead, their chance arrived to remove the last of Alabama's powerful, New Deal triumvirate and to mount a counterattack against federal intervention in their economic, political, and, potentially, their social affairs. To lure the Alabama electorate away from Roosevelt, Hill's opponents revived the issue of race, largely dormant since the disfranchisement of Alabama's blacks in 1901. Roosevelt's creation of a Fair Employment Practices Committee (FEPC), the threat of federal laws against lynching and poll taxes, abolition of the "white primary," and the then seemingly slim possibility that federal financial aid to education might lead to school integration provided the rationale for an effort to heighten racial fears and hostilities.

This time defenders of the status quo had ample opportunity to select a more respectable spokesman than the politically rejected Tom Heflin. Their eventual choice, James A. Simpson, a prominent Birmingham corporation lawyer, had been a popular and able state legislator and protégé of former Alabama Governor Frank Dixon. Initially, Simpson was reluctant to raise the issue of race, but, eventually, he conceded that it offered his only chance to defeat an established and powerful incumbent. Simpson's attempt to light the racial fuse in 1944 fizzled, however. Most Alabamians still admired and trusted Roosevelt. The possibility that this President might lead them to the eventual breakdown of their legally segregated way of life seemed remote. In the midst of all-out war, deliberate provocation of racial hostility appeared disruptive and potentially dangerous.

Also, Hill proved his own ablest defender against those who intimated that he favored integration. Simpson and his supporters found it difficult to pin the label of an advocate of "social equality" on one who had spoken and voted against FEPC, as well as against federal laws to outlaw lynching and poll taxes, and who fervently proclaimed his dedication to continued segregation of schools and buses. But primarily because of their use of racism, opponents of Roosevelt and the New Deal persuaded almost half of Alabama's voters to cast their ballots against Hill. However, Hill's 25,000-vote majority over a major opponent, backed by powerful forces in Alabama and outside this State, added to his aura of invincibility and helped to discourage formidable challengers for 18 years.

Following the end of World War II, Alabama opponents of the New Deal, no longer constrained by patriotism, prepared for a fresh assault upon federal activism. In urging a permanent FEPC and national health insurance, Harry Truman seemed a considerably more vulnerable opponent than his predecessor. But as had Hugo Black in the aftermath of an earlier war, James E. Folsom caught the Alabama establishment by surprise. Folsom's election as Governor projected a more radical element onto Alabama's political battlefield in which, since the 1930's, only New Dealers and defenders of the *status quo ante* New Deal had warred.

After the death of John Bankhead, Jr., in 1946, Hill devoted his major attention to the elevation of his protégé, John Sparkman, to the Senate. Because Sparkman, although a veteran of five terms in the House, had no statewide following or organization, Hill placed his powerful and superbly organized machine, headed by Roy Nolen and Marc Ray ("Foots") Clement, at Sparkman's service. Even so, the Huntsville congressman had only 230 votes to spare when nominated over Simpson and Frank Boykin, a Mobile congressman with strong ties to business and lumber interests.

Although the elections of Folsom and Sparkman in 1946 represented defeats for big farmers and "big mules," that coalition regrouped to propose the Boswell amendment as a counterpoise to Folsom's plans to repeal the cumulative poll tax, to reapportion the legislature, and thereby to loosen the purse strings of state and local government. Through unabashed use of racial arguments, backers of the Boswell plan persuaded Alabama's overwhelmingly white electorate, which just had chosen a professed Jacksonian as Governor, to approve a further means of restricting the suffrage, insofar as possible, to the educated, propertied, and well-born. Hill, not daring to give his opponents an excuse to claim that he favored black voting, confined himself to warning that the Boswell amendment was designed to limit the *white* electorate and to prevent voting "by those [of] whom the Big Mules do not approve."[4] But the federal courts were left to decree the Boswell stratagem an unconstitutional violation of the fifteenth amendment.

Alarmed by the contrast between Truman's increasing commitment to civil rights and the mood of his Alabama constituents, Hill began to focus more upon the area of health than upon his long quest for federal aid to education. Anticipating the coming storm over racial issues, he relinquished his post as Democratic whip of the Senate at the end of 1946. By so doing, Hill turned aside from the path that would have led him to the position he then desired above all: Democratic leader of the United States Senate. In his stead, a brash and aggressive new Senator, a natural risktaker less fettered by his Texas constituents on the issue of race, would seize this post in 1953. Thus, Lyndon Johnson took a long stride toward the White House.

Although Hill bowed out of the national leadership of his party, he continued to lead the fight for control of the Alabama Democratic Party. Harry Truman's increasingly bolder stands for civil rights provided opponents of centralized power and the "welfare state" with a powerful weapon with which they hoped to snatch Alabama's political reins away from the State's new triumvirate of Hill, Sparkman, and Folsom. With the politically erratic and personally flawed Folsom in temporary eclipse, Hill headed the drive to elect Democratic loyalists as delegates to their party's 1948 convention and to ensure that this half of the Alabama delegation remained in place when the other half walked out of the Philadelphia hall. While loyalists had concentrated on the delegate race, Dixon and his allies, by positioning States' Rights electors

---

4. Press Release (n.d.) (available in Lister Hill Papers, Special Collections, Gorgas Library, The University of Alabama) (discussing Boswell amendment).

under the Democratic rooster, had seen to it that Alabama was the only state in which voters would be unable to cast ballots for Truman. But the defection of these nominally Democratic electors to the support of States' Rights Party candidates in 1948 had been a clever ruse rather than a valid test of the will of the electorate.

Hill and his supporters benefited from the frustration felt by many Alabamians who had wanted to vote the national Democratic ticket in 1948. Two years later, despite injection of the race issue by States' Righters, loyalists won control of Democratic Party machinery in Alabama in a statewide election for members of the State Democratic Executive Committee. Shortly thereafter, at Hill's instigation, Truman named to the federal bench one who had been instrumental in bringing about that loyalist victory. This appointee, Richard Rives, and a later Republican nominee to the United States Court of Appeals for the Fifth Circuit, Frank M. Johnson, Jr., who had been endorsed by Hill in preference to his own cousin, served on special, three-judge federal district courts that struck down segregation and discrimination in Alabama schools, parks, jury selection, higher education, voting, and legislative reapportionment.[5]

In 1950, the same year in which Claude Pepper and Frank Graham lost their Senate seats to opponents who made blatantly racist appeals, Hill easily was reelected over token opposition. In 1952, by requiring a virtually ironclad pledge of loyalty to the Democratic national nominees, the forces led by Hill barred members of the States' Rights Party from appropriating the Alabama Democratic label in a second consecutive Presidential election. With the States' Rights movement stalemated, signs of nascent Republicanism began to appear in Alabama.

Seeking a southerner to share the national ticket with Adlai Stevenson in 1952, Democrats settled upon Hill's senatorial colleague, in part because Sparkman's political base in north Alabama contained fewer blacks and, thus, seemed to exhibit less racial hostility than did Hill's home area of the Black Belt. Later, "Foots" Clement would ruminate that the greatest disappointment of Hill's career was that, although clearly the leader of Alabama loyalists and his State's senior Senator, he was not chosen to be his party's

5. *See* J. Bass, Unlikely Heroes 82 (1981).

Vice Presidential nominee in 1952.[6] With Sparkman on the ticket, Alabama Democrats beat back a strong Republican challenge, but Eisenhower received almost 40% of the popular vote.

With racial problems now on the doorstep of a Republican President, Hill, Sparkman, and Folsom prevailed again in 1954. Former Birmingham Congressman Laurie Battle, representing the "big mules" in an effort to displace Sparkman, voiced strong opposition to federal housing programs, TVA, unions, foreign aid, and the United Nations. Casting about for a racial issue, Battle charged Sparkman with having run for Vice President on a ticket advocating civil rights. A third Senate aspirant, John Crommelin, alleged that Jews (whom he called by the euphemism of "Eskimos") were conspiring with Communists to undermine the nation.[7] But an estimated 200,000 new voters, three-fourths of them white females and poor white males and one-fourth of them blacks, thronged to the polls to take advantage of a drastic reduction in Alabama's cumulative poll tax and to give overwhelming victories to Sparkman and the racially moderate Folsom. In contrast to the 10% of Alabama's voting age population that had participated in Hill's first Senate election, almost *one-third* voted in 1954. Editor Grover Hall, Jr., of the *Montgomery Advertiser*, commenting that Alabama was dominated by "Populists and Fair Dealers" led by both United States Senators from the State and its Governor, conceded that this election amounted to "a crop failure for us Plantation Whigs."[8]

Starting with the Hill-Simpson race of 1944, Alabamians had been exhorted six times to make political choices based upon racist appeals. In the referendum over the Boswell amendment, such appeals had proven irresistible. In the 1948 race for delegates to the Democratic convention, loyalists and dissidents had fought to a virtual draw. But under the adroit leadership of Lister Hill, the majority of Alabama voters, focusing upon *economic* issues, such as the improvements wrought in their lives by the New and Fair Deals, Hill's recent bills to provide hospitals and telephone service

---

6. Interview with Robert (Bob) Jones, former congressman from Alabama in Scottsboro, Alabama (June 16, 1983).

7. *See* T. Gilliam, The Second Folsom Administration: The Destruction of Alabama Liberalism, 1954-1958, at 55 (1975) (Ph. D. dissertation, Auburn University).

8. P. Smith, Loyalists and States' Righters in the Democratic Party of Alabama, 1949-1954, at 115-16 (1966) (M.A. thesis, Auburn University).

for rural Americans, and Folsom's neo-Populist policies, had expressed their gratitude and loyalty to the Democratic Party in 1944, 1950, 1952, and 1954. However, the Supreme Court decision in *Brown v. Board of Education*,[9] handed down less than 2 weeks after the 1954 victories of Sparkman and Folsom, brought what Editor Hall had termed "the pattern of good humor" in Alabama politics to an end.[10]

These campaign successes marked the apogee of Hill's leadership of progressive forces within Alabama. Although strong potential opponents still regarded Hill as unbeatable, Crommelin tried once again to defeat him in 1956 by reiterating Commelin's fears of a "Communist-Jewish conspiracy" and the impending downfall of legal segregation. Hill won 74% of Alabama voters, but Democrats, even though cracking the whip of the loyalty oath, could muster only slightly over 56% to hold Alabama in line for Stevenson and Kefauver.[11] In the aftermath of the Montgomery bus boycott of 1955, of Autherine Lucy's unsuccessful attempt to integrate The University of Alabama in 1956, and of the confrontation at Little Rock in 1957, the tide of moderation began to ebb, and the Klan reemerged. Alabama turned from moderate Governors James Folsom and Gordon Persons to outspoken segregationists like John Patterson and George Wallace.

As the atmosphere in his State became more heated, Hill, a senior Senator holding powerful committee posts, increasingly devoted his attention to national matters. He prevailed in a squabble with Oveta Hobby, Eisenhower's Secretary of Health, Education, and Welfare, over Hill's insistence that the Salk vaccine be distributed free to all the nation's children in a monumental effort to obliterate polio. In 1956 Hill steered through the Senate his proposals for federal aid to rural libraries and establishment of a National Library of Medicine. In 1958, as a consequence of the Russian launching of Sputnik, Hill, in collaboration with Carl Elliott, achieved his long-sought goal of federal aid to education in the guise of the National Defense Education Act of 1958. But to remain a viable candidate for reelection, Hill deemed it essential to sign the Southern Manifesto, protesting the *Brown* decision, and to

9. 347 U.S. 483 (1954).

10. *See* P. Smith, *supra* note 8, at 111.

11. N. Bartley & H. Graham, Southern Elections: County and Precinct Data, 1950-1972, at 6 (1978).

serve as a team captain in filibusters against the first civil rights act to pass Congress since 1875.

In his last campaign, Hill faced an openly Republican challenger, young, vigorous James D. Martin, an oil dealer, former Democrat, and former president of Associated Industries of Alabama. Initially, Martin had no illusions that he could defeat Hill by seeking to link the Senator with the "Kennedycrats," warning against further federal encroachment, and using code words to suggest racial issues. Late in this campaign, however, the forced integration of the University of Mississippi inflamed white Alabamians and almost put Martin in the Senate. President Kennedy's dramatic action in the Cuban missile crisis helped to save Hill from defeat. Hill was reelected to his fifth and final term in the Senate by a margin of 6,800 votes, less than 2% of the total vote. Forty-nine percent of Alabama voters had supported a Republican.

The use of race as a political weapon in 1962 aroused the Alabama electorate to forego its old "friends and neighbors" pattern.[12] Hill fared poorly among the predominantly white voters of his former congressional district and other counties in the Wiregrass and Black Belt. His power base contracted from statewide proportions to north Alabama and the Tennessee Valley. Despite the best efforts of union leaders, many of labor's rank-and-file in Jefferson and Mobile Counties defected to Martin. One analyst characterized the Hill-Martin race as a "critical election" in which a minority, being beneficiaries of the status quo and perceiving themselves threatened in a period of extreme tension, set in to create a mass following and mobilize voters toward a realignment—in this case, toward a two-party Alabama.[13]

Ironically, Hill had attracted some new enemies by 1962: many Alabama doctors, including some launched on their careers through the GI Bill of Rights cosponsored by Hill, joined the coalition of his opponents. In so doing, they fought to defeat the author of the Hill-Burton Hospital Act, the public official most responsible for expanding the research activities of the National Institutes of Health, the sponsor of the National Library of Medicine, and

---

12. J. Young, A Republican Challenge to Democratic Progressivism in the Deep South: Alabama's 1962 United States Senatorial Contest 201-02 (1978) (Ph. D. dissertation, Auburn University).

13. *Id.* at 268-69. *See generally* Burnham, *The Alabama Senatorial Election of 1962: Return of Inter-Party Competition*, 26 J. of Pol. 798 (1964).

the individual generally credited with having done more for the health of Americans than any other nonmedical person in the nation's history. The fact that so many doctors and their wives actively opposed him in 1962 hurt and disillusioned Hill. Seeking an explanation of this apparent paradox, he concluded bitterly that old-time practitioners of the healing art, such as his father, had been replaced by "merchants of medicine."[14]

Mulling over the election of 1962, the *Montgomery Advertiser* perceived a further irony: Democratic policies had transformed "an impoverished, helpless mass" into a "broad affluent middle class . . . increasingly . . . unwilling to take chances with social experimentation."[15] Hill's old, white constituency, many of its members elevated in economic status largely because of federal activism, was tilting toward Republicanism. In 1965 Hill would see his onetime House seat occupied by a Republican. In 1969 Hill would retire rather than risk possible defeat by facing another strong challenger couching economic interests in racial terms. His Senate seat would go to a nominal Democrat who opposed most of the policies of the national party. After the death of James Allen, this seat eventually would be held by Jeremiah Denton, Alabama's first Republican Senator since Reconstruction—and also its first Catholic Senator. In comparison with the specter of further intrusion by the federal government in matters regarding race and society, Catholicism had faded as a political bugaboo in Alabama.

At some point during the tumult that followed the *Brown* decision, Hill deemed it prudent to remove the photograph of Hugo Black from its position of prominence in his home. For his part, Justice Black, author of the Supreme Court majority opinion that "Ole Miss" must admit James Meredith, felt some resentment that, while he was being subjected to tremendous criticism back home, Hill was mouthing racial shibboleths. Two old friends, publicly at odds over the issue of race, drifted apart.[16]

Acts of expediency, while making the public careers of Hill

14. Letter from Mike Manatos to Larry O'Brien (Feb. 5, 1963) (available in Lyndon Johnson Papers, Lyndon Johnson Presidential Library, Austin, Texas).

15. J. Young, *supra* note 12, at 238.

16. Interview with Elizabeth Black, widow of Justice Hugo Black, in Arlington, Virginia (Mar. 17, 1985); interview with Virginia Foster Durr, sister-in-law of Justice Hugo Black, in Montgomery, Alabama (July 22, 1983); interview with Henrietta Hill Hubbard, daughter of Senator Lister Hill, in Montgomery, Alabama (May 27, 1983).

and Black possible, also exacted their price. The brouhaha over Black's onetime Klan membership deeply distressed his sensitive wife, Josephine, could have cost him his seat on the High Court, and to this day shadows his career. By defecting from the Catholic Church, Hill grievously wounded his devout mother and sisters and incurred the scorn of Montgomery's small Catholic community. Fearful of the coming storm over civil rights, he turned aside from his quest of the post of Democratic leader of the Senate and later found himself passed over for his party's Vice Presidential nomination in favor of a fellow Alabamian, seemingly less vulnerable on this crucial matter. In the late 1930's, Hill and Black had been regarded by keen observers in Washington as men of potential Presidential stature. Both these highly capable and ambitious men had dreamed of occupying the White House. But one was exposed to the nation as a former Klan member. The other, to survive politically, consistently opposed civil rights legislation. Thus, the Presidency became an unattainable goal.

Hill and Black had one final experience in common: at the zenith of their careers, both suffered obloquy from large numbers of fellow Alabamians who eventually fell captive once again to political manipulation over the emotional issue of race. Black's record on the Court, in particular on the *Brown* and *Engel v. Vitale*[17] decisions, led many Alabamians to denounce him as "a nigger lover"[18] and "a traitor to the South";[19] in 1961 his son and namesake would feel compelled to forsake his own political ambitions and to leave a state in which he and his family frequently were harassed and to which his father could not return "without being treated like a leper."[20] Black's former neighbors in the small, isolated community of Ashland have blocked a move to build a library there in memory of their distinguished fellow citizen and have given little support to the idea of restoring his boyhood home.

In 1962 in protest against integration of the University of Mississippi, thousands of Alabama voters voted, so the *Montgomery Advertiser* later reflected, "to sacrifice Hill . . . who had done more for them and all Americans than any man the state has ever sent

---

17. 370 U.S. 421 (1962).
18. H. Black, My Father: A Remembrance 211 (1975).
19. *Id.* at 209, 211.
20. *Id.* at 214.

to Washington."[21] Fifty-seven percent of the voters in Hill's home city of Montgomery favored Martin; the *Montgomery Advertiser* chose to sit out this race without endorsing either candidate. Prominent Montgomerians castigated Hill with the special fury that many upper-income Americans reserve for those whom they perceive to have deserted, like Franklin Roosevelt, the interests of their class. After Hill led loyalists in redeeming the Alabama Democratic Party from the States' Righters, a friend reported that he had achieved a new distinction: many in Montgomery now hated him even more than they hated Hugo Black.[22]

But "big mules," physicians, and other well-to-do Alabamians did not constitute the majority of those who vehemently excoriated Black and Hill. Bitterest pill of all, the loudest hue and cry arose from white Alabamians whose quality of life had improved dramatically following the Great Depression, due in no small measure to Hugo Black's and Lister Hill's long devotion to their cause.

21. The Montgomery Advertiser, Jan. (n.d.), 1968 (clipping available in Hill Papers, Alabama State Department of Archives and History, Montgomery, Alabama).

22. Letter from Jesse B. Hearin to Lister Hill (Jan. 18, 1952) (available in Lister Hill Papers, Special Collections, Gorgas Library, The University of Alabama).

THE EARLY SOCIAL AND POLITICAL PHILOSOPHY OF HUGO BLACK: LIQUOR AS A TEST CASE

*Paul L. Murphy**

The career of a nationally prominent figure like Hugo Black quickly gets out of focus as his latter-day achievements and accomplishments become better known and more significant. Scholars begin looking for the origins of his meaningful ideas, his significant concepts and doctrines, often on the assumption that they must have been there from the start and that later achievements constitute the fulfillment of lifelong commitments developed at an early age. Thus, we learn from political scientists who have assessed Black's career on the United States Supreme Court that many of the values which pervaded his judicial career were implicit in his youthful experience and his general intellectual foundations. One commentator claims that Black had faith, "from his early contact with Populism, 'that people had the right, through *their* government, to [control] their daily lives' ";[1] that Black had a great faith in the wisdom and good judgment of the common people; and that he always had "felt that full and open debate on public issues (guaranteed the people by the First Amendment) would clear out misconceptions and reduce the potency of the emotions."[2] Thus, he was, apparently from the start, "an absolute defender of those rights."[3] Black also was an incipient New Dealer, almost from the beginning of his career and before he ever left Alabama. Further, "there [was] remarkable continuity in Black's political thought.

---

* Professor of History and American Studies, University of Minnesota. B.A. 1947, College of Idaho; M.A. 1948, Ph. D. 1953, Univerity of California at Berkley.

1. H. Ball, The Vision and the Dream of Justice Hugo L. Black: An Examination of a Judicial Philosophy 2 (1975) (quoting J. Frank, Mr. Justice Black, The Man and His Opinions 11-12 (1948)) (emphasis in original).

2. H. Ball, *supra* note 1, at 3.

3. *Id.*

[As] a critic of corporate wealth and power . . . he [was] concerned with helping to improve the lot of the American worker. He . . . always favored an America in which dissent thrives on unrestricted freedom of speech. These ideas [through his career were] firm and immutable."[4]

This is marvelous rhetoric and wonderful hagiography but quite inadequate and misleading history. In fact, if one wants to talk about hagiography, Black arguably emerges as a leader to be idealized and idolized. This image arises from an accurate acknowledgment that many of his later ideas, especially on human rights and personal freedom, constituted rejections of his earlier, far more narrow views and showed his ability to grow with the times, to adapt as a good pragmatic politician to changing human needs, and to come up with new solutions to old problems. Thus, the Black of the Supreme Court was in many ways a very different Black than Black the Senator, Black the police court judge, Black the county prosecuting attorney, or Black the boy growing up in the Alabama of the pre-World War I period.

To test the thesis, then, suggests the need to look at liquor, both in its consumption and in attempts to control that consumption, and to the prohibition movement to see where Black fits in that regard. Justification for this necessity is that, in the years prior to the 1930's, the politics of prohibition were a central factor in both Alabama history and Black's own personal history and that the way in which he approached the issue, or where he found himself regarding the issue, tells a great deal both about that issue and about the man and his career. This Article deliberately does not try to argue that Black's attitudes toward prohibition, or, for that matter, the general public's attitude toward prohibition, were a bellwether of later behavior. The Article does suggest that they are revealing of Black's intellectual and political career, particularly given the wide spectrum of reactions. This, in turn, was because prohibition represented a type of social control with very interesting and generally negative implications regarding individual freedom and individual rights. A bit of history puts this in proper setting. Drink and its excesses had troubled Americans almost from the beginning of settlement in Massachusetts Bay. The Massachusetts Code of 1648 criminalized immoral behavior and assigned

---

4. Berman, *Hugo Black: The Early Years*, 8 CATH. U.L. REV. 103, 115 (1959).

government the responsibility of punishing that behavior at its own initiative and expense. Drunkenness was one manifestation of that immoral behavior, and the authorities were expected to contain it for the betterment both of society and the individual victimized by it.[5] The nineteenth century, however, sharply modified this trend, and the use of law to enforce morality gave way, in a variety of circumstances, to a more *laissez-faire* attitude. Generally, the majority of Americans in those years felt it inappropriate for the government to attempt to control behavior that had no substantial significance except about the morality of the actor. Such matters, according to the majority, were best left to religious, educational, and other social influences—to informal forms of social control. Hostility toward statism and ongoing commitment to the principles of limited government ran high in those years, as did the feeling that the local community could and would deal with immorality in its own normally private way.

The Progressive America in which Hugo Black grew up was to some degree a throwback to the earlier times. Society not only had become complex but evil and filled with sin. The individual was in many ways at the mercy of a variety of massive and relentless forces that he or she individually could not control. Hence, the concept of stewardship and the moral responsibility of natural leaders within the society grew. To the stewards, moral uplift and a more efficient functioning of society could be achieved best by a responsible upper class of committed citizens, conscious of the need for imposing stable policies to hold together a turbulent, threateningly disintegrating, and distressingly changing society. This need further entailed turning to law in the hopes of improving conditions under which morality could and would emerge eventually.

But the legal and constitutional implications of this shift were startling to a generation raised on *laissez-faire* and especially to a generation apprehensive over the beginnings of public regulation, particularly at the national level. To accept such a view of positive government necessitated rethinking the relationship of the federal government to the states as well as to the individual. More precisely, acceptance meant rethinking the old concept of "police

5. Flaherty, *Law and the Enforcement of Morals in Early America*, in LAW IN AMERICAN HISTORY (D. Fleming & B. Bailyn eds. 1971).

power," which, prior to this time, had been solely a justification for social legislation at the state level. Thus, when the Progressives set out to deal with the alcohol problem, the saloon, and drunkenness in all its antisocial manifestations, their actions and their attitudes, while mollifying many good citizens, disturbed and troubled many others.

Generally, the broader policy considerations underlying this move created the greatest unease. Should the consumption of alcohol be made criminal? Would ending that consumption attain the perfectability of man? Was the government responsible for saving people from themselves, with their acquiescence irrelevant? Should the rights of the community and the welfare of the broader society constitute a higher priority than the freedom of the individual being coerced legally? Should cultural pluralism be a factor in any way? Should cultural differences, for example, that immigrant and ethnic groups came out of a culture where beer and wine were natural and integral parts of social and even family activities, carry any weight? Or was prohibiting booze an important way of heating up the melting pot and removing undesirable ethnic traits from those who would like to be true Americans?

Prohibition, then, opened up a wide range of issues, political, moral, ethical, legal, and personal, especially in the sense of how much a free society should coerce the free individual in making personal choices about his or her lifestyle and what constituted acceptable behavior. Alabama and Hugo Black had to face those issues as well, and the range of approaches that the confrontation elicited was intriguingly broad and complex.

But before examining that immediate situation, look at the way recent historians have attempted to create typologies for those involved in prohibition. One group of scholars has operated on the more traditional set of assumptions that those pushing prohibition the hardest were generally rural, agrarian, nineteenth-century-oriented Americans, usually retrogressive in their political purposes and out to restore a simpler American culture in which the centralizing forces of a developing urban and industrial social system did not seduce and pollute healthy and moral social living. These historians saw prohibition as "a pseudo-reform—a pinched parochial substitute for reform, [which represented] the final victory of the defenders of the American past."[6] Richard Hofstadter wrote: "On the rock of the Eighteenth Amendment, villiage American made its last stand."[7] Prohibition was enduring rural localism's and evangelical Protestantism's "drive to protect its cultural heritage against erosion."[8] Thus, as Norman Clark has written, the prohibitionists sought to "restore the lost purity of the great agrarian dream."[9]

On the other side, other modern scholars such as James Timberlake, Paul Carter, and Lawrence Levine see prohibition as an aspect of Progressivism and point to prohibitionists' commitment to efficiency and progress. They recognize the modernity of the prohibitionists' positive conception of the state, although they believe it was accompanied by an anachronistic style of politics with both religious and absolutistic characteristics. They also stress that prohibition was a means of social control and an aspect of heightened nationalism, plus an effort by a resurgent middle class to reassert its control over American urban life.[10]

Later synthesizers have argued that the two views need not be mutually exclusive. Prohibition indeed may have been an attempt to restore a simpler America, but the people leading the movement were not all ignorant boobs or intolerant fundamentalists. A great many were middle-class people, well educated and well informed, holding professional positions, residing in cities or suburbs—people who had traveled and seen the world and, thus, had a more cosmopolitan orientation than nonprofessional, poorly educated, rural residents of low mobility and little experience. But this also meant that these leaders, because they were more sophisticated, not only understood the growing social science literature on the problems and danger of alcoholism, but realized the impor-

6. R. WIEBE, THE SEARCH FOR ORDER, 1877-1920, at 301 (1967). *See generally, e.g.*, J. GUSFIELD, SYMBOLIC CRUSADE: STATUS POLITICS AND THE AMERICAN TEMPERANCE MOVEMENT (1963); Hayes, *Political Parties and the Community-Society Continuum*, in THE AMERICAN PARTY SYSTEMS, STAGES OF POLITICAL DEVELOPMENT 152 (W. Chambers & W. Burnham eds. 1967).

7. R. HOFSTADTER, THE AGE OF REFORM 289 (1955).

8. Hayes, *supra* note 6, at 174.

9. N. CLARK, THE DRY YEARS: PROHIBITION AND SOCIAL CHANGE IN WASHINGTON 127 (1965).

10. *See generally, e.g.*, P. CARTER, THE DECLINE AND REVIVAL OF THE SOCIAL GOSPEL: SOCIAL AND POLITICAL LIBERALISM IN AMERICAN PROTESTANT CHURCHES, 1920-1940 (1956); L. LEVINE, DEFENDER OF THE FAITH: WILLIAM JENNINGS BRYAN: THE LAST DECADE, 1915-1925 (1965); J. TIMBERLAKE, PROHIBITION AND THE PROGRESSIVE MOVEMENT 1900-1920 (1963).

tance of turning to effective political organization in a modern society and adopting techniques that maximized the possibility of the success of their movement. This knowledge did not mean necessarily that their values were not still relatively provincial, but it did mean that they combined the best of modern approaches with the aspiration to attain a value system which they felt desirable to restore.

The movement also had an important power dimension. Resurgent elements in the middle class were using prohibition as an instrument for reasserting their control over American urban life. Significantly, they were willing to use the power of the state to create or sustain a particular conception of community. Even more significantly, they had made the intellectual shift from the primarily negative conception of the state prevalent in the nineteenth-century temperance movement (the law ought not to sanction the liquor trade) to the more positive conception of the state inherent in the prohibition movement (the state ought to suppress the manufacture of alcoholic beverages). They had not made, however, the corresponding shift from the religious and absolutistic style of politics characteristic of the nineteenth century to the secular and pluralistic style more typical of the twentieth. Furthermore, they were conscious of the political pressures generated from within the society by ethnic and other pressure groups constantly threatening to reshape the state and to redirect its power. Hence, the frantic drive existed among many to establish their desired policy by constitutional amendment and, thus, to place it beyond the reach of a mere majority rule.

A look at Alabama and Hugo Black against this backdrop presents an intriguing task, especially to see where Black fit, which values he embraced, and which he rejected. A profile of the local scene is helpful to reach that end.

The liquor issue in Alabama was to some degree a microcosm of the issue at the national level but with clear regional variations. The temperance movement had grown in the State in the late nineteenth century. Controversy about the form it should take continually frustrated its success. The State had tried the license system, the oldest form of liquor regulation, but with far from satisfactory results. High license fees reduced the number of liquor dealers, but concentrated control of the traffic in the hands of a few men with political power. But legal enactment also made territories dry. When this happened, they frequently were flooded with liquor from adjacent wet areas. Thus, "[l]ocal option, so widely hailed as the great solution, was a disappointment; [for years,] most of the counties had voted wet in the local option elections."[11]

But other approaches existed. Many advocated a system of state dispensaries, run by a state dispensary commission. That practice was attempted in the years between 1900 and 1908, yet the plan was not terribly successful. "Blind tigers," a version of later speakeasies, and private whiskey jugs indicated the public's general complacency regarding the liquor traffic. Further, true drys never accepted it; they felt it was a shameful compromise with the devil, particularly because critics of the dispensary claimed that, far from discouraging drunkenness, it helped to promote it. In the good old days, a man bought a small drink and drank it quietly in the saloon. With the new system, according to the law, he must buy at least a half pint at a time. He then took his bottle outside and often treated his friends on the streets or highways. Thus, particularly among blacks, public drunkenness was increasing, along with alarming problems of law and order, including disturbing the peace.

All these factors tended to produce calls for group action. One of the vital results was a move to organize a state Anti-Saloon League in Alabama.[12] Effective local option was the immediate goal, and interim steps were to be taken to elect legislators committed to that end. The League was organized in 1904 and later began issuing the *Alabama Citizen* as its official organ. It sought political action to attack drink, although, from the beginning, it proclaimed itself to be nonpartisan.[13] Opposition did occur, however. The *Birmingham Ledger*, for example, maintained that local option was better than some forms of prohibition, "but a man does not like a county where one side of a branch is prohibition and the other is not . . . . Alabama ought to have one law for all her people."[14] Other organs expressed similar views.

In time, after much local controversy, action was taken in this direction, with a move for statewide prohibition as the result. In November 1908 the Alabama Senate, 32 to 2, passed a bill to that

11. J. Sellers, The Prohibition Movement in Alabama, 1702-1943, at 87 (1943).
12. *Id.* at 102.
13. *Id.* at 102-04.
14. Birmingham Ledger, Feb. 16, 1907.

effect that earlier had been approved by the House. But, when put into operation, noncompliance grew rapidly, and even the ultimate validation of the prohibitory statute by the highest court in the State did not secure its enforcement. The result was that, in short order, the influential *Alabama Courier* maintained that the law was a complete failure. One could get all the booze one wanted in any prohibition town because the people did not back prohibition.[15] This statement was particularly true in turbulent Jefferson County, in which defiance was both strong and outspoken.

Response from the temperance forces was to move for a statewide constitutional amendment, an idea that had been around since the 1890's, but which now took on new and important meaning and drew new dry support. This 1909 action was hailed as the "finest that ha[d] ever been drawn in all the attempts of the various states to . . . enforce the statutes enacted against the storage and sale of alcoholic concoctions."[16] In providing for searching, raiding, and confiscating the property of lawbreakers, the action was described as "the most drastic prohibition law ever brought to the attention of any legislature."[17] But while it passed both houses of the legislature by large margins (70 to 29; 23 to 10), it was turned back by popular amendment after a vigorous and frenetic campaign throughout the State.

To this set of varied approaches, one also must add the nationally growing feeling, again reflected in Alabama politics, of the need for a federal constitutional amendment in the prohibition area. This move had its supporters and critics and took on heavy political significance as the sides took shape and, occasionally, shifted in this era. Alabama Congressman Richmond P. Hobson, who had served in Congress since 1906, was a zealous prohibitionist. He offered a prohibition amendment to the federal Constitution in 1913. His action, however, at that time was denounced by a majority of the representatives from Alabama. The reasons were politically important. States' rights and local self-determination

15. Alabama Courier, Aug. 12, 1908. As the editor argued in a later issue, when "the public opinion is not behind the movement, it is impossible to enforce the measure, and prohibition that does not prohibit, is worse a thousand times than the open bar room." *Id.*, Aug. 26, 1908.

16. The Birmingham News, July 28, 1909, at 2, col. 1; *see* H.R. 172, 1909 Leg., Special Sess., 1909 J. of H.R. (Special Sess.) 507.

17. Montgomery Journal, Aug. 5, 1909, at 1, cols. 5-6.

had been the keystone of Alabama politics since the 1870's. Federal solutions to local problems had been resisted vigorously and, at times, passionately. Oscar W. Underwood spoke for a substantial portion of the population when he called the move "an attempt to rob the States of their jurisdiction over police matters, in part to destroy the right of local self-government, and to establish a precedent that would concentrate the power of all government in the government established here in Washington."[18] The passage of such a bill, Underwood declared, would not eliminate the evils of intemperance, but would destroy local supervision of the liquor traffic and deprive the government of much revenue.[19] In the long run, only four of ten Alabama representatives voted in favor of Hobson's resolution.

But public reaction was also sufficiently overt to be noticed. As Norman Clark has pointed out, "[i]n Alabama, for example, citizens were gathering in public meetings to declare that while the liquor traffic in their state was 'as dead as the men who lived before the flood,' they would not allow the federal government to take from them what in the 1870s their fathers had taken from the federal government—the right to determine their own affairs in Alabama. [They would never] yield in their dedication to states' rights, even if the issue were Prohibition."[20] When Hobson and Underwood ran against each other for the Senate in 1914, even though Hobson had all the "good" people on his side and Underwood had all the "bad" (including the Wholesale Liquor Dealers of America), Underwood won. Hobson subsequently blamed the defeat upon the liquor forces, and the campaign did stimulate new enthusiasm for prohibition. The trend led the legislature again to pass a statewide prohibition law. Then Governor Emmet O'Neal left office rather than veto it. But, as he did, he bitterly scorned the legislature for "wantonly [having] ravished the cherished and inalienable rights of the people."[21]

But the rights of the people, at least to the extent that they represented any sense of capacity for individual choice, were not primarily in the minds of legislators. Thus, "[t]o place further re-

---

18. 52 CONG. REC. 519 (1913) (statement of Oscar W. Underwood).

19. *Id.* at 521.

20. N. CLARK, DELIVER US FROM EVIL: AN INTERPRETATION OF AMERICAN PROHIBITION 123-24 (1976).

21. Birmingham Ledger, Jan. 18, 1915.

strictions on the consumption of liquor, the legislature passed an act in February 1915 which prohibited liquor advertisements in newspapers, magazines, on bill boards, or in any other form. Again, Governor Charles Henderson exercised his veto prerogative. He returned the bill with the comment that he did not think the law could be effective."[22] The interstate commerce clause of the United States Constitution protected liquor advertising, he argued. "[A]dvertising could not be stopped by legislation."[23] The law would serve only as a further irritant. But the House passed the bill over his veto and despite expressed concern by the local press that "newspapers publishing liquor advertisements would be forced by such a law into a role of virtue which they had no right or desire to assume."[24]

Prohibition and the liquor issue, to be focused fully, however, must be seen vis-a-vis other issues of the time. Was this a liberal position or a conservative one? Here the record is complex. For some politicians, prohibition was another of the Progressive reforms, a liberal move that went hand in hand with a positive attitude toward other forms of social legislation, from minimum wage laws to maximum hour laws to child labor laws. Certain leaders, however, were both pro-prohibition and antilabor. A figure like Oscar W. Underwood, for example, opposed the principle of prohibition and favored local option. At the same time, he saw the labor movement as a form of bolshevism. The Ku Klux Klan, reactivated in Alabama during World War I and "the most powerful political force in Alabama during the 1920's,"[25] affected a kind of pseudo radicalism on social issues. It fought against the corporations, for the common people, and against "Catholic intolerance." In economically depressed areas, its leaders stressed raising wages by cutting off the influence of cheap, immigrant labor. They saw prohibition as, to an extent, a cultural movement. It was a way of striking at Catholics and Jews and south European foreigners, whom the Klan saw as imposing alien and foreign values, such as the use of wine and beer, upon Christian Americans. They also saw prohibition as an instrument for law and order and as a way of

22. J. Sellers, *supra* note 11, at 185.

23. *Id.*

24. *Id.*

25. M. Silverstein, Constitutional Faiths: Felix Frankfurter, Hugo Black, and the Process of Judicial Decision Making 106 (1984).

getting at bootleggers, crime, and the infiltration into the State of undesirable outside influences.

Some scattered voices, nervous about social control imposed by a distant national government, saw the issue as a form of destruction of individual freedom of choice in the name of imposing a type of monolithic societal morality, unjustifiable in an open and free society. Such leaders had little faith in experts as agents of progress in the modern state. They feared that, if liberalism meant favoring the centering of more power in Washington government bureaus, it was potentially more a danger than a solution.

Early in his career, Hugo Black came upon, and eventually came to terms with, the complexities of the liquor issue and the prohibition question. At the personal level, his favorite brother, Pelham, a lawyer whom he idolized, was drowned after a drinking spree when Hugo was 16.[26] The tragedy seemed to verify his father's warning "that alcohol was a demon which lured good men to their destruction."[27] The episode led to Black's becoming personally and ultimately a "dry" Baptist teetotaler, a position that he took publicly; for example, in the senatorial primary of 1926, he claimed that he had never in his life tasted whiskey. The circumstances of Pelham's death also may help to explain Black's sensitivity to the liquor issue and its centrality in his life. As a "heart" person, responding to his own feelings and instincts about what was right and wrong, he early saw liquor as a source of evil and had little need for empirical and statistical validation in that regard.

In those pre-war years, the body of research findings on the effects of alcohol, both on the individual and upon society, increased. The findings tended to support the case for total abstinence. Researchers claimed that they had discovered "that alcohol [did] not warm the body, that it [was] a depressant rather than a stimulant, and that it depresse[d] the higher mental functions as well as muscular control . . . . In 1915 a report on life insurance statistics held that as few as two drinks a day would shorten the life of a robust man. [Certain] highly regarded studies demonstrated to the satisfaction of many intelligent people a close rela-

---

26. V. Hamilton, Hugo Black: The Alabama Years 22-23 (1972) (citations omitted).

27. V. Hamilton, *supra* note 26, at 23; Dowe, *Hugo Black's Childhood in Clay County: No. 1: 'Best Dressed Boy in Ashland' Begins Brilliant Career*, Alabama Journal, July 4, 1960, at 2-A, col. 3.

tionship between alcohol and insanity."[28] The researchers generally also "believed that alcoholic parents produced degenerate children."[29] From a different tack, many scientists were lowering their estimate of what constituted harmless doses of liquor. American psychiatrists and neurologists at a national meeting in 1914 declared alcohol to be a poison. Educators, such as Charles Eliot, President of Harvard, after studying scientific findings, advocated total abstention.[30] "Moreover, investigators in the new social sciences supplied a mass of statistics to show relationships between alcohol and crime, prostitution, and poverty. Since studies in scientific management regularly stressed efficiency and sobriety, some American industrial interests, most notably several railroad companies, had actually ordered their employees not to drink at any time, on or off duty."[31] Nothing indicates, however, that Black turned to such support to undergird his position. He essentially distrusted the elite of any stripe, and he had no faith in experts as agents of progress.[32] What he did trust were his own understanding of human nature and, as a student of history and a devotee of "conflict" history, the lessons of his own experience and the experiences of his day, especially as they applied to the "common man." Here he learned from the "real world," a world that he confronted early on when, as a young attorney, fresh out of the University of Alabama Law School and almost penniless, he arrived in Birmingham in September 1907 to begin his career.

Birmingham, at the time, had many of the attributes of a frontier city. As William Rogers has written, its boomtown atmosphere produced a "movement to the city [which] was accompanied by a frequently radical changing way of life."[33] One Alabama editor "still unsophisticated enough to be outraged at Birmingham's mo-

---

28. N. Clark, *supra* note 20, at 121-22.
29. *Id.*
30. *Id.*
31. *Id.*
32. Black, throughout his career, remained unimpressed by the legal realists and their heavy emphasis upon empirical support for legal positions. His opinions did not rely upon social science data and pure logic. As Wallace Mendelson has argued, "Mr. Justice Black seem[ed] satisfied to leave recondite matters for those who are specially competent to deal with them . . . ." W. Mendelson, Justice Black and Frankfurter: Conflict in the Court 39 (1961). An "idealist, he concentrate[d] heavily on the outcome of the immediate case." *Id.* at 40.
33. W. Rogers, The One-Gallused Rebellion: Agrarianism in Alabama, 1865-1896, at 95-96 (1970).

res . . . warned its inhabitants, 'Watch out that God don't yet shower his wrath on a town and a people that so persistently desecrate the Sabbath. Remember the fate of Sodom and Gomorrah.' "[34] "Birmingham's citizens[, Rogers argues,] allowed their emotions such unbridled freedom that the town become known for its two *M*'s—minerals and murders."[35]

But one might also add an L. Only a few months after Hugo Black took a part-time job as a police court judge for the city, hearing cases against persons charged with minor crimes, the liquor issue erupted. The city, which previously had adopted prohibition, reversed itself and, led by Commissioner A.O. Lane, for whom Black was an informal protégé and who favored taxpaying, licensed saloons over "blind tigers," voted wet. The result was both an increase in homicides and arrests and an increase in business for Black's court. Black, who frequently had been lenient regarding excessive fines, especially for victimized blacks, became extremely tough on prohibition violators, particularly those who continued to patronize the "blind tigers." He was known to stun certain citizens by $500 fines and 90-day jail sentences for prohibition violations. However, in one case, he released charged blacks, despite the testimony of police officers. In the process, he gained a reputation for fair procedure, particularly toward the more powerless members of society. This reputation stood him well as he began to contemplate a more ambitious political career.

These years further helped to shape Black's attitudes toward people, toward government, and toward the law. Black always had identified with the poor and the victims of the abuse of power in society. For him, given this identification with plain Americans, an obligation existed to oppose people of privilege when that privilege was being abused. He also felt an instinctive commitment to equal justice. This viewpoint did not mean, however, that Black had an idealistic attitude toward the capacity of powerless individuals. He was well aware of human frailties and the inability of the weak individual to stand up against both the temptations of the flesh and the power of the establishment. So, while he was convinced that people were able to govern themselves and to make up their minds about their own destinies, and while he was hopeful that

34. *Id.* at 96 (quoting Anniston Weekly Watchman, Aug. 23, 1887).
35. W. Rogers, *supra* note 33, at 96.

they would exert their own political power to make the system deliver for them what they needed, he was also aware that many institutional arrangements would preclude easy success in this area. Private power would not surrender easily its privilege. Elites were seldom altruistic, and they normally worked for their own self-interest.

Yet given his Jeffersonian orientation, Black instinctively distrusted the state, at least in his early career. However, he was prepared to concede that a necessary balance was important. While freedom should be the rule and restraint the exception, the state could move to create a more healthy social climate. Political power could be used to improve people's lives. More specifically, it could be a device for combating the evils of industrial civil society. As his confrontation with political reality became greater and more realistic, he moved more in this direction. Thus by the mid-1920's, when he was ready to enter national politics, he was prepared to accept that reform and the implications of government power were linked inextricably.

But while some have seen him as a classical liberal before that time, such an argument has to be treated cautiously. Given a choice between individual freedom and the need for a healthy community, Black instinctively chose the latter, particularly when it seemed the freedom might not be used with a sense of moral restraint and obligation. This position may help explain how he could accept the Ku Klux Klan. That organization was almost a prototype of antiliberal, right-wing communitarianism, advocating, and indeed taking, actions against those, from bootleggers to foreign immigrants, whose attitudes and behavior threatened the traditional closed community. Alabama was known especially, as Virginia Hamilton has pointed out, as a State in which dissent was suppressed and conformity was enforced. Classical or traditional liberalism, and especially a civil libertarian position, was virtually out of the question. Thus, those who contend that they can find in Black's early career an example of his first amendment absolutism fail to understand that early career and its strictures. Again, the liquor issue is a good indicium.

We have mentioned the Alabama Legislature's 1915 law prohibiting liquor advertisement "in newspapers, magazines, on billboards, or in any other form." Alabama editors argued that this ban clearly violated freedom of the press. When Black, then Solicitor of Jefferson County, attempted to prevent by injunction the sale of newspapers containing liquor advertisements, his action was deplored by the city court of Birmingham, which declared the measure unconstitutional. Black then personally appealed the case to the Alabama Supreme Court, which heard it as *State ex rel. Black v. Delaye.*[36] Delaye, a newsstand owner in Birmingham, had been arrested for selling out-of-state newspapers with liquor ads in defiance of the state antiadvertising liquor law. His attorneys had argued that the law violated the commerce clause of the United States Constitution and also had contended that the statute constituted an improper exercise of the state's police power. Black argued that the law did not contravene any of the provisions of the state or federal constitutions, but was a perfectly proper exercise of that police power. No first amendment issue was raised, much less was argued. When the Alabama Supreme Court unanimously reversed the Birmingham city court, Black was vindicated.[37]

During this same period, Black's name began to become a statewide code word for prohibition enforcement. As a special attorney for the state Attorney General's office in 1916, he was called in to prosecute a major whiskey ring, which had smuggled over a half million dollars worth of illegal alcohol into the small town of Girard, Alabama. The town conveniently was located just across the river from Columbus, Georgia. In all, twenty-two separate cases arose out of the Girard raid. Black early made known his presence by asking for a court order to destroy immediately $600,000 worth of alcohol. When the defendants protested the seizure and destruction of their property and claimed officials had lacked specific search warrants, the issue went to the Alabama Supreme Court. There, the justices decided that the State had been justified in the procedure; the lack of warrants had been cured, the court maintained, by the discovery of illegal goods. This illegal possession distinguished the situation from cases involving lawful

36. 193 Ala. 500, 68 So. 993 (1915).

37. In maintaining that the law was a proper use of state police power, the Alabama Supreme Court reasoned that the state possessed the power to ban alcohol advertisements as a corollary to its power to outlaw the alcohol itself. If the state may ban sales, it may ban solicitation for those sales. As authority for this reasoning, the Alabama court relied on the United States Supreme Court's opinion in Delamater v. South Dakota, 205 U.S. 93 (1913), in which the Court ruled that an advertiser could not use the protections of the commerce clause to evade a state prohibition law. Solicitation for illegal sales could not receive constitutional protection. *Id.*

property.[38]

After service in World War I and his return to the State, Black's reputation apparently still held. By that time, prohibition was a national policy. But Mobile, previously the center of wetness in the State and a sailor town, continually chafed under such restrictions, and local business men found ways to slake sailors' thirsts outside the law. Federal agents were alert and in November 1923 seized thousands of quarts of illegal liquor. A federal grand jury indicted 117 prominent Mobilians, including the Chief of Police, P.J. O'Shaughnessy, and charged them with conspiracy to bribe the district attorney to release them. By this time, the federal Justice Department decided that a special assistant attorney should be assigned to the case, and Attorney General Harlan Fiske Stone turned to Black, who so vigorously had prosecuted prohibition violators in Girard 7 years earlier. " 'The only real soldier, in times of peace, is the man who walks in obedience to the law,' Prosecutor Black told the court,"[39] as he set out to gain convictions. Midway through the trial, he dropped the conspiracy charges against some of the defendants, but this strengthened the Government's case against those remaining. Ultimately, eleven men, including Police Chief O'Shaughnessy, were convicted.[40] These "booze trials" further made the name of Hugo Black synonomous with rigid prohibition enforcement, specifically, and the dry cause, generally.

When Black ran for the United States Senate in 1926, he campaigned on a platform castigating concentrated wealth, power trusts, railroad systems, high tariffs, and government cliques. He also stressed the prohibition issue and charged that his opponents were politically dry but personally wet. In addition, possibly because of his affiliation with the Ku Klux Klan, he took a strong "societal morality" and antimelting pot position and suggested that the latter idea was dangerous to our national inheritance.

Now securely in a Senate seat, Black quietly could reassess his position and could begin viewing the political world with a broader, national perspective. By the late 1920's, a significant decline of the old "dry," labor, and Klan coalition, which had been so

---

38. Hemmelweit v. State *ex rel.* Dedge, 200 Ala. 203, 203, 75 So. 961, 961 (1917).

39. V. HAMILTON, *supra* note 26, at 109 (quoting Hugo L. Black).

40. V. HAMILTON, *supra* note 26, at 110 (citing Birmingham News, May 22, 1924, at 1, cols. 7-8; May 10, 1924, at 1, col. 1).

vital to Black's electoral success, had occurred. This change again was freeing for him. During the Al Smith Presidential campaign of 1928, Black took a relatively cautious position. While he opposed Smith's nomination, he was not prepared to resort to the hyperbole and demagoguery of his fellow Senator, Tom Heflin.[41] Nonetheless, although he soft pedaled Smith's Catholicism, he was clear in his position that a Catholic Yankee " 'as wet as the ocean' "[42] was hardly in a position to represent well southern democracy.

In the years from 1929 to 1933, the "new" Black slowly but steadily continued shucking off his earlier Jeffersonian misgivings about positive government. He also began to show a new concern both for balancing liberty and order more heavily on the liberty side and for the political expedience of modifying his hard-nosed prohibition stand.

In a 1929 Senate debate over an amendment to the Smoot-Hawley Tariff, banning the importation of seditious and salacious publications, Senator Black declared himself opposed to censorship. He maintained that "the American citizen should be persuaded in no way except by logic and reason."[43] He saw such restriction as threatening because of the power it vested in customs officials. He opposed any plan to ban the distribution of literature, he further argued, "so long as the juries in the States, where public sentiment is made, have it within their power to condemn the distribution of that literature as being deleterious to the morals of their people."[44] Thus, although Black feared the control of literature by an agency of the state, his similar fear was apparently not present when the same power was exercised by juries in the name of the people. The posture hardly suggests unrestrained freedom and still partakes of a strong "societal morality" view. Nonetheless, it reflects an important contrast with his position on the liquor advertisement issue of some years earlier. It also may reflect the growing national civil liberties consciousness of the 1920's, which

---

41. V. Hamilton, *supra* note 26, at 150-51.

42. *Id.* at 151 (quoting letter from James Esdale to W.F. Zumbraum, Apr. 14, 1928 (available in Papers of J. Thomas Heflin, University of Alabama Library [hereinafter cited as Heflin Papers]; letter from James Esdale to J. Thomas Heflin, Apr. 14, 1928 (available in Heflin Papers)).

43. Frank, *Hugo L. Black*, in The Justices of the United States Supreme Court: Their Lives and Major Opinions 2327 (L. Friedman & F. Israel eds. 1969).

44. 72 Cong. Rec. 4469 (1929) (statement of Hugo L. Black).

notably had been absent in the pre-war years.[45]

One reality was clear on the liquor question by this time: prohibition was not only increasingly unenforceable, but was producing open defiance, major problems of law and order, and general public cynicism. Black still was playing this cool. In 1932 he accepted an appointment, urged by Senator George Norris, as the "dry" on a special subcommittee studying modification of the eighteenth amendment. In agreeing to serve, however, he protested that the Senate had better "spend all its time trying to remedy unemployment . . . instead of listening to personal opinions on prohibition."[46] Noting "that many Alabama drys, recognizing the futility of enforcing prohibition, now favored modification,"[47] the *Birmingham Post* at this point argued: "If Senator Black will face the facts squarely, he, too, may change his mind."[48] Black's antennae were up. In the Alabama Democratic primary of 1932, four aspirants challenged Black, with prohibition the central issue of the primary. The result was a necessary run-off between Black and Thomas E. Kilby. Kilby demanded to know Black's views on prohibition, called him "wiley Hugo,"[49] and "declared that Black had tricked the drys by waiting until after the primary to announce that he favored a nationwide referendum on the"[50] subject. Now, sensing the need to mend fences, Black defended himself by maintaining that he was a Jeffersonian Democrat who believed that the people themselves should decide the fate of prohibition.

Securely reelected, Black, during the 1932-33 lame duck session of Congress, voted for the twenty-first amendment, which repealed the eighteenth. He also told the Senate he favored resubmission of the eighteenth amendment to the voters only if states were assured of the right to prohibit liquor sales within their boundaries. In July 1933 Alabamians voted to repeal the eighteenth. Although dry militancy, stealthily aided by bootleggers, was far from dead, the issue ceased to be a major consideration as far as Black's own senatorial career and ultimate national prominance

45. *See generally* P. Murphy, World War I and the Origin of Civil Liberties in the United States (1980).

46. V. Hamilton, *supra* note 26, at 199.

47. *Id.* at 200.

48. Birmingham Age-Herald, Dec. 30, 1931; Birmingham Post, Jan. 1, 1932, at 4, col. 2, *both quoted in* V. Hamilton, *supra* note 26, at 200.

49. V. Hamilton, *supra* note 26, at 206.

50. *Id.* at 207.

were concerned.

Thus, in conclusion, I would maintain that the Hugo Black of the prohibition era was neither the New Deal Senator of the 1930's or the Associate Justice of the '40's, '50's, and '60's. Clearly, he was representing sensitively and well the people of Alabama in those early years. He was prepared to trim his sails on the liquor issue as the political winds changed. He certainly was beginning to put together a coherent and consistent political posture when it came to the question of individual freedom and societal needs. However, the years of the New Deal, a Second World War, the McCarthy era, and a long period of service on the bench were necessary to produce the Black of the later years. He was far from being there even as late as 1933. Yet, his capacity to grow, his capacity to adapt, and his common sense pragmatism did make possible important changes and the emergence of the judicial statesman of the Warren Court era.

HUGO LA FAYETTE BLACK AS UNITED STATES SENATOR

*David A. Shannon**

In May 1934, when Hugo Black had been in the Senate for about 5 years, a rather brief encounter with Senator Daniel O. Hastings of Wilmington, Delaware, revealed Black's style in Senate debates. One could describe the style as very polite, maybe too polite at times, but *tough*.

In the second session of the 73d Congress, five "bail out" bills passed Congress, including one bill to facilitate reorganization of corporations, H.R. 5884. The Great Depression had put many corporations through the wringer; they needed a more flexible law. Senators Black and Hastings were members of the Judiciary Committee; each was an able lawyer. Their basic difference on H.R. 5884 was that Hastings' interest was purely local and Black's was primarily national. Most American corporations had been incorporated in Delaware because its laws were the loosest and most generous to incorporated companies. Hastings was determined to keep it that way and thereby to provide to Delaware attorneys a continuing lucrative practice. Black wanted to share the practice with the other forty-seven states.

In the debate, Black clearly indicated that he wished "simply to provide, if there is any question raised, that the court shall automatically send [the bankruptcy case] to such other Federal courts as may have jurisdiction of the matter." Borah of Idaho, who regarded himself as the ablest constitutional lawyer in the nation, agreed with Black, but Borah's pompous remarks and digressions must have annoyed Black.

Hastings, seeing that the drift of the discussion was going against him, offered an amendment. He suggested that the clause

---

* Commonwealth Professor of History, The University of Virginia. B.S. 1941, Indiana State College; Ph. M. 1946, Ph. D. 1951, University of Wisconsin.

be changed to the following: "Or, if the principal place of business or the place where the principal assets are located is in doubt, then the territorial jurisdiction in which the company was incorporated." Black asked, "Doubt in whose mind?" Others said his question was well taken. Hastings retreated again. He suggested new language:

> Or, if the principal place of business or the place where the principal assets are located is controverted, then in the territorial jurisdiction in which it was incorporated, provided that the court *may*, upon petition, direct a transfer . . . to any territorial jurisdiction where the corporation has a substantial portion of its assets . . . .

Black had won his position, but he saw a possible escape for Hastings. Black moved to insert "shall" for "may," and the Senate accepted his motion. He had won the polite little battle.

Let me now go back to Hugo Black's origins, his special talents, his career in Alabama, and then his first term as a Senator in the 70th Congress, 1927 to 1929. Later, I shall discuss his activities in subsequent Congresses, 1930 to 1937.

Congress has a long tradition of permitting each congressman or Senator to write his autobiography for each session's *Congressional Directory*. Black's biography for 1934 was as follows:

> Hugo La Fayette Black, Democrat of Birmingham, was born in Clay County, Ala., February 27, 1886; attended public school at Ashland, Clay County, Ala., LL. B., University of Alabama, 1906. Lawyer; captain Eighty-first Regiment Field Artillery, World War; married; elected November 2, 1926, to the Senate for the full term of six years, and reelected November 8, 1932.[1]

The terse statement was all he wrote: five lines of print.

In contrast, Senator J. Hamilton Lewis of Illinois submitted a biography of forty-seven lines to the same *Directory*. Ham Lewis was a bizarre character. He sported a *pink* beard—not red, not orange—and wore flamboyant clothes. Ostentatiously polite, he always answered his telephone with the same question: "To whom, may I ask, have I the pleasure of speaking?" He was in the Senate

---

1. Black's modest entry in the *Directory* provides the bare bones of his career. For a fuller account, see generally V. HAMILTON, HUGO BLACK: THE ALABAMA YEARS (1972). This work both is well written and is well researched. I have used it to good advantage for a book I presently am writing on FDR and the Congress, as well as for this Article. I am indebted to her for her work.

for 14 years, rarely speaking in debate and without ever introducing a public bill or even an amendment. Identifying two more different Senators than Black and Lewis would be difficult.

Named for Victor Hugo, an indication of his parents' reading taste, Black's earliest years were in a village called Harlan, in which his father operated a general store and his mother served as postmistress. In 1889, when Hugo was not quite four, the family moved to Ashland, the county seat (population 350) so that the children could receive a better education. For Hugo, the better schooling was very effective; he became an omnivorous reader, and later, he developed the skill of reading a line of print at a glance. He subsequently became a student at Ashland College, a combination of high school and junior college. For the youthful Black, it was a godsend. Besides his required studies and wide reading on his own, he actively participated in debate. The youngster's frequent attendance of trials at the Clay County courthouse well may have had at least as important an effect on his future. He found the trials absorbing, but not yet had he determined to become an attorney.

Orlando, one of Black's older brothers, had gone to medical school and had become a promising young physician. Orlando and his mother urged Black to study medicine, and he followed their advice. His record at the Birmingham Medical College was spectacular; in 9 months he completed the curriculum for the first 2 years. The following summer he worked for Orlando as an assistant. At summer's end, however, Orlando agreed with Hugo that a career in medicine was not for him. In the fall, he enrolled in the University of Alabama School of Law. Again, he was diligent and brilliant. He was one of seven who graduated with grades of 95 or better, and he accomplished this feat while sitting in on lectures in history, political economy, and English.

He returned to Ashland, bought a set of law books, rented an office, and waited for clients to walk in. Few came. Most Ashlanders made a rational decision and took their legal problems to older lawyers. Would *you* engage an attorney only a few months over 20? The next year he moved to Birmingham.

The decision to move in 1905 was among the most important of his career because it removed him from bucolic Clay County to a booming and growing city already well on its way to becoming one of the country's major industrial cities. Having moved to an urban community, he steadily became more urbane.

Interestingly, for a man who, for compelling political reasons, would become a member of the Ku Klux Klan—which in 1937 would become an embarrassment—Black's first important case in Birmingham was representing a black man. Early in this century, southern governments commonly leased convicts to private employers. William Morton legally had been leased to the Tennessee Coal, Iron, and Railway Company, but illegally had been forced to serve an additional 22 days beyond his sentence. One of Birmingham's most important attorneys represented the company. Black won the case, and the opposing lawyer later complimented Black on the way that he represented his client.

By subsequent standards, labor relations in Birmingham were backward. Wages were low, hours were long, and peremptory firings were commonplace. Black soon established a reputation as a labor lawyer, though he took other cases, too. His fees were not as generous as those received by attorneys who represented employers, but he was still under 25, and his income was not bad for a fledgling lawyer.

Growing rapidly and more progressively than other southern cities, Birmingham reorganized its municipal government by creating a city commission of three members. A.O. Lane, the judge in the *Morton* case, became the commissioner of public safety. Rather quickly, Lane discarded the expensive and inefficient municipal court and appointed Black judge of the recorder's court, which really was a low-level police court. The young judge ran his court in both a judicious and remarkably efficient way. On his first day as judge, he tried and decided thirty cases in two hours. He insisted that all those arrested, mostly drunks, gamblers, and prostitutes, be present at 8:30 a.m., a ghastly hour for these people. Black adjourned court by late morning. His judicial salary was $1,500 a year, and he was free to practice law in the afternoon; the country boy made good in the big city!

In the fall of 1912, however, Black, age 26, resigned from the recorder's court. He and his law partner, David J. Davis, were doing well in their practice. Further, the young Black rather clearly was beginning to think about getting into politics. The idea possibly had been in the back of his mind for a long time. I have a hunch that it was.

Jefferson County, which surrounds Birmingham, was to have

an election in 1914 for solicitor, which other states frequently call county prosecutor. Many county politicians aspired to the job, among them Harrington P. Heflin, whose brother, Tom, would be elected to the Senate in 1920; Z.T. Rudulph, the county's establishment candidate; F.D. McArthur, a long shot; and Black. Black prepared an intelligent election strategy. Because his experience in that part of the country was confined to Birmingham, he drove his Model T throughout Jefferson County, even into remote villages; his rural background proved to be advantageous. His political advertisements were inexpensive and clever: every day he ran a small ad with his picture and such slogans as "Hugo Black will make a good solicitor—ask the judges" and "the gamblers are against this man for solicitor."

Even during the campaign, Black, foreshadowing his special interest in civil liberty when he sat on the United States Supreme Court, sought an injunction when Birmingham's city court penalized the owner of a newsstand that sold magazines advertising liquor. Subsequently, he took the case to the Alabama Supreme Court and won his constitutional point. Alabama was dry, but that was not the issue; it was fairness. Black himself supported prohibition. Indeed, in spring 1924 he successfully served as special prosecutor in the Mobile booze trials. The trials made him favorably known throughout the State, although renown in Alabama already had come his way in 1923 when he had persuaded the Supreme Court of the United States unanimously to accept his arguments in *Lewis v. Roberts*.[2]

Earlier in the 1914 campaign for prosecutor, Black had won handily with 6,843 votes, 2,271 more than the second-place Heflin. He ran as a candidate for reelection in 1916, but he lost. Davis, his former law partner, was also a candidate, and Black's opponents effectively used the question, "Do you want two former law partners . . . in the criminal court?"

Black returned to his law practice, but within a matter of months, America declared war against Germany, and Black joined the army in the spring of 1917. He served as a captain of the 81st Field Artillery and as regimental adjutant from November 1917 to December 1918. The army did not send him overseas. No reason exists to believe that his becoming a soldier was motivated politi-

2. 267 U.S. 467 (1925).

cally. Yet, given the war spirit and the pride Americans took in their role in 1917-18, young servicemen who had political aspirations enjoyed an advantage over those who had not served. Then 32 years old, the ex-soldier returned to Birmingham and resumed his lucrative law practice; in 1925 his income was about $40,000.

Black clearly had decided to run for the Senate though senatorial salaries were then only $10,000. Much depended upon the decision of Oscar W. Underwood, who had been in the House and Senate for 31 years and who aspired to be President. Underwood's desire to be the Chief Executive had made it unlikely he could win reelection to the Senate in 1926 because he had not supported the Ku Klux Klan; paradoxically, it would have been foolish of him to do so because of his desire to be President. In Alabama, however, where the Klan was still strong, his failure to support the Klan made Underwood's chances slim. On July 1, 1925, Underwood announced he would not run for the Senate. Black *was* a Klan member, but in July he submitted a letter of resignation. The Alabama Grand Dragon replied: "I'll keep [the resignation] in my safe against the day when you'll need to say you're not a Klan member."[3] Thus, as Professor Hamilton shrewdly has observed, "Black had all the advantages of Klan support and none of the disadvantages of membership."[4]

Black announced his candidacy. His major opponents were Thomas E. Kilby, a wealthy manufacturer and former governor; John H. Bankhead, Jr., a corporate attorney and coal mine operator; and Judge James J. Mayfield, another member of Alabama's establishment. Still another was an ardent prohibitionist, Lycurgus Breckenridge Musgrove, understandably known as "Breck." For that matter, all the main contenders took a solid dry position.

Black had a sensible electoral plan. Realizing that he was not well known in many counties, he vigorously stumped the whole state. In his speeches, he made the point that Kilby, Bankhead, and Mayfield were of the wealthy establishment. Among his opponents, only "Breck" Musgrove had a common man image and was a friend of labor.

In the primary system then in use, voters could cast first and second preferences. Black received 71,916 first choice and 12,961

3. V. HAMILTON, *supra* note 1, at 119-20.
4. *Id.* at 120.

second choice votes to become the winner. Bankhead came in second, Mayfield third, Musgrove fourth, and Kilby last. Given Alabama's overwhelming preference for Democrats, Black easily defeated the Republican candidate, Edmund H. Dryer, in the general election with about 80% of the vote. Black became the junior Senator from Alabama on December 26, 1926.

Fortunately for Black, President Coolidge did not call a special session of Congress, and the 70th Congress did not begin until early December 1927. Black had nearly a year to study the Senate's procedures and, realizing how green he was, to undertake a remarkable program of serious reading. Among the works he read were the records of the 1787 Constitutional Convention, many of the works of the ancient Greeks and Romans, and Rousseau, Montesquieu, and Locke. His additional reading of the writings of Thorstein Veblen provokes special interest.

Black ordinarily was not one to back out of a fight he considered right, but he waffled on support of Alfred E. Smith when Smith became the Democratic Presidential candidate in 1928. Smith was Catholic and, therefore, an untouchable in the South. Black said that, except for the immigration issue, the New Yorker represented "a clarion call to progressive democracy." Thereafter, Black kept as low a profile as possible, a prudent choice under the circumstances.

He was best at investigating practices that he deemed wasteful and reeking of special privilege. In his first term, he took on the United States Shipping Board, an agency intended to improve the American merchant marine. When GOP senators prevented him from launching an investigation, Black pointed out on the floor that the agency had forty-seven lawyers, who in 1927 had studied only 258 cases, an average of only 5.5 cases per lawyer. He did succeed in getting the Senate to cut its appropriation to $10,000 for *outside* lawyers.

After Roosevelt's inauguration, Black had greater success in his war with the Shipping Board. In 1933 he became chairman of a Special Committee to Investigate Air and Ocean Mail Contracts. He told the Senate that the subsidies were exorbitant. One owner of ships, Black said, had received in 1929 a salary of $50,000 plus dividends of $74,000 for the shipowner's company, of which he was the principal share owner. In 1932 the same company had received subsidies of $1.2 million. Black moved to amend an appropriation bill that would forbid paying employees of these firms a salary of more than $17,500 a year. After a brief discussion, the Senate accepted his amendment without a vote. Apparently, FDR, for reasons never revealed, put pressure on the somewhat pliable House leadership to make the subsidies more generous. One conference committee of the House and Senate failed to reach an agreement. However, in a second conference committee meeting, on the very last of the Hundred Days, the House conceded and accepted the Black amendment.

In December 1932, during the lame-duck session of the 72d Congress, Black introduced a bill, generally called the 30-hours bill, and conducted hearings. Because so little time remained before the convening of the 73d Congress in 1933, passage of his bill was impossible. He introduced it again in March 1933, had it referred to the Judiciary Committee, of which he was a member, and submitted the committee's favorable report in late March. Its chances of passage appeared to be strong.

The Black bill's central provision was to prohibit interstate commerce of the products of manufacturing and mining produced by workers who labored more than 30 hours a week or 6 hours a day. The bill exempted unprocessed agricultural commodities. It also included a 2-year "sunset" clause to provide that the law would expire in 2 years.

Most of the bill's critics, who included Roosevelt, dismissed it simply as a "share the work" measure. Black and his supporters, however, saw the bill as a means generally to stimulate the economy. His report put it: "The channels of interstate commerce are dried up . . . because men without jobs cannot buy. It is manifest . . . that our economic structure cannot be rehabilitated until our people can work at fair wages and thus buy the things they need."

Black argued that his bill would reduce industrial competition, *without violating the antitrust laws*, because all manufacturing and mining companies would be subject to the same standards of days and hours worked. His bill's weakness was the absence of a minimum wage provision. He told the Senate that the Supreme Court "expressly [had] ruled . . . that any minimum wage law would contravene the Constitution," but that he personally did not object to a minimum wage.

Public opinion on the bill, of course, was divided. Most of the letters that he received from working men were favorable, as were those from some corporate officials. Indeed, an Alabama textile executive urged him to support a quite similar idea. Other businessmen strongly opposed it and prepared letters against it, which they persuaded their employees to sign, not a difficult task in those days of precarious employment.

Joe Robinson, the Senate Democratic majority leader, introduced an amendment to change the hours limit to 35, very probably at FDR's request. An indication of the Black bill's popularity in the Senate was the defeat of the amendment, 41 to 48. Democrats voted against it, 35 to 20, quite a rebuff to the majority leader. That afternoon, the Senate passed Black's bill, 53 to 30.

In her memoirs, Frances Perkins reported that FDR opposed the bill on various grounds, but the real reason for his resistance was that he was considering an idea that later in 1933 would become the National Industry Recovery Act (NIRA). Using the strength he had with the compliant House leadership, Roosevelt prevented the Black bill from getting to the floor of the House.

Black knew he had been licked. To a Birmingham constituent he wrote: "[M]y 30 hour bill has been stopped . . . . The President has indicated that he is going to send a message asking for some kind of substitute." In May 1933 FDR recommended NIRA. The administration bill did not pass easily, but it passed, and its Title I, an extremely favorable provision for manufacturers and mine operators, substituted for the Alabamian's bill. Black voted for passage of NIRA, but he did not give up. He introduced his measure once more in 1935, only to have it fail again. In that year he wrote a constituent: "[I]f the 30 Hour week had been adopted . . . instead of employing three million people . . . we would have reemployed more than ten million." In 1938, however, Black's position, in a watered-down version, passed Congress and became law as the Fair Labor Standards Act. Interestingly, in Black's papers at the Library of Congress, he had his papers on the 1933 and 1935 bills in the same file as the 1938 law. By then, of course, Black was an Associate Justice of the Supreme Court. Apparently, he saw the three bills as of a single piece and purpose.

Recall that Black in 1933 had stated that to include a minimum wage provision in his bill would have been unconstitutional. Title I of NIRA had such a provision, even though FDR had told Secretary Perkins he considered Black's bill to be unconstitutional. The irony in Black's and Roosevelt's positions is strong, especially in light of the Supreme Court's decision on May 27, 1935, *A.L.A. Schechter Poultry Corp. v. United States*,[5] in which the Court unanimously held NIRA unconstitutional. Which statesman was the better lawyer? Only the "sunset" provision of the Black bill survived in NIRA.

Trying to determine whether Senator Black was liberal, conservative, or somewhere in between is useful. For several reasons, however, the effort presents some difficult questions. Sometimes Senators are ambivalent about a measure or amendment; they like some features and dislike others. Sometimes they have understandings with other Senators, the President, or someone else that amount to a reciprocal, "you scratch my back and I'll scratch yours," agreement. Sometimes, on a minor issue or one in which their constituents hold little interest, Senators fundamentally are uninterested. Sometimes, too, they vote against or for a bill or amendment because they have quarreled with a colleague and wish to "stick him" when the time is propitious. We must assume that Black, at least occasionally, might have yielded to such impulses in some situations, though I cannot cite any.

Nevertheless, to try to define Black's essential ideology is worth the undertaking. Let us begin with the 73d Congress, 1933-34. The first Senate roll call of 1933, of course, was on the Emergency Banking Bill, which saved the American banking system. Black voted for it, as did all but a very few. I see no ideological implications in his vote; it was simply a necessity during one of the nation's most serious crises.

His second vote in 1933 was on an amendment moved by Senator LaFollette on the Economy bill, which would have reduced salary cuts of civil service workers. Black voted nay. He voted for Tom Connally's weak amendment on salary cuts as well as for passage of the Economy bill. These votes reflected a conservative position by Black.

Some interest arises from Black's vote, along with almost all Senators, for the 3.2 beer. Only the professional prohibitionists, such as Morris Sheppard of Texas, voted nay. Nevertheless, I see no ideological implications.

On March 6, 1933, FDR sent Congress a message and bill on agriculture. After 7 weeks of debate, it became the Agricultural

5. 295 U.S. 495 (1935).

Adjustment Act (AAA). Senators introduced dozens of amendments. Most lost; a few passed.

Still engaged with his 30-hours bill, Black did not vote on Burton K. Wheeler's 16-to-1 silver amendment, Bryan's cause of 1896. He voted on only two roll calls. He voted yea on a much watered-down and almost useless compromise on silver, which carried by a majority of twenty, and he voted yea on passage of AAA, one of the sixty-four Senators who did so. Black's few votes prevent our knowing much about his views on the subject. Alabama, of course, was still part of the Cotton Kingdom, and Black must have been interested in the bill. His vote on the watered-down silver roll call may or may not indicate anything at all. One only can speculate about what he thought about silver legislation. Wheeler's amendment was a good proposal in 1933 simply because it would have improved the plight of debtors, especially farmers, but Black's opinion about Wheeler's defeat on the 16-to-1 amendment is an unknown quantity.

Black's position on TVA is clear. He argued and voted against Vandenberg's crippling amendment but for John Bankhead's less restrictive one, which lost, thanks to Senator Norris's strong speech against it. Black voted for TVA's passage. Only twenty Senators voted against it.

This short description of Black and TVA is too simplified. Bankhead's amendment related to fertilizer's method of production, not its desirability. The matter was technically complicated, politically regional, and passionately disputed. Bankhead's amendment would require the use of the cyanamide process, then in use at Niagara Falls. Norris argued that the equipment then in place in the Valley was antiquated and that it required about "80,000 horsepower to operate at capacity producing a product which would have to sell at a loss, making it impossible to use the power elsewhere." Becoming emotional, Norris questioned his colleagues' inability to see the Power Trust's interest in the amendment: "Is it not a fact that while they would rather have the power themselves, and if they cannot get it, would like to have the Government utilize it where it would not do anybody any good and do them no harm?" Norris had been admired widely on both sides of the aisle since his days in the House, and his speech was persuasive. Huey Long called for the yeas and nays on Bankhead's amendment requiring manufacture by the cyanamide process. The motion failed badly, 12 for to 73 against. All those voting for it were Democrats, all but two of them from the deep South.

Norris's reasons for opposing Bankhead's amendment appear to be persuasive, and Black's vote for it strikes me as out of character. Perhaps his constituents clamored for the cyanamide process so vigorously that he yielded to their views even though he would not be up for reelection until 1936. Other explanations also may exist.

Before the 1933 session ended, Huey Long introduced an amendment that would limit annual incomes to $1 million and gifts to $5 million. Black voted against it, as did forty-nine others, but, surprisingly, Robert Reynolds of North Carolina voted for it when even Hattie Caraway of Arkansas, supposedly in Long's pocket, voted nay.

Normally, the second session of a Congress is a rather dull affair. Usually, they are short, if for no reason other than that congressmen and Senators want to get back to their districts and states. Congressmen return to campaign for reelection, as do Senators in the last year of their term. Reelected in 1932, Black and others enjoyed a happy position, but they liked to return to their states to keep in touch with their constituents' views.

One could not describe the 1934 session as exciting, but it considered some interesting issues. Three deserve treatment: a tax on alcoholic beverages, the Gold Reserve Act of 1934, and the Independent Offices Appropriation (IOA) for 1935.

To start a session with an essentially silly bill to tax alcoholic beverages was bizarre, but the Senate did. It proposed a tax of $3 on a gallon of wine and $5 on spirits imported from nations in default of their war debts. To believe such a tax would be effective during a world-wide depression was wildly optimistic, but the bill passed. Black voted for it, but so did William Gibbs McAdoo, Senator from California, the country's largest wine-producing state. McAdoo obviously did not understand his State's wine industry; in 1933 he had urged that the 3.2 beer bill include 3.2 wine. California's senior Senator, Hiram Johnson, quickly straightened him out.

The Gold Reserve Act, urged by Roosevelt, was a rather dull, but necessary, subject. Democrats and Republicans had a consensus for it. Black voted yea on passage, and the bill carried by a large majority.

The IOA bill, however, was a very hot potato, just as it had been in the 1933's appropriation. The American Legion urged a plan that would restore the pensions of wounded solders to approximately the same status as before the Economy Act of 1933, which FDR urged strongly and which passed easily on January 20, 1933. The Economy Act was one of Roosevelt's major blunders, both economically and politically. Why reduce pensions during a depression, especially when the effect would be further to reduce buying power?

The American Legion in 1934 prepared a plan to restore the veterans' cuts of 1933 and a political program to get it passed. Only about 16 years since the Armistice, when memories were still sharp, passage of the proposal seemed likely. FDR bitterly was opposed to it, and he worked with a very conservative organization in New York and New England against it. Debate on the bill was passionate. Pat McCarran of Nevada urged an amendment that the Legion approved, and the measure passed by one vote. Black voted against it. Dr. Henry Hatfield introduced another amendment; Black did not vote. Congress, sensitive to Legion pressure, passed a bill essentially like the veterans' plan, and FDR vetoed it. On March 27 the House overrode the veto, and the Senate overrode it the next day. The effect was to stimulate the economy by infusing it with $228 million. Black voted with Roosevelt all the way, against McCarran's amendment and against the override.

Why FDR vetoed it is a puzzle. Was he simply bull-headed? Did he have a personal distaste for the Legion? Did he not realize that an override was probable? Black's motive may have been to stay in FDR's good graces at least until he could try again on the 30-hours bill in 1935. But if that was his motive, it failed.[6]

Congress assembled on January 3, 1935, for a session that would be long and would pass an impressive number of liberal bills. That session would become the high tide of the New Deal. In the Senate, the first issue was whether or not to accept Roosevelt's request to join the World Court. In retrospect, the heat FDR's request provoked seems quaint, but, undeniably, it was a very hot issue then. Hiram Johnson led the opposition to it. Like so many liberals of the time, he was an isolationist. Johnson succeeded in preventing the necessary two-thirds majority; thus, the Senate rejected the request. Black voted for the World Court. Loyalty to

---

6. The author would appreciate any information or theory of explanation anyone has.

FDR may have influenced his vote—the second try for the 30-hours bill had not yet come up—but the South was more internationalist than the West.

McCarran's amendment to the Work Relief Bill, which carried by one vote, was an important issue. The amendment proposed by Cutting, Republican Senator of New Mexico, to provide up to $30 million for the nation's public schools, carried by a large margin. Black voted for each. Joe Robinson, however, succeeded in getting both these amendments out of the final appropriation bill. Black's vote for final passage probably reflected nothing more than a sense that the appropriation was necessary—better a weaker bill than none. Thus, the Alabamian's record on Work Relief indicated voting with the Senate's more liberal members.

In 1935 Wright Patman of Texas got a bill through the House to fund a bonus to World War veterans with new and inflationary greenbacks and immediately to pay the veterans. The Senate rather quickly followed suit. Black voted for it. Setting a precedent, Roosevelt addressed a joint session of Congress and delivered a long and very strong plea to reject the bill. The House overrode FDR's subsequent veto. The Senate voted for override 54 to 40, but the yea votes were insufficient to meet the required two-thirds majority. Black voted to override. In January 1936 Congress voted overwhelmingly for what was essentially the same bill, and again FDR vetoed it. This time both houses successfully overrode the veto, and in June vouchers for more than $1.5 billion were mailed to veterans, which thereby strongly stimulated the economy. In 1935 Black had voted twice for the bonus, but in 1936 he voted against it. His switch on the very popular bonus bill of 1936 presents an enigma, especially when he had 2 years before he came up again for reelection. He could not have been thinking of a Presidential nomination to the Supreme Court because it was common knowledge that Joe Robinson would fill the first vacancy on the Court.

Black's voting record on Robert F. Wagner's bill to create the National Labor Relations Board in 1935 demonstrated Black's consistent support for the Act, despite FDR's quiet opposition to it until very late in the game. He voted against Millard Tyding's crippling amendment, which Tyding admitted in debate had been drafted by the National Association of Manufacturers, and Black voted for passage of the Wagner Act. Only twelve senators voted against it. The new law, together with the Social Security Act and Sam Rayburn's holding company measure, were gut issues. The Wagner Act gave an enormous boon to the labor movement, and for Black, it must have provided solace for the second defeat of his 30-hours bill in April. When the Supreme Court approved the Wagner Act in 1937. the effect was at least partially to get buying power in the hands of workers, which, of course, had been the main purpose of Black's pet bill.

The holding companies bill and Social Security Act did not pass until near the end of the session, the holding company law passing first. Two crippling amendments would have made the holding company bill almost useless, and Black voted against them and cast a yea on passage. On three Social Security amendments that would have prevented its effectiveness, Black voted nay. One of them, incidentally, was by Daniel Hastings, the Delaware Senator that Black had handled so deftly in the colloquy on the bankruptcy act in 1934. Black was among the seventy-seven Senators who voted for Social Security. Six Senators voted against the bill. Two of them, each with about 2 years to go before the end of their term, voted nay. Neither of them was around for the next Congress. The other four had terms that did not expire until later. Such was the people's overwhelming support for Social Security.

On February 26, 1937, Black voted for a motion to provide pensions for retired Supreme Court members. The proposal came directly from the Judiciary Committee. Fortunately for Black's long-term reputation, given his nomination to the Supreme Court on August 19 of that year, 72 days had passed between his vote in February and his being recommended for the Court. Further, Black was not a member of the Judiciary Committee in 1937, having left the committee when Congress convened in 1935.

Black favored, but participated little, in the debates on the Court packing proposal—or Court reform, if you prefer—that Roosevelt submitted on February 5, 1937. Joe Robinson, the majority leader, fought hard to get the measure through, although he was in an awkward position because, by then, everyone knew FDR would nominate him to the Court when a seat was open. At first, it appeared that the Court bill would pass despite the disapproval of Vice President John N. Garner, who, after a clerk had read the message, held his nose with one hand and pointed his thumb down with the other. Burt Wheeler led the opposition, and the Republicans, though strongly opposed, thought it wise to remain quiet and to let the Democrats fight among themselves. Wheeler's arguments diminished Democratic support, especially when Democratic Senators learned from their constituents that the plan was unpopular. McCarran, for one, had favored the scheme until a 2-week tour of his vast state changed his mind.

The battle climaxed in a very hot, Washington July. Joe Robinson died of a heart attack on July 14. (It was ironic that the conservative Robinson would die on Bastille Day.) Robinson had been very popular among conservative Democrats, and their hero's death had the effect of further reducing Democratic support. Many of them thought that Roosevelt's Court packing plan and Robinson's struggle for it had killed him. From that time on, Court packing steadily slid downhill. On the special train returning from Robinson's funeral at Little Rock, scores of Democrats spent their time discussing Court packing; most opposed it. To defeat it, the votes of freshman Senators were necessary. Once back in Washington, Prentiss Brown of Michigan called a meeting of eight freshmen. After a 2-hour meeting on July 20, Brown announced that they had enough votes to recommit the bill. The move killed Court packing. The long fight was over. Incidentally, during the trip back from Little Rock, Democrats had made many critical comments about Roosevelt. Clearly, a large number of Democrats had soured on him and were not prepared to support his positions as they had been previously. The bipartisan conservative coalition had come into being. Indeed, FDR had important difficulties with his own party from 1937 until about 1940, when isolationist versus interventionist issues became paramount.

In May 1937 Justice Willis Van Devanter announced his retirement and, thus, left a vacancy on the Bench. Roosevelt had not made a nomination during the Court fight. On August 12 he sent a note to the Senate to inform it that he nominated Black. Four days later the Senate Judiciary Committee favorably confirmed the nomination 63 to 16. On August 19 Black resigned from the Senate.

Thus ended the legislative career of Senator Hugo La Fayette Black. He took his seat as Associate Justice of the Supreme Court on the traditional first Monday of October. He resigned from the Court on September 17, 1971, and died 8 days later.

A great legislator he had been; he became an even greater, and more famous, Justice of the Court.

Hugo Black and the Golden Age

*J. Mills Thornton III**

The sheer variety of the twentieth-century southern political figures who have at one time or another been called Populists must give the historian pause. Jimmy Carter, George Wallace, James Folsom, Eugene Talmadge, Strom Thurmond, Theodore Bilbo, Huey Long, Orval Faubus, Ross Barnett, Sam Ervin, Jesse Helms, even the anti-Semitic propagandist Gerald L. K. Smith—all have been identified by commentators as standing in the Populist tradition. It also is worth noting that southern black politicians essentially never are called Populists, though no mass political movement occurred in all of southern history, with the exception of the Reconstruction Republicans, in which black participation was a more significant element. These two observations alone should be sufficient to make the student suspicious when he finds Hugo Black's judicial philosophy attributed to a Populist intellectual heritage. The careful scholar would wish to see that heritage defined quite specifically, and he would want to know precisely how and when it exerted its influence on Black.

The looseness with which the term "Populist" is bandied about is not, however, the only warning signal. Investigation reveals Hugo Black's background in Clay County in the years of the Populist Revolt to have been one exceedingly unlikely to have sensitized him to the Populist perspective.[1] Black's father, La Fayette Black, was politically unsympathetic not only to Populism proper but even to its watered-down Bryanite free silver version; in 1896 La Fayette Black voted for the Goldbug ticket of Palmer and Buckner. Furthermore, the elder Black was just the sort of man who would have seemed the apotheosis of evil from the perspective of Populist true believers: the proprietor of a general store in the county seat of Ashland, La Fayette Black earned a substantial part of his income from advancing

*Professor of History, University of Michigan. A.B. 1966, Princeton University; Ph.M., 1969, Ph. D. 1974, Yale University.

1. See generally V. Hamilton, Hugo Black: The Alabama Years 3-28 (1972) (discussing Black's family background and youth).

to area farmers credit secured by crop liens.[2]

Hugo Black grew up in a relatively bustling county seat, in a family atmosphere fashioned by an economically prosperous and politically conservative father, and by the examples of ambitious and upwardly mobile siblings, among them a doctor, a lawyer, and a merchant.[3] That young Hugo internalized many of the attitudes which surrounded him is evidenced sufficiently by his refusal to be satisfied with the limited education afforded by Ashland College, from which he received his initial diploma; by his determination—against some financial odds—to attend the University of Alabama; by his selection of law as his career, after a brief flirtation with medicine; and by his decision, shortly after his admission to the bar, to settle and practice in Alabama's booming metropolis, Birmingham.

The likelihood appears to be small that a young man from such a background would have rooted his developing personal and political ideology in a sympathy for the doctrines of the isolated farmers who were attracted to the banner of Populism, doctrines that reflected deep fears of and hostility toward the expanding market economy which threatened to overwhelm and to marginalize them. Such an explanation for the origins of Black's outlook would need the clearest evidence, given its inherent implausibility. But, in fact, no contemporary evidence at all indicates that Black felt any enthusiasm for Populism; we have only nonspecific assertions of such a sympathy by later commentators.

If, therefore, the roots of Black's judicial philosophy are not likely to be found in Populism, do other, more credible sources, explain his emerging attitudes? Three influences on Black in his early manhood suggest a positive response to the question: his membership in the Ku Klux Klan, his passionate attachment to prohibition, and the strong orientation of his law practice toward personal injury suits against corporations. An additional source may have been another ideological tradition deeply influential in Alabama, a tradition that by Black's time was more generalized than Populism and of which Populism is, in a sense, a subset: Jacksonianism.

The Ku Klux Klan of the 1920's too seldom is recognized as a

---

2. See generally B. PALMER, "MAN OVER MONEY," THE SOUTHERN POPULIST CRITIQUE OF AMERICAN CAPITALISM (1980) (discussing the southern Populists' ideology, in general, and their hostility to merchants and crop liens, in particular).

3. See generally Turner, Understanding the Populists, 67 J. AM. HIST. 354 (1980-1981) (remarking that rural isolation is important in forming the Populist outlook).

fountainhead for liberalism in later decades, and Hugo Black's involvement with the Klan very often is understated. Both are profound errors, whose sources, however, are entirely understandable. To be sure, thinking of the Klan as a breeding ground for liberals is quite difficult. Its highly unpleasant tactics in the 1920's included intimidation, masked floggings, and strident rhetorical condemnations of Catholics and Jews. Senator Black himself, during his struggle for confirmation to the Supreme Court, first attempted to minimize his earlier role in the Klan; and later admirers' attempts to prove that the Senator's account of his activities was an accurate one are hardly surprising.[4] But however easily one may explain the origins of these misinterpretations, they nevertheless have served to obscure an important element in the formation of Black's judicial philosophy and, hence, have contributed to the acceptance of the false notion that his philosophy's roots lie in Populism.

To take the second misconception first, careful investigation makes it clear that Black's involvement in Klan activities[5] was extensive and ardent. One of his law partners, Crampton Harris, was cyclops of the largest Birmingham klavern. Two of his closest friends and associates, Ben Ray and Hugh Locke, were among the Klan's most vocal public spokesmen. In the battle over the expulsion of the klansman, demagogue, and anti-Catholic bigot, Senator Tom Heflin, from the Democratic Party in 1929, Ben Ray was the leader of the pro-Heflin forces on the State Democratic Executive Committee, and Hugh Locke was Heflin's gubernatorial runningmate on the bolters' ticket in the general election of 1930.[6]

Black first gained statewide attention as the attorney who successfully defended a fundamentalist Protestant preacher who had murdered a Catholic priest in Birmingham in 1921—a defense that featured explicit appeals to racial and religious prejudice. In 1922 Black defended the Birmingham City Commission in impeachment proceedings founded on its refusal to prosecute masked floggers. In 1923 he officially joined the Klan at a public ceremony attended by some 25,000 spectators. Alabama's Grand Dragon, James Esdale, actively managed Black's senatorial campaign in 1926, and there is

---

4. See e.g., J. FRANK, MR. JUSTICE BLACK: THE MAN AND HIS OPINIONS 38-45, 95-108 (1949) (Frank is particularly guilty of such extenuation.).

5. See generally V. HAMILTON, supra note 1, at 46-170.

6. For a more detailed account of this episode, see generally Thornton, ALABAMA POLITICS, J. THOMAS HEFLIN AND THE EXPULSION MOVEMENT OF 1929, 21 Ala. Rev. 83 (1968).

no doubt that the Klan's massive support supplied him with the margin of victory in that election. Indeed, Black himself did not doubt it at the time. At a great Klan celebration shortly after the order's triumphs in the 1926 Democratic primary, Black told the audience: "I do not feel that it would be out of place to state to you here on this occasion that I know that without the support of the members of this organization I would not have been called, even by my enemies, the 'Junior Senator from Alabama.' "[7] He went on to praise the Klan for "loving the pride of Anglo-Saxon spirit" and for remaining "true to the heaven-born principles of liberty which were written in the Constitution of this country, and in the great historical documents, straight from the heart of Anglo-Saxon patriots. . . ."[8]

Black's intimate association with the Klan hardly can be denied. The role of the Klan in contributing a group of distinguished leaders to Alabama liberalism is noted less often. Yet the development is a fascinating and an important one. Black is certainly the most prominent of these men at the national level. But in the history of Alabama, quite a number of others join him. After Black, the best known is Bibb Graves, the Yale graduate and cyclops of the Montgomery klavern who was elected governor with Klan votes in the same primary in which Black was elected to the Senate and who was chosen for a second term in 1934.[9]

Perhaps Black's closest parallel is Judge Richard Rives. Said to have been an active member of the Montgomery klavern, Rives was a law partner of two close relatives of Congressman and Senator Lister Hill. Rives served for many years as a general superintendent of Hill's political affairs at home. In the late 1930's and early 1940's, Rives met the early stirrings of efforts by blacks to obtain voting rights as the attorney for several Black Belt Boards of Voting Registrars. He successfully defended the Montgomery County Board and the Macon County Board in separate test cases brought by blacks during and just after World War II. In Montgomery city politics in the 1920's and 1930's, Rives was a leading opponent of Montgomery's staunchly anti-Klan mayor, William A. Gunter. Yet, despite these rather unpromising credentials, Richard Rives, once appointed to

7. V. HAMILTON, supra note 1, at 137 (quoting Sprigle, Stenographic Transcript of the Klorero Proceedings, Pittsburgh Post-Gazette, 1937, reprinted in New York Times, Sept. 15, 1937).

8. Id. at 138.

9. For a discussion of Graves' liberalism, see generally Gilbert, Bibb Graves as a Progressive, 1927-1930, 10 Ala. Rev. 15 (1957).

the United States Fifth Circuit Court of Appeals by President Truman, promptly revealed a judicial philosophy almost identical to that of Hugo Black. That these two former Klansmen came to espouse from the bench attitudes so markedly sympathetic to civil liberties and civil rights is no coincidence. Lister Hill, a third Montgomerian, also may be added to this list. Though Hill apparently was not so active in the Montgomery klavern as were Graves and Rives, the family of which he was the most prominent spokesman was allied closely with the Klan in its wars with Mayor Gunter and the Montgomery Advertiser's Grover C. Hall. Yet, Hill in Congress pursued an unswervingly liberal course on all questions other than those involving race. A third example from the ranks of the judiciary is Justice Joel Brown of the Alabama Supreme Court. Actively sympathetic with the Klan, Justice Brown was the sole member of the court to support Senator Heflin's position in the suit seeking to prevent Heflin's expulsion from the Democratic Party. In the 1940's, however, Brown became known for stinging dissents from opinions approving questionable procedures in the trials of blacks. Perhaps his most eloquent dissent appeared in his opinion in Ex parte Taylor,[10] a capital conviction of a black teenager for the rape of a white girl.

A particularly striking example of the tendency for former Klansmen to embrace liberal causes in later decades arose during the battles of the Dixiecrat years. In 1929 anti-Klan elements in command of Democratic party machinery set out to crush the Klan's power in state politics by barring from the Democratic primary any candidate who had failed to support the party's Presidential nominee, Al Smith, in the preceding year's election. Because of the Klan's vitriolic hostility to Smith's Catholicism, those expelled under this rule included a great many of the Klan's leading politicians. Pro-Klan forces under the leadership of Ben Ray vigorously, though unsuccessfully, fought this proposal in the Democratic Executive Committee. The anti-Klan forces insisted that all Democrats were under an obligation to support the party ticket, and the Klansmen denounced such enforced support for an obnoxious candidate as a violation of fundamental freedoms. In 1948, at the time of the Dixiecrat revolt, in many cases the same cast of characters played out the same drama, but the roles exactly were reversed. The leaders of the Loyalist faction, who insisted on a rule barring from subsequent pri-

10. 249 Ala. 667, 671, 32 So. 2d 659, 661 (1947) (Brown, J., dissenting).

maries any candidate who had opposed Truman in 1948, were in large part the Klan sympathizers who had denounced expulsion for failure to support Smith in 1928. When the Loyalists captured control of the Executive Committee in 1950, Ben Ray became state party chairman. The anti-Klan forces of 1929 and 1930 were not the backbone of the Dixiecrat States' Rights leadership and insisted on obedience to the dictates of conscience. Like the stripes on the Confederate battle flag, the two factions had crossed each other and had ended up in opposite corners.[11]

The reasons for this peculiar migration are complicated. The enforcement of party loyalty in 1929 meant holding the surging popular revolt represented by the Klan triumphs of 1926 within the bounds of the balanced power-sharing arrangements between poor whites and wealthy planters and industrialists, which had been erected at the Constitutional Convention of 1901. The enforcement of party loyalty in 1949 strengthened the hand of the forces who, under the leadership of Governor James Folsom, had managed to place the 1901 system on the defensive and who, even at this moment, were attacking its very heart—malapportionment of the Alabama Legislature. That pair of observations, however, forces us to recognize the Klan of the 1920's for what it was: a mass protest movement of poorer and more marginalized whites, whether urban, small town, or rural.[12] The politicians affiliated with it were led to associate with, and thereby increasingly were sensitized to the viewpoints and the circumstances of, the poor whites who constituted the bulk of its membership. That experience explains in part the number of Alabama's leading liberals of the 1930's, 1940's and 1950's who came from the Klan's ranks.

But if the Klan is to be seen as a mass protest movement, seeking a definition of its ideological orientation becomes necessary. What attitudes did the Klan communicate to its members? A part of the answer to that question is all too obvious. An important element in its appeal relied upon the manipulation of racial and religious prejudice to create scapegoats upon whom its less well-to-do members could blame their hard lot. However, the Klan has more appeal than this merely negative aspect. Hugo Black had praised it for being "true to

---

11. For a more thorough discussion on the Dixiecrats episode, see generally W. Barnard, Dixiecrats and Democrats: Alabama Politics 1942-1950, at 95-124 (1974).

12. See generally Thornton, supra note 6 (advancing these arguments in greater detail).

the heaven-born principles of liberty which were written in the Constitution of this country." Are we to take this accolade as simply empty oratory? I think not. I believe that Black saw something in the Klan difficult to see at this distance. To understand this perspective, a brief look at the other cause with which Black was most enamored in the 1920's, prohibition, becomes important. The step from the Klan to prohibition is a very short one. The Montgomery Advertiser commented in the fall of 1929: "In Alabama it is hard to tell where the [Anti-Saloon[League ends and the Klan begins."[13] The two organizations worked closely together in their political and lobbying efforts. The Klansmen embarked on many of their nocturnal flogging expeditions to enforce prohibition. Hugo Black was most definitely not alone in coupling the two enthusiasms. While Black's defense of the murder of the Catholic priest in 1921 first gained him statewide notice, his real fame before his election to the Senate resulted from his appointment in 1924 as a Special United States Attorney to handle the prosecution of more than 100 public officials and prominent citizens in Mobile, including future Congressman Frank Boykin, who had been indicted for participation in a bootlegging conspiracy. His vigorous conduct of the trial unquestionably proceeded from his own deeply felt prohibitionist convictions. In 1916 he had served as a special state prosecutor in a similar bootlegging case in Phenix City and had done his duty with equal zeal on that earlier occasion.

What drew together in the minds of Black and a great many far humbler Alabamians admiration for the Klan and for prohibition? In the booming 1920's, with suddenly shortened women's skirts, rapidly rising divorce rates, and flaming youth, the feeling was abroad in the land—and especially among more poorly educated Americans from fundamentalist and less cosmopolitan backgrounds—that a falling off from the standards of conduct of earlier years had occurred. The Klan attempted the public enforcement of morality through the pressure of community vigilantism upon deviants, and the prohibition movement sought to compel the universal adoption of its principles of private moral conduct through legal and constitutional mechanisms. Both drew much of their emotional appeal from this sense of the necessity to restore America to an earlier, happier time. The belief that American morality was in a marked decline,

13. The Montgomery Advertiser, Nov. 13, 1929.

that the republic itself was threatened by that decline and by the alien forces which played upon it, and that the preservation of all that the United States had come to mean in the world depended upon the restoration of the faith, attitudes, and modes of behavior that had distinguished the nation's founding years characterized the outlooks both of Klansmen and of prohibitionists. Of course, their outlooks were characterized too, by a certain intellectual rigidity, by an historical absolutism which refused to recognize that the age of America's founding fathers, like all ages, was filled with complexities and cross-currents. Rather, the period of our national youth easily came to seem to them a golden age.

All these attitudes influenced Hugo Black. Black was appealing to them when, at the great Klan gathering of 1926, and quite sincerely, he breathed his

> undying prayer that this [Klan] will carry on, sacredly true to the real principles of American manhood and womanhood, revering [the] virtue of the mother of the race, loving the pride of Anglo-Saxon spirit—and I love it—true to the heaven-born principles of liberty which were written in the Constitution of this country, and in the great historical documents, straight from the heart of Anglo-Saxon patriots.[14]

The genius of restoration fairly sings beneath these sentiments.

One more element added to the compound of influences on the early manhood of Hugo Black: the nature of his law practice. From the time that Black first entered private practice in Birmingham in 1907, he had taken on many personal injury lawsuits against corporations. When he returned to private practice in 1919, after service in World War I, he devoted himself almost exclusively to these cases. A practice of this kind necessarily emphasized to him the least admirable traits of corporate America. Day after day, in his office and in the courtrooms of Jefferson County, he saw unfold before him stories of incompetence or, worse, insouciance on the part of the managers of Birmingham's mines and mills in discharging their responsibility to protect the health and safety of their employees. When workers became the victims of these managerial attitudes, he saw corporations respond by employing every device of bureaucratic and legal delay to avoid compensating the often financially desperate injured. Unsurprisingly, the conviction began to grow in his

---

14. V. HAMILTON, supra note 1, at 138.

mind that capitalist enterprise was guided primarily by motives of heartless greed. This perspective obscured or slighted many far more positive contributions of corporations to the life of the community. Black's sample of employer-worker relations was by its very nature an unrepresentative one. It is hardly a source of wonder that Black's professional experience should have engendered in him a growing hostility towards the wealthy industrialists of Birmingham, men whom he easily came to see as supercilious, self-satisfied, and blind to the social costs of their exploitative conduct.

These three sources of influences—the restorationist ideology of prohibition; the sensitivity to the fears and aspirations of the marginalized whites formed in the Klan and the Klan's own powerful restorationism; and the image of a pitiless capitalism devoid of any public spirit not wrung from it by law, gained from his legal practice in Birmingham—accounted for the genesis of the principal components of Hugo Black's later judicial philosophy. Black's absolutist devotion to the Bill of Rights, his antipathy towards all exploitative or manipulative concentrations of power (expressed, toward government, both in his generous conception of the constitutional limitations upon it when he understood it to be defending the powerless, and in his indignant strict construction when he understood it to have become itself despotic), and his peculiarly romantic notion of the republic's early history and of the motives of the Constitution's framers, all are adumbrated in the ideological orientation derived from these early experiences.[15] Black's idiosyncratic reading of American history, so much commented upon, particularly can be seen hiding within the restorationist fervor of his youth. To think of the Constitution as an institutional arrangement crafted by practical and conservative men of affairs who sought to deal with specific political, economic, social, and moral problems was emotionally foreign to him. Rather, he perceived the Constitution to be the written emanation of a democratic faith, summoning later generations to defend in their own time the shining vision which, he believed, had informed the republic's birth, standing as a judgment against the unworthy deviations of subsequent lesser ages. Professor Gordon Wood has taught historians to think of the intellectual movement

---

15. The most thorough study to date of Black's Supreme Court tenure is G. DUNNE, HUGO BLACK AND THE JUDICIAL REVOLUTION (1977). However, Dunne's acceptance of the notion that Black's views had their roots in Populism mars this work's careful scholarship.

from the Revolution to the Constitution as characterized by a hesitant empiricism, motivated by the necessity to chasten rampant democracy while also preserving popular discipline upon government. One suspects that Justice Black would have approached such an account of the origins of the Constitution from precisely the same perspective as that of a Creationist encountering the evolutionary theories of Charles Darwin.[16] So necessary was the Bill of Rights for Black, so much an embodiment of fixed and fundamental principle rather than a product of historical circumstance, that he even convinced himself that every provision of it, every jot and tittle, inevitably was implied by the Fourteenth Amendment's simple phrase "the privileges of immunities of citizens of the United States." This religion—for such it was—reflects the inflexible absolutist fundamentalism and the condemnation of the delinquencies and the mistaken accretions of our latter days that had typified the Klan-prohibitionist culture in which the young Black had moved.

These attitudes are apparent in almost all of Black's constitutional writings, but perhaps in none more clearly than in his 1964 opinion for the Court in the case of Wesberry v. Sanders. This landmark decision requires that all of a state's congressional districts must be substantially equal to each other in population. In appealing to the Supreme Court, attorneys for Wesberry, a resident of Atlanta, Georgia, whose congressman represented double the population in an average Georgia district and treble the population in its smallest one, had relied primarily on the equal protection clause of the Fourteenth Amendment. But Black in his opinion never reached the Fourteenth Amendment claim. He had disposed of the question at hand far earlier—in fact, at the very birth of the republic. He held that congressional districts were required to be equal in population by the terms of the first article of the original Constitution, when it says, "The House of Representatives shall be composed of members chosen every second year by the people of the several states."

In his opinion, Black recited the story of the "Connecticut compromise" at the constitutional convention, noting correctly that under the terms of this agreement, the states were to have equal

---

16. Compare G. Wood, The Creation of the American Republic 1776-1787 (1969) (a portrait of the motives of the Framers); with Wesberry v. Sanders, 376 U.S. 1 (1964) (Black's portrait of the motives of the Framers).

representation in the Senate, but representatives were to be allotted to the states in proportion to their population. He cited the arguments of the delegates from the large states that justice required that a greater number of people have a greater number of representatives. And because the House of Representatives reflected in its structure the views of the large states' delegates, he deduced that their arguments in favor of proportional representation in Congress necessarily implied also a desire to have the congressional districts within the states equal to each other in size. He thus reached the conclusion that the unadorned words "by the people of the several states, " required in and of themselves that congressional districts must be of equal population. This view of the matter, he wrote, vindicates "our Constitution's plain objective of making equal representation for equal numbers of people the fundamental goal for the House of Representatives. That is the high standard of justice and common sense which the Founders set for us."

For the dissenters in this six-to-three decision, Justice John Marshall Harlan called Black's reasoning "whimsical." The historian can only agree. In the first place, the very text of the first article itself is against Black's reading of it. The Constitution allots additional representatives to states for three-fifths of their slaves, inhabitants who not only could not vote but were not even citizens. It requires that every state have at least one representative, no matter how small its population. And, in exactly the same sentence which contains the phrase upon which Black focused, it incorporates all the disfranchising sex, age, and property tests of the various state constitutions, by requiring that no one could vote for a member of the federal House of Representatives who was not eligible to vote for a member of his state legislature's House of Representatives. The "high standard of justice" to which Black appealed, demanding that every person's vote be equal to every other person's, was, to say the least of it, not very evident in these companion provisions.

The textual objections to Black's position, which are advanced in Harlan's dissent, would appear conclusive by themselves. But the consideration of the rationale for popular election actually put forward at the constitutional convention by the proponents of that mode of choosing representatives, renders Blacks' account of their intentions simply untenable. As Gordon Wood and other careful students of the making of the Constitution point out, the principal goal of the framers was to develop some institutional mechanism which, without abandoning the principles of popular self-government, would still compel the electorate to select as its officials men whom the framers would regard as sufficiently well-educated, honorable, and experienced to be able to see what was actually in the voters' long-term best interests, rather than demagogues who would pander to what the framers considered the voters' own narrow and ill-informed notions of what would be good for them. At the convention, two possible strategies for achieving this goal emerged. The first rested on what James Madison called "refining appointments through successive filtrations"—that is, having the voters elect the state legislators, the state legislators elect the federal Congress, and the Congress elect the president, for instance. The reasoning behind this strategy was that, if the electorate were small enough, the persons doing the electing could know the candidates personally, and thus could distinguish the demagogues from the honest statesmen. But this strategy had been tried in a number of the state constitutions, and had not proven entirely successful.

The second, and newer, strategy found its chief exponents in James Wilson of Pennsylvania and James Madison of Virginia. It rested on the direct election of the official from a very large district. The theory behind this approach was that if the district were large enough geographically, it would be physically impossible for a demagogic candidate to meet the majority of the voters and make personal pledges to them. The electorate, in the absence of such personal contact, would be obliged to rely on what today is called "name recognition," that is, the voters would have to vote for the candidate whose background, breeding and career had prepared him for the office, the candidate who had a "district-wide name." The constitutional convention, of course, ended up using elements of both strategies in the document that it drafted. But the House of Representatives was based essentially entirely on the latter strategy, the large-district method. In designing the House, the delegates considered the most crucial provision one that we today almost never notice: the requirement that no district contain fewer than 30,000 persons. The Constitution provides no maximum population; a district could not be too large for the framers' purposes. But they believed that no district could be formed embracing as many as 30,000 people which would not be so vast as to preclude participatory democracy, or as they would have put it, demagogy. Of course, developments which the founding fathers could not have foreseen—enormous increases in population density, the creation of political parties, and the increasing perfection of mass-marketing techniques—rather rapidly rendered the insights which underlay the large-district scheme irrelevant to its operation in practice. But once we understand those insights, and the goals which they were designed to effect, we must recognize Black's portrait of the framers' motives for what it is: arrant sentimentalism.

Were we able to present this analysis to Black himself, there can be no doubt at all that his reaction to it would be the same as his reaction actually was to Justice Harlan's critique in his trenchant dissent: Black would reject it. No matter how massive may be the evidence for the elitist presumptions and aims of the framers—and it is quite massive, indeed—Black would not, could not, accept its validity, because if he were to do so, he would thereby in effect abandon the restorationist vision which gave meaning to his life and work. He was unwilling to follow the far more hard-minded, but far less judicially acceptable, example of his colleague William O. Douglas in frankly seeking to shape constitutional requirements to reflect his own concept of what was just. For Black, the ideals which had formed the Constitution, the ideals of the men who had written and ratified it, were themselves already truly just. The evil of later and lesser eras had obscured the luster of those ideals. But to achieve the just society for which the republic ought to stand, there was no need to impose new constitutional requirements; they had only to be recovered, and restored to their rightful place.

The attribution of Black's emerging attitudes to his experiences with the Klan, prohibition, and an apparently unfeeling big business has the virtue of finding their origins in influences whose importance to him, unlike that of Populism, is fully demonstrable. We can prove that these forces really existed in and shaped his early life. But our task is not yet done. A critic reasonably might object to restorationism, the belief that the republic's natal years were a golden age, and a deep and bitter hostility to the monopolistic power of corporate America were both central to the doctrines of the Populist revolt. Even if Black absorbed these notions through intermediate movements and circumstances, the critic might ask, are not their ultimate origins to be discovered in Populism? Let me attempt to answer that objection.

The home environment of Black's boyhood was virtually the antithesis of a Populist one. Many enthusiasts of the Klan and prohibition movements were like Black in this regard. The Klan and prohibitionism were mass movements of protest against the social and moral climate of modern America, as was Populism; yet the constituencies to which the Klan and prohibitionism appealed were different from that of Populism. Indeed, the Klan-prohibition constituency was more nearly comparable to that of Progressivism than to that of Populism.[17] The Klan, and to a somewhat lesser extent prohibition, appear to have drawn many of their adherents from Alabama's small towns and cities, and from the lower-middle as well as the lower classes. Membership in an organized religious denomination, Protestant and usually fundamentalist, also seems to have been normal among them.[18] Populism, on the other hand, found its most enthusiastic support in the most rural and isolated areas; any frequent contact with the wider world—even the presence of a village nearby, or regular attendance at an organized church—militated against allegiance to the Populist crusade.[19]

What, then, accounts for Populism's sharing with the Klan and prohibition movements of 30 years later such powerful and ruling concerns? My own notion is that the mass protests both of the 1890's and of the 1920's drew upon attitudes general, though appearing in a variety of guises, in the political culture of Black's Alabama and inherited from the ideology that had dominated the State in the Antebellum period—Jacksonianism.

The source of antebellum political divisions, and the fears on which they were founded, is to be sought in the same phenomenon that later generated Populism: the expansion of the market economy in rural America in the years between the War of 1812 and World War I. Resistance to the marketplace implied a conception of the meaning of freedom widely held in the Jacksonian generation and undergirding the program of Jackson's party, the Democrats, a party dedicated to defending the ethic of subsistence agriculture. For Democrats, freedom was something that the citizenry had gained in the American Revolution and that it now held by right, but that evil, antidemocratic forces were attempting to take away. A

---

17. See generally S. HACKNEY, POPULISM TO PROGRESSIVISM IN ALABAMA (1969) (carefully distinguishing these two constituencies in Alabama).

18. I venture these generalizations with some confidence, yet they are based entirely upon impressionistic evidence. The returns from the 1926 Democratic primary (for the Klan) and from the county option referenda of 1906 and 1907 and the repeal referendum of 1935 (for prohibition) would provide a good basis for a quantitative investigation of this subject and would be a welcome addition to our knowledge.

19. My conception of Populism is much influenced by Turner, supra note 3, though I believe that his notion of the temporal specificity of the social developments which he cites is erroneous.

man was free when he was dependent on no one else for his livelihood and welfare. Movements and institutions whose success would diminish the autonomy of the individual were, thus, by definition, aristocratic and inimical to the American experiment. Jacksonians saw themselves as fighting to preserve in its purity the revolutionary ideology of Thomas Jefferson, an ideology that they believed to be threatened with subversion by urban, commercial, broad constructionists. Democrats campaigned for the abolition of property qualifications for voting and office-holding because they hoped that a broadened electorate would be able to use the government to restrict the growth of corporations and, ultimately, to destroy them. They conceived of their political party as a sort of trade union of the electorate, through which ordinary citizens, individually weak, could band together and use their numbers to counterbalance the power of the wealthy. The Democracy's enthusiasts usually were concentrated in those areas most insulated from market agriculture. Alabama was one of the party's chief strongholds, and within Alabama, its bastions were the hill counties of the northern part of the State.

In the years between the Mexican War and the Civil War, as America entered upon a period of unexampled economic prosperity, the Jacksonian movement gradually lost its social and ideological coherence. A group of ambitious younger Democratic politicians, who generally accepted the label "Young America," began to use aspects of Jacksonianism, especially its devotion to laissez-faire and strict constructionist doctrines, in ways that defended commercial and industrial interests, instead of attacking them. The ideas that originated with Young America often have been called, though quite misleadingly, "social Darwinism." Adopted in most instances as well by the leaders of the Republican Party during the 1850's, these ideas became the ideology of America's dominant culture after the Civil War. The Populist revolt stood squarely against them. For that reason, Populism appears on the surface to repudiate so many articles of the Jacksonian creed: Jacksonianism favored a hard money, wholly specie circulation, but Populism liked a soft money, inflationary policy; Jacksonianism favored a small and inactive government, but Populism supported an expansive, highly active one; Jacksonians would have been horrified by any suggestion of federal intervention in the agricultural economy, but the Populists' subtreasury scheme sought just that: Jacksonians stood for individual autonomy, but Populists stood for the cooperative commonwealth. In all these respects, the doctrines preached by the Redeemer Democrats in the

South in the 1880's and 1890's remained truer to the precedents of Jacksonianism than did the remedies proposed by the Farmers' Alliance and the People's Party. Yet, clearly, the Populists had their own strong claim on the Jacksonian legacy. The Populists' agrarianism, their suspicion of the ethic of the marketplace, their hostility towards great corporations and other manipulative power centers, and their defense of the isolated and the marginalized all had precise counterparts in Jacksonianism. In short, Jacksonian ideology, having bifurcated at midcentury, had become by the end of the century so generalized a part of the social faith that aspects of it were to be found across the entire southern ideological spectrum.[20]

One element of the Jacksonian creed descended to all its heirs: its restorationist analysis of American history. An essential component of Jacksonianism was the sense that powerful forces in American life were betraying the Revolution and that the Democratic party was engaged in a crusade to defeat their machinations and to restore the republic to the virtues of its founding years.[21] An identical viewpoint is to be found in Populism. But, although seldom noted, an analagous position marked the Redeemers' outlook as well. After the Civil War, Redeemer politicians began to claim that the essence of the Confederate cause had been not the defense of slavery but to defense of the purity of the Constitution. They depicted their own Democracy's states' rights, laissez-faire, low tariff platform as an extension of this sacred movement. The belief that the United States following the Civil War had deserted its founding Jeffersonian doctrines permeated all social and economic classes in the late nineteenth- and early twentieth-century South. Thus, Klansmen and

20. Not all the developments discussed in these paragraphs have been studied as thoroughly as they deserve. For some detailed discussion of these developments, see generally S. HAHN, THE ROOTS OF SOUTHERN POPULISM: YEOMAN FARMERS AND THE TRANSFORMATION OF THE GEORGIA UPCOUNTRY, 1850-1890 (1983); M. HOLT, THE POLITICAL CRISIS OF THE 1850'S (1978); H. WATSON, JACKSONIAN POLITICS AND COMMUNITY CONFLICT: THE EMERGENCE OF THE SECOND AMERICAN PARTY SYSTEM IN CUMBERLAND COUNTY NORTH CAROLINA (1981). The loss of coherence in Jacksonianism in the 1850's produced a similar disintegration of orthodoxy within Whiggery. As Professor Holt emphasizes, the economic positions of the parties converged in the final ante-bellum decade. Consequently, elements of the Whig faith are to be found mixed with elements of Jacksonianism in the doctrines of both Redeemers and Populists in the later years of the century.

21. See M. MEYERS, THE JACKSONIAN PERSUASION: POLITICS AND BELIEF (1960) (correctly emphasizing the restorationist theme in Democratic doctrine, though conceding a greater enthusiasm for upward social mobility among Democrats than actually was usual among the true believers).

prohibitionists in the 1920's did not have to rely on Populism to teach them restorationist attitudes. At least a mild restorationism was almost a characteristic of being a white southerner in the period. The Klan and prohibition merely were intensifying and playing upon sentiments widespread in the culture and present in it since antebellum times.

If Hugo Black were here today, we cannot doubt the principal source that he himself would cite for his philosophy. He would tell us that its roots lay primarily in the thought of Thomas Jefferson. We know that he spent much time throughout his life studying and reflecting upon Jefferson's writings. Black's Jefferson, however, was a romanticized, I may even say, a modernized Jefferson—Jefferson the democrat and civil libertarian, not Jefferson the believer in a natural aristocracy. Black's understanding of Jefferson was, in other words, a Jacksonian understanding of him. Black's belief that he was a disciple of Jefferson, as powerful as it was, was no stronger than Andrew Jackson's own. But it is not the spirit of the eighteenth-century Age of Reason, implicit in all of Jefferson's ideas, which one encounters in Hugo Black; it is the spirit of egalitarian democracy; it is the spirit of the Jacksonians.

Far too much Southern historiography has failed to challenge the rank perversion of the region's history that depicts the region as having been dominated thoroughly by conservatism. Populism seems to be the one liberal movement whose importance in shaping the southern past all concede. Consequently, when they encounter a southern liberal like Hugo Black, too many scholars are puzzled by his liberal manifestations and rush to label the challenge to their preconceptions a recrudescence of the Populist crusade. The time has come to outgrow that tendency. We now must recognize the many and diverse sources of liberalism in the South's intellectual heritage. The careful study of the experiences and the thought of Hugo Black, and of the many other southern political leaders like him, is certainly the first step towards the general acceptance of such a position.

ETHICAL BACKGROUND OF HUGO BLACK'S CAREER: THOUGHTS PROMPTED BY THE ESSAYS OF SHELDON HACKNEY AND PAUL L. MURPHY

*Bertram Wyatt-Brown**

President Hackney refers to the outsider-insider character of what we might call the Hugo Black enigma.[1] I confess to veering toward the outsider polarity myself. I am not a lawyer, not an Alabamian, not even a southerner, by birth at least, nor a specialist in politics, law, or the recent South. But I do have some credentials, though far less interesting or appropriate than President Hackney's connections with Hugo Black. My father, an Episcopal minister, originally from Eufaula, Alabama, shared so many of the values and attitudes and even authoritarian mistrust of Demon Rum, "economic royalists," and Yankee-style unmannerliness and hypocrisies that the Associate Justice of the Supreme Court seems almost like a kinsman. So many southerners like Black and my father loyally believed the Democratic Party to be an organization not of blind reaction and special interests but of vision and reform, warm camaraderie and great leadership. Most gratifying for them both—and many others—was the selection of Franklin Roosevelt as President of the United States. To one, he was a political hero; to the other, he was a near saint if Episcopalians were ever to revive beatification—an unlikely event in FDR's case.

Though southerners of this kind are familiar, aspects of their lives are remote to us. We can identify with graduate student Hackney's puzzlement about why southerners of Hugo Black's gen-

---

* Richard J. Milbauer Professor of History, University of Florida. B.A. 1953, University of the South; B.A. (Hon.) 1957, King's College, Cambridge University; M.A. 1961, Cambridge University; Ph. D. 1963, Johns Hopkins University.

1. Hackney, *The Clay County Origins of Mr. Justice Black: The Populist as Insider*, 36 Ala. L. Rev. 835, 839-40 (1985).

eration found public demonstrations for Negro civil rights so protofascist and threatening, especially in light of the Justice's concern for the "little man."[2] For Hugo Black, crowd unruliness violated the rightness of things; it was a question of dignity, order, and seemliness. Hidden assumptions about class and race exist in such concepts without for a moment conjuring up that ugly label "racism." Historians like Professor Murphy and President Hackney have the job of recapturing that "old-fashioned" mentality, an adjective Black often proudly used to describe his own views. They describe the mentality with erudition here, but have avoided the spell of sentimentality and nostalgia for the good old days,[3] which were not really all that good.

Three areas that the Articles discuss in whole or part can be amplified: the character of law and liberty as understood in the South; the fraternal impulse; and the question of personal ambition and self-understanding. Although abolitionists, civil rights workers, and Yankee historians usually have taken a different view, the South's legal profession was much fairer and more professional than its outside reputation would indicate. Eugene Genovese, the dean of southern antebellum scholars, has observed the remarkable degree of high jurisprudence with which slave cases had been handled in those benighted pre-Civil War days, setting ample precedent for Black's early and vigorous defense of Birmingham blacks and his lifetime courtroom fairness to minorities. Able attorneys, sometimes without fee or favor, defended helpless clients with the same tricks of the craft and oratorical exertion that they gave to more lucrative trials.[4]

The South's intellectual life always has centered upon religion and law. Both influences, as Hackney points out, strongly were intertwined in Hugo Black's makeup.[5] One of Black's remarks was instructive; the Justice once referred to the Constitution as "my legal Bible,"[6] a union of two chief sources of wisdom: law and

2. *Id.* at 835.

3. *Id.* at 839-42; Murphy, *The Early Social and Political Philosophy of Hugo Black: Liquor as a Test Case*, 36 ALA. L. REV. 861, 871-79 (1985).

4. *See generally* E. GENOVESE, ROLL, JORDAN, ROLL: THE WORLD THE SLAVES MADE 25-69 (1974); B. WYATT-BROWN, SOUTHERN HONOR: ETHICS AND BEHAVIOR IN THE OLD SOUTH 389 (1982).

5. Hackney, *supra* note 1, at 842-43.

6. H. BLACK, A CONSTITUTIONAL FAITH 41 (1968), *quoted in* Snowiss, *The Legacy of Justice Black*, in 1973 THE SUPREME COURT REVIEW 241.

scripture. No doubt his devout mother, Martha Toland Black, had much to do with her son's strong moral, religious, and antiliquor commitment. But the law was equally important to Black's development. Being more exclusive and requiring lengthier education than the ministry, the law took precedence in intellectual and, perhaps, even in popular terms. Historians' delay in realizing the significance of law in American culture is curious, particularly when compared with the attention devoted to church and theological matters. Part of the problem has been the legal profession itself, which has encouraged a narrowly constitutional, parochial view of its own history. We certainly will not understand Hugo Black's contribution to American jurisprudence simply by going over his record case by case. Clearly, the organizers of the Hugo Black centennial symposium have recognized that limitation and have brought together not just constitutional experts, members of the bar, and office holders but specialists in political and social history, too, to address the main point, the significance of law in southern life and its relation to Hugo Black's early career.

Surely a good trial offered country folk as much opportunity for participatory entertainment as any tent meeting. The courthouse was the secular temple of every county. As Virginia Hamilton notes in her persuasive biography, young Hugo Black could be found in the Ashland courtroom when his friends were at play.[7] The proceedings displayed rules for order, hierarchy, process, ritual, and drama. There, good more visibly and immediately was sundered from evil than in Sunday services in which the same Manichaean division had to be described abstractly or with monotonously familiar Biblical stories.

For most school boys, the courthouse was a very fascinating place, but for Black, the intrigue was more than that. The chance to do justice for all was part of the cultural life and lore of the region. The concept of liberty was basic, but its meaning was different from its definition in the civil rights era. Despite the loss of both sovereignty and slavery in the Civil War, southern whites continued to assume that liberty was the right to self-dependence, to defend one's home, property, and neighborhood against encroachments of alien forces. Public tranquility, it was thought, required strict adherence to group conformities about race, moral

---

7. *See* V. Hamilton, Hugo Black: The Alabama Years 18 (1972).

constraints, and place in the order of society. As Professor Hackney comments in his Alabama study, *Populism to Progressivism in Alabama*, reform Governor Comer who signed the Prohibition Act of 1907 expected the measure to restore "moral vigor everywhere"[8] in the State. Although the measure was a sour disappointment to its supporters, Governor Comer was not alone in holding that initial conviction.

In his concise review of revisionist scholarship on temperance, Professor Murphy argues that the twentieth-century antiliquor movement throbbed to a middle-class beat, even in the South. Bourgeois reformers sought, for the first time, state powers "to create or sustain a particular conception of community."[9] In one sense, he is accurate. Southern Progressives differed from traditionalists in their willingness to use government even at risk to states' rights doctrine. Whether the designation "middle-class," however, tells us much about why so many Americans, and particularly southerners, advocated an end to liquor consumption is not so certain. But whether upper- or just middle-class, the "respectable" people, to use a current term, since time out of mind have known kinfolk—father, son, brother, uncle, cousin—ruined by alcohol. As Professor Murphy notes, Hugo Black's brother Pelham, a lawyer, died under circumstances suggesting overindulgence.[10]

The difference was that, in earlier southern history, nobody dreamt that government could or should legislate sobriety. Such vices as intemperance were seen as personal failings for which society had no responsibility. As in other areas of southern life, a regional fatalism about these matters only slowly surrendered to more hopeful ideas of human nature and institutional possibilities. Instead, resignation and puzzlement over sad examples of broken humanity prevailed. However, as a Birmingham police court judge and solicitor and, later, as a Mobile prosecutor, Black was devoted to the new theory of governmental aggression for public good. The idea was the common Progressive wisdom of the day. Even if it implied criticism of hard-drinking foreigners in American society, the whole rationale was basically innocent and unselfconscious, narrow spirited though it was. Assiduously, Black enforced the

---

8. S. Hackney, Populism to Progressivism in Alabama 305 (1969).
9. Murphy, *supra* note 3, at 866.
10. *Id.* at 871.

statutes with color blindness in a manner in keeping with his notions of liberty and public need. Like Jefferson, he believed that primary power should reside in the hands of a consensus-making community—what then was called popular will. Southern and, indeed, rural American custom placed individuals within a community and family context so that, as Walker Percy once remarked, the difference between the private and solitary sphere and the public one scarcely existed. Thus, the independent householder had the freedom to do as his neighbors did on the foundations of mutual respect before the public and of equality before the bench. Justice Black's belief in ordered community relationships gave coherence to his life and judicial decisions.

In his early legal practice, Black championed the rights of a once independent yeomanry lately caught in the toils of impersonal and monolithic companies: steel, railroad, and utility combines that threatened the sanctity of proud community and individual life. No mystery or paradox existed at all in this effort that some might choose to identify wholly with Populism. First, as a young stranger in Birmingham, no clients except the down and out were likely to cross his legal threshold. They could not afford better; he could not afford to turn them away. At that time, no modern-day firms existed in Alabama, even in industrial Birmingham, to recruit and train young law school graduates. Second, he could identify with the "plain folk," not because he belonged to that class, but because, like Tom Watson, Huey Long, and even Lyndon Johnson, he came from people of unpretentious but genuine refinement and place in society. He shared with his working-class clients the manly ideal. According to this prescription, man must be free to earn and have respect because he is free from material and social dependency. When that sense of selfhood is threatened or ruined, a man becomes slave, a status forbidden by the fundamental law of the land. Populism itself was an attempt to right the scales of justice both in terms of economic reform and psychological esteem. Both old ideas and new methods constituted that cause, a cause that Clay County residents had cherished during Black's childhood.

No paradox or irony was involved in his advocacy of prohibition on the one hand and anticorporatism on the other. At the same time, both helped to sustain freedom and community harmony. The law, he always believed, was the best means for keeping alive the Jeffersonian and Jacksonian vision of self-respect and dignity. The chief thread of continuity that can be discerned in Black's early and late Supreme Court rulings consisted in his understanding of the traditional proposition: the organic unity of local community with individual aspiration. Graduate student Sheldon Hackney was perplexed by Justice Black's swing toward the communal rather than the individual aspect of the equation, as Professor Hackney recognized later.[11] Although in the 1960's Black's emphasis shifted toward social stability, he always had believed that disorder, however justified in the minds of the perpetrators, violated the individual's right to protection and self-esteem.

Ideally, the inner man and his social personality reflected in the eyes of those who knew him were supposed to harmonize. Under peaceable circumstances, the public had to respect the independence of the individual, but when dangers to social order arose, the rule of community came first, the individual second, the impersonal forces of corporation or bureaucracy last. His concept of a necessary balance between the conflicting forces of society and individual was not far from that old, classical ideal of Aristotelian and stoic *media res*—prudence, restraint under provocation—a theme that certainly pervaded much of Hugo Black's voracious intellectual study. Not being an expert on his rulings, I may be far from the mark, but such are some speculations. As Daniel Berman pointed out some years ago, Hugo Black "has never in any sense been in favor of a revolutionary transformation of society."[12] To sum up, then, Justice Black was a man of honor in its Ciceronian sense and also in the most objective meaning of the term.

After that possibly self-serving designation (because I have written on the topic), I may seem perverse to claim that this proposition helps to explain his fraternal proclivities and membership in the Klan. Here we find the gregarious southerner searching for fellowship and power in the company of other men. In the South, perhaps, communal bonding had been felt more intensely than in the North. Masonry flourished everywhere for a time, but the militia, I believe, served as the southern antebellum center of male social life. But that agency fell into some disrepute following the late

11. Hackney, *supra* note 1, at 837-39.
12. Berman, *Hugo L. Black: The Early Years*, 8 CATH. U.L. REV. 103, 116 (1959).

unpleasantness, and in the 1880's and 1890's village and country men went to their lodges for fun and fellowship in the same spirit as their fathers had gone to muster. Belonging to fraternal orders was just as important to late 19th-century politicians as belonging to the militia officer corp had been for their predecessors. Hugo Black apparently loved the companionship that these societies provided through ritual and idolatry of male self-esteem. Given his truncated educational experience, he had missed out on the college fraternity experience, but he made up for it later, though always with a sobriety that his fellows probably did not share in every situation.

The impulse of the joiner strikes the academic in the way it did H.L. Mencken: as an exercise in boobery. As Alexis de Tocqueville explained early in the nineteenth century, however, "associationism" was a way of being somebody in mass democratic society. Certainly, Black was not dependent upon others to define who he was, but he nonetheless was the kind of man to enjoy telling jokes, passing along the handshake from member to member, and creating a sense of fellowship by other forms. The camaraderie was certainly preferable to the casual elbowbending at the corner saloon. In contrast with the tippling crowd, the Elks, Moose, and Civitans were organized grandly at that time. So was the Klan, at least at first. Over 1700 attended the Birmingham rally in 1923 when Black pledged himself to the Robert E. Lee chapter of the Ku Klux Klan.[13]

Difficult though understanding now may be for some of us, the decision must be seen in context. Whatever the mindlessness of Klan "mumbo-jumbo" was, it certainly cannot be classified as a pure aberration. Simple membership reflected no social pathology in itself. As the Baltimore sage noted at the time, "[i]f the Klan is against the Negro, so are all of the States south of the Mason-Dixon line [and most north of it, too, one might add]. If the Klan wears grotesque uniforms, so do the Knights of Pythias and the Mystic Shriners . . . . If the Klan lynches a Moor for raping someone's daughter, so would you or I."[14] For generations, southerners had preserved community ideals and values, first by gossip and hectoring. When the deviancy continued, they involved regulator

13. *See* V. Hamilton, *supra* note 7, at 99.
14. D. Chalmers, Hooded Americanism: The History of the Ku Klux Klan 1 (1981).

means, unruly devices stretching far back into the medieval past. A new and more secular world had arisen during and after World War I. Many Americans, and not just southerners alone, were frightened by the changes. They convinced themselves that safety lay in preserving traditional values against alien people and ideas. Black was among them. At a Klan celebration after his 1926 senatorial victory, he told the audience that they all upheld "the real principles of American manhood and womanhood . . . loving the pride of Anglo-Saxon spirit—and I love it—true to the heaven-born principles of liberty which were written in the Constitution of this country."[15] Although he never condoned lynching and lawlessness in the turbulent 1920's, he never condemned them either. The latter course would have been political suicide.

How could his notions of Anglo-Saxon brotherhood in the Klan be reconciled with his love of strict duty, rectitude, and law? First was the purely personal side. Hiram Evans, Imperial Wizard at Atlanta headquarters, and William J. Simmons, Klan founder, were both Hugo Black's Clay County contemporaries. Moreover, Evans' father had been the very judge whom young Hugo so had admired. Ties of neighborhood—not a casual consideration in southern life—played a part. Second, the old Confederate shades still rode through his mind, as they did for most other southerners, more or less in the boyish style of Faulkner's Charles Mallison. The second Klan was built upon that fund of folk memory and reverence for the "Lost Cause," a set of emotions and passions more intense than those that inspired allegiance to the Elks or Moose. Black was scarcely unique in his faith in the Civil War traditions passed down from father to son. Even at a later date, had he read the liberal revisionists of Reconstruction history that graduate student Hackney might have recommended to him, he would have thrown up his hands in disbelief. Such memories from early days did not influence necessarily his courtroom judgments or attitudes about civil rights. Instead, the recollections simply meant a fidelity to what had mattered so much to his parents and others who had lived through that tumult long ago. No less important was the question of political support. Whatever its deficiencies and bad odor, the Alabama Klan was about the only organization that could provide help for an aspiring politician cut off from the cam-

15. V. Hamilton, *supra* note 7, at 138.

paign treasure chests of the "Big Mules"—the large corporations. The industrial unions, though active, were not powerful enough. Besides, their strength did not reach into the countryside. Furthermore, veterans of the Great War were exempted from the poll tax; the exemption expanded the voting potentiality of poor whites disfranchised earlier in the century. In the struggle against the entrenched and wealthy powers of the State, many of these new voters were reachable through the Klan. The opportunity was hard to turn aside.

On matters of violence, the law and the lawless came together on this point as they had for centuries back in the southern past. By the end of the First World War, the hour was late, the view archaic and threadbare. Despite a growing modernity in the educated circles of southern life, the common folk and their small-town leaders reverted to time-worn extralegal methods in their reaction to wartime's dislocations and peacetime's moral slackness. Defense of old sanctities for female purity, male regularity, black subordination, and Anglo-Saxon and Christian conformity required stern measures of a united people or so the logic of honor ran. The point is neither to condemn nor to justify such attitudes. Sad to say, they were just a part of southern culture.

Obviously, Black pursued bootleggers in his prosecutions and spoke about immigration restrictions at Klan rallies because duty and conviction seemed to require such actions. But, in truth, raw ambition, the essential drive that politicians must have, also played a part. No officeseeker could afford to denounce the Anti-Saloon League or the Klan in 1920's Alabama. If Black's contemporary Oscar Underwood took such risks, his actions may have reflected an integrity and courage that lesser men could not muster, but his temerity was perhaps no less calculating than Black's. When, in his bid for the 1924 Presidential contest, the senior Alabama Senator denounced the Klan and the operation of the eighteenth amendment, he had his own agenda for national, as opposed to local, fame and power. The result was defeat on all fronts. Black, on the other hand, moved expertly through the political quicksands to survive the fall of Klan power and the swell of anti-Catholic sentiment that Al Smith's 1928 campaign generated.

Throughout these years, and thereafter, too, Black seemingly retained remarkable self-possession without ever indicating a sense of guilt over past wrongdoings or questionable decisions. If the original premise about the centrality of self-dependence is correct, we should not be surprised at all. The southern ethic was based upon the oneness of individual and society, leader and follower in essential faiths—not always and not in every case, but ideally so. Therefore, open admission of former sins was wholly inappropriate. To someone of Black's cast of mind, public confession would be demeaning, casting a cloud over one's claim to leadership and self-possession. Instead, remaining as tight-lipped and dignified as possible was preferable. That was how Justice Black handled the issue of Klan membership when it arose after his confirmation for the Supreme Court. The same attitude, according to Hackney, governed his approach to matters challenged by his law clerks.[16]

Real strength—and stubbornness—characterized such a temperament. Yet the remarkable fact about Justice Black was his intellectual and personal growth, as Professor Murphy points out.[17] The Supreme Court tends to mold its members in its own way. Black was intellectually malleable enough to permit its influence to shape his maturing legal thought to a degree that opened him to charges in Alabama of gross betrayal. Therefore, I do not agree wholly with Professor Hackney's interpretation mentioned at the start of this paper: "the principles of an outsider and the behavior of the insider."[18] The explanation depends upon what one means by "outsider." Certainly, it does not apply to members of the High Bench itself. In terms of Alabama or southern politics, as Hackney goes on to show, it is a slippery concept. Perhaps "outsider" covers too wide a range—from Andrew Jackson to Jimmy Carter. These and other southern leaders (for example, George Wallace in the 1960's) were outside the sophisticated eastern circles, the corporate world, and the Washington establishment, but they were isolated not at all from ordinary people who shared their mistrusts of centralism, bigness, and cultural elitism. Moreover, the southern tendency to admire mavericks tends to be deceptive. Only by being a little larger than life could the southern officeseeker be a man of the plain folk. In southern democracy, charismatic leadership depended upon that perception of differentness and yet oneness at the same time.

---

16. Hackney, *supra* note 1, at 837.
17. Murphy, *supra* note 3, at 879.
18. Hackney, *supra* note 1, at 839; *see supra* note 1 and accompanying text.

In any event, from parochial beginnings, Hugo Black matured into one of the Court's most trenchant members. In his decisions, the exclusive brotherhood of fraternal orders became the right of all to legitimate access; liberty was expanded beyond white independence. The silence of honor found expression in the fifth amendment's prohibiting coerced self-incrimination. Black was probably more perceptive and innovative about the nature of the fifth amendment than he was about most other portions of the Bill of Rights. In addition, traditional southern mistrust of central powers was fashioned into Black's hostility toward government harassment. Liberty, central to his thought, meant "the fundamental right of each man to participate in the self-government of his society,"[19] an understanding commensurate with but wider than its old communal meaning. His enthusiasm in the early days for "Anglo-Saxonism" was so diluted that by 1950 he waspishly assailed the idea that the Court should rely only on the "English-speaking peoples to determine what are immutable and fundamental principles of justice."[20] All these things were done in the name of a literalness about the Constitution that brings to mind the hardy, Old Testament orthodoxies of Clay County at the turn of the century. Thus, within the ethic of his forebears, Hugo Black found principles and means for strengthening the law's protection of self-dependence and regard for community autonomy. His rejection of Justice Douglas' sweepingly nationalistic view of the fourteenth amendment was based upon his adherence to old, States' Rights federalism. Nor did he forget the need for community safety. An offender's rights under the fourth amendment, he declared, should be limited to "make our cities a safer place for men, women and children to live."[21]

During Black's lifetime, the world as well as the man changed. After the New Deal and the Second World War, the nation, like Black himself, was less restrictive and moralistically rigid than it had been in his youth. Certainly, in reviewing Black's opinions on church and state questions, one cannot argue for a frozen uniform-

19. *In re* Winship, 397 U.S. 358, 385 (1970) (Black, J., dissenting), *quoted in* Snowiss, *supra* note 6, at 194.

20. Rochin v. California, 342 U.S. 165, 176 (1952) (Black, J., concurring), *quoted in* G. Dunne, Hugo Black and the Judicial Revolution 289 (1977).

21. Davis v. Mississippi, 394 U.S. 721, 730 (1969) (Black, J., dissenting), *quoted in* Snowiss, *supra* note 6, at 221.

ity. Instead, his stance evolved step by step, a transformation that Felix Frankfurter so forcefully urged along. But Justice Black's basic moral structure, the ideal of justice and freedom within order, existed from the start. In addition, he remained sensitive to the dangers of governmental and judicial assertions of broad power, surely a Jeffersonian and southern heritage. His later decisions on questions of criminal rights reflected a growing worry about an unraveling of the social fabric from increased crime. Nevertheless, one could argue that his concern for "the poor, the ignorant, the numerically weak, the friendless, and the powerless"[22] was based upon issues of fairness and appropriate legal procedure, not upon a liberal sense of guilt for poverty's existence, a societal flaw for which compensation should be given. That, too, fit well his devotion to the manly virtues of individual integrity so particularly revered in the South.

The dictates of honor sometimes could be dark and foreboding, especially about tolerance for dissent, as Professor Murphy observes.[23] But, in Hugo Black's hands, those dictates helped to provide the rationale for human rights and community as well as national security. According to constitutional scholars, he was not always consistent in his opinions of first amendment issues. Nonetheless, the general coherence of his decisions, balanced as they were between the exigencies of order and individual freedom, rested on well-selected parts of the self-reliant and Biblical principles upon which he was raised in Clay County. He was not one to condone license, permissiveness, or dependency at home or in society at large. His exercise of thoughtful judgment and ethical decisiveness made him a loyal southerner, a model gentleman of intellect, conviction, and humane concern, and a great jurist.

---

22. Chambers v. Florida, 309 U.S. 227, 238 (1940), *quoted in* Snowiss, *supra* note 6, at 239.

23. Murphy, *supra* note 3, at 874-75.

II.
The Court Years, 1937-1971

REMARKS ON THE OCASSION OF THE JUSTICE HUGO L. BLACK CENTENNIAL

Justice William J. Brennan, Jr.

Justice Black was my colleague for fifteen years. My memories of him make this participation in the 100th anniversary of his birth a very pleasant privilege for me. I remember him particularly for the many delightful times we shared at his home or my own. He and Elizabeth were warm and engaging hosts. His menu was almost invariably steak and his steaks were always broiled to perfection. Conversation was always lively with a minimum of shop talk. His stories of his Alabama upbringing were moving, and his deep affection for his native state always apparent. He often sang hymns and songs he had learned when very young. Believe me, he was no Caruso, but his renditions never failed to move his guests. He had his own tennis court on the grounds of his beautiful home in Alexandria—as a player he gave no quarter, not even to Elizabeth when she was his adversary, and fought as hard to win as he did at the Court to get us to see a case his way. One privileged as I was to be with him so often in those surroundings and under such circumstances would soon see in him the great humanity, love, warmth and youth that made him the great human being he was.

I

Our friendship did not mean, however, that as Justices we marched to the same drummer. We had differences over how properly to interpret the Constitution, over his view that the Fourteenth Amendment applied *all* of the Bill of Rights against state power, and over his theory of absolutism in the application of the Bill of Rights against both federal and state power. Those differences led to some lively, indeed sometimes loud and vehement debates between us, but without, I can say, the slightest change in the mutual regard and respect we had for one another. Everyone who worked with him and experienced his intensity of conviction and the fervid, brilliant style with which he sought to persuade to acceptance of his views was aware that he respected those with whom he disagreed. He was not a court politician, lobbying in the invidious sense of that term. He made known his views with a clarity and force beyond the talent of most of us, but he didn't seek to impose his views if they did not sell. And he listened well, although one had to be wary that his patient attention might be only a delaying tactic to gain time to marshal arguments to demolish you.

He told me over, and over, and over again his standard of constitutional interpretation. He summed it up in his Carpentier Lectures, *A Constitutional Faith*, delivered at Columbia Law School in 1968. He there said:

> [I]t is language and history that are the crucial factors which influence me in interpreting the Constitution—not reasonableness or desirability as determined by justices of the Supreme Court.[1]
>
> . . . .
>
> I strongly believe that the public welfare demands that constitutional cases must be decided according to the terms of our Constitution itself and not according to the judges' views of fairness, reasonableness, or justice.[2]
>
> . . . .
>
> I cannot subscribe to the doctrine that consistent with [his] oath a judge can arrogate to himself a power to "adapt the Constitution to new times." The soft phrases used to claim that power for judges have siren-like appeal. For one who has a legitimate power to interpret there is at first a certain persuasive note in the constant repetition to him that in explaining a constitution meant for the ages he should not stick to its old eighteenth-century words but substitute others to make the Constitution best serve the current generation. And there is a certain appeal in the argument that the dead should not control the living.[3]

I do not think this made him an adherent of the doctrine of "original intent," currently being debated—at least, he was not an adherent to that doctrine in its most doctrinaire incarnation, which, as I understand it, would have the Justices accept that the Framers had sufficiently specific constitutional intentions that today's courts need only locate them and apply them to such areas as nuclear power, television, professional sports, environmental pollu-

1. H. Black, A Constitutional Faith 8 (1969).
2. *Id.* at 14.
3. *Id.* at 21.

tion and a host of other modern subjects that bedevil our courts. Justice Black would have none of such a crabbed authority. His demand for faithful adherence to language and history was not a demand for adherence to any particular interpretation of the precise words, but to an interpretation that adhered to the spirit and basic objective of the Constitution and the Bill of Rights—that is, to further freedom for all. It is a functional philosophy of interpretation. He asked what the particular provision under discussion was designed to achieve—what evil it was to suppress or prevent. He searched for this in history and, finding it, would decide in its light whether the circumstances in the particular case required the interpretation sought because the interpretation was necessary to achieve the goals of the provision or to prevent the evils at which it was aimed. This way of sticking to the "old eighteenth-century words," he insisted, did not "render government powerless to meet new times, new circumstances, and new conditions":

> [This] is exemplified most clearly by the Commerce Clause which gives Congress the broad, general power to regulate commerce. The fact that railroads or automobiles were unknown to the Framers does not mean that the power granted by the Constitution does not apply to them, for Congress is given power to regulate *all commerce*, and it makes no difference whether that commerce is carried on by ox wagons or jet planes.[4]

But inconsistently, as some, including me, have thought, and despite the holding in *Boyd v. United States*[5] in 1886 that the Fourth Amendment was intended to protect against "invasions . . . of the sanctity of a man's home and the privacies of life,"[6] he said:

> I can find in the Constitution no language which either specifically or implicitly grants to all individuals a constitutional "right of privacy." There are, of course, guarantees in certain specific constitutional provisions which are written in part so that they protect privacy at certain times and places with respect to certain activities. But, even though I like my privacy as well as the next person, I am nevertheless compelled to admit that the states have a right to invade it unless prohibited by some specific constitutional provision . . . . [Thus,] in *Katz v. United States*, . . . I simply could not find that the words of the Fourth Amendment prohibiting unreasonable

4. *Id.* at 8-9 (emphasis in original).
5. 116 U.S. 616 (1886).
6. *Boyd*, 116 U.S. at 630.

searches and seizures also prohibit eavesdropping . . . . I just cannot say that a conversation may be "searched" or "seized" within the ordinary and generally accepted meanings of those words.[7]

Those of us who held to the contrary in *Katz*[8] think that in the *Katz* dissent,[9] Homer nodded, for his view there hardly adheres to the spirit or objectives of the Fourth Amendment.

How different is my own view of the proper way to interpret the Constitution and Bill of Rights? I expect most would say quite different, although as often as not we agreed on result in the cases. My view is this:

> Like every text worth reading, [the Constitution] is not crystalline. The phrasing is broad and the limitations of its provisions are not clearly marked. Its majestic generalities and ennobling pronouncements are both luminous and obscure. This ambiguity of course calls forth interpretation . . . . [In interpreting it] one cannot read the text without admitting that it embodies substantive value choices . . . . To remain faithful to the content of the Constitution, therefore, an approach to interpreting the text must account for the existence of these substantive value choices, and must accept the ambiguity inherent in the effort to apply them to modern circumstances . . . . Successive generations of Americans have continued to respect these fundamental choices and adopt them as their own guide to evaluating quite different historical practices.
>
> We current Justices read the Constitution in the only way that we can: as Twentieth Century Americans. We look to the history at the time of framing and to the intervening history of interpretation. But the ultimate question must be, what do the words of the text mean in our time. For the genius of the Constitution rests not in any static meaning it might have had in a world that is dead and gone, but in the adaptability of its great principles to cope with current problems and current needs . . . . Our Constitution was not intended to preserve a pre-existing society but to make a new one, to put in place new principles that the prior political community had not sufficiently recognized. Thus, for example, when we interpret the Civil War amendments—abolishing slavery, guaranteeing blacks equality under law, and guaranteeing blacks the right to vote—we must remember that those who put them in place had no desire to enshrine

---

7. H. BLACK, *supra* note 1, at 9-10.
8. Katz v. United States, 389 U.S. 347 (1967).
9. *Id.* at 364 (Black, J., dissenting).

> the status quo. Their goal was to make over their world, to eliminate all vestige of slave caste.[10]

My view echoes Chief Justice Stone's in *United States v. Classic*:[11]

> [I]n determining whether a provision of the Constitution applies to a new subject matter, it is of little significance that it is one with which the framers were not familiar. For in setting up an enduring framework of government they undertook to carry out for the indefinite future and in all of the vicissitudes of the changing affairs of men, those fundamental purposes which the instrument itself discloses. Hence we read its words, not as we read legislative codes which are subject to continuous revision with the changing course of events, but as the revelation of the great purposes which were intended to be achieved by the Constitution as a continuing instrument of government.[12]

You may, with good reason, believe that I espouse an evolutionary concept of the Constitution. It postulates that while a thing may not be within the letter of the Constitution, yet it may be within the Constitution and within the intention of the makers because within the spirit and purpose of the Great Charter.

In that respect, at least, our visions were not squarely at odds. For as one commentator has noted, Justice Black addressed himself to his judicial task of interpretation with a clearly discernible view of what John Marshall called "the genius and character of the whole government."[13]

> The grand strategy of [his] constitutionalism [had] two aspects: he [saw] government as possessing ample, perhaps even yet hardly explored powers to act in the pursuit of the happiness of all, and he [saw] these powers as bindingly limited, with something like the same amplitude, against any entry into certain broad reserved areas of human dignity and freedom. . . . [I]t is certain that Hugo Black believe[d], with the plainest textual warrant, that our Constitution rejected that reliance [for freedom on the intrinsic general weakness of government]. He look[ed] upon the great power of government

---

10. Address by Justice William J. Brennan, Jr., Text and Teaching Symposium, Georgetown University, October 12, 1985.

11. 313 U.S. 299 (1941).

12. *Classic*, 313 U.S. at 316.

13. C. Black, *Foreward* to HUGO L. BLACK AND THE SUPREME COURT, A SYMPOSIUM xi (S. Strickland ed. 1967).

> and [found] it filled with potential for happiness; he would not seek freedom by making government weak. But he also taught, once more by [what he thought were] the plainest words of the text he so much revere[d], that there are closes of personality, walled gardens of human dignity, where this power may not enter.[14]

In sum, central to his view was a powerful government whose designated authority was to be expansively read, subject, however, to expressed limitations on that authority, usually found in the Bill of Rights. Any limitations, particularly those in the Bill of Rights, were to be applied, in his words, without any if's, and's, or but's. Thus, "Congress shall make no law" meant *no* law. There was therefore, he argued, no reason or latitude for interpretation of such commands by judges. The Framers of the Bill of Rights had used words readily understood and judges should be required to enforce and apply them as written. Substantive value choices were not for judges to make, but by and large were to be left to the people's elected representatives. Judges too, of course, most emphatically had a major responsibility. They were oath-bound to enforce and maintain the Bill of Rights in exactly the form it was written. He conceded no authority in judges to balance those rights against governmental interests, large or insignificant. He insisted that *Korematsu v. United States*,[15] which allowed the government to confine Japanese citizens in concentration camps during World War II, was not a departure from that view—we were at war for our survival and that alone justified striking a balance in favor of the military judgment.

Thus it could be said that:

> A distinct philosophy concerning constitutional law runs through all of his work. It is a highly controversial philosophy, and it has been often misstated by critics and by friends as well. But for better or worse it has indelibly marked the Court and the law. It represents Justice Black's unique contribution, for while other Justices have shared his views on issues, none have produced such a comprehensive and individual philosophy.[16]

---

14. *Id.* at x-xii.

15. 323 U.S. 214 (1944).

16. Reich, *The Living Constitution and the Court's Role*, in HUGO L. BLACK AND THE SUPREME COURT, A SYMPOSIUM, *supra* note 13, at 133.

II

I should like now to turn to another subject—that of the extension of the restraints of the Bill of Rights against state power. Justice Black forthrightly stated his position in *A Constitutional Faith.* He said:

> In 1947, in a dissenting opinion in *Adamson v. California*, . . . I made clear my view that the Fourteenth Amendment made the Bill of Rights applicable to the states. The reasons for this view are based on my reading of the history of the Amendment's adoption . . . . In my judgment that history demonstrates that the language of the first section of the Fourteenth Amendment, taken as a whole, was thought by most of those responsible for its submission to the people, and by most of those who opposed its submission, sufficiently explicit to guarantee that thereafter no state could deprive its citizens of the privileges and protections of the Bill of Rights. Of course I am aware of the attacks made upon my historical beliefs, but all I can say is that such attacks simply have not convinced me that I am wrong.[17]

But, as he admitted,

> I have never been able at any one time to get a majority of the Court to agree to my belief that the Fourteenth Amendment incorporates *all* of the Bill of Rights' provisions (the first eight Amendments to the Constitution) and makes them applicable to the states . . . . The Court has, however, . . . adopted a theory of selective incorporation of different Bill of Rights' provisions . . . . [I]n *Palko v. Connecticut*, . . . the Court, speaking through Mr. Justice Cardozo, was careful to emphasize that "immunities that are valid as against the federal government by force of the specific pledges of particular amendments have been found to be implicit in the concept of ordered liberty, and thus, through the Fourteenth Amendment, become valid as against the states" and that guarantees "in their origin . . . effective against the federal government alone" had by prior cases "been taken over from the earlier articles of the federal bill of rights and brought within the Fourteenth Amendment by a process of absorption."[18]

---

17. H. Black, *supra* note 1, at 34.

18. *Id.* at 36-37 (emphasis in original) (quoting Palko v. Connecticut, 302 U.S. 319, 324-26 (1937)).

Justice Black's reaction to the Court's going only part way with him was completely in character. Said he:

> With the *Palko* case the Supreme Court adopted the principle that those Bill of Rights' provisions which are fundamental and essential to the concept of ordered liberty are made applicable to the states through the Fourteenth Amendment. While I have made it clear that I believe *all* of the Bill of Rights' provisions are made applicable to the states through the Fourteenth Amendment, I have not objected to and indeed have supported the one-at-a-time process of absorption . . . . "If the choice must be between the selective process of the *Palko* decision applying some of the Bill of Rights to the States, or . . . applying none of them, I would choose the *Palko* selective process."[19]

Little wonder that Mr. Justice Black was magnanimous. He had lost a skirmish but had certainly won the war. For through this process of selective incorporation, a process which I have subscribed to in preference to Justice Black's view, the Court "has held that the Fourteenth Amendment guarantees against infringement by the states the liberties of the First Amendment, the Fourth Amendment, the Fifth Amendment's privilege against self-incrimination, the Sixth Amendment's rights to notice, confrontation of witnesses, compulsory process for witnesses, and the assistance of counsel, and the Eighth Amendment's prohibition of cruel and unusual punishments."[20] And under *Malloy v. Hogan*,[21] these guarantees "are all to be enforced against the States under the Fourteenth Amendment according to the same standards that protect those personal rights against federal encroachment."[22]

His achievement was not only in gaining agreement that the Fourteenth Amendment applied most, even if not all the guarantees to the States. Perhaps as striking was his success in persuading the Court of the speciousness of the argument that applying any of the Bill of Rights to the States "interferes with our concept of federalism in that it may prevent states from trying novel social and economic experiments."[23] I fully agreed with him

19. *Id.* at 37 (emphasis in original) (quoting Adamson v. California, 332 U.S. 46, 89 (1947) (Black, J., dissenting)).
20. *Id.* at 38.
21. 378 U.S. 1 (1964).
22. *Malloy*, 378 U.S. at 10.
23. H. BLACK, *supra* note 1, at 40.

in his belief "that under the guise of federalism the States should [not] be able to experiment with the protections afforded our citizens through the Bill of Rights."[24] He aligned himself, as I do, with Justice Goldberg who said in *Pointer v. Texas*,[25]

> [t]o deny to the States the power to impair a fundamental constitutional right is not to increase federal power, but, rather, to limit the power of both federal and state governments in favor of safeguarding the fundamental rights and liberties of the individual . . . . [T]his promotes rather than undermines the basic policy of avoiding excess concentration of power in government, federal or state, which underlies our concepts of federalism.[26]

III

I turn finally to Justice Black's doctrine of absolutes—that, for example, when the First Amendment says "Congress shall make no law . . . abridging the freedom of speech, or of the press," "*no* law means *no* law, without exception, without any ifs, buts, or whereases, that freedom of speech means that government shall not do anything to people, or . . . move against people, either for the views they have or . . . the words they speak or write."[27] So, for him, because obscenity was "speech" and defamation was "speech," he continuously voted to strike down all laws dealing with obscene materials and all libel laws. The First Amendment said "Congress [and the states after the Fourteenth Amendment] shall make *no* law abridging freedom of speech," and judges were absolutely without authority to do other than enforce that explicit command.

The same approach was required, he thought, with respect to the Religion Clause: "Congress shall make no law respecting an establishment of religion, or prohibiting the free exercise thereof." That meant, for him, that

> [n]either a state nor the Federal government can set up a church. Neither can pass laws which aid one religion, aid all religions, or prefer one religion over another. Neither can force nor influence a person to go to or remain away from church against his will or force him to profess a belief or disbelief in any religion. No person can be

---

24. *Id.*
25. 380 U.S. 400 (1964).
26. *Pointer*, 380 U.S. at 414.
27. H. Black, *supra* note 1, at 45.

> punished for entertaining or professing religious beliefs or disbeliefs, for church attendance or non-attendance. No tax in any amount, large or small, can be levied to support any religious activities or institutions, whatever they may be called, or whatever form they may adopt to teach or practice religion. Neither a state nor the Federal Government can, openly or secretly, participate in the affairs of any religious organizations or groups and *vice versa*.[28]
>
> Thus we have the absolute command of the First Amendment . . . . And with the passage of the Fourteenth Amendment the Supreme Court has properly recognized that this command is now applicable against the states as it is against the federal government.[29]

Of course, Justice Black's understanding of the word "Congress" in the First Amendment was somewhat less absolute, for even if one concludes that the Fourteenth Amendment applies the First Amendment against the states, this would not explain why its prohibition reached beyond the legislature to executive or judicial action. I think the answer is that Justice Black's understanding of the constitutional text was less literalist than absolute: he believed that the Framers had embodied discrete and discernible value choices in the provisions of the Bill of Rights and that our duty as Justices of the Supreme Court was to enforce these choices without allowing them to be watered down in any way. Thus, he abominated the "balancing test" generally used by a majority of his colleagues during his tenure. Under that test, a compelling public interest might justify suppression of the protections of a guarantee of the Bill of Rights. He charged that this test denied citizens the protections of the first eight amendments because "balancing" allowed judges to stifle these freedoms when "the interest of the government in stifling [them] is greater than the interest of the people in having them exercised."[30] This, he said, was closely akin to the notion that neither the First Amendment nor any other provision of the Bill of Rights should be enforced unless the Court believes it is *reasonable* to do so. "I believe that the First Amendment's unequivocal command that there shall be no abridgment of

28. Everson v. Board of Educ., 330 U.S. 1, 15-16 (1947).
29. H. Black, *supra* note 1, at 46.
30. *Id.* at 50.

the rights of free speech shows that the men who drafted our Bill of Rights did all the 'balancing' that was to be done in this field."[31]

Justice Black's doctrine of absolutes thus calls upon judges to render decisions concerning the Bill of Rights not by making an ad hoc balance but by reference to an underlying balance established by the Constitution. Yet the result each of us reached in many cases, he on his absolutist approach, and I and other Justices by "balancing," was much the same. And I remember after I announced the opinion for the Court in *New York Times Co. v. Sullivan*,[32] a libel suit which balanced the plaintiff's interest in personal reputation against the defendant newspaper's right of freedom of the press, he sent me a note. The note reads, "You know, of course, that despite my position and what I wrote, I think . . . that the *Times* case . . . is bound to be a very long step toward preserving the right to communicate ideas." Again, he may have lost a skirmish but won the war. Justice Frankfurter would have commented, "Always remember it is harmony of goals not of views for which we strive here."

The 100th anniversary of the birth of any public man may justify its commemoration, but seldom has commemoration been more fitting than this of the anniversary of the birth of Hugo Lafayette Black. His place is secure in the pantheon of America's great public men. He held passionately to the view that has been the lodestar for all justices: "that law is a pathway to the good life, that the best hope of the nation is to be worked out through law, that our highest political goals are expressible and expressed in law."[33] And, as Charles L. Black, Jr., has said:

> No man makes a style, creates a mode. Even within the Court, Hugo Black . . . sat with others who faced the same way. Yet, when the list is made up of those men through whom has been chiefly worked out this nation's resolve to live greatly through law, to make a way by law for the prevailing of its democracy, to use law to increase general happiness, and yet steadfastly to express through law its respect for the individuality of man, Hugo Black's name will surely be among a very few of highest honor.[34]

---

31. *Id.* at 52.
32. 376 U.S. 254 (1964).
33. C. Black, *Foreward* to HUGO L. BLACK AND THE SUPREME COURT, A SYMPOSIUM, *supra* note 13, at x.
34. *Id.* at xii.

And Henry Abraham has said,

> Few jurists have had the impact on law and society of Mr. Justice Hugo Lafayette Black. A constitutional literalist to whom every word in the document represented a command, he, nonetheless, used the language of the Constitution to propound a jurisprudence that has had a lasting effect on the development of American constitutional law. His contributions were towering. They stand as jurisprudential and intellectual landmarks in the evolving history of the land he loved so well.[35]

All the many encomiums upon the eminent judicial career of Hugo Lafayette Black cannot help but be fatuous when compared with his own opinions and other writings that so clearly tell us his constitutional faith. It is in those writings, not in my or others' appraisals, that one discovers the extraordinary nature of this man.

What his writings reveal in bold relief is not only a mind at once brilliant and wide-ranging, but as well a man who understood the law on its most profound levels and was capable and desirous of conveying that understanding to a nation profoundly affected by his decisions. He, perhaps more than any other Justice in our history, explained to the Nation why the deepest principles of its law required, and continues to require, not only the painful revolution of racial equality, but also the strength of the Constitution and Bill of Rights so that the United States will be a country where the dignity and rights of all persons are equal before all authority. His need to explain stemmed no doubt from his empathy for all who suffer, be they black or white, and from his commitment to the South, his home.

May I close with the famous passage from his great opinion in *Chambers v. Florida*:[36]

> Under our constitutional system, courts stand against any winds that blow as havens of refuge for those who might otherwise suffer because they are helpless, weak, outnumbered, or because they are non-conforming victims of prejudice and public excitement. . . . No higher duty, no more solemn responsibility, rests upon this Court, than that of translating into living law and maintaining this constitutional shield deliberately planned and inscribed for the benefit of

---

35. H. Abraham, Justices and Presidents 213-14 (2d ed. 1985).
36. 309 U.S. 227 (1940).

> every human being subject to our Constitution—of whatever race, creed or persuasion.[37]

That he fell short of complete acceptance by the Court of all his views is neither a mark of failure nor a true measure of his success. For no Justice in our history had a greater impact on our law or on our constitutional jurisprudence. Men and women walk taller in our free country because Hugo Lafayette Black lived.

37. *Chambers*, 309 U.S. at 241.

ATTORNEY GENERAL MEESE Vs. CHIEF JUSTICE JOHN MARSHALL AND JUSTICE HUGO L. BLACK

*Arthur J. Goldberg**

Attorney General Edwin Meese, III has sharply criticized the federal judiciary, particularly the Supreme Court, for departing from the "original intent" of the Founding Fathers.[1]

Further, the Attorney General questions whether the so-called "doctrine of incorporation" (which, through the Fourteenth Amendment, applies the Bill of Rights to the states)[2] is really in accord with the Framers' wishes.[3]

Justices Brennan and Stevens have publicly taken sharp exception to the views expressed by Mr. Meese, terming them unfounded, simplistic, and anachronistic.[4]

The media understandably has enjoyed a field day with this contretemps. The protagonists might have debated in government briefs or Court opinions. Indeed, it has been so argued in many cases. Going public, however, considering the principals, is rather unprecedented, but the Court, like all our institutions, is not immune from criticism. Constitutional debate has historical origins; criticism of the judiciary is not necessarily harmful and, indeed, may be both warranted and helpful. I doubt, however, that anyone

---

* Former Associate Justice of the United States Supreme Court.

1. MacKenzie, *Why Pick on This Court When Any One Will Do?*, L.A. Daily J., Dec. 11, 1985, at 4, col. 4; Schwartz, *Attorney General's Bad Cites Are an Embarrassment to the Law*, L.A. Daily J., Dec. 11, 1985, at 4, col. 3; Rosenfeld, *The Attorney General's Dilemma*, N.Y.L.J., Nov. 20, 1985, at 2, col. 3; De Benedictis, *High Court Faces Renewed Push for Conservative Tilt*, L.A. Daily J., Oct. 4, 1985, at 1, col. 6.

2. See *infra* notes 13-17 and accompanying text.

3. Rice, *Flimflam Under the 14th*, Wall St. J., July 31, 1985, at 18, col. 4.

4. Wicker, *Quote the Words Honestly*, L.A. Daily J., Nov. 6, 1985, at 4, col. 3; *Brennan, Stevens, and the Constitution*, L.A. Daily J., Nov. 6, 1985, at 4, col. 3; Tapp, *Stevens Questions Meese Comments*, Chi. Daily L. Bull., Oct. 24, 1985, at 1, col. 2; *The Justice Erred From the Start*, L.A. Daily J., Oct. 23, 1985, at 4, col. 1; *The 20th-Century Justice*, N.Y. Times, Oct. 15, 1985, at 30, col. 1.

has envisioned a public controversy between sitting Justices and our nation's chief law enforcement officer.

In analyzing the merits of this debate, one must confess to a sense of deja vu. The subject is hardly novel; rather, it has comparatively ancient roots.

With respect to the contention of the Attorney General that the Supreme Court should adhere to the "original intent" of the Founding Fathers and is overstepping its bounds in not doing so, Mr. Meese confronts a most formidable adversary.

The Attorney General runs afoul, in judicial constitutional interpretation, of the greatest of all Chief Justices of the Supreme Court of the United States, John Marshall, who himself was an eminent Founding Father.

The core of the constitutional philosophy of Chief Justice Marshall was expressed in *McCullough v. Maryland*,[5] decided in 1819. In an oft-repeated phrase, he said: "[I]t is a *constitution* we are expounding . . . intended to endure for ages to come, and consequently, to be adapted to the various crises of human affairs."[6] Marshall added that for the Framers to have attempted to prescribe in detail in the Constitution the answers to unforeseen contingencies "would have been to change, entirely, the character of the instrument, and give it the properties of a legal code."[7] This, he observed, would be most "unwise."

Chief Justice Marshall's constitutional philosophy has been described as the evolutionary concept of the nature of our Constitution. This philosophy has been pervasive throughout our legal history and has been accepted, with few exceptions, by the federal judiciary, present and past scholars, legal and lay. A few pertinent quotations are illustrative. Then-Justice Harlan F. Stone, appointed to the Court by President Coolidge, in *United States v. Classic*[8] said:

> [I]n determining whether a provision of the Constitution applies to a new subject matter, it is of little significance that it is one with which the framers were not familiar. For in setting up an enduring framework of government they undertook to carry out for the indefinite future and in all the vicissitudes of the changing affairs of men,

---

5. 17 U.S. (4 Wheat.) 316 (1819).
6. *McCullough*, 17 U.S. (4 Wheat.) at 407, 415 (emphasis in original).
7. *Id.* at 415.
8. 313 U.S. 299 (1941).

> those fundamental purposes which the instrument itself discloses. Hence we read its words, not as we read legislative codes which are subject to continuous revision with the changing course of events, but as the revelation of the great purposes which were intended to be achieved by the Constitution as a continuing instrument of government.[9]

Justice Joseph McKenna, appointed by President McKinley, expressed the same view in *Weems v. United States*,[10] decided in 1910:

> Time works changes, brings into existence new conditions and purposes. Therefore a principle to be vital must be capable of wider application than the mischief which gave it birth. This is peculiarly true of constitutions. They are not ephemeral enactments, designed to meet passing occasions. They are, to use the words of Chief Justice Marshall, "designed to approach immortality as nearly as human institutions can approach it." The future is their care and provision for events of good and bad tendencies of which no prophecy can be made. In the application of a constitution, therefore, our contemplation cannot be only of what has been but of what may be. Under any other rule a constitution would indeed be as easy of application as it would be deficient in efficacy and power. Its general principles would have little value *and be converted by precedent into impotent and lifeless formulas*. Rights declared in words might be lost in reality.[11]

The simple fact is that the Founding Fathers, endowed with an unparalleled genius for statecraft, wrote our fundamental law in 6,000 words, general in nature and replete with ambiguities requiring judicial interpretation. This the Framers did to endow this greatest of political documents with an innate capacity for growth and adaptation to enable the Constitution to meet new needs and unforeseen contingencies. The Constitution, as Justice McKenna and many other judges have pointed out, was, in Marshall's words, "designed to approach immortality as nearly as human institutions can approach it."[12] The grand design of the Constitution is frustrated by reading it literally as a code or statute.

---

9. *Classic*, 313 U.S. at 316.
10. 217 U.S. 349 (1910).
11. *Weems*, 217 U.S. at 373 (emphasis added).
12. Cohens v. Virginia, 19 U.S. (6 Wheat.) 264, 387 (1821), *quoted in Weems*, 217 U.S. at 373.

The Constitution is a state document of inspiration. It is our legend and hope, the union of our minds and spirits. It is our defense and our protector, our teacher and our lodestar in the quest for liberty and equality. In a profound sense, simplistic invocation of the Founding Fathers' intention does injustice to their vision and grand design in framing our fundamental law.

On the "original intent" issue, it would appear that Mr. Meese, with all respect, is on a bad wicket.

The Attorney General's other criticism of the Court's constitutional philosophy, the so-called "incorporation" doctrine, is equally untenable.

Thus, all present members of the Burger Court, as did the members of the Warren Court, agree that the Fourteenth Amendment makes the fundamental guarantees of the Bill of Rights (originally designed to protect only against abridgement by Congress) obligatory on the states.

The extension of this obligation derives from the plain language of the Amendment, which reflects the intention of its framers: "No State shall make or enforce any law which shall abridge the privileges or immunities of citizens of the United States; nor shall any State deprive any person of life, liberty, or property, without due process of law; nor deny to any person within its jurisdiction the equal protection of the laws."[13]

Surely the basic safeguards of the Bill of Rights contains fundamental liberties and privileges of Americans. Denial of any of the safeguards by states is plainly a denial of due process of law prohibited by the Fourteenth Amendment. This is the essence of the "incorporation" doctrine.

In *Adamson v. California*,[14] Justice Black, dissenting for four members of the Court, had this to say about "incorporation":

> [H]istory conclusively demonstrates that the language of the Fourteenth Amendment, taken as a whole, was thought by those responsible for its submission to the people, and by those who opposed its submission, sufficiently explicit to guarantee that thereafter no state could deprive its citizens of the privileges and protections of the Bill of Rights.[15]

---

13. U.S. CONST. amend. XIV, § 1.
14. 332 U.S. 46 (1947).
15. *Adamson*, 332 U.S. at 74 (Black, J., dissenting).

Inasmuch as Justice Black's views relating to incorporation have largely prevailed, even with the present Court,[16] it would appear here, too, Mr. Meese is on a bad wicket and runs afoul of another giant of the Supreme Court, Justice Hugo L. Black.

Both President Reagan and the Attorney General are seeking to appoint "conservative" judges, in the belief that they will practice "judicial restraint" and renounce "activism."[17] I do not share their viewpoint, but I do not find it surprising or unusual that a President and an Attorney General should seek to appoint judges who are philosophically at one with them. This is common to almost every President in our country's history.

History teaches us, however, that President Reagan and Mr. Meese are in for a surprise.

President Theodore Roosevelt appointed Justice Holmes to our highest court, believing that he would be an anti-trust jurist, only to learn very early that the Great Yankee from Olympus did not share the President's views on anti-trust matters.[18] President Eisenhower appointed Chief Justice Warren and Justice Brennan. The President discovered, to his great chagrin, that these outstanding jurists departed very widely from his concepts about our Constitutional safeguards.[19] President Truman appointed Justice Tom Clark, a trusted advisor and his attorney general. All accounts indicate that this feisty President was outraged when

---

16. The number of jurors required of the states in civil cases, scarcely a fundamental right, constitutes a rather minor exception to the Burger Court's general acceptance of incorporation. *See* Colgrove v. Battin, 413 U.S. 149 (1973) (Montana federal court rule providing for six-person juries in civil trials held to be consistent with Seventh Amendment trial-by-jury guarantees).

17. The Reagan Administration's proclivity for nominating "conservative" judges to the federal bench was never more pronounced than in 1986, with the nomination of Justice William Rehnquist to succeed departing Chief Justice Warren Burger, and the nomination of District of Columbia Circuit Judge Antonin Scalia to succeed Justice Rehnquist. *Reagan Names Rehnquist to be Chief Justice*, N.Y.L.J., June 18, 1986, at 1, col. 2. The Supreme Court nominations came on the heels of the administration's notorious and successful nomination of Daniel Manion for district court judge, *see* Roberts, *Manion Wins Senate Vote, But Nomination Still 'In Flux,'* L.A. Daily J., June 27, 1986, at 20, col. 3; *Minimal Standard*, L.A. Daily J., May 19, 1986, at 4, col. 1, and the administration's equally notorious and unsuccessful nomination of Jefferson Sessions III, *see* Williams, *Judicial Nominee Queried on His Racial Attitudes*, N.Y. Times, Mar. 14, 1986, at 9, col. 4.

18. *See* Northern Securities Co. v. United States, 193 U.S. 197, 400 (1904) (Holmes, J., dissenting); S. Bent, Justice Oliver Wendell Holmes 251-61 (1932).

19. *See* J. Pollack, Earl Warren: The Judge Who Changed America 194, 200 (1979); Bender, *Is the Burger Court Really Like the Warren Court?*, 82 Mich. L. Rev. 635, 638 n.2 (1984).

Justice Clark voted against Truman's seizure of the nation's steel mills.[20] Surely President Nixon must have been nonplused by Justice Blackmun's pro-abortion decision,[21] let alone Chief Justice Burger's Watergate opinion.[22]

The decisions of the Burger Court, by and large, are further proof of the unpredictability of Presidential judicial appointees. True, the Burger Court is nibbling away at *Miranda*,[23] narrowing the exclusionary rule,[24] limiting the safeguards of the Fourth

---

20. Youngstown Sheet & Tube Co. v. Sawyer, 343 U.S. 579, 660 (1952) (Clark, J., concurring).

21. Roe v. Wade, 410 U.S. 113 (1973).

22. United States v. Nixon, 418 U.S. 683 (1974).

23. Miranda v. Arizona, 384 U.S. 436 (1966). The Warren Court decision in *Miranda* extended the Fifth Amendment privilege against compulsory self-incrimination to individuals subjected to custodial interrogation by the police. The *Miranda* decision created a presumption that interrogations in the station-house environment are inherently coercive and held that statements made under such circumstances are inadmissable unless the suspect is specifically informed of his *Miranda* rights and freely decides to forego those rights.

The Burger Court, in subsequent cases, has attempted to narrow the scope of *Miranda*. *See, e.g.*, New York v. Quarles, 467 U.S. 649 (1984) (adopted "public safety" exception to requirement that *Miranda* warnings be given before suspect's answers may be admitted into evidence; availability of such exception does not depend upon motivation of individual officers); Oregon v. Mathiason, 429 U.S. 492 (1977) (per curiam) (under certain circumstances even police-station interrogation may not be "custodial" for purposes of *Miranda*); Michigan v. Mosley, 423 U.S. 96 (1975) (if suspect invokes right to remain silent, police may, under certain circumstances, "try again" and succeed at later interrogation session); Michigan v. Tucker, 417 U.S. 433 (1974) (sanctioned admission of fruits of *Miranda* violation, but only because violation was technical and interrogation was non-coercive); Harris v. New York, 401 U.S. 222 (1971) (statements made during custodial interrogation where defendant had not waived *Miranda* rights could be introduced to impeach the defendant's credibility).

24. The exclusionary rule originated in the 1914 Supreme Court opinion of Weeks v. United States, 232 U.S. 383 (1914), wherein the Court held that evidence secured by federal agents through an illegal search and seizure was inadmissable in a federal prosecution. In 1962, the Warren Court, in Mapp v. Ohio, 367 U.S. 643 (1962), applied the exclusionary rule to state criminal procedure. Although the Warren Court continued to apply the exclusionary rule expansively, the trend suffered somewhat during the Burger Court era. *See, e.g.*, United States v. Leon, 468 U.S. 897 (1984) (Fourth Amendment exclusionary rule should not be applied to bar use in prosecution's case-in-chief of evidence obtained by officers acting in reasonable reliance on search warrant issued by a detached and neutral magistrate but ultimately found to be invalid); Nix v. Williams, 467 U.S. 431 (1984) (ultimate or inevitable discovery exception to exclusionary rule adopted: if prosecution can establish by preponderance of evidence that information inevitably would have been discovered by lawful means, then deterrence rationale has so little basis that evidence should be received); United States v. Janis, 428 U.S. 433 (1976) (Court viewed deterrent force of rule "highly attenuated" under circumstances and refused to apply exclusionary rule to federal civil tax proceeding based upon evidence illegally obtained by state police); United States v. Peltier, 422 U.S. 531 (1975) (illegally seized evidence should be suppressed only if it can be said that officer had knowledge or may properly be charged with knowledge that search was unconstitu-

Amendment,[25] tolerating some breaches in the wall of separation between church and state,[26] restricting resort to the great writ of habeas corpus,[27] becoming somewhat tolerant about coerced con-

---

tional); United States v. Calandra, 414 U.S. 338 (1974) (grand jury witness could not refuse to answer questions based on illegally seized evidence; Court deemed "speculative" and "minimal" the deterrence that might be achieved by upholding such objection).

25. *See, e.g.*, Michigan v. Long, 463 U.S. 1032 (1983) (protective search for weapons could extend to passenger part of car not occupied by suspect absent probable cause to arrest suspect or to search car); Illinois v. Gates, 462 U.S. 213 (1983) (rigid "two-pronged test" for determining whether informant's tip establishes probable cause for issuance of warrant abandoned and "totality of the circumstances" approach substituted in its place); United States v. Ross, 456 U.S. 798 (1982) (upheld warrantless search of "movable container" found in locked car truck); New York v. Belton, 453 U.S. 454 (1981) (whether or not there is probable cause to believe car contains evidence of crime, police may conduct warrantless search of entire interior of car, including closed containers, so long as there are sufficient grounds to make lawful "custodial arrest" of vehicle's occupants); Schneckloth v. Bustamonte, 412 U.S. 218 (1973) (when government seeks to justify search on consent grounds, it need not demonstrate "knowing and intelligent" waiver of Fourth Amendment rights).

26. *See, e.g.*, Lynch v. Donnelly, 465 U.S. 668 (1984) (reasoning that the Constitution does not require complete separation of church and state but does mandate accommodation, not merely tolerance, of all religions, Court concluded that city's activity in Christmas display was not in violation of Establishment Clause of First Amendment); Marsh v. Chambers, 463 U.S. 783 (1983) (upheld legislature's employment of chaplain and use of opening prayer because prayer was acceptable part of legislative activity at time Congress drafted First Amendment); Committee for Public Educ. & Religious Liberty v. Regan, 444 U.S. 646 (1980) (upheld state statute reimbursing nonpublic schools for expenses incurred in administering and scoring standardized educational achievement tests, recording and reporting data concerning student attendance, and compiling and reporting statistical information about students, staff, and facilities of each institution); Tilton v. Richardson, 403 U.S. 672 (1971) (upheld federal Higher Education Facilities Act under which federal grants were made to colleges, including religious colleges, for construction of facilities for other than religious activities); Walz v. Tax Comm'n, 397 U.S. 664 (1970) (upheld granting of exemptions from property taxes to churches as part of general exception encompassing a wide variety of non-profit institutions). *But see* Grand Rapids School Dist. v. Ball, 473 U.S. 373 (1985) (school district's shared time and community education programs, which provided classes to nonpublic school students at public expense in classrooms located in and leased from nonpublic schools, had "primary or principal" effect of advancing religion and therefore violated dictates of Establishment Clause); Stone v. Graham, 449 U.S. 39 (1980) (statute requiring posting of Ten Commandments on wall of each public school classroom in state violated Establishment Clause); Lemon v. Kurtzman, 403 U.S. 602 (1971) (statute providing 15 percent salary supplement to teachers of secular subjects in private schools and statute authorizing reimbursement of nonpublic schools for fraction of teacher salaries and instructional materials in secular subjects invalid as violations of Establishment Clause).

27. *See, e.g.*, Stone v. Powell, 428 U.S. 465 (1976) (state prisoner may not be granted federal habeas corpus relief on search-and-seizure grounds unless denied "an opportunity for full and fair litigation" of claim in state court).

fessions,[28] and cutting back on other of the Warren Court's decisions, particularly in the area of the rights of the accused in criminal cases.[29]

But! The Burger Court, with the votes of some, and in some cases all, of the recent "conservative" appointees, has never totally overruled *Miranda*.[30] The Court has reaffirmed *Reynolds v. Sims*[31]—"one person, one vote"; ordered President Nixon to turn over the Watergate tapes;[32] outlawed silent prayer;[33] legalized abortions;[34] sanctioned busing as a permissible tool for eliminating segregation in public schools;[35] and declared publication of the Pentagon Papers protected by the First Amendment.[36]

The Burger Court has not been as "conservative" as "liberals" feared or as rightists hoped. And, I predict, the same will be true of virtually all of the federal judges who have been or may yet be appointed by President Reagan. The judicial pendulum will swing,

---

28. *See, e.g.*, Michigan v. Tucker, 417 U.S. 433 (1974) (appeared to equate "compulsion" within meaning of Fifth Amendment privilege with "coercion" or "involuntariness" within meaning of pre-*Miranda* "totality of the circumstances"-"voluntariness" test). *But see* Brewer v. Williams, 430 U.S. 387 (1977) (once adversary proceedings have commenced against individual, government efforts to "deliberately elicit" incriminating statements from him—whether done openly by uniformed police officers or surreptitiously by "secret agents"—violates individuals' right to counsel).

29. *See* cases cited *supra* notes 23-25, 27-28; *see also* United States v. Gouvia, 467 U.S. 180 (1984) (effectively overruled Escobedo v. Illinois, 378 U.S. 478 (1964), by holding that Sixth Amendment right to counsel does not attach until initiation of adversary judicial proceedings); United States v. MacDonald, 456 U.S. 1 (1982) (only formal indictment or information—or else actual restraints imposed by arrest and detention—trigger speedy trial provision of the Sixth Amendment); Oregon v. Kennedy, 456 U.S. 667 (1982) (only where government conduct was intended to "goad" defendant into moving for mistrial may defendant raise bar of double jeopardy to second trial after succeeding in aborting first trial on his own motion).

30. *See supra* note 23.

31. 377 U.S. 533 (1964). The "one man, one vote" rule was reaffirmed by the Burger Court in Hadley v. Junior College Dist., 397 U.S. 50 (1970), where the Court refused to distinguish, for purposes of the apportionment rule, between elections for legislative officials and administrative officials.

32. United States v. Nixon, 418 U.S. 683 (1974).

33. Wallace v. Jaffree, 472 U.S. 38 (1985).

34. Roe v. Wade, 410 U.S. 113 (1973). As recently as 1983, the Burger Court has reaffirmed its holding that a woman has a fundamental constitutional right to have an abortion. *See* Akron v. Akron Center for Reproductive Health, Inc., 462 U.S. 416 (1983).

35. Swann v. Charlotte-Mecklenburg Bd. of Educ., 402 U.S. 1 (1971).

36. New York Times Co. v. United States, 403 U.S. 713 (1971) (Court dismissed temporary restraining orders and stays against New York Times and Washington Post and refused to enjoin the newspapers from publishing a classified study on United States policymaking in Vietnam).

as it has from time to time in the past, with changing personnel. But the clock will not be turned back on a host of libertarian Court decisions.

This leads me to a discussion of repeated attempts to categorize justices as "liberal," "activist," or practitioners of "judicial restraint."

The terms "liberal" or "activist," as applied to judges whom the President and Attorney General Meese criticize for overstepping proper bounds, are not illuminating.

The most "activist" Supreme Court in our history was that of the "nine old men of the Thirties." They usurped the power to invalidate virtually all of President Roosevelt's and Congress' New Deal legislation.[37] And this Court was perhaps the most conservative of all time.

By way of contrast, the so-called "liberal" and "activist" Warren Court in *Ferguson v. Skrupa*[38] declared:

> We refuse to sit as a "superlegislature to weigh the wisdom of legislation," and we emphatically refuse to go back to the time when courts [struck down state laws] "regulatory of business and industrial conditions, because they may be unwise, improvident, or out of harmony with a particular school of thought."[39]

Surely this opinion is the very model of judicial restraint. And the writer of this unanimous opinion was none other than that outstanding "liberal" jurist, Hugo L. Black.

It is true that all courts, present and past, in varying degrees, are activists in enforcing the liberties enshrined in the Bill of Rights, as distinguished from social and economic privileges. But, in light of the express language of the Constitution, they cannot, in fidelity to our fundamental law, do otherwise.

---

37. *See, e.g.*, Carter v. Carter Coal Co., 298 U.S. 238 (1936) (invalidated regulation of bituminous coal industry); A.L.A. Schecter Poultry Corp. v. United States, 295 U.S. 495 (1935) (National Industrial Recovery Act unconstitutional as illegitimate delegation of legislative power); R.R. Retirement Bd. v. Alton R.R., 295 U.S. 330 (1935) (Railroad Retirement Act of 1934 unconstitutional as violating Fifth Amendment due process); Panama Refining Co. v. Ryan, 293 U.S. 388 (1935) (section 9 of the National Industrial Recovery Act unconstitutional as invalid delegation of legislative power).

38. 372 U.S. 726 (1963).

39. *Ferguson*, 372 U.S. at 731-32 (quoting Day-Bright Lighting, Inc. v. Missouri, 342 U.S. 421, 423 (1952), and Williamson v. Lee Optical Co., 348 U.S. 483, 488 (1955)) (footnotes omitted).

The Bill of Rights is explicit in its terms. "Congress shall make no law respecting an establishment of religion . . . or abridging freedom of speech, or of the press."[40] "The right of the people to be secure . . . against unreasonable searches and seizures shall not be violated . . . ."[41] No "person shall be . . . deprived of life, liberty, or property, without due process of law."[42] "[T]he accused shall enjoy the right . . . to have the Assistance of Counsel for his defense."[43] "[C]ruel and unusual punishment [shall not be] inflicted."[44]

Surely it would appear that judicial activism in these areas is mandated.

Paradoxically, the Attorney General appears to be a closet believer in the Cult of the Robe. While denigrating decisions of the Court, he, at the same time, exaggerates the role of the judiciary in our constitutional scheme. The late Professor Bickel termed the judiciary to be "[t]he least dangerous branch of the American government."[45]

The mistaken belief that judicial law can fundamentally change our social and economic institutions is evidenced by the flood of young men and women to our nation's law schools and the creation of new law schools. This reflects commendable idealism and does give the bar new voices that should be heard. It is necessary, however, to bear the limitations of the judicial process in mind. Judicial law can help us ensure compliance by the government and by our citizenry with the Bill of Rights and valid laws and regulations—matters of transcendent importance. Judges can invalidate unconstitutional laws and unauthorized executive actions. This also represents the exercise of power, unknown in many countries, including some of the democratic West. Judges cannot, however, establish social and economic justice by judicial fiat.

Directing compliance with a subpoena, even one directed against a President, is one thing—that is judicial stuff; coping with

40. U.S. CONST. amend. I.

41. *Id.* at amend. IV.

42. *Id.* at amend. V.

43. *Id.* at amend. VI.

44. *Id.* at amend. VIII.

45. A. BICKEL, THE LEAST DANGEROUS BRANCH: THE SUPREME COURT AT THE BAR OF POLITICS 1 (2d ed. 1986).

our nation's economic, social and, foreign ills is another thing—that is not judicial stuff.

The courts can do nothing about the deficit, inflation, high interest rates, and unemployment; it is up to the President and Congress to provide the remedy. Yet, the consequences of the failure to reduce the deficit, to curb inflation, to lower high interest rates, and to check unemployment may be even more menacing to our democratic institutions than the clear danger to them of Watergate. The fate of the Weimar Republic is a stark example.

The courts cannot balance the budget. Only the executive branch and Congress can. The judiciary cannot seek to persuade the Soviet Union to negotiate an acceptable SALT III Treaty, as envisioned by President Reagan. But our very survival depends upon staying the hand of the nuclear clock, now advancing inexorably to midnight. Judges cannot bring peace to the Middle East—a problem of the utmost significance, which thus far has defied the best efforts of the executive branch. The judiciary lacks the power of the purse and the sword.

Even in the area of judicial competence, like the enforcement of the Bill of Rights, we must never overlook the profound teaching of Judge Learned Hand: "[A] society so riven that the spirit of moderation [liberty] is gone, no court can save. [A] society where the spirit flourishes, no court need save."[46]

The Attorney General ignores what may be at the very heart of the issues he has raised.

Our Constitution is an instrument of practical government. It is also, more importantly, a declaration of faith in the spirit of Liberty, Freedom, and Equality.

The ultimate safeguard of our liberty is the people. They are the source of our Constitution. That document's first words are: "We the People of the United States, in Order to . . . secure the Blessing of Liberty to ourselves and our Posterity, do ordain and establish this Constitution for the United States of America."[47] The people are the ultimate guardians and protectors of our liberty, not the President, not Congress, and not the judiciary.

---

46. L. HAND, *The Contribution of an Independent Judiciary to Civilization*, in THE SPIRIT OF LIBERTY: PAPERS AND ADDRESSES OF LEARNED HAND 119 (1959).

47. U.S. CONST. preamble.

And We the People, if we are to keep our constitutional faith, must always recall the admonition of Thomas Paine: "Those who expect to reap the blessings of freedom must . . . undergo the fatigue of supporting it."[48]

48. T. Paine, *The American Crisis*, in 1 The Complete Writings of Thomas Paine 102 (P. Foner ed. 1969).

JUSTICE BLACK AND LABOR LAW: SOME REFLECTIONS ON THE JUSTICE'S JURISPRUDENCE OF INDIVIDUAL VERSUS COLLECTIVE RIGHTS IN INDUSTRIAL RELATIONS

*Harry T. Edwards**

I. Introduction

A. *Jurisprudential Foundations*

It has been reported that Justice Hugo Black once read *The Greening of America*, a book authored by one of his former law clerks, Professor Charles Reich of Yale. In one passage of the book, Reich describes the purportedly discredited moral vision of those who believe that "the American dream is still possible and that success is determined by character, morality, hard work and self-denial." Justice Black wrote in the margin: "I still do."[1]

This brief anecdote seems quite unexceptional, until one recognizes that it captures Justice Black's remarkable and deeply rooted faith in the American dream and in the process and results of American democracy. He believed firmly that lawmaking is the exclusive province of legislative bodies elected by the majority of the people, that often individual desires must give way to the collective choices of that majority, and that judicial power must be exercised principally to give effect to the will of the legislature. On several occasions during his judicial career, Justice Black voted to uphold legislation that he personally viewed as abhorrent or unde-

---

* Circuit Judge, United States Court of Appeals for the District of Columbia Circuit. B.S. 1962, Cornell University; J.D. 1965, University of Michigan. The author wishes to acknowledge the research assistance of Virginia A. Seitz in the preparation of this article.

1. Snowiss, *The Legacy of Justice Black*, 1973 SUP. CT. REV. 187, 241 (quoting N.Y. Times, Apr. 22, 1972, at 33, col. 1).

sirable, because, in many areas, he believed that legislative choices must stand unfettered.[2]

Although Justice Black had an abiding faith in majority rule, it was qualified by his belief that certain individual rights are fundamental and inviolate. In particular, Justice Black considered the specific guarantees of the Constitution, particularly the First, Fifth and portions of the Sixth Amendments, to be pre-eminently important; for him, the Bill of Rights was a "unique American contribution to man's continuing search for a society in which individual liberty is secure against governmental oppression."[3] While he "cannot rightfully be regarded as the leader in the movement for 'increasing sensitivity toward human rights, and large conceptions of equality under law,' "[4] Justice Black did strongly and consistently adhere to the view that the majority could not be permitted to infringe on those individual rights that were specifically enunciated in the Bill of Rights.

Justice Black trusted majority rule precisely because he found certain individual rights to be unconditionally protected by the Constitution. His deep faith in the substantive choices of the majority sprang from his conviction that they were the product of the exercise of enlightened individuals' judgments due in large part to the protections found in the Bill of Rights. In describing Justice Black's jurisprudence, Sylvia Snowiss gave a lucid description of the symbiotic relationship between absolute individual rights and majority rule.

> The intellectual freedom secured by the First Amendment insures a thorough canvassing and dissemination of views, the necessary precondition for the emergence of a genuinely free popular will. Freedom of association joined with constitutionally protected voting rights implements this intellectual freedom by facilitating the transmission of popular will into public policy. True responsiveness is incompatible with any exception or qualification of this process.[5]

The American individualism valued by Hugo Black, then, was not that of the maverick; his vision of self-reliant America was not that of Henry David Thoreau and a life of isolation at Walden

---

2. *See, e.g.*, Harper v. Virginia State Bd. of Elections, 383 U.S. 663, 677 (1966) (Black, J., dissenting); Griswold v. Connecticut, 381 U.S. 479, 522 (1965) (Black, J., dissenting).
3. H. Black, A Constitutional Faith 3 (1968).
4. Snowiss, *supra* note 1, at 238.
5. *Id.* at 191.

Pond. Rather, the notion of individual rights cultivated by Justice Black "was a community centered, patriotic individualism, grounded not in individual differences but in shared moral virtues of hard work and self-denial."[6]

As a result of this belief in the inevitable triumph of shared values, he possessed an extraordinary trust in the choices of a legislature elected by individuals whose freedom to think, speak and vote was and is protected by the Bill of Rights. This faith lay at the heart of Justice Black's jurisprudence, including his decisions in the area of labor relations. Here we see the same respect for legislative choices conditioned only, but absolutely, upon the protection of certain fundamental individual rights.

B. *Individual Rights and the Employment Relationship*

Many aspects of Justice Black's work in labor law have been thoroughly scrutinized. There have been thoughtful treatments of his opinions pertaining to maritime workers,[7] to unions and antitrust law,[8] and to labor picketing and the First Amendment;[9] I will not rehash them. Instead, I will focus on the Justice's labor law jurisprudence on the nature of certain individual rights in the context of collective bargaining relationships, a topic of unquestionable current significance and, coincidentally, of deep and long-standing personal interest.

The period during which Hugo Black sat on the Supreme Court saw the initiation and development of all major tenets of our national labor policy. The individual's rights to join and form a union, the selection of bargaining agents by majority rule, the rule of "exclusive representation" protecting unions in bargaining relationships, the promotion of collective bargaining, the private settlement of industrial conflicts, and the peaceful resolution of labor disputes through arbitration are the fundamental principles of

---

6. *Id.* at 245.

7. *See* Rutledge, *Justice Black and Labor Law*, 14 UCLA L. REV. 501, 513 (1967); Wright, *Justice at the Dock: The Maritime Worker and Mr. Justice Black*, 14 UCLA L. REV. 524 (1967).

8. Kirkpatrick, *The Development of Antitrust*, in HUGO BLACK AND THE SUPREME COURT 195 (S. Strickland ed. 1967).

9. Kalven, *Upon Rereading Mr. Justice Black on the First Amendment*, 14 UCLA L. REV. 428 (1967); Yarbrough, *Justice Black and His Critics on Speech-Plus and Symbolic Speech*, 52 TEX. L. REV. 257 (1974).

industrial relations in the United States today; all of these principles were enunciated during Justice Black's tenure on the Court. The tenure of Justice Black also coincided with the evolution of unions into collectivities with formidable power over the economic lives of their members, an evolution which many felt threatened individual rights within the employment relationship.

Although the several goals of modern national labor policy—the peaceful, private settlement of disputes in a manner consistent with individual rights—are *theoretically* reconcilable, there is usually a tension among them in any concrete application to particular labor disputes. The *private* adjustment of industrial conflict is not always *peaceful*. Over the years, our experience with collective bargaining has made it clear that it is inevitable that the joint decisions of union and management, or of an arbitrator selected by the parties, will significantly affect—and occasionally erode or disregard—the rights of individual employees, whether these rights have been created by a statute such as Title VII of the Civil Rights Act of 1964 or by the collective agreement. Balancing these individual rights against an opposing collective interest in any given case will often require value judgments.

Justice Black's opinions in cases involving collective bargaining were true to the values which are central to his constitutional jurisprudence—"that in a democracy lawmaking is the province of legislatures elected by the people"[10] and that, at the same time, some individual rights are too precious to be infringed upon by legislatures or the courts. Thus, in the contexts of industrial relations and labor law, which are so heavily infused with statutory prescriptions, we most often find Justice Black deferring to Congress. This tendency is clearly seen in his opinions delimiting the courts' injunctive power in labor disputes pursuant to the Norris-LaGuardia Act and in his deference to the decisions of the National Labor Relations Board (NLRB) and the Railway Adjustment Board,[11] the agencies designated by Congress to make judgments about the interpretation and application of the National Labor Relations Act (NLRA) and the Railway Labor Act. In the area of labor relations, Justice Black clearly understood that

---

10. J. Magee, Mr. Justice Black: Absolutist on the Court 19 (1979).

11. *See* Republic Steel Corp. v. NLRB, 311 U.S. 7 (1940); NLRB v. Waterman S.S. Corp., 309 U.S. 206 (1940); NLRB v. Columbian Enameling & Stamping Co., 306 U.S. 292, 300 (1938) (Black, J., dissenting).

choices between the diverging interests of collectivities—employers and labor unions—are for Congress and its agency adjuncts.

However, weighing the rights of the union or the employer against the rights of an individual employee involved more complex considerations for Justice Black. As unions grew more powerful, Justice Black feared that institutionalized labor, like a majority government unchecked by strictures such as those embodied in the Bill of Rights, would infringe upon the liberty interests of individuals. In particular, he opposed two developing trends. First, the Supreme Court had made arbitration the centerpiece of the collective bargaining process, narrowly circumscribing the role of courts that review arbitration awards and requiring employees to pursue contractual dispute resolution procedures. Second, the Supreme Court had created the union's duty to fairly represent its members but construed that duty quite narrowly, and restricted an individual's right to sue his or her employer for breach of the employment contract to those cases in which the union had engaged in arbitrary, discriminatory, or bad faith conduct.

Justice Black vehemently denounced these decisions. He felt strongly that a worker's congressionally created right to litigate his or her legal claims against the employer, either in court or in the agency forum, could not be judicially limited without *explicit* congressional direction. Hence, he rejected any limitation on employees' access to the judicial process and mistrusted the Court's deference to arbitration, the so-called "law of the shop" and the collective agreement. He feared that private agreements and dispute resolution mechanisms established by corporate and labor bodies would erode individual liberties, contract rights, and statutory or public law choices made by Congress, and that individual employees would be left without legal remedies.

I, like many scholars of labor law, share some of the concerns expressed by Justice Black. However, there is a clear divergency in our viewpoints with respect to the proper balance to be struck between individual and collective rights in industrial relations. I believe that the amount of discretion to which a union is entitled is a function of the type of individual "right" at stake. When the real underlying dispute involves a question of overriding public law or policy,[12] then deference to the bargaining parties, or their arbitrator, is inappropriate. Contrariwise, when classical "economic" or contractual rights are at issue and no specific statutory right has been infringed, I would contend that, generally, a court has no business intruding upon the arbitral process or limiting the union's flexibility to act for the collective benefit of employees in the bargaining unit,[13] absent a violation of the extremely limited duty of fair representation.[14]

During the 1940s, 1950s, and 1960s, while Justice Black was on the Court, unions gradually obtained power of significant proportions. Often, they acted as private legislatures for their members and other bargaining unit employees, making substantive choices for all without any mitigating checks or balances in areas that are now perceived as properly subject to *public* regulation. There are certain fundamental publicly mandated entitlements that now govern the employment relationship—the right to safety on the job embodied in OSHA,[15] certain protected pension rights delineated by ERISA,[16] and the protections against race, color, sex, national origin and religious discrimination created by Title VII[17] and the Equal Pay Act.[18] In addition, in recent years, there has been an

---

12. I recognize that, as an abstraction, the public right/economic right distinction may be problematic. I utilize the phrase "public right" as a shorthand term for those aspects of the employment relationship that, by consensus, have entered the realm of public regulation. For example, the employer's right to fire an employee was formerly the quintessential classical economic issue. Modern legislation banning invidious discrimination based on race, sex, national origin or religion reveals that, under certain circumstances, the decision to dismiss an employee is now governed by public values. In addition, evolving case law and proposed legislation prohibiting "unjust dismissal" demonstrate that this entire question may be in transition between the "economic" and "public" categories. *See also* Edwards, *Alternative Dispute Resolution: Panacea or Anathema?*, 99 Harv. L. Rev. 668, 672 & n.13 (1986).

13. *See generally* Edwards, *Deferral to Arbitration and Waiver of The Duty to Bargain: A Possible Way Out of Everlasting Confusion at the NLRB*, 46 Ohio St. L.J. 23 (1985).

I apologize for this and other citations to my own work. These citations are not intended as an exercise of ego, nor as a suggestion that my writings are "authoritative" sources but only as a short-hand way to highlight certain differences between Justice Black's and my own perspectives on labor law and collective bargaining.

14. *See generally* Edwards, *The Duty of Fair Representation: A View From the Bench*, in The Changing Law of Fair Representation 93 (J. McKelvey ed. 1985).

15. Occupational Safety and Health Act of 1970, 29 U.S.C. §§ 651-678 (1982).

16. Employee Retirement Income Security Act of 1974, 29 U.S.C. §§ 1001-1461 (1982).

17. Civil Rights Act of 1964, Pub. L. No. 88-352, §§ 701-716, 78 Stat. 241, 253-66 (codified as amended at 42 U.S.C. §§ 2000e to 2000e-17 (1982)).

18. 29 U.S.C. § 206(d) (1982).

expansion of the duty of fair representation pursuant to developing judicial doctrine.[19] The contours of these publicly imposed protections were not fully evident when Justice Black wrote of his tremendous fears of unbounded union power.

Justice Black was, in a sense, prophetic; he saw the need for the interjection of public values into the employment relationship. He recognized that unions, in cooperation with employers, could not be permitted to act as mini-legislatures in certain areas; and Congress itself has now imposed certain public values on the formerly private employment relationship. Justice Black was therefore ahead of his time when he insisted that some public values that protected individuals had to override the union's otherwise unquestionable right to make decisions as the employees' representative.

Many commentators, myself included,[20] have expressed grave reservations about employers and unions, or their privately chosen arbitrators, deciding public law or policy issues. Justice Black, no doubt, would have approved of the modern public legislation and litigation of individual rights for employees. He surely would have agreed with the Supreme Court's conclusion in *Alexander v. Gardner-Denver Co.*,[21] that, with respect to questions involving overriding public law, the courts may not defer to private arbitration.[22] And, had he considered the issue, Justice Black probably would have predicted the current downturn in the union movement, attributing lost union membership to the unbridled legislative power of union organizations. Justice Black believed in the sanctity of majority rule only when there were certain inviolate individual rights to ensure enlightened legislative action. There is surely no reason to think that Justice Black would have welcomed the advent of a stagnating union movement, but it is doubtful that he would have been surprised by the events of the 1980s.

Insofar as Justice Black's jurisprudence caused him to believe that there should be certain sacrosanct public values regulating

---

19. *See generally* THE CHANGING LAW OF FAIR REPRESENTATION (J. McKelvey ed. 1985).

20. *See* Edwards, *supra* note 12; Edwards, *Arbitration of Employment Discrimination Cases: An Empirical Study*, in PROCEEDINGS OF THE 28TH ANNUAL MEETING, NATIONAL ACADEMY OF ARBITRATORS 59 (B. Dennis & G. Somers eds. 1976); Edwards, *Labor Arbitration at the Crossroads: The "Common Law of the Shop" v. External Law*, 32 ARB. J. 65 (1977).

21. 415 U.S. 36 (1974).

22. *See Alexander*, 415 U.S. at 51.

employment relations, and that these values should be principally established and enforced by public bodies, I can find little fault in his philosophy. However, in the realm of union control of daily economic matters, I must frankly acknowledge a significant difference between Justice Black's views and my own. In the regime of collective bargaining established by the NLRA,[23] I believe that unions may properly act as a legislature for purposes of decision-making on economic issues, whether the question be one of contract negotiation or contract administration, and that the union's duty of fair representation must be narrowly defined in these areas. Individuals must be trusted to select a union that may then exercise full freedom in its economic choices. Cries of individual disadvantage due to specific decisions made in this realm may not drown out the collective choice when it speaks to these issues, absent proof of arbitrary or bad-faith conduct. The Supreme Court has endorsed this view in *Metropolitan Edison Co. v. NLRB*,[24] stating specifically that "the National Labor Relations Act contemplates that individual rights may be waived by the union so long as the union does not breach its duty of good-faith representation."[25] This picture of the union as a limited legislature, absolute in certain realms but restricted when publicly-mandated individual rights are involved, is ironically a microcosm of what I see to be Justice Black's view of the American system.

Justice Black would not have conceded, as I do, that unions have virtually unrestricted power over represented employees in economic decision-making. Our differences are founded in our varying concepts of the role and function of a collective bargaining agreement. I believe that the "nature of employee rights should be determined with reference to the nature of collective bargaining, the resulting bargain, and the various interests of the affected parties."[26] Professor Archibald Cox's seminal analysis of the nature of the collective bargaining agreement suggested several reasons for allowing unions to control remedies available to employees. Professor Cox first noted that collective agreements are often deliberately

23. 29 U.S.C. §§ 151-169 (1982).

24. 460 U.S. 693 (1983).

25. *Metropolitan Edison Co.*, 460 U.S. at 707 n.11.

26. Lewis, *Fair Representation in Grievance Administration: Vaca v. Sipes*, 1967 SUP. CT. REV. 81, 100 (discussing Cox, *Rights Under a Labor Agreement*, 69 HARV. L. REV. 601 (1956)).

ambiguous or unintentionally incomplete; therefore, he asserted, continuous interpretation and rulemaking must occur in some sort of orderly fashion. Cox then contended that the uniform application of the collective agreement is vital to its integrity, and that individuals must somehow be bound to solutions agreed upon by the company and the union. Finally, he maintained that, although the interests of individual employees will inevitably conflict at times, it is the union's function—as the designated bargaining agent for all employees—to settle such disputes as part of the "political" process of industrial self-government.[27]

In another brilliant article on this subject, Professor David Feller persuasively defends the federal labor policy of nonintervention in the arbitral process.[28] Feller correctly points out that, in the typical labor contract, an important part of the bargain is the agreement that disputes between the parties will be governed by the rules contained in the contract as they may be interpreted and applied by the parties' arbitrator. When the courts intervene—as they have done in some duty of fair representation cases—and supply their own interpretation of the agreement, this undermines a critical basis of the parties' bargain.

The purposes served by a collective bargaining agreement lead me to believe, with Professors Cox and Feller, that, under our existing labor laws, unions must retain control over contractual remedies. Control of grievances by individual employees would, in my view, impose unacceptable burdens on the contractual dispute resolution machinery. In addition, it seems plain to me that many of the principal rights created by the provisions of the NLRA, are, in fact, collective, and that, therefore, it is perfectly appropriate for the union to retain the power to invoke the use of the remedial processes contained within the collective agreement. The union's statutorily conferred discretion is made effective only by a broad judicial deference to the process and results of the contractual dispute resolution mechanism—usually arbitration—and a closely confined duty of fair representation.

In contrast, Justice Black believed that, once signed, a collective agreement became just like any employment contract and that

---

27. Cox, *supra* note 26, at 625-27.

28. Feller, *A General Theory of the Collective Bargaining Agreement*, 61 CALIF. L. REV. 663 (1973).

it created clear and absolute individual rights for the employees it covered. In simple terms, he believed that the collective agreement was not analogous to a statute or a constitution, but was instead a private employment contract with one discernable correct interpretation. Unless the dispute involved was one of collective rather than individual significance, the affected individual retained an absolute right to sue the employer for any alleged contract violation. Justice Black did not believe that this succor of individual rights would have a negative impact on the union's prestige or on the viability of the arbitration process. In other words, he would have severely limited the union's role in contract administration.

Justice Black and I thus fall on opposite sides of this longstanding chasm between two different concepts of the nature of the collective agreement. I am in disagreement with Justice Black's assumption that the substantive rights of individual employees are best served by unconditional access to the courts and *de novo* judicial scrutiny. My experience has convinced me that judicial protections of substantive rights and a public forum for individual employees often results in only the illusion of gain for individual workers, for it undermines *collective* bargaining and labor arbitration which offer the best hope for the just resolution of employer-employee disputes.

It is my view that, in many aspects of labor relations, arbitration presents a superior method of dispute resolution to that held out by the judicial system and, in particular, offers the most realistic hope of redress to aggrieved individual employees. I also think that any significant expansion of the union's duty of fair representation, such as a requirement that *all* grievances be pursued to the full extent of any contractual remedy, would undermine the union's discretion to administer collective bargaining contracts and to process grievance disputes, threatening the resolution of disputes through arbitration, a vital part of the collective bargaining process. Although, like Justice Black, I firmly believe that individual workers must retain access to a judicial forum to enforce public values that transcend the employment relationship, such as those embodied in the Equal Protection Clause of the Fourteenth Amendment and in Title VII, I must ultimately conclude that, in economic matters, collective bargaining and arbitration, not individual lawsuits, give the best protection of the most individual economic rights within the employment relationship.

The gains won for individual workers by assertion of their collective strength make clear the dangers inherent in the loss of organized status.[29] Any suggestion that present-day workers can completely replace the economic protection offered by unions with that embodied in substantive statutory rights and individual litigation strikes me as somewhat fanciful. Rights enforceable only through case-by-case adjudication are often empty. Current statutory protections are not comprehensive, nor are they ever likely to be. Professor Cox has aptly summarized my view:

> Labor, management, and arbitrators must recognize that the ideals and needs of society limit their freedom of decision; but the accommodation also requires infusing labor law with many of the ideas and conventions, unknown to the law but *appropriate to group action*, which have gained acceptance in the world of labor relations.[30]

My assumptions thus differ from those of Justice Black, though we operate in a similar framework. Our ultimate philosophical leanings—that is, toward the protection of individual employees through democratic rule by the majority in the workplace—*are* identical. Like the Justice, I recognize that there are times when actions taken for group advantage demand too much individual disadvantage; again like Justice Black, I believe that Congress must decide where that line is drawn.

I also believe that the Supreme Court was true to Congress' purpose in the NLRA when it elected to favor arbitration and collective bargaining in labor relations in the *Steelworkers Trilogy*,[31] and when it limited the restraints imposed on unions by creating a narrow duty of fair representation in *Vaca v. Sipes*.[32] In Justice Black's view, however, the Court's emphasis on the protection of the collective bargaining relationship and on peaceful dispute resolution through arbitration led to an impermissible twisting of traditional contract law and statutory labor law and infringed on individual employees' rights to unconditional access to a judicial forum. By looking at Justice Black's vigorous dissents in this area and by contrasting them with opposing views, I hope to illustrate

---

29. *See* R. Freeman & J. Medoff, What Do Unions Do? (1984).
30. Cox, *supra* note 26, at 605 (emphasis added).
31. United Steelworkers v. American Mfg. Co., 363 U.S. 564 (1960); United Steelworkers v. Warrior & Gulf Navigation Co., 363 U.S. 574 (1960); United Steelworkers v. Enterprise Wheel & Car Corp., 363 U.S. 593 (1960).
32. 386 U.S. 171 (1967).

the differing choices open to judges as they attempt to effectuate congressional prescriptions setting forth substantive protections for individual workers.

II. Collective Bargaining and Individual Rights

A. *Introduction*

It is sometimes not recalled[33] that Justice Black was not a party to the early courtship between the Supreme Court and grievance arbitration, when the Court began its "love affair with arbitration."[34] Although he was a member of the Court, he did not participate in either the *Lincoln Mills*[35] decision or the *Steelworkers Trilogy*,[36] the landmark judgments of the Court that lay the groundwork for the "golden age" of arbitration.[37]

In *Lincoln Mills*, the Court held that the appellant union could get specific performance of the employer's contractual agreement to arbitrate certain grievances. This remedy, the Court decided, was not proscribed by the ban against labor injunctions in the Norris-LaGuardia Act because "[t]he failure to arbitrate was not a part and parcel of the abuses against which the Act was aimed."[38] Moreover, the Court clearly felt that "[t]he congressional policy in favor of the enforcement of agreements to arbitrate grievance disputes,"[39] embodied in section 301(a) of the Labor-Management Relations Act (LMRA),[40] was more mighty than any countervailing considerations. Given the benefit of hindsight, it now seems clear that the Court's judgment in *Lincoln Mills*—ignoring the express prohibitions of the Norris-LaGuardia Act in deference to a *policy* favoring arbitration—set the stage for

---

33. *See, e.g.*, Gould, *On Labor Injunctions, Unions, and the Judges: The Boys Market Case*, 1970 SUP. CT. REV. 215, in which the author mistakenly indicates that Justice Black "assented to both *Lincoln Mills* and the *Steelworkers Trilogy*." *Id.* at 227.

34. J. ATLESON, VALUES AND ASSUMPTIONS IN AMERICAN LABOR LAW 182 n.10 (1983).

35. Textile Workers Union v. Lincoln Mills, 353 U.S. 448 (1957).

36. *See supra* note 31.

37. Feller, *The Coming End of Arbitration's Golden Age*, in PROCEEDINGS OF THE TWENTY-NINTH ANNUAL MEETING OF THE NATIONAL ACADEMY OF ARBITRATORS 97 (1976) "[I]t is plainly true that grievance arbitrators have, especially since the *Steelworkers Trilogy*, occupied a very special place in our law." *Id.* at 98.

38. *Lincoln Mills*, 353 U.S. at 458.

39. *Id.* at 458-59.

40. 29 U.S.C. § 185 (1982). This Act is also referred to as the Taft-Hartley Act.

Justice Black's strong dissents in a number of the Court's subsequent decisions interpreting section 301.

In the *Steelworkers Trilogy* the Court made manifest its view that a fundamental policy of national labor legislation is to promote the arbitral process as a substitute for economic warfare. The Court held that, where there is an agreement to submit grievance disputes to arbitration, the courts have a very circumscribed role to play. In *United Steelworkers v. American Manufacturing Co.*,[41] the Court stated that lower courts have "no business weighing the merits of the grievance," because "[t]he agreement is to submit all grievances to arbitration, not merely those which the court will deem meritorious."[42] Likewise, courts called upon to review and enforce arbitration awards have only a limited role to play. In *United Steelworkers v. Enterprise Wheel & Car Corp.*,[43] the Court stated that lower courts should not second-guess arbitrators' judgments, but only look to see whether the award "draws its essence from the collective bargaining agreement."[44] And in *United Steelworkers v. Warrior & Gulf Navigation Co.*,[45] the Court made clear that the nature of a collective bargaining agreement is different from that of most contracts: "it is a generalized code to govern a myriad of cases which the draftsmen cannot wholly anticipate;"[46] moreover, it is supplemented by the "common law of a particular industry or of a particular plant."[47] The labor agreement, in other words, is a constitution of industrial self-government, in which the knowledgeable arbitrator plays an integral part. Thus, "a reviewing court's role is strictly limited to determining whether the arbitrator exceeded his or her authority under the agreement. The court is not to concern itself with whether the arbitrator resolved the issue correctly."[48]

Significant portions of modern labor policy have been built upon the foundation of *Lincoln Mills* and the *Steelworkers Trilogy*. In the years that followed these decisions, it became apparent that the installation of arbitration as the centerpiece of national

---

41. 363 U.S. 564 (1960).
42. *American Mfg. Co.*, 363 U.S. at 568.
43. 363 U.S. 593 (1960).
44. *Enterprise Wheel*, 363 U.S. at 597.
45. 363 U.S. 574 (1960).
46. *Warrior & Gulf*, 363 U.S. at 578.
47. *Id.* at 579.
48. Edwards, *supra* note 13, at 35.

labor policy would affect (Justice Black would say distort) all related doctrinal decisionmaking. In the labor law context, the Court's interpretation of contract law, of federal statutory labor law, and of the union's duty of fair representation was affected, either explicitly or implicitly, by its devotion to the arbitral process. In each of these areas, Justice Black struggled to hold the line for his jurisprudential framework. He believed that the pre-eminence accorded to arbitration twisted traditional contract law, contravened the congressional choices embodied in the Norris-LaGuardia Act, and violated individual employees' rights to judicial process.

As will be made evident below, despite my strong adherence to the arbitral process, I am sometimes in agreement with Justice Black's laconic dissents. However, much more than did Justice Black, I believe that the selection of a union as an exclusive bargaining representative profoundly alters the employer-employee relationship and gives rise to institutional interests that ultimately protect more individuals' rights. On economic issues, Congress intended that workers receive protection through their collective, rather than their individual activities. I believe that the Supreme Court's nurturance of the arbitral process, controlled by the exclusive bargaining representative, best serves that goal.

B. *The Impact of Arbitration on Statutory Provisions: The Norris-LaGuardia Act*

In the 1960s, the national labor policy favoring arbitration collided with the equally strong anti-labor injunction policy embodied in the Norris-LaGuardia Act. In Justice Black's view, the mandate of that Act was unequivocal, and thus Congress' will was clear. Justice Black viewed the Court's rejection of the express mandate of Congress in *Boys Markets, Inc. v. Retail Clerks Union, Local 770*[49] as yet another example of the Court's policy preference for arbitration improperly eroding the force of a legislative command.

Section 4 of the Norris-LaGuardia Act bars federal courts from issuing injunctions "in any case involving or growing out of any labor dispute."[50] Section 13 of the Act defines a labor dispute

---

49. 398 U.S. 235 (1970).
50. 29 U.S.C. § 104 (1982).

as "any controversy concerning terms or conditions of employment, or concerning the association or representation of persons in negotiating, fixing, maintaining, changing, or seeking to arrange terms or conditions of employment."[51] To Justice Black, this statutory language was crystal clear. As he once noted, even *unlawful* conduct engaged in as part and parcel of a labor dispute may not be enjoined because: "Congress passed the Norris-LaGuardia Act to curtail and regulate the jurisdiction of courts, not, as it passed the Taft-Hartley Act, to regulate the conduct of people engaged in labor disputes."[52] In Justice Black's view, only Congress could cut back on the prohibitions of the Norris-LaGuardia Act.[53]

In 1961, Justice Black wrote for the majority in *Sinclair Refining Co. v. Atkinson*,[54] a case in which the Court held that the Norris-LaGuardia Act prohibited federal courts from utilizing injunctions to enforce collective bargaining agreements pursuant to section 301 of the LMRA. To him the issue was purely one of statutory interpretation. He had no difficulty concluding that the Court could not undercut an explicit prohibition of the Norris-LaGuardia Act, and enjoin a strike simply in order to provide equitable relief for the violation of a contractual no-strike provision, when, in Justice Black's view, Congress had expressly refused to do so.

To anyone who understood Justice Black's jurisprudential leanings, the framing of the issue in *Sinclair* instantaneously revealed its ultimate resolution: "whether § 301 of the Taft-Hartley Act . . . *impliedly* repealed § 4 of the pre-existing Norris-LaGuardia Act?"[55] An express congressional command would never, according to Justice Black, be repealed by implication attributable to a *judicially* created labor policy to foster the peaceful resolution of disputes through arbitration:

> The argument to the contrary seems to rest upon the notion that injunctions against peaceful strikes are necessary to make the arbitration process effective. But whatever might be said about the merits of this argument, Congress has itself rejected it. In doing so, it set the limit to which it was willing to go in permitting courts to

---

51. 29 U.S.C. § 113 (1982).
52. Marine Cooks & Stewards, AFL v. Panama S.S. Co., 362 U.S. 365, 372 (1960).
53. Order of R.R. Telegraphers v. Chicago & N.W. Ry. Co., 362 U.S. 330, 342 (1960).
54. 370 U.S. 195 (1962).
55. *Sinclair Ref. Co.*, 370 U.S. at 196 (emphasis added).

effectuate the congressional policy favoring arbitration and it is not this Court's business to review the wisdom of that decision.[56]

Moreover, as Justice Black pointed out, the Court's refusal to allow strikes called in violation of a collective agreement did not directly impair arbitration or the policy favoring it because employers retained the right to obtain an order compelling arbitration of any dispute covered by the arbitration provision of a collective agreement. "At the most, what is involved is the question of whether the employer is to be allowed to enjoy the benefits of an injunction along with the right which Congress gave him in § 301 to sue for breach of a collective agreement."[57]

Several years later, however, the Court reversed itself on this question in *Boys Markets*, deciding, *inter alia*, that the national policy favoring arbitration mandated a different result. In Justice Black's view, this choice flew in the face of a congressional decision and showed little judicial respect for the "proper division of functions between the branches of our Federal Government."[58] Justice Black could not abide the decision in *Boys Markets* because the Court relied on a judicial policy choice to override an explicit legislative enactment.

The majority in *Boys Markets* concluded that a congressional "shift in emphasis" had occurred—from protection of the fledgling labor movement to the peaceful resolution of industrial disputes. Hence, *Sinclair* no longer made a "viable contribution to federal labor policy,"[59] and a different accommodation or reconciliation of the older statute, the Norris-LaGuardia Act, with the newer statute, the LMRA, was required.

A number of labor law scholars have recognized that "the overruling of *Sinclair* had to be based on policy considerations despite legislative history."[60] It is true that in *Lincoln Mills* the Supreme Court had relied heavily on the notion that an agreement to arbitrate is the *quid pro quo* for a contractual no-strike clause, thus furnishing some justification for the Court's inclination to en-

56. *Id.* at 213.

57. *Id.*

58. Boys Markets, Inc. v. Retail Clerks Union, Local 770, 398 U.S. 235, 261 (1970) (Black, J., dissenting).

59. *Id.* at 249.

60. Atleson, *The Circle of* Boys Market: *A Comment on Judicial Inventiveness*, 7 INDUS. REL. L.J. 88, 95 (1985).

force a promise to arbitrate. Logically extended, this *quid pro quo* thesis can carry the baggage of the decision in *Boys Markets*. But, as Justice Black understood, the equitable relief granted in *Lincoln Mills*—an injunction compelling arbitration—was not wholly inconsistent with the Norris-LaGuardia Act, whereas a *Boys Markets* injunction *against* a strike was flatly at odds with the basic proscription of the Act. Nevertheless, the majority in *Boys Markets* held to the *quid pro quo* analysis and to their policy judgment favoring arbitration:

> Even if management is not encouraged by the unavailability of the injunction remedy to resist arbitration agreements, the fact remains that the effectiveness of such agreements would be greatly reduced if injunctive relief were withheld. Indeed, the very purpose of arbitration procedures is to provide a mechanism for the expeditious settlement of industrial disputes without resort to strikes, lockouts, or other self-help measures. This basic purpose is obviously largely undercut if there is no immediate, effective remedy for those very tactics that arbitration is designed to obviate.[61]

Not surprisingly, Justice Black dissented sharply in *Boys Markets*. His substantive position on this question had been set forth in *Sinclair*, and he disagreed with the Court's interpretation of the statutes on the merits. The main focus of his opinion, however, was the expression of his view that the Court had intruded into the legislative realm. He felt that after the Supreme Court had interpreted a statute, it "[became] what this Court has said it is."[62] Any reinterpretation was "neither more nor less than an amendment: it is no different in effect from a judicial alteration of language that Congress itself placed in the statute."[63] This point was highlighted, Justice Black noted, by the fact that Congress had considered, but failed to adopt bills seeking to enact precisely the reinterpretation at issue.

In *Boys Markets*, Justice Black found "the laws involved [to be] the focus of strongly held views of powerful but antagonistic political and economic interests."[64] All the more reason, he asserted, for the Court to defer to legislative choices:

---

61. *Boys Markets*, 398 U.S. at 249.
62. *Id.* at 257 (Black, J., dissenting).
63. *Id.* at 257-58 (Black, J., dissenting).
64. *Id.* at 256 (Black, J., dissenting).

> It is the Congress, not this Court, that responds to the pressures of political groups, pressures entirely proper in a free society. It is Congress, not this Court, that has the capacity to investigate the divergent considerations involved in the management of a complex national labor policy. And it is Congress, not this Court, that is elected by the people. This Court should, therefore, interject itself as little as possible into the law-making and law-changing process. Having given our view on the meaning of a statute, our task is concluded, absent extraordinary circumstances. *When the Court changes its mind years later, simply because the judges have changed, in my judgment, it takes upon itself the function of the legislature.*[65]

It is obvious that the judicial disagreements that surfaced in *Sinclair/Boys Markets* go to some of the most critical points of Justice Black's jurisprudence on collective bargaining. As one scholar has noted:

> The Court's belief that no-strike promises must be enforced by injunction lies at the heart of *Boys Market*. It should be noted that [Justice] Brennan was saying that *Sinclair*, in deferring to a congressional statute, would upset the *judicially* created policies of the Court in section 301 cases.[66]

This is precisely what Justice Black found objectionable.

Unions routinely agree to arbitrate disputes; however, such contractual provisions do not necessarily mean that they will eschew any form of self-help. Yet, the Supreme Court, relying heavily on its *quid pro quo* analysis, decided in *Boys Markets* that, where there is an express no-strike clause, injunctions are necessary to fully protect an employer's bargain and to encourage employers to agree to arbitration clauses. It was not the *substance* of this choice that Justice Black opposed. Contrary to the views of some, he did not possess an inevitable pro-labor orientation.[67]

---

65. *Id.* at 258 (Black, J., dissenting) (emphasis added).

66. Atleson, *supra* note 60, at 101 (emphasis omitted).

67. There are those who have attributed Justice Black's labor law decisions to a pro-labor result orientation. *See, e.g.*, W. MENDELSON, JUSTICES BLACK AND FRANKFURTER: CONFLICT IN THE COURT 39-41 (1966). This view profoundly over-simplifies the Justice's jurisprudence. Justice Black has reversed the Board when its actions clearly contravened congressional intention. *See* H.K. Porter Co. v. NLRB, 397 U.S. 99 (1970). In addition, the Justice has upheld state legislature outlawing the closed shop. *See* Lincoln Fed. Labor Union v. Northwestern Iron & Metal Co., 335 U.S. 525 (1949); AFL v. American Sash & Door Co., 335 U.S. 538 (1949).

Rather, Justice Black objected to the Court's decision to reverse a prior statutory interpretation and to disregard the explicit command of the Norris-LaGuardia Act and the legislative history of section 301 of the LMRA merely because a majority of the Justices were of a view that such a choice was "necessary to defend the integrity of arbitration agreements."[68]

A curious postcript to the *Sinclair/Boys Markets* debate may be found in the Court's ruling in *Buffalo Forge Co. v. United Steelworkers*,[69] decided after Justice Black's tenure on the Supreme Court. In *Buffalo Forge*, the Court held that a federal court could not enjoin a "sympathy strike" (supporting a sister union) pending an arbitrator's decision as to whether the strike was forbidden by the express no-strike clause in a collective bargaining agreement to which the striking union is a party. Adhering strictly to the *quid pro quo* analysis of *Boys Markets*, the Court concluded that no injunction could issue against a sympathy strike because the underlying dispute did not involve an arbitrable issue. In other words, even though the strike might be banned by the parties' no-strike agreement, it could not be enjoined because it did not concern a matter that was grievable under the parties' arbitration clause.

Although four members of the Court, including Justice Brennan (who authored the majority opinion in *Boys Markets*), dissented in *Buffalo Forge*, the decision would appear to follow inexorably under the rigid *quid pro quo* analysis.[70] Justice Black surely would have agreed with the result reached by the majority in *Buffalo Forge*, but only because he believed that, under the Norris-LaGuardia Act, a federal court may never issue an injunction against a strike pursuant to a labor dispute.

Buffalo Forge also highlights the arguably failing wisdom of the Court's continued, and patently strained, reliance on the *quid*

---

68. Atleson, *supra* note 60, at 102. Although the validity of the Court's factual assumptions was not questioned by Justice Black, it has been pointed out that the inclusion of arbitration clauses in collective agreements had continued to *grow*, not decline, after *Sinclair*. *See id.*

69. 428 U.S. 397 (1976).

70. The dissent in *Buffalo Forge*, also relying on the *quid pro quo* analysis, argued that "the question [of] whether the sympathy strike violates the no-strike clause is an arbitrable issue. If the court had the benefit of an arbitrator's resolution of the issue in favor of the employer, it could enforce that decision just as it could require the parties to submit the issue to arbitration." *Buffalo Forge*, 428 U.S. at 426 (Stevens, J., dissenting).

pro quo thesis. Both the majority and dissenting opinions declare an allegiance to *quid pro quo*, and neither is terribly convincing. It has always seemed to me, for example, that the Court would feel compelled to order an employer to fulfill a contractual obligation to arbitrate even if the union had an *express* contractual right to strike over an arbitrable issue. This result would fly in the face of the *quid pro quo* thesis, but it would surely adhere to the pro-arbitration policies underlying the Court's judgments in *Lincoln Mills* and the *Steelworkers Trilogy*. If the Court had focused more on the specific contractual right at issue—the promise to arbitrate *or* the promise not to strike—and less on artificial notions of *quid pro quo*, the confusion seen in *Buffalo Forge* might have been avoided. For Justice Black, the issue would have been much more simple: he would have said that the Court should not have abandoned its position in *Sinclair* in the first place.

C. The Distortion of Traditional Contract Law

Although the *Sinclair/Boys Markets* opinions are probably his best known in the field of collective bargaining, Justice Black's powerful series of dissents in the arbitration area began with *Local 174, Teamsters v. Lucas Flour Co.*[71] In that case the Court held that, where the collective agreement provides that certain disputes shall be settled exclusively by grievance arbitration, a strike called as a result of a grievable dispute is a violation of the collective agreement, *even when the agreement does not contain a no-strike clause*. The Court reasoned that "a contrary view would be completely at odds with the basic policy of national labor legislation to promote the arbitral process as a substitute for economic warfare."[72]

Justice Black's response was direct and succinct; he found the decision of the majority in *Lucas Flour* to be a gross perversion of contract law:

> [T]he job of courts enforcing contracts [is] to give legal effect to what the contracting parties actually agree to do, not to what courts think they ought to do . . . . I have been unable to find any accepted principle of contract law—traditional or otherwise—that permits

---

71. 369 U.S. 95 (1962).
72. *Lucas Flour Co.*, 369 U.S. at 105.

> courts to change completely the nature of a contract by adding new promises that the parties themselves refused to make in order that the new court-made contract might better fit into whatever social, economic, or legal policies the courts believe to be so important that they should have been taken out of the realm of voluntary contract by the legislative body and furthered by compulsory legislation.[73]

Justice Black's literalist interpretation was clear: the Supreme Court could not decide to *imply* a no-strike clause in a collective agreement merely because the parties had agreed to arbitration.

In the absence of an explicit congressional command, the Court's action in *Lucas Flour* appeared to Justice Black to badly distort traditional contract law. The historic importance to unions of the right to strike made incredible the suggestion that a union would, "without knowing it, impliedly surrender[] the right to strike."[74]

> To say that the right to strike is inconsistent with the contractual duty to arbitrate sounds like a dull echo of the argument which used to be so popular that the right to strike was inconsistent with the contractual duty to work—an argument which frequently went so far as to say that strikes are inconsistent with both the common law and the Constitution.[75]

Moreover, section 7 of the NLRA granted employees the right to engage in concerted activity. The importance of one such activity—the strike—was also reflected in section 13 which stated: "[n]othing in this Act, except as specifically provided for herein, shall be construed so as either to interfere with or impede or diminish in any way the right to strike. . . ." The Court's action thus appeared to Justice Black to contravene an explicit congressional command.

Nor, speaking fairly, could one derive the majority's result from "traditional" contract law. Assuredly, Justice Black wrote, implied contractual promises may "sometimes be found where there are facts and circumstances sufficient to warrant the conclusion that such was the intention of the parties."[76] However, one may not impose or imply a contract term, especially one so signifi-

---

73. *Id.* at 108 (Black, J., dissenting).
74. *Id.* at 109 (Black, J., dissenting).
75. *Id.* (Black, J., dissenting).
76. *Id.* at 109-10 (Black, J., dissenting).

cant as a no-strike clause, without even "one scrap of evidence [of intent] in this record."[77]

Justice Black obviously could not fathom the erosion of traditional concepts of contract law to further a judicial *policy* in favor of arbitration. He did not reject absolutely the notion that a collective bargaining agreement was somehow a different animal from a regular contract. In fact, he implicitly recognized certain differences in his majority opinion in *Detroit & Toledo Shore Line Railroad Co. v. United Transportation Union*,[78] wherein he noted "[i]t would be virtually impossible to include all working conditions in a collective-bargaining agreement. Where a condition is satisfactorily tolerable to both sides, it is often omitted from the agreement . . . ."[79] Yet, this construct fell far short of characterizing collective agreements as constitutional documents inherent within which are the entire array of national labor policies which, in their turn, alter the proper interpretation of any given phrase in the contract.

In Justice Black's view, the employees' right to strike had *not* been contracted away in *Lucas Flour*; rather it had been outweighed, in the eyes of the Court, by another interest—namely, the pre-eminence of the arbitral process purportedly embedded in the LMRA. And here is the crux of Justice Black's objection, completely understandable given his jurisprudential framework: why should a plainly stated statutory protection created by Congress, that "took more than 50 years for unions to have written into federal legislation,"[80] be outweighed by a policy that *the Court* had imposed upon a second statute, namely the LMRA? In his eyes, the Court had impermissibly raised *its* national labor policy over that enacted by Congress and had, along the way, misused contract law and undermined sections 7 and 13 of the NLRA. By equating an agreement to arbitrate with an agreement not to strike, Black concluded, the Court had imposed an unbargained-for agreement upon parties. Although he agreed that "settlements by arbitration

---

77. *Id.* at 110 (Black, J., dissenting).

78. 396 U.S. 142 (1969).

79. *United Transp. Union*, 396 U.S. at 154-55. *See also* Conley v. Gibson, 355 U.S. 41, 46 (1957).

80. Local 174, Teamsters v. Lucas Flour Co., 369 U.S. 95, 109 (1962) (Black, J., dissenting).

are desirable,"[81] he believed that such a sentiment could not justify the imposition of contract terms on unwilling parties. This was particularly true when any such approach was "certainly contrary to the industrial and labor philosophy of the Taft-Hartley Act . . . that . . . was enacted on the view that the best way to bring about industrial peace was through voluntary, not compelled, labor agreements."[82]

Justice Black's opinion in *Lucas Flour* was premised upon his assumption that a collective agreement *was* a traditional bargain and should therefore be subject to the common law of contract. As will be fully developed in the following section, I am in disagreement with this fundamental assumption. Justice Black's view was, however, a logical outgrowth of his convictions that the Court was required to enforce the express statutory mandate of Congress and that a labor agreement was a typical contract. He felt that Congress had directly forbidden the Government to dictate the terms of the parties' collective agreement and had expressly protected the employees' right to strike, and that the Court had undermined these clearly articulated goals by ignoring traditional contract law and deciding that they were outweighed by the policy decision to promote arbitration—a choice which, if it could be found at all in the LMRA, was implicit, rather than express.

D. The Right to Judicial Process

1. *The required use of contractual dispute resolution machinery.*—Our federal labor laws seek to enhance worker interests and to promote industrial peace by fostering a system of employee organization and collective bargaining.[83] Inevitably then, the individual interests of members of the bargaining unit are occasionally sacrificed for the combined or collective interest.[84] One interest that has been limited is the ability of the individual to litigate his or her suit under the employment contract. Courts have required employees to utilize the contractual dispute resolution machinery—usually culminating in arbitration—in lieu of judicial

81. *Id.* at 110 (Black, J., dissenting).

82. *Id.* (Black, J., dissenting). *See also* H.K. Porter Co. v. NLRB, 397 U.S. 99, 103-04 (1970).

83. *See* 29 U.S.C. § 151 (1982).

84. *See* J.I. Case Co. v. NLRB, 321 U.S. 332 (1944).

process, and have allowed unions to retain exclusive control over their negotiated grievance machinery, subject to their duty of fair representation. I will argue below that, absent any overriding public law question, it is perfectly proper to require the parties to use their own grievance-arbitration machinery to resolve any contractual disputes; I also believe that the union, as a signatory to the contract and as the employees' bargaining agent, should be mostly free to determine how and when to process grievances under a collective agreement.

In my view, the subordination of the individual right to sue the employer is necessary to further the principles of collective bargaining embodied in the NLRA. Justice Black, however, was vehemently opposed to what he called "compulsory arbitration."[85] He felt that the right to litigate one's claims in court was somehow fundamental, possibly rising to a constitutional level, and was, at the very least, unlimited absent a congressional mandate to the contrary.

Justice Black was surely correct in observing that nowhere is it explicitly written in the NLRA that, when represented by a union, individual employees lose the right to sue their employer for a breach of the employment contract. The first definitive step towards the loss of this right was taken in *Republic Steel Corp. v. Maddox*,[86] in which the Court held that Charlie Maddox could not sue his employer for severance pay without first attempting to utilize a three-step grievance process laid out in the collective bargaining agreement.

Justice Black characterized the holding in *Republic Steel* as "revolutionary,"[87] a decision "to expand apparently without limit the kind of claims subject to compulsory arbitration."[88] As one might expect, he objected first and foremost because he felt that the decision was not true to congressional intent. As Justice Black interpreted *Lincoln Mills* and the *Steelworkers Trilogy*, the Court had merely "expressed its preference for arbitration when used to avoid industrial warfare by heading off violent clashes between

85. Local 174, Teamsters v. Lucas Flour Co., 369 U.S. 95, 110 (1962) (Black, J., dissenting).

86. 379 U.S. 650 (1965).

87. *Republic Steel Corp.*, 379 U.S. at 660 (Black, J., dissenting).

88. *Id.* (Black, J., dissenting).

powerful employers and powerful unions"[89] or to prevent "semi-public controversies, which are more in the nature of power struggles between giants than ordinary justiciable controversies involving individual laborers."[90] He did not read these cases as saying "that an ordinary laborer whose employer discharges him and then fails to pay his past-due wages or wage substitutes must, if the union's contract with the employer provides for arbitration of grievances, have the doors of the courts of his country shut in his face."[91] Bad enough, thought Justice Black, to defer to the *result* of arbitration; now the Court would find primary jurisdiction in that private forum.

The dissent in *Republic Steel* is particularly interesting because it provides the most complete explanation of Justice Black's jurisprudential and substantive reasons for mistrusting arbitration. In his eyes, the Court committed two egregious errors. First, the decision removed certain breach of contract claims from state court jurisdiction because the collective agreement called for compulsory arbitration and thereby deprived Charlie Maddox of a judicial hearing. Justice Black could not fathom this limitation on judicial review of individual contract claims:

> Employees are thus denied a judicial hearing and state courts have their ancient power to try simple breach-of-contract cases taken away from them—taken away, not by Congress, I think, but by this Court. Today's holding is in my judgment completely unprecedented, and is the brain-child of this Court's recent consistently expressed preference for arbitration over litigation in all types of cases and for accommodating the wishes of employers and unions in all things over the desires of individual workers.[92]

Here again we see Justice Black's consistent objections—that the national labor policy preferring arbitration is a construct of the Court,[93] not of Congress, and that it warps other explicit or well-established legal principles. Justice Black concluded: "I cannot and

89. *Id.* at 666 (Black, J., dissenting).
90. *Id.* at 663 (Black, J., dissenting).
91. *Id.* at 664 (Black, J., dissenting).
92. *Id.* at 662-63 (Black, J., dissenting) (footnote omitted).
93. Elsewhere in the opinion Justice Black stated sharply: "In thus deciding on its own, or deciding that Congress somehow has decided, to expand apparently without limit the kinds of claims subject to compulsory arbitration . . . the Court interprets federal law in a way that is revolutionary." *Id.* at 660 (Black, J., dissenting).

do not believe any law Congress has passed provides that when a man becomes a member of a labor union in this country he thereby has somehow surrendered his own freedom and liberty to conduct his own lawsuit for wages."[94]

Nor was Justice Black even certain that Congress "*constitutionally* could" "pass[] any law which justifies any inference at all that workers are barred from bringing and courts from deciding cases like [*Republic Steel*]."[95] He described the employee's breach of contract claim as implicating the "ancient, treasured right to judicial trial[] in [an] independent court[] according to due process of law." He then elevated this right to constitutional status:

> [T]he difference between my Brethren and me in this case is not simply one concerning this Court's function in interpreting or formulating laws. There is also apparently a vast difference between their philosophy and mine concerning litigation and the role of courts in our country . . . . It was in Magna Carta, the English Bill of Rights, and other such charters of liberty, that there originally was expressed in the English-speaking world a deep desire of people to be able to settle differences according to standard, well-known procedures in courts presided over by independent judges with jurors taken from the public. Because of these deep-seated desires, the right to sue and be sued in courts according to the "law of the land," known later as "due process of law," became recognized. That right was written into the Bill of Rights of our Constitution and in the constitutions of the States. Even if it be true, *which I do not concede*, that Congress could force a man in this country to have his ordinary lawsuit adjudicated not under due process of law, *i.e.*, without the constitutional safeguards of a court trial, I do not think that this Court should ever feel free to infer or imply that Congress has taken such a step until the words of the statute are written so clearly that no one who reads them can doubt.[96]

In Justice Black's view, the constitutional right to a trial had been displaced by what he disparagingly referred to as "the comparatively standardless process of arbitration"[97] and the " 'common law' of the plant."[98] The process, as he saw it, was deficient in many ways:

94. *Id.* at 670 (Black, J., dissenting).
95. *Id.* at 663 (Black, J., dissenting) (emphasis added).
96. *Id.* at 669-70 (emphasis added) (citation omitted).
97. *Id.* at 665 (Black, J., dissenting).
98. *Id.* at 667 (Black, J., dissenting).

> [It] carries no right to a jury trial as guaranteed by the Seventh Amendment; arbitrators need not be instructed in the law; they are not bound by rules of evidence; they need not give reasons for their awards; witnesses need not be sworn; the record of proceedings need not be complete; and judicial review . . . is extremely limited.[99]

Moreover, according to Justice Black, the Court's preference for arbitration demonstrated a lack of appreciation for the plight of the individual laborer and an excessive concern for the institutional interests at stake. The interests of both the employer and the union in a uniform and exclusive method for the orderly settlement of employee grievances, the enhancement of the union's prestige with employees, and the benefit to the employer "in having a complicated procedural system which dissatisfied employees are here compelled to follow, which ends up in binding arbitration and which relieves the employer of a lawsuit"[100] could not outweigh, in Justice Black's eyes, the individual's right to receive his unpaid wages. The majority opinion in *Republic Steel* stated that, until an injured employee attempts to use the contractual arbitration procedures and fails, "it cannot be said" that they are inadequate.[101] Justice Black's vintage response was clear: "I think it can be said . . . and I say it."[102]

Justice Black's literalist view of labor law often raised compelling arguments, but there is another side to the coin. In his determination to protect individual employees from institutional power, Justice Black may have refused to give full breadth to the statutory scheme for collective bargaining and its necessary implications. Although Justice Black rejected the notion, deference to the process and results of arbitration follows naturally from the decision to foster private, collectively-organized industrial relations. And the success of collective bargaining is inextricably tied to the preservation of the integrity of the parties' negotiated grievance-arbitration procedures. Thus, during Justice Black's tenure, a majority of the Supreme Court properly recognized that, with respect to the classical "economic" issues of collective bargaining,[103] judges should leave the parties to their contractual dispute resolu-

99. *Id.* at 664 (Black, J., dissenting).
100. *Id.* at 667 (Black, J., dissenting).
101. *Id.* at 653.
102. *Id.* at 668 (Black, J., dissenting).
103. *See* Fournelle v. NLRB, 670 F.2d 331, 340 (D.C. Cir. 1982).

tion machinery. This view prevailed over the objections of Justice Black because it was understood that judges will cause "harsh and unnecessary intrusions into the parties' private system of governance and dispute resolution"[104] when they undertake to decide the merits of such "economic" grievances.

Professor David Feller developed this theory in his aforementioned article on *A General Theory of the Collective Bargaining Agreement.*[105] His thesis is that, in the typical collective bargaining contract, a significant part of the bargain is the agreement that disputes between the signatories will be settled by the rules contained in the contract as interpreted by an arbitrator. If courts interject themselves and interpret the agreement, a crucial basis of the bargain is undermined.

Thus, a collective bargaining agreement is *not* a contract between the employer and each individual employee, the breach of which may be settled via a court suit by the employee. Instead, as Professor Feller argues, it is a set of rules that govern employer and employee conduct. Any remedy for violation of these rules must be supplied by the contract, and not by policies or laws external to the agreement. This view is in harmony with that put forward by another leading labor law scholar, Professor Theodore St. Antoine, in his paper on the arbitrator as "contract reader."[106] St. Antoine points out that, "[s]o long as [the arbitrator] is dealing with a matter duly submitted to him, . . . [he] is speaking for the parties, and his award *is* their contract."[107] When seen from this perspective, the arbitration process has the advantage of providing both the union and the employer with some predictability and control over the consequences of any contractual breach.

Under the Feller thesis, the bargain struck by the parties contemplates only enforcement of the collective agreement. Interpretation of this agreement by a court or a jury and the imposition of remedies created by external law are normally beyond the purview of the private contract and may be characterized as unjustified intrusions into the arbitration process. When the union and

104. Edwards, *supra* note 14, at 101.

105. Feller, *supra* note 28.

106. St. Antoine, *Judicial Review of Labor Arbitration Awards: A Second Look at Enterprise Wheel and Its Progeny*, in PROCEEDINGS OF THE 30TH ANNUAL MEETING, NATIONAL ACADEMY OF ARBITRATORS 29 (B. Dennis & G. Somers eds. 1978).

107. *Id.* at 35 (emphasis in original).

the employer sign a collective agreement, they decide what their respective rights are and routinely provide that disputes over those rights should be submitted to arbitration. Under these circumstances, courts do not abdicate their responsibilities when they defer to solutions reached by arbitrators; the parties have relieved the courts of any such responsibilities by the lawful terms of their private agreement. I believe that, so long as there

> are no overriding public law questions [implicated], it is perfectly appropriate to compel the parties to use their own grievance-arbitration machinery to resolve their contractual disputes.
>
> In short, waiver of individual rights under the NLRA [subject, of course, to the duty of fair representation] is totally consistent with the principles of *collective* bargaining, including majority rule and exclusive representation, that underlie the Act.[108]

Indeed, I think that experience has shown that mandatory use of the arbitral process effectuates the protection of more individual rights than would individual lawsuits.

2. *The proper scope of the union's duty of fair representation: extinguishing individuals' meritorious claims.*—The Supreme Court long ago recognized in *Steele v. Louisville & Nashville Railroad Co.*[109] and *Tunstall v. Brotherhood of Locomotive Firemen & Enginemen*[110] that "the congressional grant of power to a union to act as exclusive collective bargaining representative, with its corresponding reduction in the individual rights of the employees so represented, would raise grave constitutional problems if unions were free to exercise this power to further racial discrimination."[111] To avoid these problems, the Court construed our national labor laws to include an implicit duty of fair representation. Initially, the union's duty of fair representation was very narrowly conceived—limited closely to its constitutional roots. But, over time, the duty has been extended to cover cases involving claims other than just invidious discrimination. Under current law, an exclusive bargaining agent must fairly represent all employees in a bargaining unit, both in contract negotiations[112] and in the

108. Edwards, *supra* note 13, at 31 (emphasis in original). *See also* Metropolitan Edison Co. v. NLRB, 460 U.S. 693, 706-07 n.11 (1983).

109. 323 U.S. 192 (1944).

110. 323 U.S. 210 (1944).

111. Vaca v. Sipes, 386 U.S. 171, 182 (1967) (citing *Steele*, 323 U.S. at 198-99).

112. Ford Motor Co. v. Huffman, 345 U.S. 330 (1953).

enforcement and administration of the resulting collective agreement.[113] Thus,

> [u]nder this doctrine, the exclusive agent's statutory authority to represent all members of a designated unit includes a statutory obligation to serve the interests of all members without hostility or discrimination toward any, to exercise its discretion with complete good faith and honesty, and to avoid arbitrary conduct.[114]

The duty of fair representation is the compromise fashioned by the Supreme Court to deal with the reality of the inherent (and constant) tension between individual rights and majority rule in collective bargaining. With a union as the employees' bargaining agent, it is inescapable that many group decisions will disadvantage some individual members. Thus, the Court concluded that some checks must be placed on majority rule, but, at the same time, that the basic benefits of collective bargaining must be preserved.

Justice Black would surely argue that an individual employee should never be made to sacrifice arguable contract claims; I would maintain that, unless the contract says otherwise, the alleged rights under a collective bargaining agreement are not "individual" in nature and therefore no sacrifice is involved. Individuals retain their constitutional and statutory rights, such as those embodied in Title VII, but in all other instances the union satisfies its duty of fair representation to an individual employee when it acts in good faith in negotiating and administering the contract. Hence, the union properly retains exclusive control over the ultimate disposition of all individual employees' disputes with the employer, subject only to an extremely limited duty of fair representation. Justice Black, on the other hand, believed that a collective agreement, like any other employment contract, created contract rights enforceable by individuals in court. Under this theory, the union's choices after negotiation of an agreement would be tightly restricted, and any facially valid grievance claims would have to be pursued.

The first real suggestion by the Court that unions might possess exclusive control of employees' individual grievances appeared

113. Humphrey v. Moore, 375 U.S. 335 (1964).
114. *Vaca*, 386 U.S. at 177 (citing *Humphrey*, 375 U.S. at 342).

in *Smith v. Evening News Association.*[115] In that case, an employer had refused to permit union members to report to work during a strike by a second union while allowing nonunion employees to continue working regular hours. In dicta, the Court reserved the question of "whether an employee who has suffered the kind of damages here alleged arising from breach of a collective bargaining agreement can file a lawsuit for himself under § 301" or "must step aside for the union to prosecute his claim."[116] Justice Black responded strongly to the suggestion that any such limitation could be contemplated:

> I cannot believe that Congress intended by the National Labor Relations Act either as originally passed or as amended by § 301 to take away rights to sue which individuals have freely exercised in this country at least since the concept of due process of law became recognized as a guiding principle in our jurisprudence. And surely the Labor Act was not intended to relegate workers with lawsuits to the status of wards either of companies or of unions.[117]

Obviously, Justice Black seemed to believe that it would be equally oppressive and unfair for an individual employee to be a "ward" of a company or a union. I frankly think that this notion badly misconceives the ideal and the reality of collective bargaining.

In the years following his dissent in *Republic Steel*, Justice Black struggled to hold a small piece of high ground for individual employees aggrieved by the actions of their employers. In *Simmons v. Union News Co.*,[118] Justice Black dissented from the Court's refusal to grant certiorari in an unusual case. The petitioner was an employee at a restaurant lunch counter at which profits had slumped dramatically. Suspecting stealing of some sort, but without a concrete object of suspicion, the company and the union initially agreed to temporarily lay off the petitioner and four other employees, and thereafter agreed to permanently discharge the five workers when profits increased substantially during the period of their layoff. The petitioner sued her employer, claiming that she had been discharged without "just cause," but her action was dismissed when the appellate court determined that "just

115. 371 U.S. 195 (1962).
116. *Smith*, 371 U.S. at 204 (Black, J., dissenting).
117. *Id.* at 205 (Black, J., dissenting).
118. 382 U.S. 884 (1965), *denying cert. to* 341 F.2d 531 (6th Cir. 1965).

cause" under the collective agreement was whatever the union and the employer had jointly decided it was. This result flowed logically from the parties' joint, exclusive control of the grievance machinery.

In a written tone of restrained outrage, Justice Black asserted that even *Republic Steel* "purported to preserve the right of an employee to sue his employer if his union refused to press his grievances."[119] The union, he stated, has no "right to negotiate away alleged breaches of a contract claimed by individual employees."[120] In a passage which previews his dissent in *Vaca v. Sipes*, Justice Black reprimanded the Court:

> Although this Court has gone very far in some of its cases with reference to the power of a collective bargaining union to process the personal grievances of its members, it has not yet gone so far as to say that where there is a personal grievance for breach of a collective bargaining agreement, the employee can be deprived of an independent judicial determination of the claim by an agreement between the union and the employer that no breach exists. But this is exactly what was done to petitioner . . . .[121]

Fearful of the joint power of employers and unions, Justice Black felt that legal principles and a public forum were the last (and fast disappearing) bastion for the individual employee. In his usual, penetrating manner, the Justice aptly observed: "The sum total of what has been done here is to abandon the fine, old American ideal that guilt is personal."[122] This analysis was correct. However, what Justice Black had refused to accept was that, since the enactment of the NLRA, certain *rights* were no longer competely personal in the context of the employment relationship—rather, these rights, like worker strength, had their roots in the collectivity.

For Justice Black, the final step in the evolution of the duty of fair representation occurred in 1967 when the Court decided *Vaca v. Sipes*.[123] In that case, Benjamin Owens, a bargaining unit employee, sought to pursue a complaint under a contractual grievance

---

119. *Simmons*, 382 U.S. at 886 (Black, J., dissenting).

120. *Id.* at 887 (Black, J., dissenting).

121. *Id.* at 886 (Black, J., dissenting).

122. *Id.* at 888 (Black, J., dissenting). *See also* NLRB v. Indiana & Michigan Elec., 318 U.S. 9 (1943) "Under our government guilt is personal; it cannot, or at least should not, attaint the innocent . . . ." *Id.* at 31 (Black, J., dissenting).

123. 386 U.S. 171 (1967).

procedure. When the union refused to appeal the grievance or to seek binding arbitration under the contract, Owens filed suit against his union and a separate suit against his employer for breach of contract.[124] The Supreme Court held that, before employees can sue their employer under section 301 of the LMRA for breach of contract, they must not only prove that any contractual remedies were exhausted, but also must demonstrate that the attempt was frustrated by " 'arbitrary, discriminatory, or . . . bad faith' " conduct by the union.[125]

Justice Black *was* willing to concede that, when an employee's sole or fundamental complaint is against the *union*, a breach of the statutory duty of fair representation occurred only when arbitrary, discriminatory or bad faith conduct occurred. A union could make a good faith decision not to pursue a grievance and not incur any liability in making that choice. However, he vehemently asserted that the same standard should *not* apply to cut off an individual's lawsuit "where the employee's primary complaint was against his employer for breach of contract and where he only incidentally contended that the union's conduct prevented the adjudication, by either court or arbitrator, of the underlying grievance."[126] The Court's opinion made it clear that a union could quite legitimately, and without breaching its duty, make a good faith decision not to pursue a meritorious grievance and that the employee would have no recourse against either the union *or* the employer. This result was, in Justice Black's view, wholly unsupportable, because it created the possibility that the merits of a grievance might *never* be determined either by an arbitrator or a jury, and that a potentially guilty employer might be "allowed to hide behind, and [be] shielded by, the union's conduct."[127]

Justice Black's position was clear: "[A]n employee should be able to sue his employer for contract violation or, if arbitration must be preferred to lawsuits, the employee's union should have an absolute duty to exhaust contractual remedies in the employee's

---

124. Thus, the Court actually did not need to reach the question of whether Mr. Owens had a good claim against his employer in order to dismiss the action against the union in *Vaca*, but it seized the occasion nonetheless.

125. *Vaca*, 386 U.S. at 203-04 (Black, J., dissenting).

126. *Id.* at 207 (Black, J., dissenting).

127. *Id.* at 205 (Black, J., dissenting).

behalf."[128] His reasons were stated concisely: "I simply fail to see how it should make one iota of difference, as far as the 'unrelated breach of contract' by [the employer] is concerned, whether the union's conduct is wrongful or rightful."[129]

This conclusion follows inexorably from Justice Black's conception of the nature of the collective agreement. Although he conceded that the process of contract negotiation was collective, he treated the rights created thereby as individual contract rights, and did not believe that collective interests might exist in the context of an apparently individual struggle with an employer. Even less could he concede that these collective interests might outweigh those of an individual claim, however meritorious.

Justice Black correctly pointed out that the *Vaca* decision could not be ascribed to the Court's preference for arbitration because "arbitration [was] precisely what Owens sought and preferred."[130] However, the Court's decision in *Vaca* sprang from the same solicitude for the union's prestige and for peaceful institutional relationships between unions and employers that had brought forth its preference for and deference to arbitration. As Justice Black asserted, the "real reason" for the *Vaca* decision was that it " 'further[ed] the interest of the union as statutory agent.' "[131] Furthering the union's interest in *Vaca* was thought to further control by the employer and the union of the grievance process which, in turn, would nurture peaceful dispute resolution. Based on this same reasoning, the Court had developed its preference for arbitration.

In labor unions, as in many groups, there is the "need for coercion implicit in attempts to provide collective goods to large groups."[132] When a labor organization negotiates and administers the collective agreement, it often restricts its individual members' economic liberty in order to provide the group with collective goods. Even Justice Black did not dispute, and indeed endorsed, the union's right to decide finally any question involving a "dispute of general importance affecting all or many of the union's

---

128. Lewis, *supra* note 26, at 102.

129. *Vaca*, 386 U.S. at 205 (Black, J., dissenting).

130. *Id.* at 207 (Black, J., dissenting).

131. *Id.* at 209 (Black, J., dissenting).

132. M. Olson, The Logic of Collective Action: Public Goods and the Theory of Groups 71 (1965).

members."[133] In all other situations, however, in which group interests conflicted with those of an individual employee, it was evident that the Justice favored "a nearly absolute power in the individual to demand a forum—either court or arbitrator—to dispose of an individual grievance."[134] He dismissed the majority's concerns for the dispute resolution process, saying that he could find "no threat to peaceful labor relations or to the union's prestige" in such an arrangement. It is here that Justice Black and I differ, for I see a grave threat. I am convinced that this concept of absolute individual economic rights is, in fact, inconsistent with the scheme of the NLRA.

Section 9(a) of the NLRA provides that a bargaining representative designated by the majority of employees in an appropriate unit "shall be the exclusive representative of all the employees in such unit."[135] It is an unfair labor practice for any employer to refuse to bargain collectively with any such representative, and the union's right to bargain with the employer extends to both the negotiation and the administration of the agreement. By this statutory scheme, "Congress has seen fit to clothe the bargaining representative with powers comparable to those possessed by a legislative body both to create and restrict the rights of those whom it represents."[136]

The analogy of a union with a legislative body is an apt one. Where there is a majority vote for a union representative who is then presumed to act in the group's interest, the actions of that representative inevitably will restrain the interests of some individuals. But these restraints are not objectionable if they represent the choices of the majority, and if they are not contrary to overriding public law. Curiously, Justice Black fully accepted this principle with respect to legislative action: in such circumstances, duly elected legislators were free (within the bounds of the Bill of

133. Republic Steel Corp. v. Maddox, 379 U.S. 650, 664 (1965) (Black, J., dissenting).

134. Lewis, *supra* note 26, at 101.

135. I recognize that Professor Clyde Summers relies on a proviso to § 9(a) of the NLRA for statutory support of his individual rights theory, even in the face of contractual provisions placing control of the grievance process in the hands of the union. *See* Summers, *Individual Rights in Collective Agreements and Arbitration*, 37 N.Y.U. L. REV. 362 (1962). I am in accord with Professor Cox's contrary interpretation of § 9(a). *See* Cox, *supra* note 26, at 624. This debate is not important in the present context, however, because Justice Black did not found his individual rights theory on § 9(a).

136. Steele v. Louisville & Nashville R.R., 323 U.S. 192, 202 (1944).

Rights) to make *economic* choices for individual citizens. Justice Black did not believe that any individual was entirely free from coercion in his or her economic life. However, the Justice apparently did not draw a parallel between Congress and unions, even though his brethren on the Court had found that Congress had conferred upon unions the full power to exercise majority rule.

Justice Black was an ardent proponent of the New Deal and a harsh critic of the Supreme Court when its "nine old men" attempted to thwart the will of the majority on economic matters by striking down FDR's proposed legislation.[137] Yet, he objected to attainment by labor unions of certain types of coercive economic power over individuals. Justice Black had several bases for these objections. First, as he stated in *Republic Steel*, he was not sure that Congress constitutionally could restrict an individual employee's right to file a suit on the contract against his or her employer. This objection is subject to the same critique Black himself made against the "nine old men" of the New Deal era, and I will not belabor it here. Furthermore, it is very difficult to view an individual's right to sue on a private employment contract as somehow fundamental, especially when the individual is not even a signatory to the contract.

In fairness, it must be recalled that Justice Black's objections were also, in part, the product of his inability to perceive a congressional command that unions obtain such control over contractual grievance procedures. In my view, however, both the statute and the well-established policies that underlay its enactment logically implicated the restrictions on individual behavior so objectionable to Justice Black. In particular, I find persuasive the analysis of Professor Cox who observed that, prior to the passage of the NLRA, "[t]he law fell into disrepute in the world of labor relations because it failed to meet the needs of men," and that, therefore, "[t]he principles determining legal rights and duties under a collective bargaining agreement should not be imposed

---

137. In the economic legislation of the New Deal, many restrictions were imposed upon behavior of individuals, and Black firmly supported the right of the majority to do so. For example, in March 1937, Senator Black stated: "A bare majority of the members of the Supreme Court of the United States have been for a number of years assuming the right on their part to determine the reasonableness of state and federal laws. The Constitution never gave that majority any such power." Frank, *Hugo L. Black*, in III The Justices of the United States Supreme Court 1789-1969, Their Lives and Major Opinions 2330 (L. Friedman & F. Israel eds. 1969).

from above; they should be drawn out of the institutions of labor relations and shaped to their needs."[138]

As Professor Cox noted, there are powerful reasons for concluding that the union ought to control the dispute resolution process with the employer, up to and including the litigation decision. First, and most obviously, if the injury is to a collective interest, then the union is best qualified to prosecute the claim. Even when any identifiable individual has been injured, "the group interest is often involved to an equal degree."[139] Second, "[t]he group may be affected by the future implications of the ruling to an extent that far outweighs the individual claims to damages."[140] Both adjudication and litigation create rules for the future—rules made without the participation of the majority representative if the individual is permitted to go it alone. Third, union control of all grievances increases the probability of uniformity, both in the prosecution and outcome of grievance charges. Frivolous claims may be screened out. Fourth, union control may to some extent prevent the utilization of the grievance machinery as a battleground for inter- or intra-union rivalries. Dissidents may not employ the dispute resolution process to build prestige or to create friction without regard to the merits of their claims.

Finally, and most importantly, union control comports with our notion of the bargaining representative as a responsible legislative body:

> When the interests of several groups conflict, or future needs run contrary to present desires, or when the individual's claim endangers group interests, the union's function is to resolve the competition by reaching an accommodation or striking a balance. The process is political. It involves a melange of power, numerical strength, mutual aid, reason, prejudice, and emotion. Limits must be placed on the authority of the group, but within the zone of fairness and rationality this method of self-government probably works better than the edicts of any outside arbiter.[141]

Awarding to individual employees the absolute right to prosecute their claims ignores section 8(a)(5) of the NLRA and the policy interests described above. In that situation, the employee is

---

138. Cox, *supra* note 26, at 604-05.
139. *Id.* at 625.
140. *Id.*
141. *Id.* at 626-27 (footnote omitted).

left in the same economic isolation with the same implications that led to the original enactment of the NLRA. In my view, giving employees an unconditional right to sue allows a certain dangerous delusion to take root—that this right alone protects the individual employee. In fact, employees will be faced with an expensive lawsuit to obtain a small sum of money with many possible contingencies and with few risk-taking lawyers available to them. An individual rights theory serves only as a cosmetic for the plain reality of the situation—the economic strength and benefits secured by individual workers have been obtained through *collective* action.[142] Any pretense that the situation is otherwise undermines collective activity and, it is my belief, ultimately damages the welfare of individual workers.

I do not mean to sound like a spokesperson for organized labor. Although I do believe in collective bargaining, I recognize its limitations and can see certain glaring flaws in the union movement. However, I would leave it to union leaders to clean house and to chart new paths to overcome any perceived "crisis in unionism." Collective bargaining in the private sector has had an important place in American society, and will continue to determine individuals' economic rights in the workplace until Congress says otherwise.

III. Conclusion

There is an extraordinary earnestness, symmetry, power and persuasiveness in the labor law opinions of Justice Black. While, ultimately, I have disagreed with many of his principal tenets, I have been unable simply to dismiss Justice Black's views. Indeed, I have felt constantly pressed to reassess my own thinking as I have parsed the philosophical linings of Justice Black's opinions.

In his labor law opinions, as in all areas of his jurisprudence, Justice Black exhibited his profound concern for individual rights without which majority rule becomes simply another form of tyranny. He believed "not only that the focus of democracy should be kept on the individual but that the Constitution as a whole [was] designed to keep it there."[143]

---

142. *See* R. Freeman & J. Medoff, *supra* note 29.

143. Dilliard, *The Individual and the Bill of Absolute Rights*, in Hugo Black and the Supreme Court, *supra* note 8, at 129.

Justice Black's solicitude for individuals and his faith in the judicial process led him to the conclusion that individuals' rights were best served by unlimited access to judicial process. And although his position has not been accepted in the area of individual workers' economic claims, his view has been vindicated by the Supreme Court in employment cases where either employers or unions violate individual rights that implicate important public values. In an age dominated by collective interests, the jurisprudence of Justice Black acts as a constant signal of caution. As Professor Reich once observed about Justice Black: "[A]s a judge he has become like a figure from the Old Testament, who never ceases to warn and to affirm that all governments are instituted among men to secure to *individuals* their inalienable rights . . . ."[144]

144. Reich, *The Living Constitution and the Court's Role*, in HUGO BLACK AND THE SUPREME COURT, *supra* note 8, at 161 (emphasis added).

JUSTICE BLACK AND THE FIRST AMENDMENT

*Anthony Lewis**

No judge in our now nearly 200 years of constitutional history has been so closely identified with the First Amendment as Hugo Black. It was his passion for more than three decades on the Supreme Court. I remember talking with Justice Black at a time, in the 1960s, when the Court was under heavy political attack because of its decisions on legislative apportionment and the First Amendment. Justice Black had created in dissent, in 1946,[1] the idea that the Constitution commanded equality in representation and that judges could enforce that command—the idea that became the law in 1964 with *Reynolds v. Sims*,[2] the one man-one vote decision. Now Congress was threatening to overrule that decision. Justice Black thought the congressional critics might succeed in that effort, I found, but the possibility did not seem to trouble him greatly. What did concern him was the First Amendment cases and their critics. "I don't believe they'll ever touch the First Amendment," he said—with a fierceness that I thought reflected both commitment and anxiety.

I plan to talk today about Justice Black's contributions to freedom of speech and press. It is a subject so large that, of course, it can be touched only glancingly. There is a universe of Hugo Black's thought on free speech and a free press. And yet, there is a curiosity about it. In all that he wrote on those themes, Justice Black hardly ever spoke for a majority of the Supreme Court.[3] If you look for opinions of the Court in which he sounded his belief

---

* Columnist, New York Times; Lecturer on Law, Harvard Law School. B.A. 1948, Harvard University.

1. Colegrove v. Green, 328 U.S. 549, 566 (1946) (Black, J., dissenting).

2. 377 U.S. 533 (1964).

3. Justice Black wrote the majority opinion for the Court in only six cases dealing primarily with freedom of speech or press: United Mine Workers of Am., Dist. 12 v. Illinois State Bar Ass'n, 389 U.S. 217 (1967); Mills v. Alabama, 384 U.S. 214 (1966); Talley v. California, 362 U.S. 60 (1960); Lincoln Fed. Labor Union No. 19129 v. Northwestern Iron &

in freedom of expression, I believe you will find only one of fundamental significance. That opinion was in *Bridges v. California*,[4] decided in 1941 near the beginning of Justice Black's career on the bench.[5]

Only one early case—but what a case. *Bridges v. California* gives us an extraordinary insight into Hugo Black's view of free speech and how that view affected the Court and the country.

First, a brief reminder of the facts. The Court in *Bridges* actually decided two cases, which reversed convictions of the *Los Angeles Times* and of Harry Bridges, a union leader, for contempt of the California courts. In each case the alleged contempt consisted of a critical public comment, made outside the courtroom, about a matter pending before a judge. The *Los Angeles Times* was fined for publishing three editorials, the most objectionable of which was headed *Probation for Gorillas?* The editorial said a judge would make "a serious mistake" if he granted probation to two members of the Teamsters Union who had been convicted of assault; the community, it said, needed "the example of their assignment to the jute mill."[6] Mr. Bridges was fined for sending a telegram to the Secretary of Labor criticizing a California judge's decision in a lawsuit between Mr. Bridges' longshoremen's union and another union.[7]

Justice Black, writing for a majority of five,[8] set aside all of the contempt convictions. Out-of-court comments on pending cases were protected, he said, by the speech and press guarantees of the First Amendment, applied to the states by the Fourteenth Amendment. Such comments could be punished only if they presented a "clear and present danger" of distorting the administration of justice,[9] and these comments did not. The four dissenters, who joined an opinion written by Justice Frankfurter,[10] said the states should

---

Metal Co., 335 U.S. 525 (1949); Martin v. City of Struthers, 319 U.S. 141 (1943); Bridges v. California, 314 U.S. 252 (1941).

4. 314 U.S. 252 (1941).

5. Justice Black was nominated for the Supreme Court by President Roosevelt on August 12, 1937. He was confirmed by the Senate on August 17, 1937, and took his seat on October 4, 1937. *See* 302 U.S. iii n.3 (1937).

6. *Bridges*, 314 U.S. at 272 n.17.

7. *Id.* at 276-77 n.20.

8. Justice Black's opinion was joined by Justices Reed, Douglas, Murphy, and Jackson.

9. *Bridges*, 314 U.S. at 263.

10. *Id.* at 279 (Frankfurter, J., dissenting). Justice Frankfurter's dissent was joined by Chief Justice Stone, Justice Roberts, and Justice Byrnes.

be free to punish as contempt any out-of-court comment that had a tendency to interfere with a pending case. They agreed that two of the *Los Angeles Times* editorials were "not close threats to the judicial function."[11] But they said the state courts should have the power to punish those responsible for the publication of *Probation for Gorillas?* and the Bridges telegram.

In that bare account, the *Bridges* case probably does not seem very exciting. But for the members of the Supreme Court at the time, it was a matter of intense passion. The case was argued twice, in October of 1940 and again a year later. The feelings that were engaged are obvious from the very first sentence of Justice Frankfurter's dissenting opinion: "Our whole history repels the view that it is an exercise of one of the civil liberties secured by the Bill of Rights for a leader of a large following or for a powerful metropolitan newspaper to attempt to overawe a judge in a matter immediately pending before him."[12] Those feelings were on display in the courtroom when the *Bridges* opinions were announced on December 8, 1941, the day after the attack on Pearl Harbor. Justice Frankfurter kept in his files a note that one of his fellow dissenters, Justice Byrnes, sent him after Frankfurter had orally summarized his opinion. The note is with the Felix Frankfurter Papers in the Harvard Law School Library. Justice Byrnes wrote: "What you have just done justifies continuance of the practice of announcing decisions. If you suffered in its delivery, you can be assured its delivery caused suffering to those who differed with you."[13]

Justice Black's file of material on the *Bridges* case is in his papers in the Library of Congress. There, and in the Frankfurter papers, one learns a surprising fact. Justice Frankfurter first had a majority with him in *Bridges*. He circulated a draft opinion of the Court. Justice Black circulated a dissent. From those drafts we can begin to sense why they cared so deeply about the *Bridges* case and why *Bridges* still matters.

After stating the facts in his draft opinion of the Court, Justice Frankfurter turned to history. The power of judges to punish comment on their work as contempt is, he said,

---

11. *Id.* at 298 (Frankfurter, J., dissenting).

12. *Id.* at 279 (Frankfurter, J., dissenting).

13. Note from Justice Byrnes to Justice Frankfurter (Dec. 8, 1941) (in the Felix Frankfurter Papers, Harvard Law School Library [hereinafter Frankfurter Papers]).

> deeply rooted in history. It is part and parcel of the Anglo-American system of administering justice .... It is believed that all the judicatures of the English-speaking world, including the courts of the United States and of the forty-eight states, have from time to time recognized and exercised the power ....[14]

Justice Black read history differently. In his draft dissent he said,

> the first and perhaps the basic fallacy of the Court's opinion is the assumption that the vitalizing liberties of the First Amendment can be abridged ... by reference to English judicial practice, either current, recent or remote .... In my judgment, to measure the scope of the liberties guaranteed by the First Amendment by the limitations that exist or have existed throughout the English-speaking world is to obtain a result directly opposite to that which the framers of the Amendment intended .... Perhaps no single purpose emerges more clearly from the history of our Constitution and Bill of Rights than that of giving far more security to the people of the United States with respect to freedom of religion, conscience, expression, assembly, petition and press than the people of Great Britain had ever enjoyed .... The First Amendment is proof conclusive that the framers of our government were well aware of the suppression of conscience and expression that had been indulged in abroad, both in England and elsewhere, and intended by the First Amendment to see that they did not happen here.[15]

Those opposing views of history survive in the two published opinions, edited but no less strong. Justice Frankfurter's dissent puts it that "the power exerted by the courts of California is deeply rooted in the system of administering justice evolved by liberty-loving English-speaking peoples."[16] Justice Black's opinion of the Court says: "No purpose in ratifying the Bill of Rights was clearer than that of securing for the people of the United States much greater freedom of religion, expression, assembly, and petition than the people of Great Britain had ever enjoyed."[17]

In that disagreement about the meaning of history we can see something more profound: a conflict over the nature of the First

14. Frankfurter, Draft Opinion in *Bridges* (in the Frankfurter Papers).

15. Black, Draft Dissent in *Bridges* (in the Hugo Black Papers, Library of Congress [hereinafter Black Papers]).

16. *Bridges*, 314 U.S. at 284 (Frankfurter, J., dissenting).

17. *Id.* at 265.

Amendment. Justice Frankfurter saw the Amendment, as he saw much of the Constitution—as a natural development of English traditions, a part of a continuum. Justice Black saw the First Amendment as something very new and distinctively American. Benno Schmidt strikingly summed it up by saying that Justice Black's opinion in the *Bridges* case was "a judicial Declaration of Independence for the First Amendment, freeing it from English law."[18]

That was evidently so on the particular issue of the right to comment on pending litigation—the issue of fair trial and free press as we have come to call it. The *Bridges* case put American law on that subject on a very different basis. So it remains, for in England it is still contempt for a newspaper to print anything except the most anodyne stuff about a pending criminal case, while in this country no Supreme Court decision since *Bridges* has found the "clear and present danger" of prejudicing the judicial process required to justify punishment of out-of-court comments. The particular issue no doubt agitated Justice Frankfurter, who worried all his life about "trial by newspapers." But he must have cared so deeply about *Bridges* because he also understood that Justice Black's opinion signaled a basic shift in attitudes toward freedom of expression; he understood that it was a declaration of independence from English law.

In Benno Schmidt's view,[19] *Bridges* was one of three such declarations by the Supreme Court. The first, in 1931, was the decision in *Near v. Minnesota*,[20] establishing a First Amendment presumption against the validity of any prior restraint of the press. Chief Justice Hughes, writing for a five-to-four majority,[21] relied on Blackstone's statement that English law disfavored "previous restraints."[22] But Blackstone meant by that phrase something very different from the court injunctions that were at issue in the *Near* case; he meant administrative censorship of the kind practiced in Tudor and Stuart times, when nothing could be printed without the approval of an official licenser. Under the guise of continuity

18. B. Schmidt, Remarks at the University of Arizona (unpublished).

19. *Id.*

20. 283 U.S. 697 (1931).

21. Chief Justice Hughes was joined by Justices Holmes, Brandeis, Stone, and Roberts. Justices Van Devanter, McReynolds, and Sutherland dissented with Justice Butler.

22. *Near*, 283 U.S. at 713 (quoting 4 W. BLACKSTONE, COMMENTARIES *151).

Hughes liberated American expression from a much more confining English tradition. Again, we can still see the results: judges in England today enjoin the publication of articles and books claimed to be libelous and even restrict the showing of television programs that might violate commercial confidences[23]—actions unthinkable in American courts.

What *Near* did to free our law of prior restraints from English tradition, and *Bridges* our law of contempt, the 1964 decision in *New York Times Co. v. Sullivan*[24] did for libel. Justice Brennan found in a regretted episode of American history—the Sedition Act of 1798[25]—evidence that our Constitution outlawed the old English practice of punishing critical comment on public officials even when the criticism was false. The controversy over the Sedition Act, Justice Brennan said, "first crystallized a national awareness of the central meaning of the First Amendment"[26]—namely, the American people's right, as Madison put it, "of freely examining public characters and measures."[27] The *Sullivan* opinion relied on *Bridges* in reasoning that officials, like judges, must be strong enough to bear criticism.[28] I think it is plain that Justice Black's opinion laid an essential foundation for the *Sullivan* case and its great advance in freedom of expression.

There is another crucial way in which *Near*, *Bridges*, and *Sullivan* are linked. The earlier Supreme Court cases on freedom of speech—the decisions after World War I in which Holmes and Brandeis often disagreed with the majority[29]—focused on the harm that speech could do. The issue between the majority and the dissenters was how serious and imminent the prospective harm had to be before an authority could step in and punish the speech. Justice Black viewed free speech in terms not of the harm but of the good it could do. "[I]t is a prized American privilege to speak one's

---

23. *See, e.g.*, British Steel Corp. v. Granada Television Ltd. [1981] 1 All E.R. 417.

24. 376 U.S. 254 (1964).

25. Ch. 74, 1 Stat. 596 (1798). Congress allowed this Act to lapse in 1801 according to its own provision.

26. *Sullivan*, 376 U.S. at 273.

27. Virginia Resolutions of 1798, *reprinted in* 4 Elliot's Debates on the Federal Constitution 554-55 (J. Elliot 2d ed. 1836). James Madison was the author of the Virginia Resolutions of 1798.

28. *Sullivan*, 376 U.S. at 273.

29. *E.g.*, Whitney v. California, 274 U.S. 357, 372 (1927) (Brandeis, J., concurring); Schaefer v. United States, 251 U.S. 466, 482 (1920) (Brandeis, J., dissenting); Abrams v. United States, 250 U.S. 616, 624 (1919) (Holmes, J., dissenting).

mind," he said in his published opinion in *Bridges*, "although not always with perfect good taste, on all public institutions."[30] He added that "an enforced silence" in comment on judges "would probably engender resentment, suspicion, and contempt much more than it would enhance respect."[31]

Similarly in *Near*, a case in which a newspaper devoted to attacking city officials as corrupt had been enjoined as scandalous and malicious, Chief Justice Hughes found affirmative reasons for a free press. The growth of crime and official malfeasance, he said, "emphasizes the primary need of a vigilant and courageous press."[32] And then, in *Sullivan*, Justice Brennan spoke of our "profound national commitment to the principle that debate on public issues should be uninhibited, robust, and wide-open, and that it may well include vehement, caustic, and sometimes unpleasantly sharp attacks on government and public officials."[33] All three decisions, then, took a positive view of the value of free speech—a very American, populist view. There is a passage in Justice Black's draft dissent in *Bridges*, one that does not appear in the published opinion, that makes even clearer the distinctively American and populist attitude underlying his commitment to free speech. It is the very opening of the draft:

> First in the catalogue of human liberties essential to the life and growth of a government of, for, and by the people are those liberties written into the First Amendment to our Constitution. They are the pillars upon which popular government rests and without which a government of free men cannot survive.[34]

How did Justice Black's dissenting position in *Bridges* become the opinion of the Court? Justice Frankfurter's papers tell us the answer. After the case was first argued, on October 18 and 21, 1940, the Court voted six-to-three to affirm the contempt convictions of Harry Bridges and, on the one editorial, the *Los Angeles Times*. In the majority were Chief Justice Hughes and Justices McReynolds, Stone, Roberts, Frankfurter, and Murphy. The dissenters were Black, Reed, and Douglas. On February 1, 1941,

30. Bridges v. California, 314 U.S. 252. 270 (1941) (footnote omitted).
31. *Id.* at 270-71.
32. Near v. Minnesota, 283 U.S. 697, 720 (1931).
33. New York Times Co. v. Sullivan, 376 U.S. 254, 270 (1964).
34. Black, Draft Dissent in *Bridges* (in the Black Papers).

Justice McReynolds retired. That left a five-to-three majority for affirmance. Justice Frankfurter circulated his draft opinion of the Court. His files show notes of agreement from several justices. On May 30, Stone wrote him: "I am happy to join in your opinion in the *Contempt Cases*, and only hope that it will go down. I am bound to say, however, that this is more hope than expectation."[35] And then there is a letter, undated, from Justice Murphy. It says: "The still-new robe never hangs heavier than when my conscience confronts me. Months of reflection and study compel me to give it voice. And so I have advised the Chief Justice and Justice Black that my vote in Numbers 19 and 64 must be in reversal."[36] The Court was now divided four-to-four in the contempt cases, and they were put over for reargument. At the end of the term, Chief Justice Hughes retired, leaving only three votes to affirm the contempt convictions. The two new members who took their seats in October divided on *Bridges*. Justice Byrnes made a fourth vote for affirmance, and Justice Jackson cast a fifth for reversal. Justice Black had his majority.

A curious footnote can be added. Justice Reed, when he responded to the Frankfurter draft, wrote: "Beautifully done. I agree with it all except the conclusion. My dogmatism makes me say your dogmatism is right as to two [contempt convictions] and wrong as to the others. Too bad that we are required to express our literary preferences on editorials or telegraphs 3000 miles from the scene."[37] Justice Frankfurter replied:

> Thank you very much, dear Stanley, for your characteristic generosity. Apparently that which is fundamental with me is of no moment to you, namely, that striking down state action by declaring it UNconstitutional entails a wholly different quality of judgment from that involved in letting state action prevail. To describe the denial of power that this decision denies to the states of the union as an expression of "our literary preferences" . . . is, I am bound to say, a delightful euphemism. If it is merely a difference of "literary prefer-

35. Letter from Justice Stone to Justice Frankfurter (May 30, 1941) (in the Frankfurter Papers).

36. Letter from Justice Murphy to Justice Frankfurter (1941) (in the Frankfurter Papers).

37. Note from Justice Reed to Justice Frankfurter (1941) (in the Frankfurter Papers).

> ences" then by all the canons of constitutional adjudications we ought to stay our hands.[38]

That reply to Justice Reed—testy, I think it is fair to call it—shows how much was at stake for Justice Frankfurter in the case. Even more dramatic evidence of his feelings, and more surprising, is a note that he wrote on the face of one copy of his draft opinion of the Court. It reads as follows:

> According to my custom in sending Brandeis all my draft opinions *after* he retired—circulating to him as to the sitting justices—I sent this to him. When shortly thereafter I saw him he said[,] "That's a very fine opinion of yours. I assume that you have a unanimous Court." "Certainly not," I replied & told him that I may not have even a majority & that Black was writing. To which he said "Black & Co. are going mad."[39]

I should not leave unquestioned any assumption that Justice Brandeis would in the end have disagreed with the Black view in *Bridges* if he had still been on the Court. No doubt fair trial was an important value for him, and he might well have been reluctant to limit the power of judges to punish comments threatening that fairness. But it is also true that Louis Brandeis considered freedom of speech a positive good, and he made the case for that belief with compelling eloquence. "Those who won our independence," he said in his concurring opinion in *Whitney v. California*,[40]

> believed that freedom to think as you will and to speak as you think are means indispensable to the discovery and spread of political truth. . . . [T]hey knew that order cannot be secured merely through fear of punishment for its infraction; that it is hazardous to discourage thought, hope and imagination; that fear breeds repression; that repression breeds hate; that hate menaces stable government; that the path of safety lies in the opportunity to discuss freely supposed grievances and proposed remedies . . . .[41]

Those were also Hugo Black's beliefs.

---

38. Letter from Justice Frankfurter to Justice Reed (Dec. 2, 1941) (in the Frankfurter Papers) (emphasis in original).

39. Note by Justice Frankfurter on Frankfurter, Draft Opinion in *Bridges* (1941) (in the Frankfurter Papers) (emphasis in original).

40. 274 U.S. 357 (1927).

41. *Whitney*, 274 U.S. at 375 (Brandeis, J., concurring).

That files from Justice Black's years on the Supreme Court are in the manuscript collection of the Library of Congress may surprise some of you. It surprised me. I had read the affecting book by Hugo Black, Jr., *My Father: A Remembrance*,[42] and was gripped by his account of the burning of certain of Justice Black's papers at Black's insistence near the end of Black's life.[43] I assumed that all his Court papers were destroyed. That is not so. Those that went were Justice Black's notes of what was said at the conferences of the Court, or so I now believe. Case files including preliminary drafts of opinions remain. And there are letters—thousands of them. Reading here and there in those files taught me much about a man I thought I knew, and I want to share a few of my impressions.

First, he made clear in his own letters why he was determined to destroy his conference notes. As early as 1956, he wrote Professor Edmond Cahn of the New York University Law School that he had never thought

> the diaries or memoranda of public men containing their contemporary personal impressions could be anything but one-sided. . . . All of us know that incidents that may loom high at the time they occur are frequently forgotten in a very short time because of their triviality. Then, too, one-sided writings leave wrong impressions when published long after they are jotted down. I am inclined to think that public officials can be better judged by their public utterances than by their private correspondence, memoranda, and diaries.[44]

Those inclinations were evidently confirmed for him by an episode that took place in 1970. On April 22 of that year, S. Sidney Ulmer, professor of political science at the University of Kentucky, wrote Justice Black[45] asking permission to quote a note found in the Burton papers that Black had written to Justice Burton. Over the next six months the Justice and Professor Ulmer exchanged nearly twenty letters. It is a fascinating correspondence, at times bristling, at other times hilarious.

---

42. H. Black, Jr., My Father: A Remembrance (1975).
43. *Id.* at 250-52, 254-55.
44. Letter from Justice Black to Professor Edmond Cahn (Nov. 1, 1956) (in the Black Papers).
45. Letter from Professor S. Sidney Ulmer to Justice Black (Apr. 22, 1970) (in the Black Papers).

Justice Black said he would prefer not to have his note to Burton published.[46] Professor Ulmer replied that scholars have an obligation to understand the inner workings of the Supreme Court. He added: "You may care to know that I am preparing a paper on 'The Longitudinal Behavior of Hugo LaFayette Black and Environmental Change' for presentation at the annual meeting of the American Political Science Association."[47] Justice Black, still regretting intrusions into the Court's privacy, nevertheless withdrew his objection to the use of his letter to Justice Burton. He added: "I wish you success in your article on 'The Longitudinal . . . .' "[48] Professor Ulmer sent him the paper, complete with a graph headed "Linear and Quadratic Regression of Time on Hugo L. Black's Votes in Civil Liberty Cases 1937-1967."[49] Justice Black commented: "I must admit your title is an enigmatic one for me because I am not too familiar with the system of measuring opinions or other writings by the longitudinal test. At any rate, I am sure your address represents your honest views."[50]

The correspondence then took a serious turn. Professor Ulmer sent the Justice a paper on the School Desegregation Cases[51] that he was to deliver in November of 1970 at a meeting of the Southern Political Science Association.[52] On the basis of Justice Burton's elliptical conference notes, the paper said that Justice Black had told his colleagues he was opposed to segregation, but if a majority voted to uphold its constitutionality, he would agree.[53] After an ambiguous exchange, Justice Black wrote Professor Ulmer: "[I]f you are saying that under any circumstances I would have voted to

46. Letter from Justice Black to Professor Ulmer (May 4, 1970) (in the Black Papers).

47. Letter from Professor Ulmer to Justice Black (May 7, 1970) (in the Black Papers).

48. Letter from Justice Black to Professor Ulmer (May 15, 1970) (in the Black Papers).

49. Letter from Professor Ulmer to Justice Black (June 19, 1970) (in the Black Papers).

50. Letter from Justice Black to Professor Ulmer (July 15, 1970) (in the Black Papers).

51. Brown v. Board of Educ., 349 U.S. 294 (1955); Bolling v. Sharpe, 347 U.S. 497 (1954); Brown v. Board of Educ., 347 U.S. 483 (1954).

52. Letter from Professor Ulmer to Justice Black (July 24, 1970) (in the Black Papers).

53. *See* Letter from Justice Black to Professor Ulmer (Aug. 7, 1970) (in the Black Papers).

continue to hold that segregation was constitutional then your statement is not correct."[54]

Returning to the question of scholars examining the inner workings of the Court, Professor Ulmer quoted Karl Llewellyn as saying that judges had made a fetish of secrecy.[55] To this Justice Black replied:

> I knew the late Karl Llewellyn very well and agreed with much of what he wrote. But if he meant by the remarks you quoted that the Court's conferences should be held out in the open before radio or television, I disagree with him. . . . I hope you will understand fully from this letter that there is no earthly reason why you and I should think less of one another because we happen to disagree. Disagreements are the life of progress.[56]

The amazing thing is that Justice Black really lived by that standard. Most of us are thinner skinned than we like to admit. Much as we may believe in free speech as a principle, we are not comfortable with criticism and sharp disagreement. Justice Black was, or so one would have to conclude from looking at his letters. Again and again, he showed an ability to keep disagreement from becoming personal dislike or resentment.

In 1963, for example, he received a letter from Dean Erwin N. Griswold of the Harvard Law School. It said: "Dear Justice Black, [w]ith trepidation, and with great respect, I am sending you herewith a copy of the Leary Lecture which I am giving in Salt Lake City on Wednesday evening, February 27th."[57] It was a lecture attacking Justice Black's constitutional views. The Justice replied:

> There was no reason at all for you to feel "trepidation" in sending me a copy of the lecture which you gave . . . on February 27th. Perhaps that was a very appropriate time for you to give a lecture about my philosophy since it happened to be my birthday. As you can guess, I disagree with most of the constitutional principles you advocated in your lecture. As a matter of fact, I am of the opinion that you could not possibly think my constitutional philosophy is any more dangerous than I think is the constitutional philosophy you

---

54. Letter from Justice Black to Professor Ulmer (Sept. 8, 1970) (in the Black Papers).

55. Letter from Professor Ulmer to Justice Black (Oct. 15, 1970) (in the Black Papers).

56. Letter from Justice Black to Professor Ulmer (Oct. 22, 1970) (in the Black Papers).

57. Letter from Dean Griswold to Justice Black (Feb. 27, 1963) (in the Black Papers).

> expressed in the lecture. Nevertheless, as I wrote John Frank today, my admiration for you—and my respect for your sturdy integrity—are such that I am compelled to admit that your championship of your views causes me to hope that maybe they are not as dangerous as I still believe they are.[58]

When I read that, I thought I would look at the letter to John Frank to which the Justice referred. Could he really have been so generous about Dean Griswold? He could. He told John Frank: "While I disagree with most of the things he said, not one word he said caused me to feel any less respect or regard for him as a citizen and as a champion of that which he believes to be right."[59]

There was a serenity in Justice Black that comes through in his correspondence. I do not mean he was angelic—far from it. He was in the battle, not above it. As a judge, and as a politician before that, he was a tenacious fighter. But he retained his composure under attacks that would have left most of us embittered.

In 1938, during his first term on the Court, Marquis Childs published an article in *Harper's* magazine saying that Justice Black had "shocked his colleagues" by "blunders" resulting from his "lack of legal knowledge" and his "deficiencies in background and training."[60] The article caused a great stir. Years later Childs sent the Justice some pieces of his with a letter including this gracious apology: "A long time ago, for a variety of reasons, including my own lack of knowledge and experience, I did you a great disservice and I have had cause often since to regret this . . . ."[61] Justice Black replied:

> First let me say that I am not at all sure you ever did me any "great disservice." Even if you had, your letter . . . would be nonetheless welcome. I have never believed that a man's decisions in matters of public importance should be influenced to any extent whatever by personal feelings about individuals.[62]

Justice Black was an unflagging advocate of freedom of the press even though his own experience with the press was not always happy. That is an understatement. After he was nominated

58. Letter from Justice Black to Dean Griswold (Mar. 13, 1963) (in the Black Papers).
59. Letter from Justice Black to John Frank (Mar. 12, 1963) (in the Black Papers).
60. Childs, *The Supreme Court Today*, 176 HARPER'S 581, 582 (1938).
61. Letter from Marquis Childs to Justice Black (Jan. 30, 1961) (in the Black Papers).
62. Letter from Justice Black to Marquis Childs (Feb. 21, 1961) (in the Black Papers).

and confirmed as a member of the Court, the *Pittsburgh Post-Gazette* published a series of articles stating that Justice Black had been a member of the Ku Klux Klan and had concealed that fact.[63] We know that as a matter of history, but few of us can remember or imagine the virulence of the attacks that were made on Hugo Black by the press then. The *New York Herald-Tribune* called him "a humbug and a coward."[64] A *Washington Times* editorial was headed, "Mr. Justice Faustus."[65] The *Washington Post* said "the elevation of a Klan intimate to the Supreme Court" was "humiliating and degrading."[66] A *New York Times* editorial ended with this sentence: "At every session of the court the presence on the bench of a justice who has worn the white robe of the Ku Klux Klan will stand as a living symbol of the fact that here the cause of liberalism was unwittingly betrayed."[67]

Justice Black did not forget those words. He once mentioned that *New York Times* editorial to me. I think he was indicating that association with the *Times* did not start me out with a claim on his affections! To add another personal note, I found in his files in the Library of Congress a copy of a magazine article I wrote about the Court. Justice Black had scribbled comments all around the margins, and they were not compliments. Looking back at the piece, I am chagrined to see how certain I was about uncertainties, how knowing about things I really did not know. But none of that, or the far deeper reasons he had for irritation at newspaper writers, moved him an inch from his belief in freedom of the press. I suppose he might have agreed with a letter of Thomas Jefferson's that he quoted in his *Bridges* opinion. Jefferson said:

> I deplore . . . the putrid state into which our newspapers have passed, and the malignity, the vulgarity, and mendacious spirit of those who write them. . . . These ordures are rapidly depraving the public taste.
>
> It is however an evil for which there is no remedy, our liberty depends on the freedom of the press, and that cannot be limited without being lost.[68]

---

63. Pittsburgh Post Gazette, Sept. 13, 1937.
64. *A Humbug and a Coward*, N.Y. Herald Tribune, Oct. 2, 1937.
65. *Mr. Justice Faustus*, Wash. Times, Sept. 23, 1937.
66. *Fake Liberalism*, Wash. Post, Sept. 16, 1937.
67. *Mr. Black's Reply*, N.Y. Times, Sept. 23, 1937.
68. Bridges v. California, 314 U.S. 252, 270 n.16 (1941).

In other ways Justice Black put principle ahead of personal feelings. He was an intensely private man, but he dissented when a majority of his colleagues found protections of privacy in the Constitution.[69] And he defended *Life Magazine*'s right to publish an intrusive and fictionalized story about James Hill that he would have resented as much as Mr. Hill.[70] He voted to allow the showing of any movie and the publication of any book despite charges of obscenity,[71] though he was old-fashioned about those things himself. Elizabeth Black, in her new book,[72] has a diary item of July 27, 1966, saying: "Jojo and I went to the matinee of Liz Taylor and Richard Burton in *Who's Afraid of Virginia Woolf?*, which Hugo refused to see because he heard it was filthy."[73]

Paul Freund said of Justice Black that he was "without doubt the most influential of the many strong figures"[74] who sat on the Supreme Court during his decades there. That statement is certainly true of his influence on First Amendment issues. He changed forever the way the Court and all of us think about freedom of speech and freedom of the press.

And yet, as I said at the start,[75] there is the curious fact that he wrote very few majority opinions sustaining claims of freedom of expression. When the Court moved in his direction, as it did in many cases, he was not given, or did not take, the opportunity to write his former dissenting views into law—as he did on the right to counsel in the *Gideon*[76] case, vindicating his dissent of 20 years earlier in *Betts v. Brady*.[77]

The fact is that Justice Black's oft-proclaimed belief in First Amendment absolutes never commended itself to a majority of his colleagues. So when the Court took a more libertarian view on, for example, the rights of the Communist Party and its members, the opinion was written by a justice who could hold a majority to-

---

69. *See, e.g.*, Griswold v. Connecticut, 381 U.S. 479, 507 (1965) (Black, J., dissenting).

70. Time, Inc. v. Hill, 385 U.S. 374, 398 (1967) (Black, J., concurring).

71. *See, e.g.*, Mishkin v. New York, 383 U.S. 502, 515 (1966) (Black, J., dissenting); Ginzburg v. United States, 383 U.S. 463, 476 (1966) (Black, J., dissenting).

72. E. Black, Mr. Justice and Mrs. Black (1986).

73. *Id.* at 148.

74. P. Freund, On Law and Justice 222 (1968).

75. *See supra* note 3 and accompanying text.

76. Gideon v. Wainwright, 372 U.S. 335 (1963).

77. 316 U.S. 455, 474 (1942) (Black, J., dissenting).

gether by taking a less doctrinaire approach.[78] But Justice Black's influence was there nonetheless, from *Bridges* near the beginning to the Pentagon Papers case[79] at the end. Even when Justice Black objected in a concurring opinion that the Court had not gone far enough, it often had gone a considerable distance toward his polestar. He was generous enough to say as much to the author of what I think was the most important opinion of the Court on freedom of expression after *Bridges*: *New York Times Co. v. Sullivan*.[80] On February 26, 1964, shortly before *Sullivan* was decided, Justice Black circulated a draft of his concurring opinion. He also sent a note to Justice Brennan saying: "You know of course that despite my position and what I write, I think you are doing a wonderful job in the *Times* case and however it finally comes out it is bound to be a very long step toward preserving the right to communicate ideas."[81]

His dissenting opinions also performed a vital function in keeping the hope of free expression alive in hard times. What Justice Black did in those dissents was to pierce all the rationalizations about the Communist threat and remind us of what was really going on. Thus, in *Dennis v. United States*[82] in 1951, the Court sustained the conviction of Communist Party leaders for conspiring to teach and advocate the overthrow of the Government by force. The majority opinion by Chief Justice Vinson might have led the uninformed person to believe that a group of men heading a powerful movement were about to overthrow our system, when, of course, the defendants were a ragtag group who had never attracted significant support in America and had never threatened anyone. Justice Black said in his dissent that he wanted to emphasize at the outset

---

78. *Compare* the opinion of the Court by Justice Goldberg in Gibson v. Florida Legislative Investigation Comm., 372 U.S. 539 (1963) *with* Justice Black's concurrence in that case, *id.* at 558.

79. New York Times Co. v. United States, 403 U.S. 713, 714 (1971) (Black, J., concurring).

80. 376 U.S. 254 (1964).

81. *See* B. Schwartz, Super Chief: Earl Warren and His Supreme Court—A Judicial Biography 534 (1983). Justice Brennan replied: "Hugo, [t]hat . . . means as much to me as if you formally joined the opinion—I'm most grateful." Note from Justice Brennan to Justice Black (undated) (in the Black Papers).

82. 341 U.S. 494 (1951).

> what the crime involved in this case is, and what it is not. These petitioners were not charged with an attempt to overthrow the Government. They were not charged with overt acts of any kind designed to overthrow the Government. They were not even charged with saying anything or writing anything designed to overthrow the Government. The charge was that they agreed to assemble and to talk and publish certain ideas at a later date: The indictment is that they conspired to organize the Communist Party and to use speech or newspapers and other publications in the future to teach and advocate the forcible overthrow of the Government.[83]

In *Dennis* Justice Black was true to what Sigmund Freud called "the reality principle." And he was true again in 1959, in *Barenblatt v. United States*,[84] when a five-to-four majority[85] upheld the contempt conviction of a Vassar instructor who refused to answer questions of the House Committee on Un-American Activities about Communist associations. The Court balanced Congress' need to investigate against the individual interest of the instructor in privacy of belief and held that the governmental interest must prevail. Justice Black disliked the whole idea of judges balancing interests in that way, and he said so again in his dissent.[86] But if there was to be a balancing test, he said, the Court had weighed the wrong factors. It had left out, he said,

> the real interest in Barenblatt's silence, the interest of the people as a whole in being able to join organizations, advocate causes and make political "mistakes" without later being subjected to governmental penalties for having dared to think for themselves. It is this right, the right to err politically, which keeps us strong as a Nation.[87]

Looking back at that scoundrel time in American history, I think no realist can disagree with Justice Black. He simply pointed out what was happening: that people were being held to obloquy, made jobless, and sent to prison for their political ideas and associations. Unlike the example of the Sedition Act, there has been

---

83. *Dennis*, 341 U.S. at 579 (Black, J., dissenting).

84. 360 U.S. 109 (1959).

85. Justices Frankfurter, Clark, Whittaker, and Stewart joined Justice Harlan's majority opinion. Chief Justice Warren and Justices Douglas and Brennan dissented with Justice Black.

86. *Barenblatt*, 360 U.S. at 137-46 (Black, J., dissenting).

87. *Id.* at 144 (Black, J., dissenting).

no President or Congress decent enough to make amends to those punished in the Red Scare. But the standard of right and reality—the constitutional standard—is still there in Justice Black's words.

Justice Black never gave up trying to persuade the Court and the country that they were wrong when they limited free expression. He was relentless in the pursuit of his constitutional vision. How I wish he were still with us, piercing the sophistries that have sustained the government's power to censor the writings of former government employees for the rest of their lives[88] and to keep Americans from traveling to Cuba.[89]

Virginia Durr, in her recent book *Outside the Magic Circle*,[90] wrote of Justice Black's passionate attachment to the First Amendment. "He felt that when people couldn't discuss issues," she said, "then nobody could be free. That's one reason I always had such a feeling of safety around him."[91]

A feeling of safety: It is a crucial insight into Justice Black and the First Amendment. He was a Jeffersonian populist, an old-fashioned radical whose ideas were anathema to many, but who had an enormous influence for freedom. That was so, surely, not just because he was so determined, but because he was himself such a happy example of freedom. He taught us that free speech should be prized, even when not in perfect taste, for its own liberating sake—and for the security it gives a democratic society. And there it was, in him: security, the inner confidence of a free man. He loved battling Felix Frankfurter. He also loved Felix Frankfurter.

Hugo Black's serenity still has the power to inspire us. "There is hope, however," he said at the end of his dissent in *Dennis*, "that in calmer times, when present pressures, passions and fears subside, this or some later Court will restore the First Amendment liberties to the high preferred place where they belong in a free society."[92]

---

88. Snepp v. United States, 444 U.S. 507 (1980) (per curiam).
89. Regan v. Wald, 468 U.S. 222 (1984).
90 V. Durr, Outside the Magic Circle (1985).
91. *Id.* at 167.
92. Dennis v. United States, 341 U.S. 494, 581 (1951) (Black, J., dissenting).

JUSTICE BLACK AND THE LANGUAGE OF FREEDOM

*Irving Dilliard**

Some of our Presidents, Jefferson, Lincoln, and Woodrow Wilson among them, are well remembered for their use of language. Indeed, it would be difficult even to think of the 1863 dedicatory speaker at Gettysburg without recalling his effectiveness in the choice of words. His choice was so striking that the words he spoke come to us today.

Supreme Court jurists may not be as strongly set in the national mind for their formulation of thought into expression. Yet, when we say the name of John Marshall, we hear the great Chief Justice's words in *Marbury v. Madison*:[1] "The government of the United States has been emphatically termed a government of laws, and not of men."[2]

A century and a quarter later, Justice Oliver Wendell Holmes, Jr., a veteran of the Civil War, gave us words in the case of the pacifist Rosika Schwimmer that cannot be recited too often: "[I]f there is any principle of the Constitution that more imperatively calls for attachment than any other, it is the principle of free thought—not free thought for those who agree with us but freedom for the thought that we hate."[3]

In *Gitlow v. New York*,[4] Holmes disposed readily of the notion that the central figure of that case was given to political inciting. It took the plain-spoken Holmes only five words to say it: "Every idea is an incitement."[5] If the legal scholar from Massachusetts may be quoted once more, let us remember that it was he who

---

* Professor Emeritus, Princeton University. Publications include ONE MAN'S STAND FOR FREEDOM: MR. JUSTICE BLACK AND THE BILL OF RIGHTS (1963).

1. 5 U.S. (1 Cranch) 137 (1803).
2. *Marbury*, 5 U.S. (1 Cranch) at 163.
3. United States v. Schwimmer, 279 U.S. 644, 654-55 (1928) (Holmes, J., dissenting).
4. 268 U.S. 652 (1925).
5. *Gitlow*, 268 U.S. at 673 (Holmes, J., dissenting).

said: "Certitude is not the test of certainty. We have been cocksure about too many things that were not so."[6]

Holmes' frequent colleague in Supreme Court opinions, Justice Louis D. Brandeis, possessed an exceptional skill in turning thoughts into words to remember. One of his most memorable passages awaits us in his opinion in *Whitney v. California*:[7]

> Those who won our independence by revolution were not cowards. They did not fear political change. They did not exalt order at the cost of liberty. To courageous, self-reliant men, with confidence in the power of free and fearless reasoning applied through the process of popular government, no danger flowing from speech can be deemed clear and present, unless the incidence of evil apprehended is so imminent that it may befall before there is an opportunity for full discussion.
>
> If there be time to expose through discussion the falsehood and fallacies, to avert the evil by the process of education, the remedy to be applied is more speech, not enforced silence. Only an emergency can justify repression. Such must be the rule if authority is to be reconciled with freedom. Such, in my opinion, is the command of the Constitution. It is therefore always open to Americans to challenge a law abridging free speech and assembly by showing that there was no emergency justifying it.[8]

Brandeis put words together so effectively that still other instances are in order:

On the Power of Facts.—"Nine-tenths of the serious controversies which arise in life result from misunderstanding, result from one man not knowing the facts which to the other man seem important, or otherwise failing to appreciate his point of view. A properly conducted conference involves a frank discussion of such facts—patient, careful argument, willingness to listen and to consider."[9]

On Thinking.—"Human nature, like the inanimate, seeks the path of least resistance. To think hard and persistently is painful."[10]

---

6. *Quoted in* Dilliard, *Foreword* to MR. JUSTICE BRANDEIS: PRESS OPINION AND PUBLIC APPRAISAL 1 (I. Dilliard ed. 1941).

7. 274 U.S. 357 (1927).

8. *Whitney*, 274 U.S. at 377 (Brandeis, J., concurring).

9. *Quoted in* MR. JUSTICE BRANDEIS: PRESS OPINION AND PUBLIC APPRAISAL 17 (I. Dilliard ed. 1941).

10. *Id.* at 36.

On the Legal Profession.—"Able lawyers have, to a large extent, allowed themselves to become adjuncts of great corporations and have neglected the obligation to use their powers for the protection of the people. We hear much of the 'corporation lawyer,' and far too little of the 'people's lawyer.' The great opportunity for the American bar is and will be to stand again as it did in the past, ready to protect also the interests of the people."[11]

On Democracy.—"Our great beneficent experiment in democracy will fail unless the people, our rulers, are developed in character and intelligence."[12]

On Occupations.—"Every legitimate occupation, be it profession or business or trade, furnishes abundant opportunities for usefulness, if pursued in what Matthew Arnold called 'the grand manner.' It is, as a rule, far more important *how* men pursue their occupation than *what* the occupation is which they select."[13]

On Liberty Through Law.—"The great achievement of the English-speaking people is the attainment of liberty through law."[14]

On the People.—"There is no subject so complex that the people cannot be interested in it and made to see the truth about it if pains enough be taken."[15]

On Regulation.—"When property is used to interfere with that fundamental freedom of life for which property is only a means, then property must be controlled. This applies to the regulation of trusts and railroads, public utilities and all the big industries that control the necessities of life. Laws regulating them, far from being infringements on liberty, are in reality protections against infringements on liberty."[16]

On Government's Example.—"Decency, security and liberty alike demand that government officials shall be subjected to the same rules of conduct that are commands to the citizen. In a government of laws, existence of the government will be imperiled if it fails to observe the law scrupulously. Our Government is the potent, the omnipresent teacher. For good or ill, it teaches the whole

---

11. *Id.* at 41.
12. *Id.* at 69.
13. *Id.* at 75 (emphasis in original).
14. *Id.* at 84.
15. *Id.* at 97.
16. *Id.* at 114.

people by its example. Crime is contagious. If the Government becomes a law-breaker, it breeds contempt for law; it invites every man to become a law unto himself; it invites anarchy. To declare that in the administration of the criminal law the end justifies the means—to declare that the Government may commit crimes in order to secure the conviction of a private criminal—would bring terrible retribution. Against that pernicious doctrine this court should resolutely set its face."[17]

The desire to continue quoting from Justice Brandeis needs to be limited, strong though it may be. A final choice is the following:

On a Free People.—"Those who won our independence believed that the final end of the State was to make men free to develop their faculties; and that in its government the deliberative force should prevail over the arbitrary. They valued liberty both as an end and as a means. They believed liberty to be the secret of happiness . . . ."[18]

If these early paragraphs have been devoted to others, including especially Justice Brandeis, there are reasons for this devotion. President Wilson appointed Brandeis to the Supreme Court in 1916. Thus, it soon will be just seventy years since Brandeis took his seat on our highest tribunal. Another reason to emphasize Brandeis is that he was a senior justice when President Franklin D. Roosevelt appointed United States Senator Hugo LaFayette Black to the supreme bench in 1937. Brandeis continued to serve until 1939, when he retired after twenty-three years of distinguished jurisprudence.

This means that Brandeis and Black were colleagues during the terms embracing 1937-39. Black could hardly have influenced Brandeis in any way in that time, and in any event, Justice Felix Frankfurter, who came onto the Supreme Court during the joint Brandeis-Black tenure,[19] reported that Brandeis became critical of aspects of the Black viewpoint.[20] Even so, it is not difficult at all to

---

17. Olmstead v. United States, 277 U.S. 438, 485 (1928) (Brandeis, J., dissenting).

18. Whitney v. California, 274 U.S. 357, 375 (1927) (Brandeis, J., concurring).

19. President Roosevelt nominated Justice Frankfurter for the Supreme Court on January 5, 1939; he was seated on January 30, 1939, fourteen days before Justice Brandeis' resignation from the Court on February 13, 1939. *See* 306 U.S. III nn.2-3 (1938).

20. *See* Noonan, Book Review, 9 Sw. U.L. Rev. 1127, 1131 (1977) (reviewing G. Dunne, Hugo Black and the Judicial Revolution (1977)).

believe that Brandeis' heroic life and work had bearing on the new Justice from the Deep South.

In one of the early opinions in which he spoke for the entire court, *Chambers v. Florida*,[21] Justice Black made effective use of the direct, unmistakable language that was to characterize an important aspect of his long tenure on the Supreme Court. The issue was "whether proceedings in which confessions were utilized and which culminated in sentences of death upon four young Negro men in the State of Florida, failed to afford the safeguard of that due process of law guaranteed by the Fourteenth Amendment."[22]

Following an outrageous murder, the accused tenant farmers were held in closest confinement without access to friends or counsel for five days. During that time they were questioned almost continuously in an atmosphere highly hostile and by officials whose manner was most abusive. Here are the final paragraphs of Justice Black's prevailing opinion:

> [P]etitioners were subjected to interrogations culminating in Saturday's . . . all-night examination . . . . [T]hey steadily refused to confess and disclaimed any guilt. The very circumstances surrounding their confinement and their questioning without any formal charges having been brought, were such as to fill petitioners with terror and frightful misgivings. Some were practical strangers in the community; three were arrested in a one-room farm tenant house which was their home; the haunting fear of mob violence was around them in an atmosphere charged with excitement and public indignation. From virtually the moment of their arrest until their eventual confessions, they never knew when just any one of them would be called back to the fourth floor room, and there, surrounded by his accusers and others, interrogated by men who held their very lives—so far as these ignorant petitioners could know—in the balance. The rejection of petitioner Woodward's first "confession," given in the early hours of Sunday morning, because it was found wanting, demonstrates the relentless tenacity which "broke" the petitioners' will and rendered them helpless to resist their accusers further. To permit human lives to be forfeited upon confessions thus obtained would make of the constitutional requirement of due process of law a meaningless symbol.
>
> We are not impressed by the argument that law enforcement methods such as those under review are necessary to uphold our

---

21. 309 U.S. 227 (1940).
22. *Chambers*, 309 U.S. at 227.

laws. The Constitution proscribes such lawless means irrespective of the end. And this argument flouts the basic principle that all people must stand on an equality before the bar of justice in every American court. Today, as in ages past, we are not without tragic proof that the exalted power of some governments to punish manufactured crime dictatorially is the handmaid of tyranny. Under our constitutional system, courts stand against any winds that blow as havens of refuge for those who might otherwise suffer because they are helpless, weak, outnumbered or because they are non-conforming victims of prejudice and public excitement. Due process of law, preserved for all by our Constitution, commands that no such practice as that disclosed by this record shall send any accused to his death. No higher duty, no more solemn responsibility, rests upon this Court, than that of translating into living law and maintaining this constitutional shield deliberately planned and inscribed for the benefit of every human being subject to our Constitution—of whatever race, creed or persuasion.

The Supreme Court of Florida was in error and its judgment is *reversed.*[23]

For our next selection of the language of Justice Black, let us reach more than twenty years beyond *Chambers*. The case is *In re Anastaplo.*[24] The Black opinion speaks not for the Court, but for a minority of four—Chief Justice Earl Warren, Justice William O. Douglas, Justice William J. Brennan, Jr., and a much distressed Black.[25] When I wrote an article about the case and its effects for a different Hugo Black Symposium a few years ago,[26] the *Anastaplo* decision was described as "a shame and a reproach."[27] To the extent that it is still in force, the decision continues to be just that.

Here is what happened in this too-little-known case: George Anastaplo was born November 7, 1925, in St. Louis, Missouri, to natives of Greece. They moved to the small coal-mining town of Carterville, Illinois. After Anastaplo was graduated from high school with an excellent record, he enrolled at the University of Illinois. But, unfortunately, Pearl Harbor had been attacked, and Hitler had brought the United States into war across the Atlantic.

---

23. *Id.* at 239-242 (footnotes omitted) (emphasis in original).

24. 366 U.S. 82 (1961).

25. The majority of five consisted of Justice Frankfurter, Justice Clark, Justice Harlan, Justice Whittaker, and Justice Stewart.

26. *See* Dilliard, *Mr. Justice Black and In re Anastaplo*, 9 Sw. U.L. Rev. 953 (1977).

27. *Id.* at 955.

After only one semester, George Anastaplo, barely seventeen, underweight, and with a heart murmur, volunteered. He was assigned to the Army Air Corps, which turned him into a navigator, awarded him wings, and commissioned him a Second Lieutenant. For more than three years, he served in the Pacific, North African, Middle Eastern, and European theaters of operation. He held his own with men who were older and physically stronger than himself. He was not yet twenty when V-J Day came in 1945.

George Anastaplo had seen so much of the world at war that he believed the peace was not yet won. So he continued his service for another year while thousands of others hurried home. Mustered out in 1947, he went into the reserves and resumed his long-delayed college education. He was accepted at the University of Chicago for the fall term. That was some six months away, so he made use of the intervening time by enrolling in courses at Southern Illinois University.

At the University of Chicago, he took on a double schedule of courses and did so well that he was awarded the degree of Bachelor of Arts, accompanied with Phi Beta Kappa honors, only a year later. He then entered the University of Chicago Law School where his distinctions included membership in the Order of the Coif. Ordinarily, the passing of the bar examination comes after law school graduation. With George Anastaplo it was the other way. He passed the bar examination in the fall of 1950 and was graduated first in his class the *next* year. He was now twenty-five by the calendar, but, taking out the thirty-eight months of military service, he was, in a sense, still only twenty-one!

In view of both Anastaplo's military and educational record, how could anyone have been more sure of prompt admission to the practice of law in Illinois or any other state? After passing the bar examination in August 1950, and well before he was graduated the following June, George Anastaplo filed, on October 26, 1950, a completed questionnaire required by the Illinois Bar's Committee on Character and Fitness. It required the applicant to summarize his or her views of the principles underlying the Constitution of the United States. Also included were affidavits on the applicant's moral character and general fitness to practice law.

In stating his views about the fundamental principles of the United States government, the applicant aligned himself with the historic precepts of the Declaration of Independence and of the Constitution itself. He wrote that "the most important" principle

> is that such government is constituted so as to secure certain inalienable rights, those rights to Life, Liberty and the Pursuit of Happiness (and elements of these rights are explicitly set forth in . . . the Bill of Rights). *And, of course, whenever that particular government in power becomes destructive of these ends, it is the right of the people to alter or abolish it and thereupon to establish a new government.* This is how I view the Constitution.[28]

This reference to the basic principles of the Declaration of Independence, in the event of the assumption of power by a tyrant, led to questioning by a two-member subcommittee. This interrogation opened the way for more questioning as to the applicant's political beliefs and affiliations. Respectfully taking the position that these were improper questions and outside the scope of legitimate inquiry, George Anastaplo declined to name his political ties. When asked if he was a member of the Communist Party, his answer was that the question was improper and not relevant any more than if he were asked whether he was a Republican or a Democrat.[29]

A committee member went so far as to ask the applicant whether he believed "in the Deity." George Anastaplo said he did not consider that what he might or might not believe about a deity should be connected with his qualification to practice law. The committee member then rejoined with his conviction that attitude toward a "Supreme Being" had a "substantial bearing upon . . . fitness to practice law."[30] Thereupon the applicant, acting as his own counsel, showed his elders that questions bearing on religion had been declared unconstitutional in Illinois in 1870![31]

All that was thirty-five years ago. The application was denied. Anastaplo's appeal went to the federal courts. There were more hearings and rehearings.[32] The believer in the Constitution would

---

28. *Anastaplo*, 366 U.S. at 99 (Black, J., dissenting) (emphasis in original).

29. Dilliard, *supra* note 26, at 957.

30. *Anastaplo*, 366 U.S. at 102 (Black, J., dissenting).

31. *See id.* at 102-03 n.4 (Black, J., dissenting).

32. After the Committee first denied Anastaplo admission to the bar in 1951, Anastaplo filed a petition and appeal in the Illinois Supreme Court. The Illinois court, however, denied the petition. *In re* Anastaplo, 3 Ill. 2d 471, 121 N.E.2d 826 (1951). Anastaplo then took his case to the United States Supreme Court, where the appeal was treated as a petition for writ of certiorari. The petition was denied on February 28, 1955. 348 U.S. 946

not change his position. He stood his ground. The division in the Illinois Supreme Court was four-to-three and the three supported the applicant wholeheartedly.[33] In 1961 the United States Supreme Court finally passed on the issue, with Justice John M. Harlan speaking for the majority of five, which also included Justices Felix Frankfurter, Tom Clark, Charles Whittaker and Potter Stewart.[34] Justice Black, speaking for the four dissenters,[35] strongly criticized the majority's "balancing" of repression against freedom to determine which is "the wiser governmental policy under the circumstances of each case."[36] Here are words from Justice Black that should be unforgettable:

> The effect of the Court's "balancing" here is that any State may now reject an applicant for admission to the Bar if he believes in the Declaration of Independence as strongly as Anastaplo and if he is willing to sacrifice his career and his means of livelihood in defense of the freedoms of the First Amendment. But the men who founded this country and wrote our Bill of Rights were strangers neither to a belief in the "right of revolution" nor to the urgency of the need to be free from the control of government with regard to political beliefs and associations. Thomas Jefferson was not disclaiming a belief in the "right of revolution" when he wrote the Declaration of Independence. And Patrick Henry was certainly not disclaiming such a belief when he declared in impassioned words that have come on down through the years: "Give me liberty or give me death." This country's freedom was won by men who, whether they believed in it or not, certainly practiced revolution in the Revolutionary War.[37]

(1955). In the same month, the United States Supreme Court denied Anastaplo's petition for rehearing. 349 U.S. 908 (1955). Thereafter, the Illinois Supreme Court requested the Committee to allow a petition for rehearing filed by Anastaplo with the Committee, in light of two recent United States Supreme Court opinions that addressed similar issues as those presented in the Anastaplo case. 8 Ill. 2d 182, 163 N.E.2d 429 (1959). As a result, the Committee conducted five hearings between February 28 and May 19, 1958. The Committee again denied Anastaplo admission to the Illinois bar, and the Illinois Supreme Court reviewed the Committee's decision once again. *See infra* note 33 and accompanying text.

33. *In re* Anastaplo, 18 Ill. 2d 182, 163 N.E.2d 429 (1959) (per curiam); *see* Dilliard, *supra* note 26, at 959 n.33.

34. *Anastaplo*, 366 U.S. at 82.

35. Besides Justice Black, the four dissenters consisted of Chief Justice Warren, Justice Brennan, and Justice Douglas.

36. *Anastaplo*, 366 U.S. at 112 (Black, J., dissenting).

37. *Id.* at 112-13 (Black, J., dissenting).

In view of the title of my part of this program, *Justice Black and the Language of Freedom*, I cannot possibly do better than quote his final four paragraphs from *Anastaplo*:

> Since the beginning of history there have been governments that have engaged in practices against the people so bad, so cruel, so unjust and so destructive of the individual dignity of men and women that the "right of revolution" was all the people had left to free themselves. As simple illustrations, one government almost 2,000 years ago burned Christians upon fiery crosses and another government, during this very century, burned Jews in crematories. I venture the suggestion that there are countless multitudes in this country, and all over the world, who would join Anastaplo's belief in the right of the people to resist by force tyrannical governments like those.
>
> In saying what I have, it is to be borne in mind that Anastaplo has not indicated, even remotely, a belief that this country is an oppressive one in which the "right of revolution" should be exercised. Quite the contrary, the entire course of his life, as disclosed by the record, has been one of devotion and service to his country—first, in his willingness to defend its security at the risk of his own life in time of war and, later, in his willingness to defend its freedoms at the risk of his professional career in time of peace. The one and only time in which he has come into conflict with the Government is when he refused to answer the questions put to him by the Committee about his beliefs and associations. And I think the record clearly shows that conflict resulted, not from any fear on Anastaplo's part to divulge his own political activities, but from a sincere, and in my judgment correct, conviction that the preservation of this country's freedom depends upon adherence to our Bill of Rights. The very most that can fairly be said against Anastaplo's position in this entire matter is that he took too much of the responsibility of preserving that freedom upon himself.
>
> This case illustrates to me the serious consequences to the Bar itself of not affording the full protections of the First Amendment to its applicants for admission. For this record shows that Anastaplo has many of the qualities that are needed in the American Bar. It shows, not only that Anastaplo has followed a high moral, ethical and patriotic course in all the activities of his life, but also that he combines these more common virtues with the uncommon virtue of courage to stand by his principles at any cost. It is such men as these who have most greatly honored the profession of the law—men like Malsherbes, who, at the cost of his own life and the lives of his family, sprang unafraid to the defense of Louis XVI

> against the fanatical leaders of the Revolutionary government of France—men like Charles Evans Hughes, Sr., later Mr. Chief Justice Hughes, who stood up for the constitutional rights of socialists to be socialists and public officials despite the threats and clamorous protests of self-proclaimed superpatriots—men like Charles Evans Hughes, Jr., and John W. Davis, who, while against everything for which the Communists stood, strongly advised the Congress in 1948 that it would be unconstitutional to pass the law then proposed to outlaw the Communist Party—men like Lord Erskine, James Otis, Clarence Darrow, and the multitude of others who have dared to speak in defense of causes and clients without regard to personal danger to themselves. The legal profession will lose much of its nobility and its glory if it is not constantly replenished with lawyers like these. To force the Bar to become a group of thoroughly orthodox, time-serving, government-fearing individuals is to humiliate and degrade it.
>
> But that is the present trend, not only in the legal profession but in almost every walk of life. Too many men are being driven to become government-fearing and time-serving because the Government is being permitted to strike out at those who are fearless enough to think as they please and say what they think. This trend must be halted if we are to keep faith with the Founders of our Nation and pass on to future generations of Americans the great heritage of freedom which they sacrificed so much to leave to us. The choice is clear to me. If we are to pass on that great heritage of freedom, we must return to the original language of the Bill of Rights. We must not be afraid to be free.[38]

Justice Black's historic use of the language of freedom was soon followed by a remarkable petition for a rehearing by George Anastaplo.[39] Not a member of the bar, but acting as counsel *pro se*, on June 19, 1961, he addressed the Supreme Court in part as follows:

> Perhaps it is true that petitioner "took too much of the responsibility of preserving [his country's] freedom upon himself." But he was young enough to hope that Americans who would not heed old precepts might yet learn from new examples . . . .
>
> It is only by an ungenerous disregard of the record as it developed, of the kind of challenges petitioner alone faced and of the

38. *Id.* at 113-16 (Black, J., dissenting) (footnotes omitted).

39. The petition for rehearing was summarily denied. *In re* Anastaplo, 368 U.S. 869 (1961).

manner in which he met them, that the action of the Illinois authorities has been upheld. The record—both before the Committee and on appeal—that record of testimony and briefs remains as a guide to reforms that are needed in the education and character of the American bar.

Petitioner is satisfied he has acted as one ought. He is further satisfied that his action will continue to serve the best interests of the bar and of the country. The generous sentiments of the dissenting opinions in Chicago, in Springfield, and in Washington keep alive hopes for the success of efforts to make the institutions and laws of our people a reflection of decency and perhaps even of nobility.

Petitioner leaves in the hands of the profession—lawyers, law teachers and judges alike—the career he might have had. He trusts he will be forgiven if he retains for himself only the immortal lines of another exile: "Then he turned back, and seemed like one of those who run for the green cloth at Verona through the open fields; and of them seemed he who triumphs, not he who loses."[40]

Between such early opinions as the strong majority voice in *Chambers v. Florida*[41] and the moving dissent from *Anastaplo*, more than two decades after *Chambers*, Justice Black employed the language of freedom time after time. Here are some representative instances:

Betts v. Brady.[42]—"The right to counsel in a criminal proceeding is 'fundamental.' It is guarded from invasion by the Sixth Amendment, adopted to raise an effective barrier against arbitrary or unjust deprivation of liberty by the Federal Government . . . . Any other practice seems to me to defeat the promise of our democratic society to provide equal justice under law."[43]

Jones v. Opelika.[44]—"The opinion of the Court sanctions a device which in our opinion suppresses or tends to suppress the free exercise of a religion practiced by a minority group. This is but another step in the direction which *Minersville School District v. Gobitis* took against the same religious minority, and is a logical extension of the principles upon which that decision rested. Since

---

40. *See* I. DILLIARD, ONE MAN'S STAND FOR FREEDOM: MR. JUSTICE BLACK AND THE BILL OF RIGHTS 414-15 (1963). Anastaplo was quoting DANTE, INFERNO XV 121-24.

41. 309 U.S. 227 (1940).

42. 316 U.S. 455 (1942).

43. *Betts*, 316 U.S. at 475, 477 (Black, J., dissenting).

44. 316 U.S. 584 (1942).

we joined in the opinion in the *Gobitis* case, we think this is an appropriate occasion to state that we now believe that it also was wrongly decided. Certainly our democratic form of government, functioning under the historic Bill of Rights, has a high responsibility to accommodate itself to the religious views of minorities, however unpopular and unorthodox those views may be. The First Amendment does not put the right freely to exercise religion in a subordinate position. We fear, however, that the opinions in these and in the *Gobitis* case do exactly that."[45]

West Virginia State Board of Education v. Barnette.[46]—"Words uttered under coercion are proof of loyalty to nothing but self-interest. Love of country must spring from willing hearts and free minds, inspired by a fair administration of wise laws enacted by the people's elected representatives within the bounds of express constitutional prohibitions. These laws must, to be consistent with the First Amendment, permit the widest toleration of conflicting viewpoints consistent with a society of free men."[47]

In re Summers.[48]—"Under our Constitution men are punished for what they do or fail to do and not for what they think and believe. Freedom to think, to believe, and to worship, has too exalted a position in our country to be penalized on such an illusory basis."[49]

United States v. Lovett.[50]—"When our Constitution and Bill of Rights were written, our ancestors had ample reason to know that legislative trials and punishments were too dangerous to liberty to exist in the nation of free men they envisioned. And so they proscribed bills of attainder . . . . Much as we regret to declare that an Act of Congress violates the Constitution, we have no alternative here."[51]

Foster v. Illinois.[52]— "The Court seems to fear that protecting these defendants' right to counsel to the full extent defined in the

---

45. *Jones*, 316 U.S. at 623-24 (Black, Douglas, and Murphy, JJ., dissenting) (citation omitted).
46. 319 U.S. 624 (1943).
47. *Barnette*, 319 U.S. at 644 (Black and Douglas, JJ., concurring).
48. 325 U.S. 561 (1945).
49. *Summers*, 325 U.S. at 578 (Black, J., dissenting).
50. 328 U.S. 303 (1946).
51. *Lovett*, 328 U.S. at 318.
52. 332 U.S. 134 (1947).

Bill of Rights would furnish 'opportunities hitherto uncontemplated for opening wide the prison doors of the land,' because, presumably, there are many people like Betts, Foster and Payne behind those doors after trials without having had the benefit of counsel. I do not believe that such a reason is even relevant to a determination that we should decline to enforce the Bill of Rights."[53]

Ludecke v. Watkins.[54]—"It is not amiss, I think, to suggest my belief that because of today's opinion individual liberty will be less secure tomorrow than it was yesterday. Certainly the security of aliens is lessened, particularly if their ideas happen to be out of harmony with those of the governmental authorities of a period. And there is removed a segment of judicial power to protect individual liberty from arbitrary action, at least until today's judgment is corrected by Congress or by this Court."[55]

Feiner v. New York.[56]—"In this case I would reverse the conviction, thereby adhering to the great principles of the First and Fourteenth Amendments . . . . I regret my inability to persuade the Court not to retreat from this principle."[57]

Joint Anti-Fascist Refugee Committee v. McGrath.[58]—"In this day when prejudice, hate and fear are constantly invoked to justify irresponsible smears and persecution of persons even faintly suspected of entertaining unpopular views, it may be futile to suggest that the cause of internal security would be fostered, not hurt, by faithful adherence to our constitutional guarantees of individual liberty. Nevertheless . . . it surely should not be amiss to call attention to what has occurred when dominant governmental groups have been left free to give uncontrolled rein to their prejudices against unorthodox minorities."[59]

Dennis v. United States.[60]—"Public opinion being what it now is, few will protest the conviction of these Communist petitioners. There is hope, however, that in calmer times, when present pressures, passions and fears subside, this or some later Court will

53. *Foster*, 332 U.S. at 140-41 (Black, J., dissenting).
54. 335 U.S. 160 (1948).
55. *Ludecke*, 335 U.S. at 183-84 (Black, J., dissenting) (footnote omitted).
56. 340 U.S. 315 (1951).
57. *Feiner*, 340 U.S. at 329 (Black, J., dissenting).
58. 341 U.S. 123 (1951).
59. *McGrath*, 341 U.S. at 145 (Black, J., concurring).
60. 341 U.S. 494 (1951).

restore the First Amendment liberties to the high preferred place where they belong in a free society."[61]

Sacher v. United States.[62]—"Preference for trial by a jury of laymen over trial by lawyer-judges lies behind the constitutional guarantee of trial by jury. I am among those who still believe in trial by jury as one of the indispensable safeguards of liberty."[63]

Zorach v. Clauson.[64]—"State help to religion injects political and party prejudices into a holy field. It too often substitutes force for prayer, hate for love, and persecution for persuasion. Government should not be allowed, under cover of the soft euphemism of 'co-operation,' to steal into the sacred area of religious choice."[65]

Irvine v. California.[66]—"It has been suggested that the Court should call on the Attorney General to investigate this record in order to start criminal prosecutions against certain California officers. I would strongly object to any such action by this Court. It is inconsistent with my own view of the judicial function in our government. Prosecution, or anything approaching it, should, I think, be left to government officers whose duty that is."[67]

Yates v. United States.[68]—"The First Amendment provides the only kind of security system that can preserve a free government—one that leaves the way wide open for people to favor, discuss, advocate, or incite causes and doctrines however obnoxious and antagonistic such views may be to the rest of us."[69]

Trop v. Dulles.[70]—"The statute held invalid here not only makes the military's finding of desertion final but gives military authorities discretion to choose which soldiers convicted of desertion shall be allowed to keep their citizenship and which ones shall thereafter be stateless. Nothing in the Constitution or its history lends the slightest support for such military control over the right to be an American citizen."[71]

---

61. *Dennis*, 341 U.S. at 581 (Black, J., dissenting).
62. 343 U.S. 1 (1952).
63. *Sacher*, 343 U.S. at 23 (Black, J., dissenting).
64. 343 U.S. 306 (1952).
65. *Zorach*, 343 U.S. at 320 (Black, J., dissenting).
66. 347 U.S. 128 (1954).
67. *Irvine*, 347 U.S. at 142 (Black, J., dissenting).
68. 354 U.S. 298 (1957).
69. *Yates*, 354 U.S. at 344 (Black, J., concurring in part and dissenting in part).
70. 356 U.S. 86 (1958).
71. *Trop*, 356 U.S. at 104-05 (Black, J., concurring).

Barenblatt v. United States.[72]—"Ultimately all the questions in this case really boil down to one—whether we as a people will try fearfully and futilely to preserve democracy by adopting totalitarian methods, or whether in accordance with our traditions and our Constitution we will have the confidence and courage to be free."[73]

Smith v. California.[74]—"Censorship is the deadly enemy of freedom and progress. The plain language of the Constitution forbids it. I protest against the Judiciary giving it a foothold here."[75]

Uphaus v. Wyman.[76]—"My guess is that history will look with no more favor upon the imprisonment of Willard Uphaus than it has upon that of Udall, Bunyan or the many others like them. For this is another of that ever-lengthening line of cases where people have been sent to prison and kept there for long periods of their lives because their beliefs were inconsistent with the prevailing views of the moment . . . . [The Constitution] was drafted by men who were well aware of the constant danger to individual liberty in a country where public officials are permitted to harass and punish people on nothing more than charges that they associate with others labeled by the Government as publicans and sinners."[77]

Wilkinson v. United States.[78]—"I can only reiterate my firm conviction that these people [who would set aside First Amendment freedoms] are tragically wrong. This country was not built by men who were afraid and it cannot be preserved by such men . . . . Where these freedoms are left to depend upon a balance to be struck by this Court in each particular case, liberty cannot survive."[79]

Konigsberg v. State Bar.[80]—"No witness could be found throughout the long years of this inquisition who could say, or even who would say, that Konigsberg has ever raised his voice or his hand against his country. He is, therefore, but another victim of

---

72. 360 U.S. 109 (1959).
73. *Barenblatt*, 360 U.S. at 162 (Black, J., dissenting).
74. 361 U.S. 147 (1959).
75. *Smith*, 361 U.S. at 160 (Black, J., concurring).
76. 364 U.S. 388 (1960) (per curiam).
77. *Uphaus*, 364 U.S. at 400-01 (Black, J., dissenting).
78. 365 U.S. 399 (1961).
79. *Wilkinson*, 365 U.S. at 422-23 (Black, J., dissenting) (footnote omitted).
80. 366 U.S. 36 (1961).

the prevailing fashion of destroying men for the views it is suspected they might entertain."[81]

Communist Party v. Subversive Activities Control Board.[82]—"I would reverse this case and leave the Communists free to advocate their beliefs in proletarian dictatorship publicly and openly among the people of this country with full confidence that the people will remain loyal to any democratic Government truly dedicated to freedom and justice—the kind of Government which some of us still think of as being 'the last best hope of earth.' "[83]

With his reliance on "the last best hope of earth," we conclude our selection of quotations from the opinions of Hugo LaFayette Black. They comprise the language of freedom and more. For surely in our time no one has used words more devotedly to express the fundamental principles of the United States of America.

81. *Konigsberg*, 366 U.S. at 80 (Black, J., dissenting).
82. 367 U.S. 1 (1961).
83. *Communist Party*, 367 U.S. at 169 (Black, J., dissenting).

JUSTICE HUGO BLACK: CRAFTSMAN OF THE LAW

*Gerald T. Dunne**

While Justice Black's renown justly rests upon his clarion opinions in constitutional law, especially in the areas of personal liberty, I would like to turn from that subject matter to another area that is less exciting, more humdrum, and yet just as full of the juice of life and law to suggest another dimension of his talent.

This is the area of commercial law, primarily the law of debtors and creditors, where the Justice exhibits a particularly fine touch as a writer and reader of statutes. Here, as elsewhere, we encounter his judicial aspiration that "[n]o higher duty, no more solemn responsibility, rests upon this Court, than that of translating into living law and maintaining [the] constitutional shield deliberately planned and inscribed for the benefit of every human being subject to our Constitution."[1] Surely it is not amiss to point out that such a shield protects property and contract every bit as much as it protects liberty. As Black said in dissent in *Amalgamated Food Employees Union Local 590 v. Logan Valley Plaza*,[2] "I believe that, whether this Court likes it or not, the Constitution recognizes and supports the concept of private ownership of property."[3] Indeed, Justice Black summed up the proper balance between personal rights and property rights in a comment on the 1968 Chicago protestors: "They've got a right to talk where they have a right to be."[4] I submit that this perspective exhibits Black in the idiom which Holmes used to apotheosize Lemuel Shaw—as a judge whose strength

> lay in an accurate appreciation of the requirements of the community whose officer he was. Some, indeed many, . . . could be named

---

*McDonnell Professor of Justice in American Society, Saint Louis University.

1. Chambers v. Florida, 309 U.S. 227, 241 (1940).
2. 391 U.S. 308 (1968).
3. *Logan Valley Plaza*, 391 U.S. at 330 (Black, J., dissenting).
4. G. Dunne, Hugo Black and the Judicial Revolution 416 (1977).

> who have surpassed him in accurate technical knowledge, but few have lived who were his equals in their understanding of the grounds of public policy to which all laws must ultimately be referred.[5]

This understanding makes Black, like Shaw, the "great *magistrate*."[6]

To begin with Black as a writer of statutes, we will look at legislation that bears his name, the Black-Connery Bill[7]—the cornerstone of the Fair Labors Standards Act of 1938.[8] Now into its second half-century, the legislation certainly has had a run for its money. Its remarkable survival in essentially its original form was surely predicted by Senator William Borah, a conservative Republican, who made the following tribute to the Bill's fundamental fairness: "[B]ear in mind . . . that the New Deal wages-and-hours bill . . . was rewritten by [Black's] committee under his influence. While in my opinion, it is not a desirable bill, yet it is far saner and wiser than when he took hold of it."[9]

Black's reading of statutes involves a more complex syntax, of which two instances may be taken as archetypal. One was the ferocity and fire of his reaction to the Jackson dissent in *Jewell Ridge Coal Corp. v. Local No. 6167, United Mine Workers*[10] which quoted the Senator to refute the Judge.[11] More lineal and analytic is Black's majority opinion in *Glass City Bank v. United States*,[12] which extended a federal tax lien to after-acquired property thereby refuting the charge of literalism which often has been uncritically applied to his judicial work.

Another illustration of Black's ability to probe beneath the letter of a statute for the nuances of legislative intent appears in his reading of union shakedowns out of the Federal Anti-Racketeering Act of 1934.[13] As Justice Byrnes, who wrote for the Court

---

5. O.W. HOLMES, JR., THE COMMON LAW 106 (1881).
6. *Id.* (emphasis in original).
7. S. 2475, 79th Cong., 1st Sess., 81 CONG. REC. 7750 (1935).
8. 29 U.S.C. §§ 201-219 (1982).
9. G. DUNNE, *supra* note 4, at 56 (quoting Senator William Borah).
10. 325 U.S. 161 (1945).
11. *Jewell Ridge*, 325 U.S. at 176-77 & n.5 (Jackson, J., dissenting); *see* G. DUNNE, *supra* note 4, at 235-36.
12. 326 U.S. 265 (1945).
13. Ch. 569, 48 Stat. 979-80 (1934) (predecessor of the Hobbs Act, 18 U.S.C. § 1951 (1982)).

in *United States v. Local 807 of International Brotherhood of Teamsters*,[14] later put it, "Justice Black and I knew what the Senate really meant."[15]

Interestingly, even when Black did not get his way with the Court, such was his capacity to appeal to the brooding spirit of the law that one of his dissents on statutory construction would eventually become ruling law[16]—the highest tribute of all. Such was precisely the case as to his insistence on according bankruptcy wage priority to health and welfare contributions in *United States v. Embassy Restaurant, Inc.*[17] Here he hit hard with one of his aphorisms which could take the opposition out with a single punch and which constitutes his stylistic hallmark: "It is hard for me to see how they could not be 'wages.' The payments are certainly not gifts."[18] This thrust certainly was the elemental force which promoted congressional reversal of the majority position and codification of Black's dissent in section 507(a)(4) of the Bankruptcy Reform Act of 1978.[19]

The same sensitivity to the demands of common sense and the practicalities of the world at large surely emerge in the judicial craftsmanship of *Texas v. New Jersey*,[20] when Black steered brilliantly between doctrinaire extremes. Here, working without a rule of decision in the area of the Court's original jurisdiction, he forged a conclusion which integrated federalism and fairness into an unprecedented multi-state escheat process.

I would like to offer as a datum symbolic of Black's craftsmanship in the law the case of *Pearlman v. Reliance Insurance Co.*[21] I chose it in part because it has surfaced in a special way in my own life, thanks to the assumption of responsibility by St. Louis University School of Law of publication of the *Fidelity and Surety*

---

14. 315 U.S. 521 (1942).
15. G. DUNNE, *supra* note 4, at 217 (quoting Justice James Byrnes).
16. *See infra* notes 18-20 and accompanying text.
17. 359 U.S. 29 (1959).
18. *Embassy Restaurant*, 359 U.S. at 37 (Black, J., dissenting).
19. Pub. L. No. 95-598, 92 Stat. 2682 (codified as amended at 11 U.S.C. §§ 100-151326 (1982)). "Paragraph (4) overrules *United States v. Embassy Restaurant*, 359 U.S. 29 (1958), which held that fringe benefits were not entitled to wage priority status. The bill recognizes the realities of labor contract negotiations, where fringe benefits may be substituted for wage demands." S. REP. No. 95-989, 95th Cong., 2nd Sess., *reprinted in* 1978 U.S. CODE CONG. & AD. NEWS 5855.
20. 379 U.S. 674 (1965).
21. 371 U.S. 132 (1962).

Newsletter of the Torts and Insurance Practice Section of the American Bar Association. In *Pearlman* Black showed the sure, deft touch of the great English chancellors—Nottingham, Hardwicke, and Eldon—in shaping a legal doctrine which exhibits both an organic intellectual continuity with the past rules of law, a pragmatic accommodation to present needs, and, above all, a sensitivity to fairness and justice which lies below the level of collective consciousness.

An aside here about equity, if I may. There is more here than the child's "that's not *fair*"; rather, the appeal is to a fundamental consonance with the meta-law,[22] so to speak, to which all rules of conduct must be referred for analysis and evolution. Moreover, here is where the great judge is called on to exhibit what Holmes called the "intuitions of public policy."[23]

As Sir John Selden reminded us in his *Table Talk*,[24] in words strongly reminiscent of Black's excoriation of the "shock the conscience" test of constitutionality:

> Equity is a roguish thing, for Law wee have a measure know what to trust too. Equity is according to [the] conscience of him [that] is Chancell[or], and as [that] is larger or narrower soe is equity. Tis all one as if they should make [the] standard for [the] measure wee call a foot, to be [the] Chancellor's foot; what an uncertain measure would this be; one chancello[r] ha's a long foot another a short foot a third an indifferent foot; tis [the] same thing in [the] Chancello[r]s conscience.[25]

Blackstone says much the same thing in warning that the unharnessed conscience of the judge may cause equity to swallow the law.[26]

Pearlman's specific equitable problem might be well called the "Miller syndrome." This syndrome finds its exemplification in the construction contractor—marginal, under-capitalized, optimistic and venturesome. It is this protagonist who today exhibits the

---

22. *See* H. Berman, Law and Revolution: The Formation of the Western Legal Tradition 8 (1983).

23. O.W. Holmes, Jr., The Common Law 1 (1881).

24. J. Selden, Table Talk of John Selden (Sir F. Pollock ed. 1927).

25. *Id.* at 43 (quoted from manuscript prepared for The Selden Society).

26. 1 W. Blackstone, Commentaries on the Laws of England 42 (Christon, Chitty, Lee, Hovenden, & Ryland ed. 1844) ("And, on the other hand, the liberty of considering all cases in an equitable light must not be indulged too far, lest thereby we destroy all law, and leave the decision of every question entirely in the breast of the judge.").

grandiose optimism of Arthur Miller's *Death of a Salesman*, a new Willie Loman riding a shoeshine and a smile, going from job to job as from pillar to post in a sequence of row-of-dominoes financing. Indeed, precisely this optimism has given us the Miller Act,[27] which ordains that for government construction, one brick cannot be laid upon another until a payment and performance bond is furnished to the United States. Since the contractor furnishes his needs hand-to-mouth from progress payments made by a lending bank, the quarrel over the contract retainage between the accommodating surety and the financing bank furnishes perhaps one of the most enduring confrontations in debtor-creditor law.

Who comes first is a source of considerable analytic difficulty. In terms of chronology the surety has an obvious primacy. Yet the bank's position has a manifest appeal. The complex, difficult, and tangled calculus was considered resolved in 1896 by Justice White in *Prairie State Bank v. United States*,[28] which was restated twelve years later in *Henningsen v. United States Fidelity & Guaranty Co.*[29] *Prairie State Bank* held that the surety has sheer equity in its favor and thereby outranks intermediate financing banks.[30] The force of the doctrine was shaken somewhat by the 1947 decision of the Court in *United States v. Munsey Trust*,[31] which implied only that a right of set-off could involve a higher equity, and yet led many to think that *Munsey* had overruled *Prairie State*. However, with a hammerstroke pronouncement in *Pearlman*, Justice Black asserted that "*Munsey* left the rule . . . undisturbed,"[32] and thereby set the doctrine magnificently to rights. *Pearlman*, however, was not without its launch difficulties; the case was virtually coincident with the advent of the Uniform Commercial Code and the amendment of section 60(6) of the old Bankruptcy Act repealing equitable liens in bankruptcy. Predictably, the young whipper-snappers of law reviews had a field day criticizing *Pearlman* both in calculus and consequences.[33]

---

27. 40 U.S.C. § 270a-270e (1982).
28. 164 U.S. 227 (1896).
29. 208 U.S. 404 (1908).
30. *Prairie State Bank*, 164 U.S. at 240-41.
31. 332 U.S. 234 (1947).
32. Pearlman v. Reliance Ins. Co., 371 U.S. 132, 141 (1962).
33. *See, e.g.*, Hoffman, *Sureties' Panacea or Narcosis? Article 9—The Uniform Commercial Code—Some Practical Aspects*, 34 INS. COUNS. J. 387 (1967); Note, *Bankruptcy—Conflicting Interests in Security—Status of Miller Act Surety*, 4 B.C. IND.

And how has *Pearlman* borne the test of time in the turbulent and dynamic context of construction finance? Professor Barkley Clark of George Washington has surveyed the field and given us a field report on the viability of *Pearlman*:

> The result is always the same: The surety company wins the retainage and the case is not governed by the priority rules of Article 9. The same analysis applies when the defalcator is a subcontractor. The surety also wins the retainage as against general creditors, receivers, or the trustee in bankruptcy of the contractor, even though no UCC filing has been made. Finally, it makes no difference that the contractor executed a legal assignment in the bond application; the surety's primary reliance is still on its equitable right of subrogation . . . . In sum, the surety companies are winning because they are successful in persuading the courts that the priority conflict falls outside the scope of Article 9.[34]

And the proof of the pudding is surely in the eating. We have now passed the twentieth anniversary of *Pearlman*, which stands unshaken. For the turbulent default-and-bankruptcy ridden world of construction financing, *Pearlman* has surely had a run for its money. Professor Clark summed up the score: "Not a single reported decision gives priority to the Article 9 financier in its battle with the surety for the retainage fund."[35]

COMM. L. REV. 748 (1963); Note, *Jacobs v. Northeastern Corp.: Surety's Dilemma—Subrogation Rights or Perfected Security Interest*, 69 DICK. L. REV. 172 (1965); Note, *National Shawmut Bank: Another Step Toward Confusion in Surety Law*, 64 NW. U.L. REV. 582 (1969); Recent Developments, *Suretyship: Subrogation Under the Uniform Commercial Code*, 65 COLUM. L. REV. 927 (1965).

34. B. CLARK, THE LAW OF SECURED TRANSACTIONS UNDER THE UNIFORM COMMERCIAL CODE ¶ 1.7[2], at 1-40 (1980).

35. *Id.* at 1-39.

JUSTICE BLACK: LOCAL CONTROL AND FEDERALISM

*Timothy G. O'Rourke**
*Abigail M. Thernstrom***

Nearing the end of a long and illustrious career on the United States Supreme Court, Justice Hugo Black wrote a number of angry dissenting opinions in cases testing the constitutionality of the Voting Rights Act of 1965.[1] Alone among the members of the Court, Justice Black objected to section 5 of the Act,[2] which required certain Southern states with a record of voting rights abuses to submit proposed changes in their election laws to the federal government for "preclearance." "Certainly if all the provisions of our Constitution which limit the power of the Federal Government and reserve other power to the States are to mean anything," Justice Black argued in *South Carolina v. Katzenbach*,[3] "they mean at least that the States have power to pass laws and amend their constitutions without first sending their officials hundreds of miles away to beg federal authorities to approve them."[4]

Three years later, in *Allen v. State Board of Elections*,[5] Justice Black reiterated his objections to section 5 in even stronger terms:

> This is reminiscent of old Reconstruction days when soldiers controlled the South and when those States were compelled to make

---

* B.A., University of Pittsburgh; M.A., Ph.D., Duke University. Associate Professor and Research Associate at the Institute of Government, University of Virginia.

**B.A., Barnard College; M.A., Ph.D., Harvard University. Visiting Lecturer, Department of Government, Harvard University. Dr. Thernstrom is the author of *Whose Votes Count? Affirmative Action and Minority Voting Rights* (1987).

1. Pub. L. No. 89-110, 79 Stat. 445 (codified as amended at 42 U.S.C. §§ 1971, 1973 to 1973bb-1 (1982)).
2. Currently codified at 42 U.S.C. § 1973a (1982).
3. 383 U.S. 301 (1966).
4. *Katzenbach*, 383 U.S. at 359 (Black, J., concurring in part and dissenting in part) (footnote omitted).
5. 393 U.S. 544 (1969).

> reports to military commanders of what they did. The Southern States were at that time deprived of their right to pass laws on the premise that they were not then a part of the Union and therefore could be treated with all the harshness meted out to conquered provinces . . . . I doubt that any of the 13 Colonies would have agreed to our Constitution if they had dreamed that the time might come when they would have to go to a United States Attorney General or a District of Columbia court with hat in hand begging for permission to change their laws. Still less would any of these Colonies have been willing to agree to a Constitution that gave the Federal Government power to force one Colony to go through such an onerous procedure while all the other former Colonies, now supposedly its sister States, were allowed to retain their full sovereignty . . . . Proposals to give judges a part in enacting or vetoing legislation before it passed were made and rejected in the Constitutional Convention . . . .[6]

That Justice Black took this stance in his dissenting opinions in these and other cases involving section 5 of the Voting Rights Act is more than a little ironic. In these cases, Justice Black advanced what appears to be the classic "states' rights" argument. He described a Constitution of enumerated federal powers and of powers reserved to the states; moreover, he harkened back to the original intent of the Founders in inveighing against a federal veto over state laws.[7] For good measure, he characterized the 1965 law as a reincarnation of Reconstruction.[8] Not surprising from a native of Alabama, it might be thought. However, the constitutional philosophy of Justice Black—expressed in almost 1200 opinions over three decades on the Supreme Court—could hardly be described as friendly to states' rights. Indeed, Justice Black urged upon the Court an expansive interpretation of congressional power under the Commerce Clause,[9] pushed for the application of the Bill of Rights to the states through a liberal reading of the Fourteenth

6. *Allen*, 393 U.S. at 595-96 (Black, J., dissenting).

7. *See id.* (Black, J., dissenting); *Katzenbach*, 383 U.S. at 358-61 (Black, J., concurring in part and dissenting in part). Justice Black also argued that section 5 impermissibly required states to seek advisory opinions from a federal court, such opinions being forbidden by the Constitution. *Katzenbach*, 383 U.S. at 357-58 (Black, J., concurring in part and dissenting in part).

8. *Allen*, 393 U.S. at 595 (Black, J., dissenting).

9. *See, e.g.*, United States v. South-Eastern Underwriters Ass'n, 322 U.S. 533 (1944).

Amendment,[10] and joined the Court's quest for racial equality in the school desegregation cases of the 1950s and 1960s.[11]

His dissents in *Katzenbach* and *Allen* notwithstanding, a concern for federalism or states' rights thus did not figure prominently in the constitutional philosophy of Justice Black. Unlike his longtime colleague on the Court, Justice John Marshall Harlan, he did not display much sensitivity to the interests of states as states within the constitutional order. His views on voting rights, however, were not as aberrant as they seem. They flowed logically from the other basic principles of constitutional interpretation to which he adhered.

Justice Black's judicial philosophy perhaps can be best characterized as a blend of democratic populism and judicial strict constructionism. He believed that the federal courts should defer to elected legislatures—both federal and state—over a broad array of policy areas.[12] For example, he recognized virtually no limits on the authority of Congress to regulate economic relations under the Commerce Clause.[13] At the same time, however, he accorded wide latitude to state legislatures in the field of economic regulation, at least to the extent that Congress had not preempted state power.[14] In short, Justice Black regarded economic regulation as a legislative domain in which the lines of federal authority would be set by Congress and not by the Supreme Court; when Congress has not acted, the Court should not, as a general matter, invoke the federal commerce power as a strait jacket on state regulatory activity.

With respect to the Bill of Rights, of course, Justice Black read the guarantees of individual liberty and due process in unequivocal terms and held that the protection afforded by the first ten amendments should apply with the same force to both the national and state governments.[15] But these views were not

---

10. *See, e.g.*, Adamson v. California, 332 U.S. 46, 68 (1947) (Black, J., dissenting).

11. *See, e.g.*, Swann v. Charlotte-Mecklenberg Bd. of Educ., 402 U.S. 1 (1971); Griffin v. Prince Edward County Bd. of Educ., 377 U.S. 218 (1964); Brown v. Board of Educ., 347 U.S. 483 (1954).

12. *See* cases cited *infra* notes 13-14; *see also* Oregon v. Mitchell, 400 U.S. 112 (1970) (federal and state control over voter qualifications in state elections); Wright v. Rockefeller, 376 U.S. 52 (1964) (state apportionment plan).

13. *See, e.g.*, *South-Eastern Underwriters*, 322 U.S. 549-53.

14. *See, e.g.*, Dean Milk Co. v. City of Madison, Wisc., 340 U.S. 349, 357 (1951) (Black, J., dissenting); Gwin, White & Prince, Inc. v. Henneford, 305 U.S. 434, 442 (1939) (Black, J., dissenting).

15. *See* Adamson v. California, 332 U.S. 46, 68 (1947) (Black, J., dissenting).

inconsistent with his belief that courts should defer to legislative will. By precisely defining civil rights and liberties, he sought to establish clear limits on legislative discretion and to reduce the likelihood that the courts would have to overrule legislative initiatives. Moreover, although incorporation of the Bill of Rights into the Fourteenth Amendment drew the Supreme Court more deeply into state policymaking, incorporation elevated the states to the same plane as the national government. By urging that both levels of government be subject to the same procedural requirements, Black sought to reduce judicial license and thus intrusiveness. His stance in the reapportionment cases likewise squared with his approach on other issues. His firm belief in deference to elected legislatures made it natural for him to support holding the United States House of Representatives, state legislatures, and local governing bodies to the "one person, one vote" standard.[16] If courts were to yield to legislatures, it followed that those legislatures must be structured democratically.

A profound respect for the democratic process thus informed Justice Black's constitutional philosophy. Constrained only by brightly marked boundaries intended to protect basic civil rights and liberties, the policymaking process would be left to those who had been popularly elected. Thus, it was up to Congress to interpret the Commerce Clause and set the boundaries of federal power.[17] Where Justice Black recognized a necessary role for courts—in cases involving legislative apportionment, as well as fundamental rights—he sought to limit judicial power by delineating constraints equally applicable to all levels of government.[18] In so doing, he sought to extricate courts from the difficult task of defining the scope and limits of federal and state authority in other areas.

In the pages that follow we attempt first to place Justice Black's judicial philosophy in historical context and then to explore the implications of that philosophy for the question of federalism. Special attention is given to Justice Black's views in cases involving federal and state economic regulation and in those involving voting rights. Although we criticize Justice Black for giv-

---

16. *See, e.g.*, Hadley v. Junior College Dist., 397 U.S. 50 (1970); Wesberry v. Sanders, 376 U.S. 1 (1964); Colegrove v. Green, 328 U.S. 549, 566 (1946) (Black, J., dissenting).

17. *See South-Eastern Underwriters*, 322 U.S. 533.

18. *See* cases cited *supra* note 16.

ing too little weight to the value of community diversity, we credit him with a more consistent and positive view of federalism than that held by most of his colleagues on the Court, particularly in the Warren era.

Justice Black: The Philosophy of a Southerner?

Appointed to the Supreme Court in 1937, Hugo Black was chosen for his views on the overriding question of economic regulation. It was an issue, of course, with profound federal overtones. As is well known, prior to Justice Black's arrival, the Court was inclined not only to look unfavorably upon congressional efforts to reach into the realm of intrastate commerce but also to view with a jaundiced eye efforts by states to regulate the marketplace.[19] Thus, in 1936 the Supreme Court both rejected congressional regulation of the coal industry as beyond the bounds of permissible federal action under the Commerce Clause[20] and struck down New York State's minimum wage law.[21]

It might be thought odd that FDR would look to the South for his first spokesman for the New Deal on the Court. But Black's commitment to Roosevelt is not at odds with Black's Southern origins. As Ladd and Hadley pointed out,

> too often overlooked is the extent to which the policy thrusts of the New Deal struck a responsive chord in Dixie. The [current] picture of the South as the most conservative region in the country leads frequently to the notion that it has always been "to the right." This tendency to impose the present upon the past is furthered by the recognition that majorities of Southern whites historically have proved reactionary on civil rights.[22]

In fact, Ladd and Hadley go on to argue that the South gave higher approval to New Deal policies than any other region in the country, as an exhaustive analysis of Gallup survey data from the

---

19. *See* cases cited *infra* notes 20-21; *see also* Hammer v. Dagenhart, 247 U.S. 251 (1918); Lochner v. New York, 198 U.S. 45 (1905).

20. Carter v. Carter Coal Co., 298 U.S. 238 (1936) (invalidating Bituminous Coal Conservation Act of 1935).

21. Morehead v. New York *ex rel.* Tipaldo, 298 U.S. 587 (1936).

22. E. Ladd & C. Hadley, Transformations of the American Party System: Political Coalitions From the New Deal to the 1970s 129-30 (1975) [hereinafter Ladd & Hadley].

1930s and early 1940s clearly indicates. "Residents of other regions, more than southerners, reflected fears that the convulsive changes of the Depression period posed a serious threat to the 'American way of life,'" they report.[23] Their picture squares with that which Dewey W. Grantham, Jr., drew in lectures in 1962. "To Southerners," he noted, "perhaps even more than to other Americans, the New Deal was symbolized by the leadership of Franklin D. Roosevelt . . . . While maintaining a high degree of personal popularity among Southern congressmen, Roosevelt also captured the minds and hearts of the Southern masses."[24]

If, as Ladd and Hadley state, Southern Democrats, as loyal members of the party, did not simply manage to swallow the New Deal, but enthusiastically accepted it, that acceptance should come as no surprise. Agrarian and other New Deal programs particularly benefitted the South, the poorest region in the nation during the Depression. During the Depression years, as the need for federal assistance grew, the region's attachment to states' rights waned. William Faulkner later said that the corridors of Washington replaced the cotton fields;[25] there was more than a little truth to his assertion. Yet the new reliance on Washington involved no threat to the structure of local power in the South. For this reason, too, the New Deal found favor. The Roosevelt administration took care not to antagonize Southern sensibilities, in considerable measure using local people in the implementation of its programs. It attempted, that is, to work closely with existing political elites.

In two respects, however, the picture that Ladd, Hadley, and others drew of Southern allegiance to the New Deal is somewhat misleading. Support for Roosevelt on the part of rank and file Democrats appears to have outlasted that of many party leaders, whose initial enthusiasm for "emergency" legislation waned once that legislation took on a more permanent cast. With the abrogation of the two-thirds rule,[26] the President's attack on the Supreme

---

23. LADD & HADLEY, *supra* note 22, at 131-32.

24. D. GRANTHAM, JR., THE DEMOCRATIC SOUTH 71 (1971).

25. The Faulkner quotation in its entirety can be found in D. GRANTHAM, JR., *supra* note 24, at 70-71.

26. Described as the "Northernization" of the Democratic Party, the Democratic Convention of 1936 eliminated the rule requiring a two-thirds vote of the delegates for nomination, thereby removing the South's veto power. *See* 10 G. TINDALL, THE EMERGENCE OF THE NEW SOUTH: 1913-1945 619 (1967).

Court,[27] the threat of an antilynching bill,[28] and the surge of reform legislation in 1937 and 1938,[29] opposition mounted. To some degree, Grantham argued, Southern conservative opponents spoke for business interests who feared the impact of a federal wage and hour law on the region's efforts to industrialize.[30] More importantly, men such as Carter Glass and Josiah Bailey felt

> threatened . . . as they had never been threatened before . . . . Not only did it seem more and more unlikely that the South could ever dominate the Democratic Party again, but it was also increasingly apparent that the national policies adopted during the thirties would ultimately strengthen organized labor, farmers, Negroes, and middle-class people sufficiently to force concessions from those who had long had the upper hand in the region.[31]

"The roots of disaffection," Tindall writes, "lay in the county-seat 'elites,' in the 'banker-merchant-farmer-lawyer-doctor-governing class.' For them the New Deal jeopardized a power that rested on the control of property, labor, credit, and local government."[32]

Support for the New Deal among Southern politicians was both short-lived and narrowly based. Not only did enthusiasm for Roosevelt flag, but from the outset such enthusiasm appears to have been for only one strand of New Deal policy: generous aid to farmers and opposition to concentrated wealth and power. Tradi-

---

27. In response to the Supreme Court's repeated invalidation of New Deal legislation as unconstitutional, President Roosevelt proposed in February 1937 to create up to fifty new federal judgeships, including six Supreme Court justices, to assist any judge who had served ten years and remained on the bench six months after his seventieth birthday. Because of adamant political opposition, however, the plan ultimately failed. For a thorough discussion of Roosevelt's "court-packing" plan, see G. TINDALL, *supra* note 26, at 619-24.

28. In 1933 the National Association for the Advancement of Colored People (NAACP), in the wake of renewed lynchings of Negroes in the South, drafted an antilynching bill which was subsequently introduced in the Senate. The bill proposed federal trials of mobsters when states failed to act, punishment of derelict officers, and damage claims against lynching counties. Opposition from Southern senators, however, prevented its enactment. *See* G. TINDALL, *supra* note 26, at 551-52 & n.38.

29. *See, e.g.*, Agricultural Adjustment Act of 1938, ch. 30, § 1, 52 Stat. 31 (codified as amended at 7 U.S.C. §§ 1281-1393 (1982)); Fair Labor Standards Act of 1938, ch. 676, § 1, 52 Stat. 1060 (codified as amended at 29 U.S.C. §§ 201-219 (1982)); Public Works Administration Extension Act of 1937, ch. 401, 50 Stat. 358.

30. *See* D. GRANTHAM, JR., *supra* note 24, at 73.

31. D. GRANTHAM, JR., *supra* note 24, at 73-74. On Southern fears that the New Deal marked the beginning of a transformation of the Democratic Party that would lead inevitably to the enfranchisement of Southern blacks, *see* Milkis, *Franklin D. Roosevelt and the Transcendence of Partisan Politics*, POL. SCI. Q., Fall 1985, at 491.

32. G. TINDALL, *supra* note 26, at 618.

tional Southern distrust of highly centralized government was not assuaged by the popular President. Congressmen from rural and small-town constituencies, Tindall reports, "did not adjust readily to the urban liberalism of labor, welfare, and housing programs."[33] Moreover—to underscore an earlier point—the conservative elite, openly opposed to the New Deal after the court-packing maneuver of 1937, emerged from the years of reform with its power intact. Although Roosevelt made sporadic and halfhearted attempts to promote the "forces of change," his decision to share control over New Deal programs with local officials reinforced the prevailing power structure. As Alan Brinkley put it:

> [N]either the Depression nor the New Deal appeared to have wrought any significant changes in the region's internal political organization or in the nature of its political leadership. In other areas of the nation, the 1930s had produced powerful new political coalitions capable of challenging and at times toppling old structures of political authority. In the South, the Depression years had produced little more than what Key described as "weak forays against the established order," forays the established order had generally countered with ease.[34]

Although it is true that a group of Southern progressives rose to prominence in the 1930s, the commitment of these progressives to many New Deal reforms was limited, their regional pride (thus opposition to federal "meddling") no less great than that of the conservatives, and their political base fragile compared to that of their conservative rivals.[35] The fragility of the progressive political base quickly became evident; most Southern progressives disappeared, changed their political tune (as Lyndon Johnson did), or tended by the end of the 1940s to find themselves more influential outside the South than within it.

Black falls into the third group. A down-the-line supporter of the New Deal, in important respects he stood outside Southern political culture, estranged from the region's existing political elite. As Sheldon Hackney pointed out, Jeffersonian ideals—a celebration of the common man and a distrust of special privilege—were

---

33. *Id.* at 631 (footnote omitted).

34. Brinkley, *The New Deal and Southern Politics*, in THE NEW DEAL AND THE SOUTH 98 (J. Cobb & M. Namorato ed. 1984).

35. Brinkley, *supra* note 34, at 103-04, 107-08.

political orthodoxy in Alabama.[36] Yet, as Paul Murphy observed, Jeffersonian misgivings about positive government were gradually shed by Black.[37] In the vanguard of advocating the aggressive use of affirmative grants of federal power, Black in 1933 introduced a bill that would have prohibited the interstate shipment of products manufactured or mined by workers who labored more than thirty hours a week or six hours a day.[38] The National Industrial Recovery Act (NIRA)[39] was in part a response to this proposal.[40] Thus, if Black, as Hackney argued, absorbed and retained the equalitarian principles of his native state—speaking for the little man, for the poor and marginalized whites, against exploitative or manipulative concentrations of private power[41]—in important respects he broke from that tradition. He accepted the modern state with its powerful and intrusive federal bureaucracy.

The point can be put another way. A commitment to the New Deal was not at odds with Southern roots, yet Hugo Black took that commitment several steps further than even "liberal" Southern politicians were generally willing to go. Fred Rodell described Black's arrival in Washington as that of "a bright new star so militantly liberal that one of [his colleagues] dubbed him an 'evangelical progressive' . . . [He was a] New Dealer for six years before there was a New Deal."[42] By the time Black was appointed to the Court, he was close to becoming a Southern renegade. Joseph Alsop portrayed his nomination as "a symbolic and defiant act."[43] "Although Black came from Alabama," William Leuchtenberg reported, "no group was unhappier about his nomination than the Southern congressmen . . . . [H]e was a Southern

---

36. Hackney, *The Clay County Origins of Mr. Justice Black: The Populist as Insider*, 36 ALA. L. REV. 835, 839 (1985).

37. Murphy, *The Early Social and Political Philosophy of Hugo Black: Liquor as a Test Case*, 36 ALA. L. REV. 861, 877 (1985).

38. For a description of the proposed bill and the political opposition thereto, see Shannon, *Hugo LaFayette Black as United States Senator*, 36 ALA. L. REV. 881, 888-89 (1985).

39. Ch. 90, 48 Stat. 195 (1933). The NIRA was subsequently held unconstitutional in A.L.A. Schechter Poultry Corp. v. United States, 295 U.S. 495 (1935).

40. Shannon, *supra* note 38, at 889.

41. Hackney, *supra* note 36, at 839-40.

42. Rodell, *A Sprig of Laurel for Hugo Black at 75*, 10 AM. U.L. REV. 1, 3 (1961).

43. J. ALSOP & T. CATLEDGE, THE 168 DAYS 269-307 (1938) *noted in* Leuchtenberg, *A Klansman Joins the Court: The Appointment of Hugo L. Black*, 41 U. CHI. L. REV. 1, 29 n.132 (1973).

liberal, and his selection signaled Roosevelt's determination to back those who were attempting to transform the conservative structure of Southern politics . . . ."[44]

That in important respects Black stood outside Southern political culture was reflected in his judicial philosophy. His philosophy cannot be fully reconciled with his Southern origins. Indeed, Justice Black's opinions on the Court exhibit scant regard for certain key elements of Jeffersonian liberalism and populist ideology: the deference to the values of the local community and the suspicion, even fear, of big government. Black's views on the Court betray his Southern experience, yet eliminate the internal contradictions of that region's tradition. In fact, Justice Black appears to have drawn upon the heritage of the South in much the same way as he read the Constitution—selecting elements to construct a coherent and consistent philosophical framework. He failed to absorb the contradictions of the Southern experience and, in striving for constitutional clarity and consistency, ignored the complexity of the Constitution itself. His opinions contain no recognition that constitutional questions—perhaps particularly those involving federalism—demand a reconciliation and balancing of fundamental, yet conflicting, principles.

The Regulation of Commerce

For all his professed insularity from politics once on the bench, Justice Black's views on questions of economic regulation were precisely those which President Roosevelt had been led to expect. His appointment marked the beginning of an epoch in which the Court abandoned the domain of economic regulation for that of civil rights and civil liberties. In 1937 a constitutional era ended and a new one began. Concern over the relationship between the individual and government replaced the preoccupation with questions of economic liberty.[45] It was a switch in focus in which Justice Black played a pivotal role. He did more than support the

44. Leuchtenberg, *supra* note 43, at 7-8.

45. This jurisprudential metamorphosis is apparent in United States v. Carolene Products Co., 304 U.S. 144 (1941), in which the Court noted that although economic regulatory measures would no longer be subject to stringent judicial review, the Court would continue independently to review government enactments that infringe upon individual liberties. *See id.* at 152-53 n.4.

Court's about-face on questions of economic regulation. He laid out a forceful and persuasive argument for the regulatory state.

Black's views on questions of economic regulation have a clear starting point. The phrase "Congress shall have power . . . to regulate commerce . . . among the several States,"[46] he believed, meant just that. Article I, that is, had assigned the regulation of interstate commerce to the legislative branch. It was thus up to Congress both to control and to define commerce. As he observed in *United States v. South-Eastern Underwriters Association*,[47] the Court's

> basic responsibility in interpreting the Commerce Clause is to make certain that the power to govern intercourse among the states remains where the Constitution placed it. That power, as held by this Court from the beginning, is vested in the Congress, available to be exercised for the national welfare as Congress shall deem necessary.[48]

Judicial deference to the legislature on Commerce Clause questions was a rule with few exceptions. Dissenting in *American Communications Association v. Douds*,[49] Black bitterly attacked a provision of the Taft-Hartley Act requiring labor union officials to deny, under oath, membership in the Communist Party. "No case cited by the Court provides the least vestige of support for thus holding that the Commerce Clause restricts the right to think," he wrote.[50] It was a rare instance in which Black viewed Congress as having overstepped the bounds of its legitimate authority to regulate interstate commerce.

Black's respect for congressional judgment in the area of commercial activity is well known. Perhaps less appreciated is his similar approach to acts of state legislatures involving economic regulation. Congressional action preempted the field. But in those areas in which Congress had remained silent, the Court, in Black's view, was bound to respect the exercise of state authority.[51] The Commerce Clause, that is, was no substantive barrier to state regulatory activity. Thus, in *Dean Milk Co. v. City of Madison,*

---

46. U.S. CONST. art. I, § 8, cl. 3.
47. 322 U.S. 533 (1944).
48. *South-Eastern Underwriters*, 322 U.S. at 552-53.
49. 339 U.S. 382 (1950).
50. *Douds*, 339 U.S. at 446 (Black, J., dissenting).
51. *See infra* notes 52-57 and accompanying text.

Wisconsin,[52] Black would have upheld a city ordinance that made unlawful the selling of pasteurized milk unless the milk had been bottled at an approved plant within a five mile radius of the city. It was a bona fide health regulation in his view. The "right to traffic in commerce for profit," he argued, should not be elevated "above the power of the people to guard the purity of their daily diet of milk."[53] Likewise, in *Gwin, White & Prince, Inc. v. Henneford*,[54] Black dissented when the Court struck down a Washington tax on the gross receipts of fruit marketers who shipped their products to other states and foreign countries. He viewed the tax as "general [and] non-discriminatory," imposed upon all businesses operating within the state.[55] The tax became, in fact, an instrument of discrimination against *intrastate* business at the point at which the burden was lifted from companies engaged in commerce which crossed state lines.[56] "[S]tate laws," he said,

> are not invalid under the Commerce Clause unless they actually discriminate against interstate commerce or conflict with a regulation enacted by Congress . . . . If valid, non-discriminatory taxes imposed in these States create "multiple" burdens, such "burdens" result from the political subdivisions created by our form of government. They are the price paid for governmental protection and maintenance in all States where the taxpayer does business.[57]

In this and other decisions Black demonstrated an acute sensitivity to the critical economic strains wrought upon state governments by the Depression and to the urgency of legislative action for which his experience both in Alabama and in the Senate had clearly prepared him. That sensitivity is explicitly articulated in *Henneford*. Thus, Black explained:

> In 1933, [the state of] Washington's system of taxation failed to supply adequate revenue to support activities essential to the welfare of its people. Mounting delinquencies due to burdensome taxes on property led the state legislature to conclude that property taxes had to be reduced . . . . [F]orced to seek new sources of revenue, the State turned—as did many other States faced with similar

52. 340 U.S. 349 (1951).
53. *Dean Milk*, 340 U.S. at 358-59 (Black, J., dissenting).
54. 305 U.S. 434 (1939).
55. *Henneford*, 305 U.S. at 442 (Black, J., dissenting).
56. *Id.* at 442-43 (Black, J., dissenting).
57. *Id.* at 446, 448 (Black, J., dissenting).

> needs—to a general, non-discriminatory excise tax upon business carried on in Washington . . . .[58]

It was a lecture in Depression economics that he had enunciated in *J.D. Adams Manufacturing Co. v. Storen.*[59]

Black's views on congressional and state legislative authority to regulate commercial activity were New Deal orthodoxy. A concomitant commitment to judicial restraint on questions of economic regulation runs through Black's opinions in *J.D. Adams*, *Henneford*, and other decisions. Thus, in *Lincoln Federal Labor Union v. Northwestern Iron & Metal Co.*,[60] Justice Black, speaking for the Court, vigorously assailed the idea that the Due Process or Contract Clauses could be used to limit state regulatory powers. Upholding right-to-work laws in Nebraska and North Carolina, he stated that "states have power to legislate against what are found to be injurious practices in their internal commercial and business affairs, so long as their laws do not run afoul of some specific federal constitutional prohibition, or of some valid federal law."[61] The point was made more explicitly in *Central Railroad v. Pennsylvania*,[62] in which Black argued against a "flexible and expansive" use of the Due Process Clause to strike down state tax laws.[63] The Commerce Clause "means that Congress can regulate commerce and that the courts cannot," he stated flatly in *Morgan v. Virginia*.[64] The issue was the constitutionality of a state law requiring bus companies to segregate black and white passengers, and Black concurred in the majority opinion only because he viewed the question as unfortunately or disingenuously closed by prior decisions.[65]

---

58. *Id.* at 443 (Black, J., dissenting) (footnotes omitted).

59. 304 U.S. 307, 317-18 & nn.4-5 (1938) (Black, J., dissenting).

60. 335 U.S. 528 (1949).

61. *Lincoln Fed. Labor Union*, 335 U.S. at 536.

62. 370 U.S. 607 (1962).

63. *Central R.R.*, 370 U.S. at 622 (Black, J., concurring). Black concurred with the majority opinion simply because he felt that the decision was adequately based on the then prevailing interpretation of the Commerce Clause and that a reconsideration of the due process issue would have been inappropriate. *Id.* (Black, J., concurring).

64. 328 U.S. 373, 386-87 (1946) (Black, J., concurring).

65. *Morgan*, 328 U.S. at 387 & n.1 (Black, J., concurring). "So long as the Court remains committed to the 'undue burden on commerce formula,' I must make decisions under it." *Id.* at 387 (Black, J., concurring).

The question, in Black's view, was often the limits of judicial competence. In *Brotherhood of Locomotive Firemen & Enginemen v. Chicago, Rock Island & Pacific Railroad*,[66] he upheld as valid safety regulations Arkansas' "full crew" railroad laws, with an attack on those who would ask the Court to indulge in legislative judgment. That judgment, in his view, would seldom be adequately informed.[67] As Black argued in *Dean Milk*, the Court could not satisfy itself that regulation of local health by means other than that which Madison, Wisconsin, had chosen would be equally effective.[68] "Comparative costs, convenience, or effectiveness [are not matters of] judicial knowledge."[69] "Only a comprehensive survey and investigation of the entire national economy—which Congress alone has power and facilities to make—can indicate the need for . . . restricting the taxing power of a State," Black stated in *Henneford*.[70] "[T]his Court is unable to make the broad national inquiry necessary to reach an informed conclusion on this question of economic policy."[71]

Trust in legislative competence and a distrust of courts on questions of economic regulation—these views held by Justice Black were precisely those, as we have earlier suggested, that Roosevelt hoped for. It was an approach which, to some degree, reinforced federalism, since it left the states relatively free from second-guessing courts on commerce, taxation, and other matters. Yet, it left states and local business vulnerable to congressional regulation almost without restraint. This is not, in fact, a theory of federalism. It was Black's belief in restricting the power of courts that gave states room to play. His views on the proper distribution of authority were but a by-product of his commitment to national and state power. One finds little support in Justice Black's opinions for an affirmative form of federalism that would proceed from

66. 393 U.S. 129 (1968).

67. *Brotherhood*, 393 U.S. at 136. "In the absence of congressional action, however, we cannot invoke the judicial power to invalidate this judgment of the people of Arkansas and their elected representatives as to the price society should pay to promote safety in the railroad industry." *Id.* at 144.

68. Dean Milk Co. v. City of Madison, Wisc., 340 U.S. 349, 358-59 (1951) (Black, J., dissenting).

69. *Id.* at 359 (Black, J., dissenting).

70. Gwin, White & Prince, Inc. v. Henneford, 305 U.S. 434, 449 (1939) (Black, J., dissenting).

71. *Id.* at 452 (Black, J., dissenting).

the Tenth Amendment to carve out a domain of protected state power.

Voting Rights I: Apportionment

In his approach to voting rights questions, deference to the legislative branch was again Justice Black's starting point. But he conditioned that deference. Legislatures apportioned by schemes systematically biased against city dwellers, for instance, did not have a democratic claim upon judicial respect equal to that of representative bodies that were truly representative.[72] Deference demanded that popularly elected bodies, in fact, reflect the popular will by the rudimentary measure of "one person, one vote."[73] That rule—like those developed in opinions involving civil liberties and commerce—should apply, he believed, with equal force to national and state legislatures.[74] Thus, dissenting in *Colegrove v. Green*,[75] he argued that population disparities among congressional districts in Illinois violated not only article I, section 2, but also the Equal Protection Clause of the Fourteenth Amendment; implicitly, the latter would equally condemn malapportioned state legislative and congressional districts drawn by a state.[76] No elected body, in Black's view, was exempt from the "one person, one vote" standard.

Some eighteen years after *Colegrove*, Justice Black wrote the Court's opinion in *Wesberry v. Sanders*,[77] holding that article I, section 2 insured the right to vote in congressional districts substantially equal in population.[78] That same year, Justice Black voted with a majority of the Court in holding that the Equal Protection Clause mandated that both houses of state legislatures be apportioned according to the "one person, one vote" principle.[79] In 1968 he voted with the majority in holding that this principle ap-

72. *See* Hadley v. Junior College Dist., 397 U.S. 50, 57-58 (1970).

73. *See* Reynolds v. Sims, 377 U.S. 533 (1964); Wesberry v. Sanders, 376 U.S. 1 (1964).

74. *See infra* notes 75-84 and accompanying text.

75. 328 U.S. 549 (1946).

76. *Colegrove*, 328 U.S. at 569-71 (Black, J., dissenting).

77. 376 U.S. 1 (1964).

78. *Wesberry*, 376 U.S. at 7-8. "[T]he command of Art. I, § 2 . . . means that as nearly as is practicable one man's vote in a congressional election is to be worth as much as another's." *Id.* (footnotes omitted).

79. Reynolds v. Sims, 377 U.S. 533 (1964).

plied to general-purpose local governments,[80] and he later wrote for the Court in extending the application of the equal population standard to a junior college district.[81] He also voted with the majority in *Kirkpatrick v. Preisler*[82] and *Wells v. Rockefeller*[83]—two 1969 decisions that, in essence, required states to justify any deviation, no matter how small, from the equal population standard in congressional redistricting.[84]

The reapportionment revolution produced deep divisions on the Court. Justice John Marshall Harlan, the most persistent critic of the "one person, one vote" principle throughout the 1960s, argued that history offered little support for the contention that article I or the Fourteenth Amendment demanded equipopulous districts.[85] Although Justice Black did not join Harlan in his near contempt for the mechanical application of precise numerical standards to legislative redistricting, Justice Black's view was more prudent than that of several of his colleagues. In two key cases,[86] Justice Black led the Court away from a far more intrusive view of fair representation than the one it was charting, with the consequence that some measure of state autonomy in the redistricting field was preserved.[87]

Wright v. Rockefeller[88] centered on an allegation that the New York legislature drew four racially gerrymandered districts in the borough of Manhattan. Writing for the Court (over vigorous dissents from Justices Douglas and Goldberg),[89] Justice Black stated that the plaintiffs had "not shown that the challenged part of the New York Act was the product of a state contrivance to segregate

---

80. Avery v. Midland County, 390 U.S. 474 (1968).

81. Hadley v. Junior College Dist., 397 U.S. 50 (1970).

82. 394 U.S. 526 (1969).

83. 394 U.S. 542 (1969).

84. *See Wells*, 394 U.S. at 545-46 (plan invalid where most populous district was 6.488% above mean and least populous district was 6.608% below); *Kirkpatrick*, 394 U.S. at 530-31 (congressional redistricting plan invalid where most populous district was 3.13% above mathematical ideal and least populous was 2.84% below).

85. *See* Wesberry v. Sanders, 376 U.S. 1, 30-41 & n.15 (1964) (Harlan, J., dissenting). "[O]ne thing seems clear; it is in the last degree unlikely that most or even many of the delegates [to the Constitutional Convention] would have subscribed to the principle of 'one person, one vote.'" *Id.* at 30-31 (Harlan, J., dissenting). *See also* Oregon v. Mitchell, 400 U.S. 112, 154-61 (1970) (Harlan, J., concurring in part and dissenting in part).

86. Fortson v. Morris, 385 U.S. 231 (1966); Wright v. Rockefeller, 376 U.S. 52 (1964).

87. *See infra* notes 88-100 and accompanying text.

88. 376 U.S. 52 (1964).

89. *Wright*, 376 U.S. at 59 (Douglas, J., dissenting); *id.* at 67 (Goldberg, J., dissenting).

on the basis of race or place of origin."[90] Decided the same day as *Wesberry v. Sanders*,[91] the *Wright* decision temporarily steered the Court away from a political thicket even more foreboding than that into which it had wandered by attacking the malapportionment question.

Justice Black's majority opinion in *Fortson v. Morris*[92] likewise rejected the radical claims advanced by four dissenters[93] and drew prudential limits on the scope of the reapportionment revolution. At issue was a provision of the Georgia constitution that required the state legislature to choose the governor from the top two candidates when no candidate had received a majority of the popular vote in a general election. At stake was the outcome of the 1966 election in which Republican Howard H. Callaway, with 47.07 percent of the vote, outpolled Lester G. Maddox and a third candidate.[94] On the basis of *Gray v. Sanders*,[95] the Supreme Court's 1963 decision invalidating Georgia's county unit system for gubernatorial elections, a district court had invalidated the provision which gave the legislature power to select the governor.[96]

The following questions were before the Supreme Court in *Fortson*: Did the constitutional provision empowering the legislature to choose the governor violate *Gray v. Sanders* (1) by removing the power of election from the people altogether, (2) by shifting the locus of decisionmaking to any legislative arena where the texture of the popular vote would be only imperfectly reflected, or (3) by shifting the power of selection to this particular Georgia legislature, which was under court order to reapportion?[97] Justice Black argued that *Gray* had not been breached because the state could vest the power of electing the governor in the legislature in the first instance and could therefore give the legislature the power

---

90. *Id.* at 58.

91. 376 U.S. 1 (1964).

92. 385 U.S. 231 (1966).

93. Justices Douglas and Fortas both wrote dissenting opinions in which Chief Justice Warren and Justice Brennan joined. *See Fortson*, 385 U.S. at 236 (Douglas, J., dissenting); *id.* at 242 (Fortas, J., dissenting).

94. *Fortson*, 385 U.S. at 236-37 (Douglas, J., dissenting).

95. 372 U.S. 368 (1963).

96. Morris v. Fortson, 262 F. Supp. 93 (N.D. Ga. 1966).

97. Reapportionment of the Georgia legislature was ordered in Toombs v. Fortson, 384 U.S. 210 (1966), *aff'g mem.*, 241 F. Supp. 65 (N.D. Ga. 1965).

to choose the governor after an election had been held.[98] Finally, and most importantly, Justice Black rejected the notion that the Georgia legislature was disqualified from choosing the governor because it was malapportioned.[99] For this assertion, he relied on *Toombs v. Fortson*,[100] in which the Court had authorized the Georgia legislature to continue to operate until May 1, 1968.

But for the views of the dissenters in the case, *Fortson* might have been a wholly unremarkable decision (although Alexander Bickel argued that it departed "indefensibly" from the majoritarian principle of prior and subsequent reapportionment cases).[101] Justice Douglas's dissenting opinion[102] (joined by Chief Justice Warren and Justices Brennan and Fortas) and Justice Fortas's dissent[103] (joined by Chief Justice Warren and Justice Douglas) contended that the Georgia legislature could not be empowered to decide the outcome of the election. Citing *Gray*, Justice Fortas claimed that it was "no less a denial of equal protection of the laws for the result of an election to be determined, not by the voters, but by the legislature on a basis which is not related to the votes cast."[104] He went on to state: "If the voting right is to mean anything, it certainly must be protected against the possibility that victory will go to the loser."[105] Giving the task of gubernatorial selection to the malapportioned Georgia legislature, he asserted, yielded essentially the result that *Gray* had prohibited.[106]

Justice Fortas's dissenting opinion contained at least two dubious ideas. That malapportionment taints a legislature's acts was the first.[107] Could it be seriously argued that the taxes levied by the Georgia legislature in 1967 were null and void because the legislature's members were not elected in accordance with the "one person, one vote" standard? It was equally doubtful that the Con-

---

98. *Fortson*, 385 U.S. at 233-34. "Not a word in the [Gray v. Sanders] opinion indicated that it was intended to compel a State to elect its governors . . . through elections of the people rather than through . . . elections by the State Assembly." *Id.* at 233.

99. *Id.* at 235.

100. 384 U.S. 210 (1966), *aff'g mem.*, 241 F. Supp. 65 (N.D. Ga. 1965).

101. Bickel, *The Supreme Court and Reapportionment*, in REAPPORTIONMENT IN THE 1970s 68 (N. Polsby ed. 1971).

102. *Fortson*, 385 U.S. at 236 (Douglas, J., dissenting).

103. *Id.* at 242 (Fortas, J., dissenting).

104. *Id.* at 243 (Fortas, J., dissenting).

105. *Id.* (Fortas, J., dissenting).

106. *Id.* at 245 (Fortas, J., dissenting).

107. *Id.* at 244-46 (Fortas, J., dissenting).

stitution might require, as the opinion implied,[108] the popular election of governors. The commitment to equally populated districts had not bound the Court to such populist purity. Had the dissenters prevailed, they would have opened a Pandora's box. Was the governor the only state executive who had to be elected? Could no local official be appointed?

Federalism questions were indirectly raised in the opinions Justice Black wrote in the area of apportionment,[109] as in those in which he dealt with questions of commerce and civil liberties.[110] He joined in the Court's push to impose the equal population standard on Congress and state legislatures.[111] Yet, he rejected the inclination of Justice Douglas and others to convert a numerical rule applicable to legislatures into a more nebulous guarantee of fair representation for racial, ethnic, or political groups[112] or into an untrammeled majoritarianism relevant to all manner of electoral mechanisms.[113] He believed in applying the "one person, one vote" standard to apportionment not only for state and local legislatures, but also for the United States House of Representatives.[114] But his approach spared the states a more intrusive and arbitrary interference based on a quest for a thorough majoritarianism.

Voting Rights II: Suffrage Qualifications and Preclearance

If Justice Black occasionally expressed reluctance to expand the scope of the reapportionment revolution, he often resisted the efforts of the Warren Court to convert the right to vote into a mandate for uniform and unrestricted national suffrage. For example, he voted against the majority when the Court struck down

---

108. *See id.* at 246-51 (Fortas, J., dissenting); *see also id.* at 240-41 (Douglas, J., dissenting).

109. *See, e.g., Fortson*, 385 U.S. at 231; Colegrove v. Green, 328 U.S. 549, 566 (1946) (Black, J., dissenting); *see also* Auerbach, *Commentary*, in REAPPORTIONMENT IN THE 1970s 76-77 (N. Polsby ed. 1971); W. ELLIOT, THE RISE OF GUARDIAN DEMOCRACY: THE SUPREME COURT'S ROLE IN VOTING RIGHTS DISPUTES 1845-1969 190 (1974).

110. *See, e.g.*, South Carolina v. Katzenbach, 383 U.S. 301, 355 (1966) (Black, J., concurring in part and dissenting in part); Dean Milk Co. v. City of Madison, Wisc., 340 U.S. 349, 357 (1951) (Black, J., dissenting).

111. *See* Lucas v. Colorado Gen. Assembly, 377 U.S. 713 (1964); Wesberry v. Sanders, 376 U.S. 1 (1964).

112. *See* Wright v. Rockefeller, 376 U.S. 52 (1964).

113. *See* Fortson v. Morris, 385 U.S. 231 (1966).

114. *See* Colegrove v. Green, 328 U.S. 549, 566 (1946) (Black, J., dissenting).

Virgina's poll tax in 1966.[115] He also found himself in the minority when the Court in 1969 invalidated a New York law limiting participation in school board elections to owners or lessees of taxable real property and to parents of school children.[116] And in 1970 he voted with a majority of the Court to strike down a federal statute mandating, *inter alia*, the eighteen-year-old vote for state and local elections.[117]

Can Justice Black's position in these cases be squared with his stance in those that dealt with malapportionment? The two lines of decisions are, in fact, distinct. They were blurred, however, by the Court. As Ward E.Y. Elliott has argued, only by means of tortured reasoning was apportionment labelled a suffrage, rather than a representation, question.[118] Elliott speculated that the Court tied apportionment issues to the right to vote—formulating the "one person, one vote" principle—in order to root the command of fair representation in the long line of Fourteenth and Fifteenth Amendment cases dealing with suffrage.[119] The command of fair representation was thus depicted as merely extending the logic of the White Primary Cases[120] and the Tuskegee racial gerrymandering case.[121] In *Reynolds v. Sims*,[122] for instance, the Court declared that the fundamental right to vote was at issue and claimed to derive the equal population standard from such suffrage cases as *Guinn v. United States*,[123] *Smith v. Allwright*,[124] and *Gomillion v. Lightfoot*.[125] Then, in turn, the Court in *Harper v. Virginia Board of Elections*[126] relied on *Reynolds* to invalidate a state poll tax.[127]

---

115. Harper v. Virginia Bd. of Elections, 383 U.S. 663, 670 (1966) (Black, J., dissenting).

116. Kramer v. Union Free School Dist., 395 U.S. 621 (1969). Justice Black joined Justice Stewart's dissent. *Id.* at 634 (Stewart, J., dissenting).

117. Oregon v. Mitchell, 400 U.S. 112 (1970).

118. W. Elliot, *supra* note 109, at 129-31.

119. *Id.*

120. Terry v. Adams, 345 U.S. 461 (1953); Smith v. Allwright, 321 U.S. 649 (1944); United States v. Classic, 313 U.S. 299 (1941); Nixon v. Condon, 286 U.S. 73 (1932); Nixon v. Herndon, 273 U.S. 536 (1927).

121. Gomillion v. Lightfoot, 364 U.S. 339 (1960).

122. 377 U.S. 533 (1964).

123. 238 U.S. 347 (1915).

124. 321 U.S. 649 (1944).

125. 364 U.S. 339 (1960).

126. 383 U.S. 663 (1966).

127. *Harper*, 383 U.S. at 667-68.

One suspects that Justice Black was not comfortable with the facile connection between suffrage and representational rights. As Elliott suggested, the right to fair representation, however it is defined, is more easily derived from the text of the Constitution than is an unrestricted suffrage right.[128] Indeed, Justice Black found the right to equipopulous congressional districts in the words of article I, section 2.[129] To be sure, as Justice Harlan contended, this reading of article I found little, if any, support in the debates of the Constitutional Convention,[130] but it was a reading that encountered no contrary provisions within the Constitution itself.

The view that the Constitution confers an unrestricted right to suffrage, however, is difficult to square with the text of the document. The Constitution contains no affirmative right to vote, but instead sets out a series of prohibitions that restrict the grounds on which the right to vote may be *denied*.[131] Justice Black did not read the Fourteenth Amendment guarantee of equal protection to foreclose its application to any and all voting rights problems—as Justice Harlan did.[132] But he balked at interpreting the Equal Protection Clause as creating an unfettered right to vote. As he observed in *Oregon v. Mitchell*:[133]

> It is obvious that the whole Constitution reserves to the States the power to set voter qualifications in state and local elections, except to the limited extent that the people through constitutional amendments have specifically narrowed the powers of the States . . . . [T]he Equal Protection Clause of the Fourteenth Amendment was never intended to destroy the States' power to govern themselves, making the Nineteenth and Twenty-fourth Amendments superfluous.[134]

---

128. W. Elliot, *supra* note 109, at 129-31.

129. *See* Wesberry v. Sanders, 376 U.S. 1, 7-8 (1964).

130. *See id.* at 30-41 (Harlan, J., dissenting); *supra* text accompanying note 85.

131. Improper grounds include race or national origin, U.S. Const. amend. XV, § 1; sex, U.S. Const. amend. XIX; failure to pay poll taxes, U.S. Const. amend. XXIV, § 1; and, age (if voter is at least eighteen), U.S. Const. amend. XXVI, § 1.

132. *See* Oregon v. Mitchell, 400 U.S. 112, 153-218 (1970) (Harlan, J., dissenting).

133. 400 U.S. 112 (1970)

134. *Mitchell*, 400 U.S. at 125-26. The *Mitchell* case involved the constitutionality of the Voting Rights Act Amendments of 1970, Pub. L. 91-285, 84 Stat. 314 (currently codified as amended at 42 U.S.C. §§ 1973, 1973b, 1973c, 1973aa-1973bb-4 (1982)). For the Court's treatment of the major provisions of the 1970 amendment, see *infra* text accompanying notes 136-38.

Justice Black's position in *Mitchell* might be called a variation on the theme of dual federalism. He advocated permitting Congress to establish suffrage standards to govern national elections and leaving the states, as well, free to set their own rules.[135] The only constraints were those specifically set by the Constitution.[136] Thus, in *Mitchell*, Justice Black approved of the power of Congress to authorize the eighteen-year-old vote for federal elections, but he rejected the power of Congress to impose the youth vote on state elections.[137] He voted in favor of prohibiting states from disqualifying voters in national elections for presidential and vice-presidential electors for not meeting state residency requirements.[138] And finally, he considered statutory action banning the literacy test to be consistent with congressional enforcement powers under the Fourteenth and Fifteenth Amendments.[139]

Thus, in this sphere, too, Justice Black put Congress and the states on the same footing; in the federal structure, each level would control its own elections. Moreover, in keeping with his stance on other issues, he advocated again the imposition of strict limits on the role of the judiciary in interpreting the Constitution. He generally accorded wider latitude to Congress in overriding state suffrage rules than he did to the Court.[140] Thus, in *Harper* he asserted that Congress might abolish poll taxes under its Fourteenth Amendment enforcement powers, but he did not join the Court in invalidating Virginia's poll tax on equal protection grounds.[141]

For Justice Black, judicial intervention in the domain of state suffrage rules could be triggered only by a clear showing that such rules breached the express prohibitions of the Constitution. He readily approved when the Court struck down Alabama's "understanding clause," which was plainly designed to exclude blacks from the electorate.[142] And in *Louisiana v. United States*,[143] a 1965

135. *Mitchell*, 400 U.S. at 117-31.

136. *Id.* at 125-26.

137. *Id.* at 117-31.

138. *Id.* at 134.

139. *Id.* at 131-34.

140. *See, e.g.*, Harper v. Virginia Bd. of Elections, 383 U.S. 663, 670 (1966) (Black, J., dissenting); South Carolina v. Katzenbach, 383 U.S. 301, 355 (1966) (Black, J., concurring in part and dissenting in part).

141. 383 U.S. at 679-80 (Black, J., dissenting).

142. Schnell v. Davis, 336 U.S. 933, *aff'g per curiam*, 81 F. Supp. 872 (S.D. Ala. 1949).

143. 380 U.S. 145 (1965).

decision abrogating Louisiana's interpretation test as a prerequisite to voter registration, he wrote:

> This is not a test but a trap, sufficient to stop even the most brilliant man on his way to the voting booth. The cherished right of people in a country like ours to vote cannot be obliterated by the use of laws like this, which leave the voting fate of a citizen to the passing whim or impulse of an individual registrar.[144]

But Louisiana's interpretation test, like Alabama's understanding clause, was a thinly veiled device to discriminate against blacks. For Justice Black, the Fourteenth and Fifteenth Amendments plainly prohibited discrimination in voting on account of race.[145] Where state voting rules did not, on their face, discriminate on the basis of race (or sex), he believed that the Court should stay its hand.[146] Recall that *Harper* invalidated Virginia's poll tax on grounds not of racial, but of economic, discrimination.[147] In words reminiscent of his writings in cases involving state economic regulation, Justice Black declared in *Harper*:

> Another reason for my dissent from the Court's judgment and opinion is that it seems to be using the old "natural-law-due-process formula" to justify striking down state laws as violations of the Equal Protection Clause. I have heretofore had many occasions to express my strong belief that there is no constitutional support whatever for this Court to use the Due Process Clause as though it provided a blank check to alter the meaning of the Constitution as written so as to add to it substantive constitutional changes which a majority of the Court at any given time believes are needed to meet present-day problems.[148]

Justice Black's approach to suffrage issues was informed by the same principles that guided him in the commerce field: deference to the legislative branches, recognition of broad congressional authority (with respect to suffrage, pursuant to article I and the various suffrage amendments), parallel treatment of national and

---

144. *Louisiana*, 380 U.S. at 153.

145. *See id.*

146. *See* Harper v. Virginia Bd. of Elections, 383 U.S. 633, 670-80 (Black, J., dissenting).

147. *Id.* at 665-70.

148. *Id.* at 675-76 (Black, J., dissenting) (footnotes omitted).

state legislatures, and an emphasis on precise rules of judicial intervention.

Given these principles, one can easily understand Justice Black's dissenting views in *South Carolina v. Katzenbach*[149] and subsequent decisions[150] involving section 5 of the Voting Rights Act of 1965.[151] Requiring certain states to preclear changes in voting laws—to seek prior federal approval before implementing them—violated several of the basic tenets upon which his philosophy was predicated. To compel preclearance was to deny presumptive validity to which all legislative acts were entitled. Moreover, it amounted to a revival of substantive due process, made more virulent by being vested (at least in part) in the executive branch rather than in the courts.[152] As Justice Black observed in his dissenting opinion in *Perkins v. Matthews*:[153]

> This permits the Federal Government to suspend the effectiveness or enforcement of a state act *before* discrimination is proved . . . . The inevitable effect of such a reversal of roles is what has happened in this case—a nondiscriminatory state practice or statute is voided wholly without constitutional authority.[154]

Conclusion

One of the ironies of Voting Rights Act decisions such as *Perkins* and *Katzenbach* is that Justice Black found himself somewhat at odds with Justice Harlan, the defender of federalism, even as Justice Black staunchly defended the rights of states against federal encroachment. Justice Harlan, of course, argued in a number of cases that history provided no support for any federal involvement in suffrage and apportionment issues based on section 1 of the Fourteenth Amendment.[155] Yet, he believed that the Fif-

---

149. 383 U.S. 301, 355 (1966) (Black, J., concurring in part and dissenting in part).

150. Perkins v. Matthews, 400 U.S. 379, 401 (1971) (Black, J., dissenting); Allen v. State Bd. of Elections, 393 U.S. 544, 595 (1969) (Black, J., dissenting).

151. Currently codified at 42 U.S.C. § 1973a (1982).

152. *See Perkins*, 400 U.S. at 402-06 (Black, J., dissenting); *Katzenbach*, 383 U.S. at 358-62 (Black, J., concurring in part and dissenting in part).

153. 400 U.S. 379, 401 (1971) (Black, J., dissenting).

154. *Perkins*, 400 U.S. at 406 (Black, J., dissenting) (emphasis in original).

155. *See supra* notes 85 & 130 and accompanying text; *see also* Carrington v. Rash, 380 U.S. 89, 97 (1965) (Harlan, J., dissenting); Reynolds v. Sims, 377 U.S. 533, 595-608 (1964) (Harlan, J., dissenting).

teenth Amendment provided clear support for congressional enactment of the Voting Rights Act of 1965 and for the preclearance provisions that were integral to it.[156] If Justice Harlan's understanding of the history of the Fourteenth and Fifteenth Amendments seemed to lead him in somewhat contradictory directions—toward rationalizing preclearance while denying federal power over apportionment—the contradictions, Justice Harlan would contend, were those of the Constitution.

Justice Black's contradictions were of a different sort. He developed a comprehensive, remarkably consistent philosophy predicated on the principles we have attempted to outline. They were principles, we have suggested, that sprung not from the Constitution itself, but from Justice Black's commitment to preserving the stature of the Court by lowering its level of activism. Thus, Justice Black sought to have the Court declare precise principles of constitutional interpretation that would provide clear guidance to the legislatures, to which Justice Black was quite willing to defer across a spectrum of policy questions.

It is not possible, however, to reconcile Justice Black's declaration that preclearance violated the Framers' intent with his assertion that translating "by the People" into "one person, one vote" would have met the Framers' approval.[157] And it is equally difficult to reconcile Justice Black's ready agreement with the notion that equal protection means that junior college districts must follow the equal population principle with his view that equal protection cannot be a basis for condemning poll taxes.[158]

Yet, to give Justice Black his due, he constructed a philosophy of constitutional law that, taken on its own terms without reference to the intentions of the Framers, has much to recommend it. Half Jeffersonian and half populist, his views have logical force and internal consistency, and in fundamental ways, they are in accord with modern notions of justice and governmental order. Like Jefferson, Justice Black looked to the legislatures to make policy,

---

156. *See, e.g., Perkins*, 400 U.S. at 397-401 (Harlan, J., concurring in part and dissenting in part); Allen v. State Bd. of Elections, 393 U.S. 544, 582-94 (1969) (Harlan, J., concurring in part and dissenting in part).

157. *Compare* South Carolina v. Katzenbach, 383 U.S. 301, 355 (1966) (Black, J., concurring in part and dissenting in part) *with* Wesberry v. Sanders, 376 U.S. 1 (1964).

158. *Compare* Hadley v. Junior College Dist., 397 U.S. 50 (1970) *with* Harper v. Virginia Bd. of Elections, 383 U.S. 663, 670 (1966) (Black, J., dissenting).

and he worked for their fair apportionment. Like Jefferson, he distrusted an unfettered judiciary and sought to construct rules of interpretation that would stay the Court's hand. And like Jefferson, he distrusted an unbridled capitalism and looked to the legislatures—federal and state—to rein it in.

Missing from Justice Black's philosophy, however, is the abiding reverence for localism that is eminently Southern and Jeffersonian. Although Justice Black's Southern origins strongly influenced his views, he lacked that attachment to the small community essential to the true believer in federalism. We have argued that he advocated considerable latitude for state action, but that latitude was merely a by-product of his desire to restrain the role of the Court. Little in Justice Black's writings suggests a constitutional theory predicated on the protection of local or state autonomy analogous to that protection which fundamental civil liberties were, in his view, entitled.

HUGO BLACK ENTERS HIS HUNDREDTH YEAR: SOME HEAVENLY REFLECTIONS ON THE CONSTITUTION

*Norman Redlich**

Almost twenty years ago I interviewed Justice Hugo L. Black for an article marking his eightieth birthday.[1] The interview was during the Court's January recess, and I travelled to Miami. There, by the side of a pool, in his car, during lunch, and strolling together, I heard Hugo Black's views on the major constitutional issues of our times—issues that he had profoundly influenced through nearly three decades on the Supreme Court. Justice Black died during the summer of 1971, and the intervening years have been marked both by constitutional developments that were on the distant horizon at the time of his death and by renewed debate over the Supreme Court's proper role in a democratic society.

Within the next year Justice Black will celebrate his hundredth birthday in surroundings somewhat less controversial, and I hope less onerous, than existed twenty years ago. The thought occurred to me that extensive preparations must already be under way for the centennial, because even within the broader time frame that marks his present environment, the first century has some special significance. One is still relatively close to the events back on earth; at the same time, the broader perspective that comes with permanent retirement has started to intrude into one's evaluation of events. Now would be the ideal time, I thought, to interview Justice Black once again so that another generation of Americans could benefit from his insights into the Constitution he loved so dearly.

---

*Judge Edward Weingeld Professor of Law, New York University School of Law. B.A., Williams College; LL.B., Yale University; LL.M., LL.D., New York University.

This essay was originally delivered as the Charles Evans Hughes Memorial Lecture, sponsored by the New York County Lawyers Association, on March 21, 1985.

1. *See* Redlich, *Justice Black At Eighty*, THE NATION, March 21, 1966, at 322.

The logistics were a bit more difficult than I had experienced during our last interview, and I will not burden this audience with the details, but at long last I knocked on the door and was greeted by the same firm handshake, the same warm welcome, and the same "let's get down to business" attitude that I recalled from two decades earlier. Hugo Black was still deeply concerned about the Constitution, the Court, and the state of freedom in the United States. He was anxious to talk about all three.

"When you . . . er . . . left the Court," I started, rather haltingly.

"You can use the word 'died,'" he said. "It doesn't offend me."

"In 1971," I continued, "the constitutional principles you had urged through the years seemed to have become the dominant themes of the Court. Did you feel a sense of satisfaction at the time?"

"In many ways, yes. By the end of the 1960s every important right in the Bill of Rights had been made applicable to the states through the Fourteenth Amendment, although the Court never accepted my correct historical analysis that the Framers of the Fourteenth Amendment intended to incorporate the Bill of Rights at the time of the Amendment's adoption. But I was satisfied with the result, if not the reasoning."

"That was a major source of controversy between you and Justice Frankfurter, and then John Harlan. Sometimes the language became quite bitter."

"It sure did," said Justice Black with a chuckle. "You're referring to my opinions in *Adamson*[2] and *Rochin*,[3] among others. Well, I did feel strongly that individual rights should depend on specific language in the Constitution and not on what individual judges thought was 'fair,' or 'fundamental,' or any other words that Felix and John could conjure out of their imaginations. Now, some people said that it really didn't matter. As long as we made the privilege against self-incrimination binding on the states, does it really make any difference if the Court did it because the privilege was written down in the Fifth Amendment, as I believed, or was 'fundamental to ordered liberty,' as Felix and John would have

2. Adamson v. California, 332 U.S. 46, 68 (1947) (Black, J., dissenting).
3. Rochin v. California, 342 U.S. 165, 174 (1952) (Black, J., concurring).

stated it? Of course, it's probably no accident that those who spouted those vague standards usually left out some of the rights written in the Bill of Rights."

"Well, why was it so important to you?" I asked. "And do you still feel that way now?"

"It was important then, and I feel even more strongly about it now. Supreme Court justices have an awesome power. They are the principal guardians of individual rights in our country. And politicians are always attacking judges who protect unpopular people. I was a politician before I was a judge, and I know how easy it is to run against judges. Franklin Roosevelt did it, and you have a President who's doing it now. When I came on the Court in 1937, we had just been through a terrible crisis because judges were creating rights that didn't exist and reading their own views of capitalism into the Constitution. We'll never know what would have happened if Hughes and Roberts hadn't changed their minds just before I was appointed. There is a limit to what the people will put up with when judges prevent them from having their own way."

"You talk about letting the people have their own way," I interrupted. "But you took the simple words 'liberty' and 'property' in the Fourteenth Amendment and tried to make the entire Bill of Rights binding on the states, with all the federal court interpretations thrown in. That's not exactly letting the people have their own way."

"But the Fourteenth Amendment was intended to do just that," he said. "I wasn't creating rights. I was just interpreting rights that were clearly intended to be given to the people of this country against infringement by the states. That's what the Fourteenth Amendment was all about. That's not abusing judicial power. It's the proper exercise of it."

"One person's abuse is another person's exercise," I replied.

"It's a big difference," he said. "I'm very fearful about the future of our rights."

"Fearful?" I said with surprise. "All of the principal rights, including the First Amendment, have been incorporated, and even some that aren't in the Bill of Rights. The Burger Court may be cutting back on the meaning of certain rights, but they don't seem to be going back to *Palko*[4] and removing rights from protection against the states. Why are you so fearful?"

"Well, things were starting to come apart in 1965 with *Griswold.*[5] There was nothing in the Constitution that created the right of 'marital privacy,' no matter how hard Bill Douglas and Arthur Goldberg poked around in penumbras and emanations and the Ninth Amendment. And then we had *Roe v. Wade,*[6] throwing out most of the states' laws against abortion and making abortion virtually an absolute right, at least in the first three months of pregnancy. And then came opinions about the sale and use of contraceptives,[7] the rights of relatives to live together,[8] and a host of other so-called rights that you can't find anywhere in the Constitution."

"You were known as a great civil libertarian," I said. "As long as the Bill of Rights was protected, rigidly enforced, and made binding on the states, why should you have objected to adding new rights, like privacy, and the right to travel, and the right to decide whether you would have a child? These are important values for a free people."

"That attitude is what is causing the Court's greatest problem today," he said sharply. "The Constitution doesn't protect 'important values for a free people.' It protects what's in the Constitution."

I suggested we take a stroll. The conversation was becoming animated.

"No, you sit right there and listen to me!" he said. "You so-called civil libertarians didn't listen when I said that by finding rights that weren't there you would destroy the rights that the Framers gave us."

"I remember your saying that when I interviewed you in Miami, but I didn't quite understand why."

"Well, I hope you understand now. When decisions are based on the written text of the Constitution, people have far more protection than when they are based on a judge's notion of what is

---

4. Palko v. Connecticut, 302 U.S. 319 (1937).
5. Griswold v. Connecticut, 381 U.S. 479 (1965).
6. 410 U.S. 113 (1973).
7. Carey v. Population Servs. Int'l, 431 U.S. 678 (1977); Eisenstadt v. Baird, 405 U.S. 438 (1972).
8. Moore v. City of E. Cleveland, 431 U.S. 494 (1977).

'fundamental.' I don't want to trust the rights of our people to the views of five justices trying to figure out what a changing society needs. I saw too many of those justices in my lifetime to be happy with their notions of freedom, and the ones I've seen since I've been up here don't make me any more comfortable."

"You're contradicting yourself. You say that we have personal freedoms because judges enforce the Constitution, and then you complain when they do."

"I don't complain when they enforce the Constitution," said Justice Black. "I complain when they enforce their own notions of what a free society should look like."

"But why should an expansive view of freedom undermine liberty?" I asked. "Why does giving a woman the right to terminate a pregnancy during the first three months threaten something like the First Amendment, or the protection against self-incrimination, or the right to counsel? One has nothing to do with the other."

"You didn't get the point twenty years ago, and you still don't. But you can be sure that Bill Rehnquist and some of the others waiting in the wings get the point. Once the Court starts to find rights that aren't set forth in the Constitution, then the Court is admitting that the text and historical intent don't matter. When justices depart from history and text, our protection depends on the personal whims of the Court. I can just hear a future justice say that if the Court is free to include a right of marital privacy in the word 'liberty,' then it is just as free to exclude the privilege against self-incrimination. And, under such an approach, a Court would feel perfectly free to interpret rights in the Bill of Rights differently against the states than as against the federal government. Don't be surprised if that approach leads the Court some day to say that 'law respecting an establishment of religion' means one thing when Congress acts and quite another thing when the states act."

"That certainly would be a constitutional revolution," I said.

"It would . . . to you and to me," Justice Black replied. "But *Roe v. Wade* was just as much a revolution to those who thought it was wrong, and if the process is freed from the text and from history, then one revolution can undo another. What may be at stake are not only the abortion decisions, but also any other decisions that a majority of the people don't like."

"Justice Black," I said timidly, "with all due respect, you haven't convinced me. If some people are angry with *Roe v. Wade*, it's not because the right to an abortion can't be found in the Constitution. It's because they profoundly disagree with the result. After all, people were angry about your school prayer decision in *Engel*,[9] and the results in *Brown*,[10] *Mapp*,[11] *Miranda*,[12] and 'one-person, one-vote' cases.[13] All of these were based on specific language in the Constitution. The fact that the Court was interpreting a right, instead of finding a new right, didn't seem to make opponents any more willing to accept a result they didn't like. People were talking about impeaching Earl Warren when the Court was doing just what you wanted it to do."

"You're not answering my argument," he said. "You're helping to prove it. Of course, the Court has to do unpopular things. The cases you mention are good examples. Sometimes the people will overturn decisions by constitutional amendment, and sometimes, when the decisions are based on interpretations, a new Court will interpret provisions differently, as has happened many times in our history. That's part of the process. But if the Court sticks to constitutional text and to history, two values are realized. First, people are more willing to accept the result because they realize that the Court is performing its designated role under our Constitution. Second, the rights that are extended to the people are more secure because they are based on something more tangible than the passing prejudices of judges."

"Are you saying that President Reagan wouldn't be trying just as hard to change the Court if the Court had confined itself to interpreting specific rights? After all, President Nixon ran for office campaigning against the interpretation your Court gave to procedural protections in the Bill of Rights. And politicians have been trying to cut down on school busing even though that was a remedy for a violation of the Equal Protection Clause. I still think people are more concerned about the result than the process. The critics of the Court simply don't like the results, and if Reagan gets

---

9. Engel v. Vitale, 370 U.S. 421 (1962).

10. Brown v. Board of Educ., 347 U.S. 483 (1954).

11. Mapp v. Ohio, 367 U.S. 643 (1961).

12. Miranda v. Arizona, 384 U.S. 436 (1966).

13. Reynolds v. Sims, 377 U.S. 533 (1964); Baker v. Carr, 369 U.S. 186 (1962).

his way, they'll change a lot more than the decisions you don't like."

"No doubt," he replied. "And it will be because the well-meaning liberals gave them the ammunition."

"I don't think that's fair," I answered. "They're cutting back on *Miranda* and *Mapp* almost weekly. Those cases were based on specific constitutional protections. You can't blame the liberals for that. Those were decisions you joined."

"I've come to look at things with a broad perspective since I've been here," he said, "and I have great concern that there is a growing movement in the country that views the Court as a political body that is imposing its values on the country without regard to the Constitution. And when people feel that way, judges may be appointed who will feel no restraint with regard to substituting their values, even if that means curtailing rights that are based on the history and text of the Constitution."

"Aren't you troubled that your approach to the Constitution is too rigid and makes it incapable of adapting to changing values, to change in science, and to change in society generally?"

"No, I'm not," said the Justice emphatically. "When people like you talk about changing times and how we need protection against computers that will invade our privacy, or against electronic gadgets that overhear conversations, or against laws that keep comatose infants alive against the judgment of their parents, I say that the people should look to their elected representatives, or perhaps to common-law courts that interpret tort and contract law, or to judges interpreting a statute. But the Supreme Court has the profoundly important, but limited, job of interpreting a constitution. I remember in *Dennis*[14] that Felix said that Holmes and Brandeis never confronted world communism, so their ideas of free speech had to be brought up to date.[15] Felix almost destroyed the First Amendment . . . . I'm afraid of people wanting to bring the Constitution up to date."

"But," I persisted, "you frequently expanded rights to cope with new attitudes and knowledge. The Chief Justice's opinion in *Brown* recognized that history was no guide to the issue of segrega-

---

14. Dennis v. United States, 341 U.S. 494 (1951).
15. *Id.* at 543-44 (Frankfurter, J., concurring).

tion,[16] and surely you could not have believed that the Sixth Amendment always guaranteed a person a right to assigned counsel in criminal cases."[17]

"It is one thing to apply specified rights to new situations," Justice Black replied. "It is another thing to create new rights to deal with new facts and attitudes."

"The difference isn't so clear to the people affected," I argued. "Was it so obvious that a company-owned town was a government entity for purposes of the Fourteenth Amendment?" I asked.

"It was to me," he replied. "In *Marsh v. Alabama*[18] we had to decide what was state action. That's the Court's proper role and the people accept it."

"You keep talking about the Court's proper role as if there's some clear line between passing laws and interpreting them, between enforcing rights and creating them."

"I think there is," he answered sharply, "and there has to be in a democracy. No one elected us."

"But the Constitution doesn't accept the principle of majority rule in every case," I argued. "It's not just the judges that flaunt the majority. Presidents can ignore Congress. A few key senators can block the majority's will. There are plenty of other examples."

"What's your point?" he asked.

"The point is that the courts have to decide cases, and constitutional issues will be raised that involve specific provisions as well as vague provisions. And the Court has to decide. Congress, the state legislatures, city councils, a President, a Governor, a Mayor—none has a monopoly on democratic legitimacy. They are all part of democratic government, and so are the courts."

"But the people can't change our decisions," he said.

"History shows that they have," I replied. "Judges' decisions aren't etched in stone. The people have brought about many changes in judicial decisions, and the people have also accepted decisions they didn't particularly like and still don't. And I don't see any pattern relating ultimate acceptance by the people to decisions that interpret a specific provision, like the privilege against self-

16. Brown v. Board of Educ., 347 U.S. 483, 492-93 (1954).

17. Gideon v. Wainwright, 372 U.S. 335 (1963).

18. 326 U.S. 501 (1946).

incrimination, or vague ones like 'privileges and immunities,' or 'liberty and property,' or the Ninth Amendment."

"Then why is the Court so unpopular today?"

"I don't think the Court is so unpopular. Some of its decisions are. Actually, the Court hasn't been on a rights-expansion spree since you left it. There's been a trend toward contracting rights. Just ask Bill and Thurgood. Inter-district busing,[19] equality of financing in public education,[20] homosexual rights,[21] age discrimination,[22] public funding of abortions,[23] rights to housing,[24] or welfare—all of these claims have been rejected."

"You still haven't answered me," Justice Black said. "Why is the Supreme Court under attack?"

"Because some people don't like the decisions in the abortion, school prayer, and busing cases. And because, despite the Burger Court, the Court is still protecting defendants' rights. Your concern, and that of many scholars, about the Court's proper role, and about interfering with democratic institutions, is entirely misplaced."

"How can you say that?" he replied angrily. "Without *Roe v. Wade* we'd probably have fifty states that make abortions illegal."

"I'm not so sure," I answered. "Some states acted before *Roe*. There are still state constitutions. Besides, I think that *Roe v. Wade* is actually more popular than your school prayer decision. Neither should be viewed as anti-democratic. Courts, both federal and state, are part of our republican form of government."

"Then why all this fuss about the role of the courts that's been going on since I left?"

"With due respect, sir, it's because too many people are caught up with the ideas you have been expressing. They're forgetting that the courts are supposed to protect rights, whether expressly stated in the Constitution, or implied from vague provisions. This isn't a popular job, and no one did it better than you. For years you were the most unpopular person in the South. You

19. Milliken v. Bradley, 418 U.S. 717 (1974).

20. San Antonio Indep. School Dist. v. Rodriguez, 411 U.S. 1 (1973).

21. Doe v. Commonwealth's Attorney, 403 F. Supp. 1199 (E.D. Va. 1975), *aff'd*, 425 U.S. 901 (1976).

22. Massachusetts Bd. of Retirement v. Murgia, 427 U.S. 307 (1976).

23. Harris v. McRae, 448 U.S. 297 (1980).

24. Lindsey v. Normet, 405 U.S. 56 (1972).

looked more democratic in your robes than Governor Wallace did in the schoolhouse door."

"I'm not immune to flattery," he said, "but I still want courts to be on a sound basis when they are doing unpopular things. That's what sustained me through the years."

I could see that I was having some effect, but Hugo Black is still a stubborn man. I decided to venture onto the dangerous ground of discussing *Roe v. Wade* on the merits, hoping that he might grudgingly find some textual support for the decision.

"Justice Black," I asked, "would you have joined the opinions of the Court that extended equal protection rights to cases of gender discrimination?"

"Well, all those cases, like *Reed*,[25] *Frontiero*,[26] and *Craig v. Boren*,[27] came after my time."

"I know," I persisted. "But how would you have voted?"

"Well, without saying how I'd vote on each specific case, I'm pretty sure I would have been on Bill Brennan's side."

"Why?" I asked.

"Because of the changing role of women." There was a long pause. He knew he was starting down a dangerous road. "Let's take a walk," I suggested.

"I know you think I'm being inconsistent," he said, as we started our walk, "but I'm not." He obviously had had time to regroup his thoughts. "The Equal Protection Clause has to be interpreted in light of society's different attitude toward groups. That's not the creation of new rights. It's the adapting of existing rights to changing mores, moral attitudes, and other societal changes. That's a normal process of constitutional adjudication. I did that in *Griffin v. Illinois*[28] when I wrote that a person's inability to pay for a transcript shouldn't deny him the right to an appeal. Differences between rich and poor in the administration of criminal justice was becoming a serious problem in the mid—1950s when *Griffin* was decided."

"Is there really a difference," I asked, "between finding new meanings for the words 'equal protection' and the words 'liberty and property without due process of law?' "

25. Reed v. Reed, 404 U.S. 71 (1971).
26. Frontiero v. Richardson, 411 U.S. 677 (1973).
27. 429 U.S. 190 (1976).
28. 351 U.S. 12 (1956).

"It's the difference between applying a written constitution and applying one's own notions of what rights people have."

"All right," I continued. "Let's stick to equal protection of the laws and to the rights of women under that concept. Wouldn't it be reasonable to argue that today, unlike in 1787 or 1868, women should be freed from legal barriers that stand in the way of their full participation in American life? Is that so different from saying that black people had to be free from the shackles of segregation in 1954 and it didn't matter, as Earl Warren wrote, what people thought in 1868 when the Fourteenth Amendment was ratified?"

"Well, I remember voting with the majority in 1948 upholding a law that said that women couldn't be employed as bartenders unless they were related to a male owner.[29] I have to admit that even by the time I left, and certainly now, there are different attitudes about men and women, and keeping a woman from earning a living denies equal protection. But it's a long step from laws that keep a woman from tending bar to giving her a right to an abortion."

"Is it?" I asked. "Isn't the real issue whether the state can impose legal barriers that prevent women from making their own choices about what they want to do with their lives? And how can they be free if they can't make the decision about child-bearing?"

"Are you saying that *Roe v. Wade* is really a case about equality and not about rights?" he asked.

"It's really about both," I replied. "Just as *Griffin* was about both. It's one thing for the criminal justice system to allow differences between rich and poor to result in unequal quality of lawyers. The Constitution probably can't deal with that unless the poor person's lawyer becomes so bad that representation is no longer effective. But when the difference between rich and poor means that the poor person can't get a transcript and because of that is denied the right to an appeal, then you said it was unconstitutional."

"Yes," said Justice Black, "but remember that there is nothing in the Constitution that says that anyone, man or woman, should be able to participate fully in American life, or however you want to state it."

---

29. Goesaert v. Cleary, 335 U.S. 464 (1948).

"That's true, and there is nothing in the Constitution that says a person has a right to an appeal. The issue is whether the state can pass laws that distinguish in something so important on the basis of gender or on the basis of wealth. And the anti-abortion laws really do single out a class—women—and say that the state is going to make criminal the one decision they must be able to make to achieve that equality. Come to think of it," I added in a weak attempt at humor, "Harry Blackmun might have cited you in his opinion."

Justice Black didn't think it was funny. "He wouldn't have dared do that. You're forgetting one important thing. The state didn't have a valid interest in keeping school children separate on account of race or denying poor people the right to lawyers or transcripts. But where does the court get the right to say that the state can't protect a fetus?"

"That's a hard question to answer," I acknowledged. "But you have to admit that you were willing, in your time, to override some pretty strongly felt state interests. People felt strongly about prayers in schools, about the threat of communism, and about the use of credible, but illegally obtained, evidence. And no one knows better than you how strongly the South felt about segregation. But once you were satisfied that there was a constitutional right involved, you were willing to override that interest. I think that if you think for a minute about the abortion issue in terms of equality for women, you might find the justification for overriding the state's concern about fetal life."

"I've got a lot more than a minute to think about it," he replied with a grudging smile. I could see that he wanted to think some more about the points I had raised. We strolled in silence and then returned to his house. He appeared anxious to change the subject.

"What has been happening back home that gives you the most concern?" I asked.

"Religion," he said, without a moment's hesitation.

"Too much or too little?"

"Too little knowledge of history, too little respect for diversity, too much talk of accommodation, people so sure that they've seen the divine light that they want the government to make everyone else see it that way, too. . . ."

Clearly, he was on a subject about which he felt deeply. He reached for his marked-up copy of the Constitution, turned to the Bill of Rights, and said, "There was nothing more important to the Framers of the Bill of Rights than the subject of religious freedom. They knew that religious differences can lead to hatred and persecution that can tear a country apart. What I don't understand . . . I can't understand . . . is how people in America can look at what is happening in the rest of the world, where people are killing each other because of religious differences, and then chip away at the constitutional rights that were put there for the very purpose of avoiding those problems. They gave us something new—a written guarantee of religious freedom, and they enforced that freedom by requiring that government and religion be separate—that government couldn't support any religions or all religions, whether through taxes, prayers, or giving money to religious schools, or putting the stamp of official approval on any religious faith."

"That's what you wrote in *Everson*,"[30] I said, referring, of course, to the famous dicta in which he had tried to lay out the meaning of the Establishment Clause.

"Yes, the paragraph that starts: 'The establishment of religion clause of the First Amendment means at least this . . . .' I never worked so hard over getting language just right as I did over that paragraph."

"But if you had it so right," I asked, "why did the Court split 5-4 in *Everson* with the majority, led by you, deciding that it was all right to reimburse parents for the cost of bus transportation for children to parochial schools. Remember, Justice Jackson said that the best precedent for your opinion was Lord Byron's Julia: 'whispering "I will ne'er consent"—consented.'[31] He meant that you set forth all the right principles and then reached the wrong result."

"Bob could turn a great phrase, and that was one of his best, but he was wrong. When I grew up in Alabama, children walked along the highways trying to get to school. It was dangerous. Reimbursing parents for the cost of bus transportion wasn't an aid to religion. It was just a means of getting school children, including those in private religious schools, off the dangerous highways and to school. That's the way I saw it, but I could understand how the

30. Everson v. Board of Educ., 330 U.S. 1, 15-16 (1947).
31. *Id.* at 19 (Jackson, J., dissenting).

dissenters considered it as an establishment. And I was always pleased that Wiley Rutledge included Madison's *Memorial and Remonstrance Against Religious Assessments* as an appendix to his dissent. It was important for the Court and the American people to understand the historical origins of the Establishment Clause."

"But doesn't *Everson* point up the problem?" I asked. "If you can accommodate religion by paying for children to get to school, then why can't you accommodate in a lot of other ways—like paying for secular subjects taught by teachers in religious schools, or even for nativity scenes, or allowing tax credits for tuition to parochial schools?"

"No . . . no . . . no . . . ," he replied, with an intensity greater than at any other point in our interview. "You've got to understand that I said in *Everson* that reimbursing for bus transportation approached the 'verge' of government power in this area. Providing bus transportation was a general benefit available to all children going to public and private school. It was for the welfare of the child and, as a safety matter, only indirectly related to education or religion."

"But you can see how the result in *Everson* could be used to justify aid to religious education under a theory that it is only to benefit the child."

"I know, and I had hoped we put an end to that child-benefit approach in *Lemon*.[32] If I had known the use that might be made of my opinion in *Everson*, I might have agreed with the dissent, but I still think that on the issue in that case I was right."

"How can you explain what is going on now?" I asked.

"There is no explanation in terms that have any relationship to what the Founders had in mind or what I wrote in *Everson, McCollum*,[33] and *Engel*, the school prayer case. *Zorach*,[34] the released-time case, was all wrong and I think Bill Douglas realized it in later years. But what this Court is doing now frightens me, I tell you. . . . When government pays to build a display of the birth of Christ, that's violating every principle of the Establishment Clause. It is endorsing religion, it is endorsing one religion, it is

32. Lemon v. Kurtzman, 403 U.S. 602 (1971).

33. McCollum v. Board of Educ., 333 U.S. 203 (1948).

34. Zorach v. Clauson, 343 U.S. 306 (1952).

using a person's tax money to support a religion he doesn't believe in. It makes non-Christians feel like outsiders. It makes a mockery of Christianity to say that it's a religious symbol that is okay because its's part of a secular holiday. . . . I just can't believe that they would approve of such a thing.[35] Bill Brennan said it all in his dissent,[36] but I would have been even angrier."

"Have you discussed it with Madison?" I asked. "He should know what he meant."

"They have a strict rule here against going back to the Founders," he replied. "They feel it would shut off debate, and that's our favorite pastime. Besides, they've probably forgotten what they really meant."

"Then how can *you* be sure?"

"I rely on what they wrote and on a study of history," he replied. Justice Black was clearly a hard man to argue with.

"How do you explain what is happening?"

"It's easy to explain. It's the same thing that happened with the Communist issue in the 1950s. Everyone was saying then that there was this Communist menace, that free speech had to be balanced against national interests, which is a fancy way of saying that constitutional rights are sacrificed to what the majority of the people think is important at any particular time. Well, now you have this strong movement for religious conformity. Preachers are becoming politically powerful by pandering to people's fears the same way McCarthy pandered to their fears thirty-five years ago. There's the fear that family values, morality, belief in God, are all being threatened and the way to deal with it is to have teachers recite prayers, or to erect religious symbols. . . ."

"Or keep women in the home, or stop abortions, or prosecute homosexuals," I interrupted. "Isn't it all part of the same movement to get the government and the Supreme Court to promote what they consider traditional American moral and religious values?"

"But the establishing of religion is the most serious," he persisted.

"Why?"

---

35. Lynch v. Donnelly, 465 U.S. 668 (1984).
36. *Id.* at 694 (Brennan, J., dissenting).

"Because America won't be the same country if people of all religious faiths can't feel that under our Constitution they are all equal. We're the only country that has religious diversity, religious freedom, and religious peace. Madison wrote that religious freedom is a beacon that lights the way for people to come here. That's still true. This isn't a Christian nation. It's a country for all—believers and nonbelievers. The Supreme Court has to stand up to those who want this to be a country only for those who share their own view of God. And let me tell you . . . religious freedom is the partner of political freedom. Every totalitarian government wants to control the churches and shut down the press because free churches and free newspapers mean that people are thinking for themselves and not accepting the government as the final authority."

"But a creche at Christmas doesn't seem that important."

"That's exactly what was said about the Regents' Prayer, and I quoted Madison in my *Engel* opinion, that we have to 'take alarm at the first experiment on our liberties.'[37] Every so-called accommodation will lead to the next one. There is already one justice, Rehnquist, who thinks that the Ten Commandments represent something secular and not religious.[38] Maybe he doesn't understand either religion or the Constitution. I understand a court has upheld a crucifix on a county seal.[39] I grew up in rural Alabama, and I know how easy it is for people to think that their religion represents the right way of life that everyone should accept. When that happens, we have a different country."

"Isn't it hard to explain to a pregnant woman carrying an unwanted pregnancy that a nativity scene at Christmas represents more of a threat to liberty than taking away her right to have an abortion?"

Justice Black spoke with a deep intensity. His answer did not come quickly. "I agree that it would be difficult. But a hungry person without money for food would regard hunger as more

---

37. Engel v. Vitale, 370 U.S. 421, 436 (1962) (quoting J. MADISON, *Memorial and Remonstrance Against Religious Assessments*, in 2 THE WRITINGS OF JAMES MADISON 183, 185-86 (G. Hunt ed. 1901)).

38. Stone v. Graham, 449 U.S. 39, 43-47 (1980) (Rehnquist, J., dissenting).

39. Johnson v. Board of County Comm'rs, 528 F. Supp. 919 (D.N.M. 1981), *rev'd sub nom. on reh'g*, Friedman v. Board of County Comm'rs, 781 F.2d 777 (10th Cir. 1985) (en banc), *cert. denied*, Board of County Comm'rs v. Friedman, 106 S. Ct. 2890 (1986).

important than the Regents' Prayer or a moment of silent prayer. And a homeless person on the street would regard a home as more important than having a lawyer if he or she was accused of a crime. But that's not the issue, is it? Even if you're right about the abortion issue, which I don't concede, you shouldn't downgrade freedom of expression and religious freedom by comparing them with the basic wants of food and clothing. The Constitution was written by people who realized that without the rights in the Bill of Rights we wouldn't be a free people. I have talked to people from countries where everyone has the basic necessities of food and clothing and shelter and jobs and where women have rights to abortions. And some day these countries may even have more advanced technology. But our Constitution wisely left economic issues to the political process and protected personal liberty through written guarantees that judges have to protect regardless of what a majority—even a Moral Majority—may want."

"I see you read the newspaper up here," I noted. "In law schools it has become fashionable to say that you grew conservative with old age in your First Amendment views."

"Yes. And some were saying that I was becoming senile or that I couldn't adjust to changing times. They were wrong."

"Have your rethought your First Amendment position?"

"Felix and Bill Douglas and John Harlan—we argue all the time. We haven't shifted much. As I recall, you were in the audience when I delivered my Madison Lecture at NYU and said that freedom of speech was absolute.[40] Felix, and others who didn't understand what I meant, reacted as if I was an ignorant country boy who had never taken a course in philosophy. 'There are no absolutes,' they said, as if anyone who thought 'no law' meant 'no law' was so stupid he shouldn't be taken seriously."

"Well," I replied, "you rejected so many free speech claims in the 1960s that you certainly gave your critics reason to question the whole idea of absolute protection for First Amendment rights."

"If you say that, then you didn't understand what I meant either."

"Well, you had no sympathy for the free speech claim of the draft card burners,[41] even though it was hard for a lot of us to see

---

40. Black, *The Bill of Rights*, 35 N.Y.U. L. REV. 865, 874 (1960).
41. United States v. O'Brien, 391 U.S. 367 (1968).

that there was anything other than free speech involved there. Or the prosecutions for burning the flag,[42] or the arm band case,[43] or the quiet, peaceful demonstration against racial segregation in a public library,[44] or the speech in front of a jail[45]—if you thought freedom of speech was so absolute, why did you reject all of those claims?"

"Because I never said that conduct was protected or that people had a right to give speeches at any time, in every place, and in any manner that popped into their heads. Burning a draft card isn't speech."

"Then why is carrying a picket sign in a labor dispute? You gave that a lot of protection in *Thornhill*,"[46] I said, warming up to the argument.

"All I said when I joined in the *Thornhill* opinion was that a law prohibiting all picketing in labor disputes was too broad. It covered both the expression of ideas and unlawful coercion. The Constitution gives absolute protection to the expression of a point of view; it doesn't protect coercion or the counseling of criminal conduct. And it doesn't protect disruption in the classroom, or burning flags or draft cards, or stopping traffic, or giving speeches in places where people have no right to be, like libraries or jails. It protects the expression of ideas in places where people have the right to give speeches and at reasonable times and in reasonable manner, and it protects that kind of speech absolutely. And it protects those ideas absolutely. That's why I predicted that the 'malice' standard in libel laws would still make it possible for people to be sued for criticizing the government,[47] and I was right. We had the same issue near the end of my time in the Pentagon Papers case,[48] and it's too bad that only the two Bills—Brennan and Douglas—came close to agreeing with me. But I'm not surprised. After 200 years people still refuse to recognize that there is no such thing as a dangerous idea, and there is no national or any other governmental interest that can override freedom of speech. That's

42. Street v. New York, 394 U.S. 576, 609 (1969) (Black, J., dissenting).

43. Tinker v. Des Moines Indep. Community School Dist., 393 U.S. 503, 515 (1969) (Black, J., dissenting).

44. Brown v. Louisiana, 383 U.S. 131, 151 (1966) (Black, J., dissenting).

45. Adderley v. Florida, 385 U.S. 39 (1966).

46. Thornhill v. Alabama, 310 U.S. 88 (1940).

47. New York Times Co. v. Sullivan, 376 U.S. 254, 293 (Black, J., concurring).

48. New York Times Co. v. United States, 403 U.S. 713 (1971).

what I said in the NYU lecture and all through the McCarthy period. That's the whole basis on which this country was founded. It is an absolute truth. Maybe it's too simple for some minds to understand, but I never had trouble with the idea. And let me tell you, I've discovered since I've been up here that there are millions of people around what you call the world who understand it very well."

"With all due respect, Justice Black," I said, "that approach may have made sense in the McCarthy era and in cases like the Pentagon Papers, but it really isn't very helpful in the free speech cases we've had since then. What do you do about campaign financing,[49] about commercial speech,[50] about corporate speech,[51] about broadcasters' claims to freedom of speech,[52] about searches of newspaper files,[53] about reporters' rights to refuse to disclose sources,[54] about the media's claims of access to prisons[55] and trials,[56] about free speech and the copyright[57] and securities laws,[58] about the right to speak on a military base[59] and on government property,[60] or the right of private citizens to place a religious symbol in a city park?[61] These are hard questions and I don't see how they are advanced by saying that 'no law' means 'no law.' "

"A lot of those questions don't involve free speech at all," he replied. "Advertising isn't speech—it's a commercial transaction. Neither is sleeping in a government park, which is another foolish

49. Buckley v. Valeo, 424 U.S. 1 (1976).

50. *E.g.*, Metromedia, Inc. v. City of San Diego, 453 U.S. 490 (1981); Central Hudson Gas & Elec. Corp. v. Public Serv. Comm'n, 447 U.S. 557 (1980); Virginia State Bd. of Pharmacy v. Virginia Citizens Consumer Council, Inc., 425 U.S. 748 (1976).

51. First Nat'l Bank v. Bellotti, 435 U.S. 765 (1978).

52. CBS v. FCC, 453 U.S. 367 (1981); FCC v. Pacifica Found., 438 U.S. 726 (1978).

53. Zurcher v. Stanford Daily, 436 U.S. 547 (1978).

54. Branzburg v. Hayes, 408 U.S. 665 (1972).

55. Houchins v. KQED, 438 U.S. 1 (1978); Saxbe v. Washington Post Co., 417 U.S. 843 (1974); Pell v. Procunier, 417 U.S. 817 (1974).

56. *E.g.*, Richmond Newspapers, Inc. v. Virginia, 448 U.S. 555 (1980).

57. Harper & Row Publishers, Inc. v. Nation Enters., 471 U.S. 539 (1985).

58. Lowe v. SEC, 472 U.S. 181 (1985).

59. Brown v. Glines, 444 U.S. 348 (1980); Greer v. Spock, 424 U.S. 828 (1976).

60. United States v. Grace, 461 U.S. 171 (1983); Heffron v. International Soc'y for Khrishna Consciousness, Inc., 452 U.S. 640 (1981); Grayned v. City of Rockford, 408 U.S. 104 (1972).

61. McCreary v. Stone, 739 F.2d 716 (2d Cir. 1984), *aff'd by an equally divided Court sub nom.* Board of Trustees v. McCreary, 471 U.S. 83 (1985).

case with which the court got involved last year.[62] And spending money for elections is just about the last thing the Framers would have associated with speech. When I was raising money for my campaigns in Alabama, I sure never thought I was giving people the opportunity to exercise First Amendment rights. They were helping me get elected so I could exercise mine. I can't believe that reporters have the right to withhold relevant information just because they're journalists."

"How should all those cases get decided?" I asked.

"The way we decided *O'Brien*, the draft card burning case. The only concern is whether the government uses means that are narrowly drawn to achieve the regulation of conduct."

"That means that such laws will almost always be upheld," I said.

"And they should be," he replied.

"But if *O'Brien* had said the draft was an outrage, you'd give him absolute protection."

"Absolutely! That's what the First Amendment means."

"So you really solve the whole problem by saying that it's either conduct or speech. And what would you do about Dr. Spock giving a speech at Fort Dix?"[63]

"The government can keep political speeches out of military bases. Soldiers can get information through newspapers, radio, and television. The base itself is for military training and not for political rallies."

"If people are allowed into the area in front of a public hospital, should they be allowed to hand out leaflets protesting about the terrible conditions in the hospital?"

"No," he said. "A hospital is for treating sick people, not for speeches."

"Not even about how they're treating sick people?" I asked.

"So," he said, "you're suggesting that people should be allowed to protest hospital conditions in front of a hospital. Would you permit them to protest President Reagan's policy in Central America in a hospital waiting room?"

"No," I said.

"Why not?"

---

62. Clark v. Community for Creative Non-Violence, 468 U.S. 288 (1984).
63. *See* Greer v. Spock, 424 U.S. 828 (1976).

"Because that has nothing to do with a hospital."

"But don't you see how you're giving the government the power to control speech?"

"I don't see that at all," I argued. "I'm extending speech into places where it might not otherwise be permitted."

"Some speech and not others," he said.

"That's right," I replied. "It depends on the place and the message. What's wrong with that?"

"I suppose you'd say that advertising is protected unless it's false or misleading or unless it urges something illegal?"

"That's what the Court has done," I replied. "And I think they're right."

"Don't you see how you're taking something precious like the First Amendment and making free speech depend on whether judges think it's a good idea to have certain types of speeches in certain places?"

"But aren't you doing the same thing by saying that something like campaign spending is conduct rather than speech, or that a park can be used for any kind of speech but that a space in front of a jail or a hospital can be shut off entirely? Your system would protect an obscene movie absolutely, but would prevent a person from delivering a political message in front of a jail or in a library. You would allow the government to ban commercial advertising of certain products, like sugar-coated cereals, just because some official agency decides that the product is bad for kids."

"That's right. The movie is the expression of ideas. The television commercial is part of the sale of a product. The Constitution places ideas out of the reach of the government, but the Commerce Clause, or state police power, allows government to regulate business. It's as simple as that."

"It's not that simple to me. You carve out a few areas and give them broad protection. But what's wrong with your system is that you deny virtually any protection for whole areas of speech that are very important to Americans. Why not give protection to some types of commercial speech, even if we don't protect deceptive advertising? Why not allow people to protest a bad hospital in front of a hospital, even if we wouldn't allow a political rally? Why not examine a law dealing with desecrating a flag and see whether the governmental interests are outweighed by the speech elements?"

"Because you would make every free speech case turn on a balancing of the governmental interest against the speech interest."

"What's wrong with that?" I asked, "as long as you tilt the scale heavily on the side of free speech?"

"Because in times of political suppression, like during the Alien and Sedition Act period, or during the First and Second World Wars, or during the McCarthy period, or when the people feared labor unions and Communists early in this century, the governmental interest will win and free speech will lose. If the government can suppress a false advertisement to protect health, then why can't the government suppress a false political idea to protect the whole country from overthrow?"

"And how does your approach prevent political suppression?"

"By carving out certain areas and giving them absolute protection and leaving other types of spoken words subject to reasonable government regulation. Remember, once you say that you can require disclosure of a campaign contribution, even though it's speech, then you can also require disclosure of membership in a political party. That's exactly what the government tried to to do to the Communists in the 1950s, and what Alabama tried to do to the NAACP until the Court stopped it.[64] It's just like what I was saying about the abortion and contraception cases. The Constitution protects some important rights. There may be others that people want protected, but that's not the job of federal judges. And when judges can decide that freedom of speech protects some toothpaste ads and not others, or some type of conduct and not others, then don't expect the courts to stand up when the government says that we have to suppress speech in order to save the country."

"Your approach to the Constitution provides a strong shield in times of suppression," I suggested, "but it doesn't provide much support for expansion of rights and liberties into new areas."

"You may be right," he replied. He became more pensive. "Maybe I wasn't a judge for all seasons. . . ."

"But you led us through the worst of times," I said.

"That's kind," he replied. "For the sake of the country, I hope we don't repeat the 1950s, and that people don't look back and say

64. NAACP v. Alabama, 357 U.S. 449 (1958).

that time has made my First Amendment ideas obsolete. But if history is any guide, those in power will once again try to silence their opponents and others who challenge the accepted wisdom. I see it happening already. And if that happens, maybe people will realize that I wasn't so naive, or simplistic, or conservative, or old-fashioned, after all."

Our time together was drawing to a close.

"Is there any one message that you'd like me to carry home?" I asked.

He grasped his copy of the Constitution and placed his other hand firmly on my shoulder. As he spoke, his voice trembled with emotion. "I've met people here from all times and places. They've been killed, jailed, tortured, and silenced because those in power didn't like their ideas, or their religion, or their politics. They come to my home here and ask to read the Constitution. They ask me whether these rights are just words on paper or are really enforced. They can't believe judges in our country have that power and that people and the government accept it. In our country, now, people want to make others conform to a true religion, or their notion of American values, or family values—the words change, but it's the same message: 'Don't speak out. Don't be different.' Tell the people back home that this Constitution and its rights make our country a special place on earth. Tell them."

Tears were in his eyes as we said goodbye. His last words to me were, "Tell them. Please tell them. Make them understand."

"I'll try," I said. "I promise I'll try."

HUGO LAFAYETTE BLACK: A BIBLIOGRAPHY OF THE COURT YEARS, 1937-1971

*Cherry Lynn Thomas**
*Jean McCulley Holcomb***

* Assistant Professor and Law Library Director, University of Alabama. B.S., M.L.S., J.D., University of Alabama.

** Assistant Law Library Director and Lecturer, University of Alabama. B.A., University of North Dakota; M.L.S., J.D., University of Alabama.

The authors wish to acknowledge the many hours of patience and meticulous attention to detail cheerfully contributed by Peggy Cook and the computer searching expertise contributed by David Lowe.

I. Introduction

In 1937 President Franklin D. Roosevelt appointed Hugo Lafayette Black, a native Alabamian and 1906 graduate of The University of Alabama School of Law, to the United States Supreme Court. Although controversy surrounded his appointment to the Court and his opinions often proved to be unpopular at home in Alabama, Hugo Black stood firmly by his convictions and his interpretation of the Constitution. Justice Black served as an Associate Justice of the Court for over 30 years in a period of wide-ranging social, political, and economic change. During his years on the Court, Justice Black championed protection of First Amendment rights, enforcement of antitrust laws, and implementation of racial desegregation.

This bibliography covers the life of Justice Black from the period of his appointment to the Court until his death. No attempt has been made here to gather information prior to that time. An excellent account of Justice Black's life before he joined the Court appears in Virginia Van der Veer Hamilton's book *Hugo Black: The Alabama Years*. A brief outline of the important events of Justice Black's life drawn from Hamilton's *Hugo Black* and from *Mr. Justice and Mrs. Black: The Memoirs of Hugo L. Black and Elizabeth Black* provides a frame of reference for the range of materials presented in the rest of the bibliography.

II. Chronology

Date	*Event*
Feb. 27, 1886	Born in Clay County, Alabama to William Lafayette and Martha Ardellah Toland Black.
1889	Family moved to Ashland, Alabama.

1903-1904	Attended one year of medical school at the University of Alabama, Birmingham, Alabama.
1904-1906	Attended the University of Alabama School of Law in Tuscaloosa and earned an LL.B.
1907	Returned to Ashland to practice law. When his office burned, he moved to Birmingham as a trial lawyer.
1911-1912	Judge of Recorder's Court while continuing the practice of law.
1915	Joined the Birmingham Chamber of Commerce.
1915-1917	Prosecutor for Jefferson County.
1917-1919	World War I: Officers Training School at Fort Oglethorpe, Georgia. Officer in the 81st Field Artillery.
1919	Entered general practice in Birmingham after World War I.
1920	Elected to the Executive Committee of the American Bar Association.
Feb. 23, 1921	Married Josephine Patterson Foster of Birmingham. They had three children: Hugo, Jr., Sterling Foster, and Martha Josephine.
1923-1925	Member of the Ku Klux Klan.
Jan. 29, 1925	First appearance before the United States Supreme Court.
1926	Elected to the United States Senate.
1932	Re-elected to the United States Senate.

1937	Appointed as Associate Justice of the United States Supreme Court. Confirmed on August 17; took Oath on August 19.
Oct. 1, 1937	First Public interview after being appointed to the United States Supreme Court.
Feb. 27, 1946	Sixtieth birthday celebration.
Feb. 27, 1951	Sixty-fifth birthday celebration.
Dec. 7, 1952	Josephine Patterson Foster (Justice Black's first wife) died.
1957	Married Mrs. Elizabeth Seay DeMeritte. Subsequently moved to Alexandria, Virginia.
June 25, 1962	Justice Black honored in proceeding for serving twenty-five full terms on the United States Supreme Court.
Feb. 27, 1966	Eightieth birthday celebration.
Apr. 25, 1967	White House reception honoring Justice Black for serving thirty full terms on the United States Supreme Court.
Dec. 3, 1968	CBS television interview broadcast.
Feb. 26, 1970	Eighty-fourth birthday celebration.
Feb. 27, 1971	Eighty-fifth birthday; clerk's dinner at the Federal City Club.
Sept. 17, 1971	Resignation from the United States Supreme Court.

Sept. 25, 1971	Died in Bethesda, Maryland. Interment in Arlington National Cemetery, Fort Myer, Arlington, Virginia.

III. Literature By or About Justice Black

A. *Introduction*

This portion of the bibliography consists of materials written by or about Justice Black. A listing of the research sources used to identify information is provided in the footnotes. Where a particular publication did not fall clearly within only one category, multiple references appear. Because the editorial policies of some indexing services mandate that articles, reviews, notes, and other materials be at least two ordinary pages or one folio page in length to qualify for inclusion, short presentations could not be identified easily.

The researchers did not search the indexes of major newspapers systematically for references about Justice Black. When other indexing sources identified newspaper articles about Justice Black, however, those which could be verified were included. An examination of the *New York Times Index* for 1971 disclosed reports of critical events in the last year of Justice Black's life. Notations of these accounts appear in the general publications category.

B. *Articles From Legal Publications*[1]

Anastaplo, *Mr. Justice Black, His Generous Common Sense and the Bar Admission Cases*, 9 Sw. U.L. Rev. 977-1048 (1977).

Armstrong, *Mr. Justice Black*, 20 Tenn. L. Rev. 638-43 (1949).

Ash, *The Growth of Justice Black's Philosophy on Freedom of Speech: 1962-1966*, 1967 Wis. L. Rev. 840-62.

Attanasio, *Everyman's Constitutional Law: A Theory of the Power of Judicial Review*, 72 Geo. L.J. 1665-1723 (1984).

---

1. Research Sources: *Index to Legal Periodicals*, *LegalTrac*, the Alabama Legal History collection of the University of Alabama School of Law Library, and the cumulative indexes of the *Alabama Law Review*, *Alabama Lawyer*, and *Cumberland Law Review*.

Baier, *Fifth Circuit Symposium—Introduction and Dedication: Mr. Justice Black (1886-1971), A Centennial Reflection*, 31 Loy. L. Rev. 415-19 (1985).
Baier, *Introduction to Hugo Black: A Memorial Portrait*, 1982 Y.B. Sup. Ct. Hist. Soc'y 72-73.
Ball, *Hugo L. Black: A Twentieth Century Jeffersonian*, 9 Sw. U.L. Rev. 1049-68 (1977).
Ball, *Justice Hugo L. Black: A Magnificent Product of the South*, 36 Ala. L. Rev. 791-834 (1985).
Barnett, Jr., *Mr. Justice Black and the Supreme Court*, 8 U. Chi. L. Rev. 20-41 (1940).
Berman, *Freedom and Mr. Justice Black: The Record After Twenty Years*, 25 Mo. L. Rev. 155-74 (1960).
Berman, *Hugo Black at 75*, 10 Am. U.L. Rev. 43-52 (1961).
Berman, *Hugo L. Black: The Early Years*, 8 Cath. U.L. Rev. 103-16 (1959).
Berman, *The Racial Issue and Mr. Justice Black*, 16 Am. U.L. Rev. 386-402 (1967).
Berman & Durr, *Hugo Black, Southerner*, 10 Am. U.L. Rev. 27-42 (1961).
Bixby, *The Roosevelt Court, Democratic Ideology, and Minority Rights: Another Look at* United States v. Classic, 90 Yale L.J. 741-815 (1981).
Black, *Hugo Black: A Memorial Portrait*, 1982 Y.B. Sup. Ct. Hist. Soc'y 72-94.
Black, *Hugo Black, The Magnificent Rebel*, 9 Sw. U.L. Rev. 889-98 (1977).
Black & Cahn, *Justice Black and First Amendment "Absolutes": A Public Interview*, 37 N.Y.U. L. Rev. 549-63 (1962).
Blaustein & Mersky, *Rating Supreme Court Justices*, 58 A.B.A. J. 1183-89 (1972).
Browning, *Hugo Lafayette Black (1886-1971)*, 5 Ala. L. Rep. 2 (Apr. 1972) (University of Alabama Law School Publications).
Cahn, *The Firstness of the First Amendment*, 65 Yale L.J. 464-81 (1956).
Cahn & Black, *Justice Black and First Amendment "Absolutes": A Public Interview*, 37 N.Y.U. L. Rev. 549-63 (1962).
Carrafiello, *Weighing the First Amendment on the Scales of the Balancing Test: The Choice of Safety Before Liberty*, 8 S.U.L. Rev. 255-300 (1982).

Case Notes, 10 Am. U.L. Rev. 64-93 (1961) (student notes on six United States Supreme Court cases in which Justice Black wrote opinions).

Cole, *Mr. Justice Black and "Senatorial Courtesy,"* 31 Am. Pol. Sci. Rev. 1113-15 (1937).

Comment, *Justice Black—Inherent Coercion: An Analytical Study of the Standard for Determining the Voluntariness of a Confession*, 10 Am. U.L. Rev. 53-61 (1961).

Comment, *Justice Hugo Black—A Question of Conscience and Consistency:* Welsh v. United States, 17 Loy. L. Rev. 105-46 (1970).

Cooper, *Mr. Justice Hugo L. Black: Footnotes to a Great Case*, 24 Ala. L. Rev. 1-13 (1971).

Cooper, *Mr. Justice Hugo L. Black: Free Man*, 17 Ala. L. Rev. 195-200 (1965).

Cooper, *Mr. Justice Hugo LaFayette Black of Alabama (1886-1971)*, 33 Ala. Law. 17-22 (1972).

Cooper, *Mr. Justice Hugo LaFayette Black of Alabama (1886-1971)*, 37 Ala. Law. 433-39 (1976) (reprint of 33 Ala. Law. 17-22 (1972)).

Decker, *Justice Hugo L. Black: The Balancer of Absolutes*, 59 Calif. L. Rev. 1335-55 (1971).

Dennis, *Overcoming Occupational Heredity at the Supreme Court*, 66 A.B.A. J. 41-45 (1980).

Dilliard, *Hugo Black and the Importance of Freedom*, 10 Am. U.L. Rev. 7-26 (1961).

Dilliard, *Justice Black and the Language of Freedom*, 38 Ala. L. Rev. 307 (1987).

Dilliard, *Mr. Justice Black and* In re Anastaplo, 9 Sw. U.L. Rev. 953-75 (1977).

Donnici, *Protector of the Minorities: Mr. Justice Hugo L. Black*, 32 UMKC L. Rev. 266-91 (1964).

Dorsen, *Mr. Justice Black and Mr. Justice Harlan*, 46 N.Y.U. L. Rev. 649-52 (1971).

Douglas, *Mr. Justice Black: A Foreword*, 65 Yale L.J. 449-50 (1956).

Dunne, *Justice Hugo Black and the Brown Decision: A Speculative Inquiry*, 39 Mo. L. Rev. 1-26 (1974).

Dunne, *Justice Hugo Black: Craftsman of the Law*, 38 Ala. L. Rev. 325 (1987).

Dunne, *Justices Hugo Black and Robert Jackson: The Great Feud*, 19 St. Louis U.L.J. 465-87 (1975).

Durr, *Hugo L. Black: A Personal Appraisal*, 6 Ga. L. Rev. 1-16 (1971).

Durr & Berman, *Hugo Black, Southerner*, 10 Am. U.L. Rev. 27-42 (1961).

Edwards, *Justice Black & Labor Law: Some Reflections on the Justice's Jurisprudence of Individual Versus Collective Rights in Industrial Relations*, 38 Ala. L. Rev. 249 (1987).

Frank, *Hugo L. Black*, 1971 L. & Soc. Ord. 1-2.

Frank, *Hugo L. Black: Free Speech and the Declaration of Independence*, 1977 U. Ill. L.F. 577-620.

Frank, *Hugo L. Black: He Has Joined the Giants*, 58 A.B.A. J. 21-25 (1972).

Frank, *Justice Black and the New Deal*, 9 Ariz. L. Rev. 26-58 (1967).

Frank, *Mr. Justice Black: A Biographical Appreciation*, 65 Yale L.J. 454-63 (1956).

Freund, *Mr. Justice Black and the Judicial Function*, 14 UCLA L. Rev. 467-74 (1967).

Freyer, *Commemorating the Centennial of Justice Hugo L. Black: An Introduction*, 38 Ala. L. Rev. 215 (1987).

Freyer, *The Justice Hugo L. Black Centennial: An Introduction*, 36 Ala. L. Rev. 789-90 (1985).

Goldberg, *Address by the Hon. Arthur J. Goldberg in Honor of Justice Hugo L. Black*, 24 Ala. L. Rev. 255-64 (1972).

Goldberg, *Attorney General Meese Vs. Chief Justice John Marshall and Justice Hugo L. Black*, 38 Ala. L. Rev. 237 (1987).

Goldberg, *Constitutional Faith: The Hugo L. Black Lecture*, 26 Ala. L. Rev. 295-307 (1974).

Gordon, *Justice Hugo Black—First Amendment Fundamentalist*, 20 Law. Guild Rev. 1-5 (1960).

Gordon & Weissman, *Mr. Justice Black at 70: The Judge and His Influence*, 16 Law. Guild Rev. 101-03 (1956).

Green, *Jury Trial and Mr. Justice Black*, 65 Yale L.J. 482-94 (1956).

Green, *Mr. Justice Black Versus the Supreme Court*, 4 U. Newark L. Rev. 113-48 (1939).

Gregory & Strickland, *Hugo Black's Congressional Investigation of Lobbying and the Public Utilities Holding Company Act: A*

Historical View of the Power Trust, New Deal Politics, and Regulatory Propaganda, 29 Okla. L. Rev. 543-76 (1976).

Grinnell, *Can Senator Black Become a Member of the Supreme Court Under the Constitution?*, 22 Mass. L.Q. 20-23 (July-Sept. 1937).

Hackney, *The Clay County Origins of Mr. Justice Black: The Populist As Insider*, 36 Ala. L. Rev. 835-43 (1985).

Haigh, *Defining Due Process of Law: The Case of Mr. Justice Hugo L. Black*, 17 S.D.L. Rev. 1-40 (1972).

Haigh, *The Judicial Opinions of Mr. Justice Hugo L. Black*, 9 Sw. U.L. Rev. 1069-1125 (1977).

Haigh, *Mr. Justice Black and the Written Constitution*, 24 Ala. L. Rev. 15-44 (1971).

Hambleton, *The All-Time, All-Star, All-Era Supreme Court*, 69 A.B.A. J. 462-64 (1983).

Hamilton, *Hugo Black: The Road to the Court*, 9 Sw. U.L. Rev. 859-88 (1977).

Hamilton, *Lister Hill, Hugo Black, and the Albatross of Race*, 36 Ala. L. Rev. 845-60 (1985).

Harlan, *Mr. Justice Black—Remarks of a Colleague*, 81 Harv. L. Rev. 1-3 (1967).

Havighurst, *Mr. Justice Black*, 1 Nat'l Law. Guild Q. 181-85 (1938).

Hobbs, *Justice Black: Qualities of Greatness*, 24 Ala. L. Rev. 11-13 (1971).

Howard, *Mr. Justice Black: The Negro Protest Movement and the Rule of Law*, 53 Va. L. Rev. 1030-90 (1967).

Hudon, *John Lilburne, the Levelers, and Mr. Justice Black*, 60 A.B.A. J. 686-88 (1974).

Hugo Lafayette Black 1886-1971, 47 Ala. Law. 128-29 (1986) (photograph).

The James Madison Lecture: "The Bill of Rights," 35 N.Y.U. L. Rev. 865-81 (1960).

Johnson, *Senator Black and the American Merchant Marine*, 14 UCLA L. Rev. 399-427 (1967).

Justice Black and the Bill of Rights, 9 Sw. U.L. Rev. 937-51 (1977) (transcript of CBS News Special in which Justice Black was interviewed by Eric Sevareid and Martin Agronsky).

Kalven, *Upon Rereading Mr. Justice Black on the First Amendment*, 14 UCLA L. Rev. 428-53 (1967).

Kalven & Steffen, *The Bar Admission Cases: An Unfinished Debate Between Justice Harlan and Justice Black*, 21 L. Transition 155-96 (1961).

Keeffe, *Justice Black Leaves His Mark*, 58 A.B.A. J. 63-65 (1972).

Kirkpatrick, *Justice Black and Antitrust*, 14 UCLA L. Rev. 475-500 (1967).

Klein, *Hugo L. Black: A Judicial View of American Constitutional Democracy*, 22 U. Miami L. Rev. 753-99 (1968).

Kornstein, *Thoughts on Thinking the Unthinkable*, 187 N.Y.L.J. 2 (1982).

Krislov, *Mr. Justice Black Reopens the Free Speech Debate*, 11 UCLA L. Rev. 189-211 (1964).

Kurland, *Hugo Lafayette Black: In Memoriam*, 20 J. Pub. L. 359-62 (1971).

Landynski, *In Search of Justice Black's Fourth Amendment*, 45 Fordham L. Rev. 453-96 (1976).

Lee, *Resolution Relative to Appointment of Hugo L. Black as a Justice of the Supreme Court of the United States*, 4 J. Marshall L.Q. 71-77 (1938).

Leuchtenburg, *A Klansman Joins the Court: The Appointment of Hugo L. Black*, 41 U. Chi. L. Rev. 1-31 (1973).

Lewis, *Justice Black and the First Amendment*, 38 Ala. L. Rev. 289 (1987).

Long, *Mr. Justice Black*, 6 Ga. L. Rev. 17-21 (1971).

McBride, *Mr. Justice Black and His Qualified Absolutes*, 2 Loy. L.A.L. Rev. 37-70 (1969).

McGovney, *Is Hugo L. Black a Supreme Court Justice de Jure?*, 26 Calif. L. Rev. 1-32 (1937).

Mauney, *Religion and First Amendment Protections: An Analysis of Justice Black's Constitutional Interpretation*, 10 Pepperdine L. Rev. 377-420 (1983).

Meador, *Justice Black and His Law Clerks*, 15 Ala. L. Rev. 57-63 (1962).

Meador, *Mr. Justice Black: A Tribute*, 57 Va. L. Rev. 1109-14 (1971).

Meiklejohn, *Public Speech in the Burger Court: The Influence of Mr. Justice Black*, 8 U. Tol. L. Rev. 301-41 (1977).

Meiklejohn, *Religion in the Burger Court: The Heritage of Mr. Justice Black*, 10 Ind. L. Rev. 645-74 (1977).

Mendelson, *Mr. Justice Black's Fourteenth Amendment*, 53 Minn. L. Rev. 711-27 (1969).

Mersky & Blaustein, *Rating Supreme Court Justices*, 58 A.B.A. J. 1183-89 (1972).

Murphy, *The Early Social and Political Philosophy of Hugo Black: Liquor As A Test Case*, 36 Ala. L. Rev. 861-79 (1985).

Note, *Legality of Justice Black's Appointment to the Supreme Court*, 37 Colum. L. Rev. 1212-16 (1937).

Note, *Reflections on Justice Black and Freedom of Speech*, 6 Val. U.L. Rev. 316-31 (1972).

Opinions of Mr. Justice Black, 10 Am. U.L. Rev. 100-15 (1961).

O'Reilly, Jr., *Hugo L. Black—Legal Craftsman*, 56 Mass. L.Q. 323-24 (1971).

O'Rourke & Thernstrom, *Justice Black: Local Control and Federalism*, 38 Ala. L. Rev. 331 (1987).

Paul, *Mr. Justice Black and Federal Taxation*, 65 Yale L.J. 495-528 (1956).

Ray, *Justice Black Adorns the Bench*, 10 Ala. Law. 455-57 (1949).

Redlich, *A Black—Harlan Dialogue on Due Process and Equal Protection: Overheard in Heaven and Dedicated to Robert B. McKay*, 50 N.Y.U. L. Rev. 20-46 (1975).

Redlich, *Hugo Black Enters His Hundredth Year: Some Heavenly Reflections on the Constitution*, 38 Ala. L. Rev. 357 (1987).

Reich, *Foreword: Mr. Justice Black as One Who Saw the Future*, 9 Sw. U.L. Rev. 845-57 (1977).

Reich, *Mr. Justice Black and the Living Constitution*, 76 Harv. L. Rev. 673-754 (1963).

Remarks of Justice William J. Brennan on the Occasion of the Justice Hugo L. Black Centennial, 38 Ala. L. Rev. 223 (1987).

Resnik, *Black, Douglas, and Absolutes: Some Suggestions for a New Perspective on the Supreme Court*, 47 J. Urb. L. 765-95 (1970).

Rice, *Justice Black, the Demonstrators, and a Constitutional Rule of Law*, 14 UCLA L. Rev. 454-66 (1967).

Rodell, *Foreword: A Sprig of Laurel for Hugo Black at 75*, 10 Am. U.L. Rev. 1-6 (1961).

Rostow, *Mr. Justice Black: Some Introductory Observations*, 65 Yale L.J. 451-53 (1956).

Rutledge, *Justice Black and Labor Law*, 14 UCLA L. Rev. 501-23 (1967).

Shannon, *Hugo La Fayette Black As United States Senator*, 36 Ala. L. Rev. 881-97 (1985).

Shores, *Justice Black and the Antitrust Laws*, 27 Antitrust Bull. 389-432 (1982).

Slayman, *Recent Books on Civil Liberties and Civil Rights*, 10 Am. U.L. Rev. 94-99 (1961).

Snowiss, *The Legacy of Justice Black*, 1973 Sup. Ct. Rev. 187-252.

Strickland, *Mr. Justice Black: A Reappraisal*, 25 Fed. B.J. 365-82 (1965).

Strickland & Gregory, *Hugo Black's Congressional Investigation of Lobbying and the Public Utilities Holding Company Act: A Historical View of the Power Trust, New Deal Politics, and Regulatory Propaganda*, 29 Okla. L. Rev. 543-76 (1976).

Sutherland, *Justice Black on Counsel and Non-Voluntary Confessions*, 14 UCLA L. Rev. 536-52 (1967).

Thernstrom & O'Rourke, *Justice Black: Local Control and Federalism*, 38 Ala. L. Rev. 331 (1987).

Thornton, III, *Hugo Black and the Golden Age*, 36 Ala. L. Rev. 899-913 (1985).

Tillett, *Mr. Justice Black, Chief Justice Marshall, and the Commerce Clause*, 43 Neb. L. Rev. 1-26 (1963).

Touchy, *The New Legality*, 53 A.B.A. J. 544-46 (1967).

Ulmer, *The Longitudinal Behavior of Hugo Lafayette Black: Parabolic Support for Civil Liberties 1937-1971*, 1 Fla. St. U. L. Rev. 131-53 (1973).

U.S. Congress, *Memorial Addresses and Tributes in the Congress of the United States*, H.R. Doc. No. 236, 92nd Cong., 1st Sess. (1972).

U.S. Supreme Court, *Proceedings Honoring Mr. Justice Black, June 25, 1962*, 370 U.S. V-VI (1961) (addresses by Solicitor General Archibald Cox and Chief Justice Earl Warren).

U.S. Supreme Court, *Proceedings in the Supreme Court of the United States in Memory of Mr. Justice Black, Tuesday, April 18, 1972*, 405 U.S. IX-LXI (1972) (addresses by Solicitor General Erwin Griswold, Acting Attorney General Richard Kleindienst, and Chief Justice Warren Burger).

Van Alstyne, *Mr. Justice Black, Constitutional Review, and the Talisman of State Action*, 1965 Duke L.J. 219-47.

Warren, *Introduction*, 14 UCLA L. Rev. 397-98 (1967).

Warren, *A Tribute to Hugo L. Black*, 85 Harv. L. Rev. 1-2 (1971).

Weissman & Gordon, *Mr. Justice Black at 70: The Judge and His Influence*, 16 Law. Guild Rev. 101-03 (1956).

Wollensak, *Hugo Lafayette Black and John Marshall Harlan: Two Faces of Constitutional Law—With Some Notes on the Teaching of Thayer's Subject*, 9 S.U.L. Rev. 1-35 (1982).

Wright, *Hugo L. Black: A Great Man and a Great American*, 50 Tex. L. Rev. 1-5 (1971).

Wright, *Justice at the Dock: The Maritime Worker and Mr. Justice Black*, 14 UCLA L. Rev. 524-35 (1967).

Wyatt-Brown, *Ethical Backgrounds of Hugo Black's Career: Thoughts Prompted by the Articles of Sheldon Hackney and Paul L. Murphy*, 36 Ala. L. Rev. 915-26 (1985).

Yarbrough, *Justice Black and Equal Protection*, 9 Sw. U.L. Rev. 899-935 (1977).

Yarbrough, *Justice Black and His Critics on Speech-Plus and Symbolic Speech*, 52 Tex. L. Rev. 257-84 (1974).

Yarbrough, *Justice Black, the First Amendment, and the Burger Court*, 46 Miss. L.J. 203-46 (1975).

Yarbrough, *Justice Black, the Fourteenth Amendment, and Incorporation*, 30 U. Miami L. Rev. 231-75 (1976).

Yarbrough, *Justices Black and Douglas: The Judicial Function and the Scope of Constitutional Liberties*, 1973 Duke L.J. 441-86.

Yarbrough, *Mr. Justice Black and Legal Positivism*, 57 Va. L. Rev. 375-407 (1971).

C. Symposia Issues

The Justice Hugo L. Black Centennial, Part 1—Hugo L. Black: Alabamian and American, 1886-1937, 36 Ala. L. Rev. 789-926 (1985).

Included articles:

Ball, *Justice Hugo L. Black: A Magnificent Product of the South*, at 791-834.

Freyer, *The Justice Hugo L. Black Centennial: An Introduction*, at 789-90.

Hackney, *The Clay County Origins of Mr. Justice Black: The Populist as Insider*, at 835-43.

Hamilton, *Lister Hill, Hugo Black, and the Albatross of Race*, at 845-60.

Murphy, *The Early Social and Political Philosophy of Hugo Black: Liquor As A Test Case*, at 861-79.

Shannon, *Hugo LaFayette Black As United States Senator*, at 881-97.

Thornton, III, *Hugo Black and the Golden Age*, at 899-913.

Wyatt-Brown, *Ethical Backgrounds of Hugo Black's Career: Thoughts Prompted by the Articles of Sheldon Hackney and Paul L. Murphy*, at 915-26.

The Justice Hugo L. Black Centennial, Part Two—Hugo L. Black: The Court Years, 1937-1971, 38 Ala. L. Rev. 215-500 (1987).

Included articles:

Dilliard, *Justice Black and the Language of Freedom*, at 307-24.

Dunne, *Justice Hugo Black: Craftsman of the Law*, at 325-30.

Edwards, *Justice Black & Labor Law: Some Reflections on the Justice's Jurisprudence of Individual Versus Collective Rights in Industrial Relations*, at 249-88.

Freyer, *Commemorating the Centennial of Justice Hugo L. Black: An Introduction*, at 215-22.

Goldberg, *Attorney General Meese Vs. Chief Justice John Marshall and Justice Hugo L. Black*, at 237-48.

Lewis, *Justice Black and the First Amendment*, at 289-306.

O'Rourke & Thernstrom, *Justice Black: Local Control and Federalism*, at 331-56.

Redlich, *Hugo Black Enters His Hundredth Year: Some Heavenly Reflections on the Constitution*, at 357-80.

Remarks of Justice William J. Brennan on the Occasion of the Justice Hugo L. Black Centennial, at 223-36.

Thernstrom & O'Rourke, *Justice Black: Local Control and Federalism*, at 331-56.

Justice Hugo L. Black: A Symposium, 9 Sw. U. L. Rev. 845-1155 (1977).

Included articles:

Anastaplo, *Mr. Justice Black, His Generous Common Sense, and the Bar Admission Cases*, at 977-1048.

Ball, *Hugo L. Black: A Twentieth Century Jeffersonian*, at 1049-68.
Black, *Hugo Black: The Magnificent Rebel*, at 889-98.
Dilliard, *Mr. Justice Black and* In Re Anastaplo, at 953-75.
Haigh, *The Judicial Opinions of Mr. Justice Hugo L. Black*, at 1069-1125.
Hamilton, *Hugo Black: The Road to the Court*, at 859-88.
Justice Black and the Bill of Rights, at 937-51 (transcript of CBS News Special in which Justice Black was interviewed by Eric Sevareid and Martin Agronsky).
Landynski, Book Review, at 1139-55 (reviewing G. Dunne, *Hugo Black and the Judicial Revolution* (1977)).
Noonan, Jr., Book Review, at 1127-37 (reviewing G. Dunne, *Hugo Black and the Judicial Revolution* (1977)).
Reich, *Foreword: Mr. Justice Black as One Who Saw the Future*, at 845-57.
Yarbrough, *Justice Black and Equal Protection*, at 899-935.

Mr. Justice Black: A Symposium, 65 Yale L.J. 449-528 (1956).

Included articles:

Cahn, *The Firstness of the First Amendment*, at 464-81.
Douglas, *Mr. Justice Black: A Foreword*, at 449-50.
Frank, *Mr. Justice Black: A Biographical Appreciation*, at 454-63.
Green, *Jury Trial and Mr. Justice Black*, at 482-94.
Paul, *Mr. Justice Black and Federal Taxation*, at 495-528.
Rostow, *Mr. Justice Black: Some Introductory Observations*, at 451-53.

Mr. Justice Black: Thirty Years in Retrospect, 14 UCLA L. Rev. 397-552 (1967).

Included articles:

Freund, *Mr. Justice Black and the Judicial Function*, at 467-74.
Johnson, *Senator Black and the American Merchant Marine*, at 399-427.
Kalven, *Upon Rereading Mr. Justice Black on the First Amendment*, at 428-53.
Kirkpatrick, *Justice Black and Antitrust*, at 475-500.

Rice, *Justice Black, the Demonstrators, and a Constitutional Rule of Law*, at 454-66.
Rutledge, *Justice Black and Labor Law*, at 501-23.
Sutherland, *Justice Black on Counsel and Non-Voluntary Confessions*, at 536-52.
Warren, *Introduction*, at 397-98.
Wright, *Justice at the Dock: The Maritime Worker and Mr. Justice Black*, at 524-35.

Tribute to Justice Black on the Occasion of His Seventy-fifth Birthday, 10 Am. U.L. Rev. 1-119 (1961).

Included articles:

Berman, *Hugo L. Black at 75*, at 43-52.
Berman & Durr, *Hugo Black, Southerner*, at 27-42.
Case Notes, at 64-93 (student notes on six Supreme Court cases in which Justice Black wrote opinions.
Comment, *Justice Black—Inherent Coercion: An Analytical Study of the Standard for Determining the Voluntariness of a Confession*, at 53-61.
Dilliard, *Hugo Black and the Importance of Freedom*, at 7-26.
Durr & Berman, *Hugo Black, Southerner*, at 27-42.
Opinions of Mr. Justice Black, at 100-15.
Rodell, *Foreword: A Sprig of Laurel for Hugo Black at 75*, at 1-6.
Slayman, *Recent Books on Civil Liberties and Civil Rights*, at 94-99.
Speeches and Articles by Mr. Justice Hugo L. Black, at 116-19.

D. Articles From General Publications[2]

Allen, *Who Exposed Black?, With Editorial Comment*, 145 Nation 308, 311-12 (1937).
Allerdice, *Ten Jurists Who Made the Court Supreme*, 117 Scholastic Update 10-11 (Nov. 30, 1984).

---

2. Research Sources: *Readers' Guide to Periodical Literature, International Index to Periodicals, Social Sciences Index, 1971 New York Times Index*, and the following Dialog Databases: America: History and Life, Magazine Index, National Newspaper Index, and United States Political Documents.

Anderson, *Black's Solitary Dissents*, 146 Nation 634-35 (1938).

Anderson, *Marquis Childs and Justice Black; With Editorial Comment*, 146 Nation 577-80 (1938).

Beth, *Mr. Justice Black And The First Amendment: Comments On The Dilemma Of Constitutional Interpretation*, 41 J. Pol. 1105-24 (1979).

Bickel, *Mr. Justice Black: The Unobvious Meaning Of Plain Words*, 142 New Republic 13-15 (Mar. 14, 1960).

Black: A Man of Parts, 7 Newsweek 21 (Mar. 14, 1936).

Black Admits Klan Link, Denies Intolerance, 31 Scholastic 14 (Oct. 16, 1937).

The Black Affair, 145 Nation 361-62 (1937).

Black and K.K.K., 124 Literary Dig. 6 (Sept. 25, 1937).

Black Back, 30 Time 50 (Oct. 11, 1937).

Black Dissenting, 141 New Republic 5-7 (July 27, 1959).

Black Friday; Pro and Con, 124 Literary Dig. 7 (Oct. 16, 1937).

Black, *I Did Join the Klan: About Fifteen Years Ago. . .*, 4 Vital Speeches 20-21 (Oct. 15, 1937).

Black in White, 30 Time 13 (Sept. 20, 1937).

Black, Jr., *Mr. Justice Black, the Supreme Court, and the Bill of Rights*, 222 Harper's 63-68 (Feb. 1961)

Black Link With Klan Causes Political Uproar, 31 Scholastic 19 (Oct. 2, 1937).

Black of Alabama, 26 Commonwealth 409-10 (1937).

Black On Libel, 59 Newsweek 80 (June 25, 1962).

Black Scandal, 30 Time 10-11 (Sept. 27, 1937).

Black: Senate Is Sorry, President Is Angry, and the Justice Is Silent, 10 Newsweek 10-11 (Sept. 27, 1937).

Burlingham, *A Matter of Character; Reply to M. Lerner, With Rejoinder*, 145 Nation 515 (1937).

Callaway, *Notes On A Kleagle*, 43 Am. Mercury 248-49 (Feb. 1938).

Case of Mr. Justice Black, 92 New Republic 200-01 (1937).

Chancey, *Justice Black's Liberalism: A Reevaluation*, 35 Negro Hist. Bull. 173-75 (Dec. 1972).

Civil Rights Rulings: What They Mean: Excerpts from Statements, 57 U.S. News & World Rep. 40-41 (Dec. 28, 1964).

Cole, *Mr. Justice Black And "Senatorial Courtesy,"* 31 Am. Pol. Sci. Rev. 1113-15 (1937).

Confessions of the Law Clerks—Extracted from the 80th Birthday of Mr. Justice Black—February 27, 1966 (privately printed 1966).

Curtis, Jr., *How About Hugo Black?*, 163 Atlantic 667-74 (May 1939).

Custom Binds Senate, and It Votes Against Its Will, 10 Newsweek 13-14 (Aug. 28, 1937).

Daniels, *Battle of the Bench*, 118 Collier's 12-13, 68-72 (Aug. 17, 1946).

Douglas, *An Intimate Memoir of the Brethren*, 130 N.Y. Times, Sept. 21, 1980 (Magazine), at 38.

Douglas vs. Black: Old Friends Fall Out, 54 U.S. News & World Rep. 20 (June 17, 1963).

Editorial, N.Y. Times, Sept. 18, 1971, at 28, col. 2.

Editorial: Of Supreme Stature, N.Y. Times, Sept. 26, 1971, IV, at 14, col. 2.

Education of Hugo Black, 145 Nation 337-38 (1937).

Elman, *Reply to J. Frank* 113 New Republic 135-36 (1945).

Engel, *Justice Black After Seven Years*, 159 Nation 404-06 (1944).

Excerpts from Justice Black's Opinions and Views, N.Y. Times, Sept. 18, 1971, at 12, col. 4.

Faith in the People, 91 Time 76 (Mar. 29, 1968).

F.D.R. Takes A Run-Out Powder on the Black Sheep, 92 New Republic 213-14 (1937).

Flynn, *Comments on Mr. Justice Black*, 92 New Republic 101-02 (1937).

For 34 Years on Bench, A Key Influence on Law, N.Y. Times, Sept. 18, 1972, at 12, col. 7.

Fortune Survey: Was the Appointment of Hugo Black to the Supreme Court a Good Choice or a Bad Choice?, 17 Fortune 92 (Jan. 1938).

Frank, *Obituary: Hugo L. Black*, 165 New Republic 15-17 (Oct. 9, 1971).

Frank, *The Divided Supreme Court, Principles or Personalities?*, 112 New Republic 833-37 (1945).

Frank, *Reply*, 142 New Republic 30 (Apr. 4, 1960).

From Songs To Sedition, 67 Newsweek 27 (Mar. 7, 1966).

Gillis, *Editorial Comment—Talent Rewarded: Mr. Justice Black*, 146 Catholic World 129-34 (1937).

Graham, *Nixon Attends Funeral in the Capitol for Justice Black*, N.Y. Times, Sept. 29, 1971, at 37, col. 1.

Grossman, *Justice Black and the Absolute*, 36 Commentary 244-48 (1963).

Hamilton, *Mr. Justice Black's First Year*, 95 New Republic 118-22 (1938).

High-Court Controversy, 114 New Republic 887 (1946).

The High Court Loses the Best of Adversaries, 78 Newsweek 20 (Oct. 4, 1971).

High Court: Silent Treatment, 27 Newsweek 29-30 (June 24, 1946).

High Court's No-Man: Black's 13 Dissents Stir Up Rumors and Denials, 11 Newsweek 26 (May 23, 1938).

Honor Among Judges, 146 Nation 577-78 (1938).

Hugo Black, Current Biography 82-84 (1941).

Hugo Black: Portrait, N.Y. Times, Feb. 18, 1940 (Magazine), at 8.

Hutchins, *Dissenting Opinion as a Creative Art*, 44 Saturday Rev. 12, 35-36 (Aug. 12, 1961).

Inside A Senate Investigation; From An Article In Harper's Magazine, February, 1936, 37 U.S. News & World Rep. 104-07 (Oct. 22, 1954).

Investigation by Headlines, 26 Time 14-17 (Aug. 26, 1935).

Issues in Jackson-Black Dispute: Press Appraisal of Effect on Court, 20 U.S. News & World Rep. 40 (June 21, 1946).

Judiciary; Slug?, 31 Time 13 (May 23, 1938).

Justice Black, Champion of Civil Liberties for 34 Years on Court, Dies at 85, N.Y. Times, Sept. 26, 1971, at 76, col. 1.

Justice Black, 85, Quits High Court, Citing His Health, N.Y. Times, Sept. 18, 1971, at 1, col. 8.

Justice Black Dies at 85; Served on Court 34 Years, N.Y. Times, Sept. 25, 1971, at 1, col. 2.

Justice Black Dissents; Turning Conservative?, 60 U.S. News & World Rep. 26-27 (Mar. 21, 1966).

Justice Black: "I Did Join, Resigned; The Case Is Closed," 10 Newsweek 12 (Oct. 11, 1937).

The Justices and Their Ladies, 43 U.S. News & World Rep. 16-17 (Dec. 27, 1957).

Klan Member on the Supreme Court? New Evidence Comes to Light, 10 Newsweek 9 (Sept. 20, 1937).

Klansman Black?, 26 Commonwealth 483-84 (1937).

Klansman Black Became Black the Inquisitor, 54 Christian Century 1189-90 (1937).

A Klansman on the Court?, 92 New Republic 256 (1937).

Lazarsfeld, *Change Of Opinion During a Political Discussion; Appointment of Senator Hugo Black to the United States Supreme Court*, 23 J. Applied Psychology 131-47 (1939).

Lerner, *Hugo Black: A Personal History*, 145 Nation 367-69 (1937).

Lerner, *Justice Black, Dissenting*, 146 Nation 264-66 (1938).

Lerner, *The Supreme Court: It's a Final Bulwark for the People Against Oppression by Unjust Laws*, 7 Holiday 73-82, 119-20, 122 (Feb. 1950).

Lewin, *Bizarre Decision By The Court: The Sometime 18-Year Old Vote*, 164 New Republic 21-22 (Jan. 2, 1971).

Lewis, *Justice Black at Seventy-Five: Still the Dissenter*, N.Y. Times, Feb. 26, 1961 (Magazine), at 13, 73-75.

Lewis, *Hugo Black—An Elemental Force*, N.Y. Times, Sept. 26, 1971, IV, at 1, col. 2.

Lewis, *Mr. Justice Black*, N.Y. Times, Sept. 20, 1971, at 25, col. 1.

Lewis, *Portraits of Nine Men Under Attack*, N.Y. Times, May 18, 1958 (Magazine), at 15-16.

Life in Court May Tame Black, Bus. Week, Aug. 31, 1937, at 14-15.

Madison, *Justice Hugo Black: Still Dissenting at 70*, 182 Nation 156-69 (1956).

Mauney, *Justice Black and First Amendment Freedoms: Thirty-four Influential Years*, 35 Emporia State Res. Stud. 1-51 (Fall 1986).

Medelman, *Do You Swear to Tell the Truth, the Whole Truth, and Nothing but the Truth, Justice Black?*, 69 Esquire 114-15, 156-66 (June 1968).

Mendelson, *Hugo Black and Judicial Discretion*, 85 Pol. Sci. Q. 17-39 (1970).

Mendelson, *Justices Black and Frankfurter: Supreme Court Majority and Minority Trends*, 12 J. Pol. 66-92 (1950).

Minority Opinion, 79 Time 53 (June 22, 1962).

Moley, *Imperfect Contrition*, 10 Newsweek 44 (Oct. 11, 1937).

Moley, *Inquisitor Comes To Glory*, 10 Newsweek 40 (Aug. 21, 1937).

Moley, *Whoso Diggeth A Pit*, 10 Newsweek 44 (Sept. 27, 1937).

Mr. Black Comes First, 26 Commonwealth 559-60 (1937).
Mr. Black's New Job, 124 Literary Dig. 5-6 (Aug. 28, 1937).
Mr. Justice Black, 78 Newsweek 40 (Sept. 27, 1971).
Mr. Justice Black Retires, 23 Nat'l Rev. 1097-98 (Oct. 8, 1971).
Murphy, *Deeds Under a Doctrine: Civil Liberties in the 1963 Term*, 59 Am. Pol. Sci. Rev. 64-79 (1965).
New Justice, 31 Scholastic 14 (Sept. 18, 1937).
New Look at the Warren Court, 47 U.S. News & World Rep. 74 (July 13, 1959).
Nine Justices, 70 Time 12-13 (July 1, 1957).
Nine New Egos, 18 Newsweek 23 (Dec. 8, 1941).
No Place For Fanatics, 100 Collier's 74 (Oct. 23, 1937).
Nock, *Picking of Hugo Black*, 42 Am. Mercury 229-33 (Oct. 1937).
Nominee No. 93, 30 Time 13-14 (Aug. 23, 1937).
Now Court Upholds States: Rulings Stand Against Communists and Unions, 40 U.S. News & World Rep. 64-66 (June 15, 1956).
Now, The Nixon Court And What It Means, 98 Time 15-16 (Oct. 4, 1971).
People in the Limelight: Mr. Justice Black, 112 New Republic 462 (1945).
People: Senator Black, 124 Literary Dig. 11 (Aug. 28, 1937).
Pollack, *Nine Men Who Defend America*, 44 Coronet 122-26 (July 1958).
The President Keeps To His Course, 54 Christian Century 1038-39 (1937).
Rebuttal for Hugo L. Black, 11 Newsweek 30 (June 20, 1938).
Recent Aquisitions of the Manuscript Division, 30 Q.J. Libr. Cong. 308-10 (1973).
Redlich, *Justice Black At Eighty: The Common Sense Of Freedom*, 202 Nation 322-26 (1966).
Rodell, *Black vs. Jackson*, 106 Forum 168-70 (1946).
Rodell, *Gallery of Justices: One Man's Dream Court*, 41 Saturday Rev. 9-11, 36-37 (Nov. 15, 1958).
Rodell, *Justice Hugo Black*, 59 Am. Mercury 135-43 (Aug. 1944).
Romero, *Justice Under Law: Hugo L. Black*, 30 Negro Hist. Bull. 12-14 (Feb. 1967).
Roosevelt Takes Out Judicial Insurance, Enrages Foes, and Upsets an Immemorial Usage, 10 Newsweek 7 (Aug. 21, 1937).

Ryan, *Due Process and Mr. Justice Black*, 151 Catholic World 36-39 (1940).

Salute to Justice Black, 145 Nation 183-84 (1937).

Schlesinger, *The Supreme Court: 1947*, Fortune 73-78, 201-12 (Jan. 1947).

Sebastian, *Klansman Black? Reply*, 26 Commonwealth 574-75 (1937).

Senator Black as Justice, 92 New Republic 60-61 (1937).

Senior Justice Retires, 98 Time 32 (Sept. 27, 1971).

A Shift In The Supreme Court: What One New Justice Can Mean, 62 U.S. News & World Rep. 67-68 (Apr. 24, 1967).

Stevens, Bailey, Kruger & Mollowitz, *Criminal Libel as Seditious Libel, 1916-65*, 43 Journalism Q. 110-13 (1966).

Still in the Storm's Center, 80 Time 9 (July 6, 1962).

The Story Behind Justices' Dispute: Clash of Ideas and Factions, 20 U.S. News & World Rep. 15-16 (June 21, 1946).

A Study in Black and White, 54 Christian Century 1255-57 (1937).

Supreme Court: Facing A Crucial Case Again . . . 8 of 9 Have New Deal or Fair Deal Connections, 32 U.S. News & World Rep. 49-51 (May 16, 1952).

The Supreme Court: The Limits that Create Liberty and the Liberty That Creates Limits, 84 Time 48-58 (Oct. 9, 1964).

Thomas, *Uncritical Support*, 145 Nation 387 (1937).

Three Points of View from the Court, 98 Time 10-11 (July 12, 1971).

The Twelve Great Justices of All Time, 71 Life 52-56 (Oct. 15, 1971).

Uproar Over School Prayer, and the Aftermath, 53 U.S. News & World Rep. 42-44 (July 9, 1962).

Vacancies on the Court, 165 New Republic 8-9 (Oct. 2, 1971).

Van Der Veer, *History at Middle Distance: Hugo Black and the K.K.K.*, 19 Am. Heritage 60-64, 108-11 (Apr. 1968).

Villard, *Issues and Men*, 145 Nation 221 (1937).

The Warren Court: Here Are the Justices Who Are Making Historic, Controversial Decisions, 43 Life 33-36 (July 1, 1957).

What the Court Said About Congressional Districts, 56 U.S. News & World Rep. 32-33 (Mar. 2, 1964).

Wrath Without Dignity, 47 Time 18-19 (June 17, 1946).

E. Articles Written By Justice Black[3]

Black, *About Edmond Cahn*, 40 N.Y.U. L. Rev. 207-08 (1965).
Black, *The Bill of Rights*, 35 N.Y.U. L. Rev. 865-81 (1960).
Black, *Dedicatory Address*, 5 J. Legal Educ. 417-23 (1953).
Black, *Democracy's Heritage: Free Thought, Free Speech, Free Press*, 1968 Britannica Y.B. 39-44.
Black, *Erie v. Tompkins*, 13 Mo. B.J. 173-76 (Oct. 1942).
Black, *Franklin D. Roosevelt*, 6 Law. Guild Rev. 396-99 (Jan.-Feb. 1946).
Black, *Franklin Roosevelt*, 12 J.B.A. Dist. Col. 150-52 (May 1945).
Black, *Inside a Senate Investigation*, 172 Harper's 275-86 (1936).
Black, *Justice Black's Warning—'I Fear for Our Constitutional System'*, 64 U.S. News & World Rep. 16 (Apr. 1, 1968).
Black, *The Lawyer and Individual Freedom*, 21 Tenn. L. Rev. 461-71 (1950).
Black, *Mr. Justice Frankfurter*, 78 Harv. L. Rev. 1521-22 (1965).
Black, *Mr. Justice Murphy*, 48 Mich. L. Rev. 739 (1950).
Black, *Mr. Justice Rutledge*, 25 Ind. L.J. 423 (1950).
Black, *Mr. Justice Rutledge*, 35 Iowa L. Rev. 541 (1950).
Black, *Reminiscences*, 18 Ala. L. Rev. 3-11 (1965).
Black, *A Supreme Court Justice Speaks His Mind on Key Issues*, 65 U.S. News & World Rep. 55-57 (Dec. 16, 1968).
Black, *There is a South of Union and Freedom*, 2 Ga. L. Rev. 10-15 (1967).
Black, *To Win the War and the Peace*, 107 New Republic 107-08 (1942).
Black, *Tribute to Elbert Tuttle*, 16 J. Pub. L. 279 (1967).
Black, *William Orville Douglas*, 73 Yale L.J. 915-16 (1964).

F. Books By and About Justice Black[4]

H. Ball, *The Vision and the Dream of Justice Hugo L. Black: An Examination of a Judicial Philosophy* (1975).
H. Black, *A Constitutional Faith* (1968).

---

3. Research Sources: *See* sources cited *supra* note 2. Additional references were provided by a search of footnotes in previously identified books, theses, and articles about Justice Black.

4. Research Source: Dialog Database: Books in Print

H. Black & E. Black, *Mr. Justice and Mrs. Black: The Memoirs of Hugo L. Black and Elizabeth Black* (P. Baier ed. 1986).

H. Black, Jr., *My Father: A Remembrance* (1975).

2 L. Blandford & P. Evans, *Supreme Court of the United States 1789-1980: An Index to Opinions Arranged by Justice* 729 (1983).

J. Cooper, *"Sincerely Your Friend:" Letters of Mr. Justice Hugo L. Black to Jerome A. Cooper* (1973).

H. Davis, *Uncle Hugo: An Intimate Portrait of Mr. Justice Black* (1965).

I. Dilliard *One Man's Stand for Freedom: Mr. Justice Black and the Bill of Rights* (1963).

G. Dunne, *Hugo Black and the Judicial Revolution* (1977).

2 P. Evans & L. Blandford, *Supreme Court of the United States 1789-1980: An Index to Opinions Arranged by Justice* 729 (1983).

J. Frank, *Mr. Justice Black: The Man and His Opinions* (1949).

V. Hamilton, *Hugo Black: The Alabama Years* (1972).

V. Hamilton, *The Senate Career of Hugo L. Black* (1968).

Hugo Black and the Bill of Rights: Proceedings of the First Hugo Black Symposium in American History on "The Bill of Rights and American Democracy" (V. Hamilton ed. 1978).

Hugo Black and the Supreme Court: A Symposium (S. Strickland ed. 1967).

Index to Microfilm Records of Handwritten Notes in the Hugo Black Collection (Washington, U.S. Supreme Court Library, 1985).

Justice Hugo Black and the First Amendment: " 'No Law' Means No Law" (E. Dennis ed. 1978).

Justices Black and Frankfurter: Conflict in the Court (W. Mendelson ed. 1961)

Justices Black and Frankfurter: Conflict in the Court (W. Mendelson 2d ed. 1966).

J. Magee, *Mr. Justice Black: Absolutist on the Court* (1980).

D. Meador, *Mr. Justice Black and His Books* (1974).

M. Silverstein, *Constitutional Faiths: Felix Frankfurter, Hugo Black, and the Process of Judicial Decision Making* (1984).

U.S. Congress, *Memorial Address and Other Tributes in the Congress of the United States on the Life and Contributions of*

Hugo Lafayette Black (H.R. Rep. Doc. No. 236, 92nd Cong., 1st Sess. (1972)).

C. Williams, *Hugo L. Black: A Study in the Judicial Process* (1950).

G. Book Reviews[5]

H. Ball, *The Vision and the Dream of Justice Hugo L. Black: An Examination of a Judicial Philosophy* (1975).

Legal Periodicals:

Carp, Book Review, 12 Hous. L. Rev. 991-94 (1975).
Edwards, Book Review, 45 U. Cin. L. Rev. 163-66 (1976).
Stephenson, Book Review, 21 Vill. L. Rev. 810-18 (1976).

General Periodicals:

Rossum, Book Review, 38 J. Pol. 505 (May 1976).
Sakmyster, Book Review, 100 Libr. J. 872 (1975).
Slotnick, Book Review, 17 La. Hist. 235-36 (1976).
Strickland, Book Review, 71 Am. Pol. Sci. Rev. 1167-69 (1977).

H. Black, *A Constitutional Faith* (1968).

Legal Periodicals:

Sultan, Book Review, 47 J. Urban L. 579 (1970).

General Periodicals:

Deutsch, Book Review, N.Y. Times, February 16, 1969, at 18.
Fox, Book Review, 93 Libr. J. 4124 (1968).
Gould, Book Review, 90 Commonwealth 176-79 (Apr. 25, 1969).
Lucey, Book Review, 120 America 535 (1969).

---

5. Research Sources: *Index to Legal Periodicals*, *LegalTrac*, *Book Review Index*, *Book Review Digest*, and the Dialog Database: Book Review Index.

Waltz, Book Review, Book World 10 (Oct. 27, 1968).

H. Black & E. Black, *Mr. Justice and Mrs. Black: The Memoirs of Hugo L. Black and Elizabeth Black* (P. Baier ed. 1986).

Legal Periodicals:

Frank, Book Review, 22 Trial 83-85 (1986).

General Periodicals:

Childress, Book Review, 111 Libr. J. 91 (1986).
MacKenzie, Book Review, N.Y. Times, April 20, 1986, at 23, col. 2.
Stuttaford, Book Review, 229 Publishers Weekly 56-57 (Jan. 17, 1986).

H. Black, Jr., *My Father: A Remembrance* (1975).

Legal Periodicals:

Collins, Book Review, 1977 Duke L.J. 1087-97.
Freund, Book Review, 89 Harv. L. Rev. 450-52 (1975).
Strickland, Book Review, 24 U. Kan. L. Rev. 711-21 (1976).

General Periodicals:

Book Review, 35 Best Sellers 285 (Dec. 1979).
Silver, Book Review, 103 Commonwealth 93-95 (Jan. 30, 1976).

I. Dilliard, *One Man's Stand for Freedom: Mr. Justice Black and the Bill of Rights* (1963).

Legal Periodicals:

Mosk, Book Review, 1 San Diego L. Rev. 135-39 (1964).
Rosenwein, Book Review, 23 L. Transition 165 (1963).
Van Alstyne, Book Review, 28 Mo. L. Rev. 675 (1963).
Weiss, Book Review, 72 Yale L.J. 1665-70 (1963).

General Periodicals:

Andrews, Book Review, 88 Libr. J. 1543 (1963).
Book Review, 40 Va. Q. Rev. XXXV (Win. 1964).
Clancy, Book Review, 109 America 669 (Nov. 23, 1963).
Grossman, Book Review, 36 Commentary 244-48 (1963).
McKay, Book Review, N.Y. Times, Sept. 1, 1963, at 7.

Madison, Book Review, 46 Saturday Rev. 29 (June 29, 1963).

G. Dunne, *Hugo Black and the Judicial Revolution* (1977).

Legal Periodicals:

Book Note, 29 Emory L.J. 305-06 (1980).
Boudin, Book Review, 90 Harv. L. Rev. 1733-45 (1977).
Clark, Book Review, 13 Tulsa L.J. 185-94 (1977).
Denonn, Book Review, 65 A.B.A. J. 238 (1979).
Landynski, Book Review, 9 Sw. U.L. Rev. 1139-55 (1977).
Losos, Book Review, 21 St. Louis U.L.J. 202-05 (1977).
Noonan, Book Review, 9 Sw. U.L. Rev. 1127-37 (1977).
Stephenson, Book Review, 63 Va. L. Rev. 1087-97 (1977).
Yarbrough, Book Review, 8 Rut.-Cam. L.J. 724-30 (1977).

General Periodicals:

Book Review, 37 Best Sellers 81 (June 1977).
Book Review, 73 Booklist 1048 (Mar. 15, 1977).
Book Review, Book World E5 (May 22, 1977).
Book Review, 14 Choice 1277-78 (1977).
Book Review, 104 Commonwealth 537 (Aug. 19, 1977).
Book Review, 13 Kliatt Paperback Book Guide 31 (Spring 1979).
Book Review, 45 Kirkus Reviews 26-27 (Jan. 1, 1977).
Book Review, 211 Publishers Weekly 76 (Jan. 17, 1977).
Book Review, 214 Publishers Weekly 74 (Oct. 9, 1978).
Caplan, Book Review, 60 New Leader 17-19 (Aug. 1, 1977).
Cortner, Book Review, 40 J. Pol. 229-31 (1978).
Dershowitz, Book Review, 82 N.Y. Times, Apr. 10, 1977, at 9.
Howard, Book Review, 82 Am. Hist. Rev. 1352 (1977).
Lieberman, Book Review, Bus. Week, May 16, 1977, at 16-20.
Mayer, Book Review, 4 Saturday Rev. 25-26 (Mar. 5, 1977).
Murphy, Book Review, 64 J. Am. Hist. 1168-69 (1978).
Silver, Book Review, 102 Libr. J. 506 (1977).

J. Frank, *Mr. Justice Black: The Man and His Opinions* (1949).

Legal Periodicals:

Armstrong, Book Review, 20 Tenn. L. Rev. 638-43 (1949).
Bloch, Book Review, 12 Ga. B.J. 43-54 (1949).
Book Note, 47 Mich. L. Rev. 735-36 (1949).

Bradford, Book Review, 2 S.C.L.Q. 198-201 (1949).
Brewster, Book Review, 27 Tex. L. Rev. 573-75 (1949).
Burns, Book Review, 35 A.B.A. J. 213-15 (1949).
Burris, Book Review, 24 N.Y.U. L.Q. Rev. 459-61 (1949).
Coblentz, Book Review, 24 Cal. St. B.J. 42-43 (1949).
Dunham, Book Review, 44 Ill. L. Rev. 263-65 (1949).
Forrester, Book Review, 23 Tul. L. Rev. 429-30 (1949).
Foster, Book Review, 2 Okla. L. Rev. 397-400 (1949).
Grant, Book Review, 37 Calif. L. Rev. 329-31 (1949).
Kunstler, Book Review, 49 Colum. L. Rev. 717-20 (1949).
Kurland, Book Review, 37 Geo. L.J. 653-54 (1949).
Lee, Book Review, 1 Ala. L. Rev. 349-52 (1949).
Miller, Book Review, 5 Loy. L. Rev. 98-99 (1949).
Minton, Book Review, 24 Ind. L.J. 299-303 (1949).
Murphy, Book Review, 27 N.C.L. Rev. 386-92 (1949).
Scanlan, Book Review, 25 Notre Dame Law. 190-92 (1949).
Spring, Book Review, 3 Rutgers L. Rev. 328-32 (1949).
Sullivan, Book Review, 23 Conn. B.J. 63-65 (1949).
Sutherland, Jr., Book Review, 34 Cornell L.Q. 687-90 (1949).
Thurman, Book Review, 1 Stan. L. Rev. 578-81 (1949).
West, Book Review, 2 U. Fla. L. Rev. 310-12 (1949).

General Periodicals:

Book Review, 16 Kirkus Reviews 587 (Nov. 1, 1948).
Book Review, 24 New Yorker 80 (Jan. 15, 1949).
Cousens, Book Review, 55 Am. Hist. Rev. 227 (Oct. 1949).
Engel, Book Review, 168 Nation 131-32 (1949).
Ernst, Book Review, N.Y. Times, Jan. 9, 1949, at 6.
Hausdorfer, Book Review, 74 Libr. J. 55 (1949).
Kunstler, Book Review, 32 Saturday Rev. Literature 27 (Jan. 15, 1949).
Powell, Book Review, 43 Am. Pol. Sci. Rev. 1039-40 (1949).

V. Hamilton, *Hugo Black: The Alabama Years* (1972).

Legal Periodicals:

Book Review, 24 Ala. L. Rev. 563-65 (1972).
Carp, Book Review, 10 Hous. L. Rev. 224-26 (1972).
Dunne, Book Review, 58 A.B.A. J. 1273-74 (1972).
Grossman, Book Review, 39 Brooklyn L. Rev. 255-58 (1972).

Newman, Book Review, 51 Tex. L. Rev. 631-35 (1973).

General Periodicals:

Book Review, 126 America 552 (1972).
Book Review, 32 Best Sellers 61 (May 1, 1972).
Book Review, 9 Choice 874 (Sept. 1972).
Book Review, N.Y. Times, Aug. 20, 1972, VII, at 20.
Brown, Book Review, 34 J. Pol. 1322 (1972).
Clark, Book Review, 68 Am. Pol. Sci. Rev. 1767-68 (1974).
Elliot, Book Review, 35 Negro Hist. Bull. 191 (Dec. 1972).
Johnson, Book Review, 97 Libr. J. 2384 (1972).
McFeely, Book Review, 59 J. Am. Hist. 754-56 (1972).
Newby, Book Review, 79 Am. Hist. Rev. 896 (1974).
Packer, Book Review, 166 New Republic 29-30 (Apr. 1, 1972).

Hugo Black and the Bill of Rights: Proceedings of the First Hugo Black Symposium in American History on "The Bill of Rights and American Democracy," (V. Hamilton ed. 1978).

Legal Periodicals:

Book Note, 45 Brooklyn L. Rev. 228-30 (1978).
Clark, Book Review, 64 A.B.A. J. 1546-48 (1978).

General Periodicals:

Book Review, 15 Choice 948 (Sept. 1978).
Keene, Book Review, 41 J. Pol. 1259 (1979).

Hugo Black and the Supreme Court: A Symposium (S. Strickland ed. 1967).

Legal Periodicals:

Agata, Book Review, 5 Hous. L. Rev. 559-62 (1968).
Ash, Book Review, 1968 Wis. L. Rev. 628-30.
Dawson, Book Review, 5 Hous. L. Rev. 563-64 (1968).
Hollingsworth, Book Review, 56 Ky. L.J. 691-93 (1968).
Howard, Book Review, 53 Va. L. Rev. 1660-66 (1967).
Keeffe, Book Review, 54 A.B.A. J. 293-94 (1968).
Keeffe, Book Review, 19 Case W. Res. L. Rev. 806-11 (1968).
Lee, Book Review, 9 Ariz. L. Rev. 550-54 (1968).
Long, Book Review, 1968 Duke L.J. 182-90.
McNulty, Book Review, 56 Calif. L. Rev. 1178-88 (1968).

Mendelson, Book Review, 1967 U. Ill. L.J. 844-47 (1967).
Schneiderman, Book Review, 33 Sask. L. Rev. 232-37 (1968).
Thomas, Book Review, 22 Sw. L.J. 394-96 (1968).
Vanderzell, Book Review, 13 Vill. L. Rev. 697-700 (1968).

General Periodicals:

Book Review, 5 Choice 264 (Apr. 1968).
Burns, Book Review, 92 Libr. J. 3049 (1967).

Justice Hugo Black and the First Amendment: " 'No Law' Means No Law" (E. Dennis ed. 1978).

General Periodicals:

Book Review, 16 Choice 143 (Mar. 1979).
Book Review, 55 Thought 231 (June 1980).
Brinkman, Book Review, 56 Journalism Q. 408-09 (1979).
Roper, Book Review, 7 History 117 (May 1979).

Justices Black and Frankfurter: Conflict in the Court (W. Mendelson ed. 1961).

Legal Periodicals:

Biddle, Book Review, 75 Harv. L. Rev. 1042-46 (1962).
Christopher, Book Review, 40 N.C.L. Rev. 657-60 (1962).
Dixon, Book Review, 30 Fordham L. Rev. 214-20 (1961).
Gordon, Book Review, 61 Colum. L. Rev. 1537-40 (1961).
Gould, Book Review, 1962 Wash. U.L.Q. 534.
Kalven, Book Review, 11 U. Chi. L.S. Rec. 22 (1963).
Kalven, Book Review, 37 Ind. L.J. 572-79 (1962).
Margolin, Book Review, 72 Yale L.J. 207-16 (1962).
Miller, Book Review, 30 Geo. Wash. L. Rev. 152-55 (1961).
Potter, Book Review, 14 Ala. L. Rev. 487-90 (1962).
Shaffer, Book Review, 37 Notre Dame Law. 743-47 (1962).
Sohn, Book Review, 23 U. Pitt. L. Rev. 248-50 (1961).
Starrs, Book Review, 39 U. Det. L.J. 265-66 (1961).

General Periodicals:

Andrews, Book Review, 86 Libr. J. 1012-13 (1961).
Beth, Book Review, 76 Pol. Sci. Q. 467 (1961).
Hook, Book Review, N.Y. Times, July 23, 1961, at 6.

Tresolini, Book Review, 55 Am. Pol. Sci. 403 (1961).

J. Magee, *Mr. Justice Black: Absolutist on the Court* (1980).

Legal Periodicals:

Collins, Book Review, 9 Pepperdine L. Rev. 287-96 (1981).
Diamond, Book Review, 67 A.B.A. J. 194-98 (1981).
Freeman, Book Review, 11 Cap. U.L. Rev. 175-80 (1981).

D. Meador, *Mr. Justice Black and His Books* (1974).

Legal Periodicals:

Bagwell, Book Review, 27 Ala. L. Rev. 209-10 (1975).
Karst, Book Review, 22 UCLA L. Rev. 1183-86 (1975).
Mersky, Book Review, 60 A.B.A. J. 898-902 (1974).
Newman, Book Review, 53 Tex. L. Rev. 406-14 (1975).
Parrish, Book Review, 20 Am. J. Legal Hist. 72-75 (1976).

General Periodicals:

Mersky, Book Review, 45 Libr. Q. 101-03 (1975).

M. Silverstein, *Constitutional Faiths: Felix Frankfurter, Hugo Black, and the Process of Judicial Decision Making* (1984).

Legal Periodicals:

Book Review, 1985 Y.B. Sup. Ct. Hist. Soc'y 131-32.
Cameron, Book Review, 1985 Pub. L. 169-71.
Clark, Book Review, 30 Am. J. Legal Hist. 191-92 (1986).
Levinson, Book Review, 3 Law & Hist. Rev. 437-40 (1985).
Re, Book Review, 30 N.Y.L. Sch. L. Rev. 217-225 (1985).

General Periodicals:

Dunne, Book Review, 90 Am. Hist. Rev. 511-12 (1985).

C. Williams, *Hugo L. Black: A Study in the Judicial Process* (1950).

Legal Periodicals:

Book Review, 12 Ala. Law. 109-10 (1951).
Cate, Book Review, 4 Vand. L. Rev. 215-17 (1950).
Christopher, Book Review, 3 Stan. L. Rev. 751-55 (1951).
Countryman, Book Review, 60 Yale L.J. 922-25 (1951).

Cumberlege, Book Review, 211 Law Times 138-39 (1951).
Durham, Book Review, 39 Geo. L.J. 515-16 (1951).
Frank, Book Review, 51 Colum. L. Rev. 261-65 (1951).
Harper, Book Review, 11 La. L. Rev. 498-500 (1951).
Lockley, Book Review, 11 Fed. B.J. 263-64 (1951).
Luce, Book Review, 99 U. Pa. L. Rev. 1043-45 (1951).
Ogburn, Book Review, 36 A.B.A. J. 1019-20 (1950).
Schlesinger, Book Review, 12 U. Pitt. L. Rev. 661-65 (1951).
Surrency, Book Review, 25 Temp. L.Q. 112-13 (1951).
Vann, Book Review, 3 Ala. L. Rev. 449-50 (1951).

General Periodicals:

Bernt, Book Review, 75 Libr. J. 2004 (1950).
Book Review, 18 Kirkus Reviews 625 (1950).
Book Review, 171 Nation 622 (1950).
Cahn, Book Review, N.Y. Times, Dec. 17, 1950, at 19.

H. *Dissertations*[6]

D. Berman, *The Political Philosophy of Hugo L. Black* (1957) (available in Rutgers University Library and from University Microfilms).

O. Devor, *Has Hugo Black Changed His Basic Tenets?* (1971) (available in Claremont University Library and from University Microfilms).

J. Gambill, *Hugo Black: The First Amendment and the Mass Media* (1973) (available in Southern Illinois University Library and from University Microfilms).

J. Mayes, *An Analytical Study of the Judicial Philosophy of Hugo Black as it Relates to Free Expression* (1973) (available in Southern Illinois University Library and from University Microfilms).

D. Pruden, *The Opposition of the Press to the Ascension of Hugo Black to the Supreme Court of the United States* (1945) (available in New York University Library and from University Microfilms).

---

6. Research Source: Dialog Database: Dissertation Abstracts Online.

I. Theses[7]

G. Doss, *Hugo L. Black and the Concept of Education* (1972) (available in University of Alabama Library).

R. Haigh, *Mr. Justice Black, Due Process of Law and the Judicial Role* (1971) (available in Fordham University Library).

V. Hamilton, *The Senate Career of Hugo L. Black* (1968) (available in University of Alabama Library).

M. Silverstein, *Liberalism, Democracy and the Court: Felix Frankfurter, Hugo Black and Constitutional Decision-Making* (1982) (available in Cornell University Library).

C. Williams, *Hugo L. Black: A Study in the Judicial Process* (1949) (available in Johns Hopkins University Library).

J. Winters, *Opinion Variation as a Measure of Attitudinal Change in the Supreme Court: A Study of the Opinions of Justice Hugo L. Black from 1957-1968* (1974) (available in University of Kentucky Library).

J. Speeches and Addresses by Justice Black[8]

Address at the Reception of Ramsey Clark, Washington, D.C. (June 12, 1967).

Alabama State Bar Association Address (July 19, 1968) (reference to this speech may be found in *Alabama Law Reporter* (University of Alabama Law School Newsletter), July 30, 1968, at 1).

Alabama State Bar Association Address, Introduction of Warren Burger (July 17, 1970).

Carpentier Lectures, Columbia Law School (March 20, 21 & 23, 1968) (These lectures provided the basis for *A Constitutional Faith.*).

Fifth Circuit Judicial Conference Address (May 13, 1966).

Fifth Circuit Judicial Conference Address (May 9-12, 1967).

Fifth Circuit Judicial Conference Address (May 21, 1969).

---

7. *See* source cited *supra* note 6.

8. Research Sources: For Justice Black's speeches and addresses delivered during the period 1937-1959, *Speeches and Articles by Mr. Justice Hugo L. Black*, 10 Am. U.L. Rev. 116-19 (1961), as well as cross references in books, articles, and theses, was used. For the period 1961-1971, Elizabeth Black's, *Mr. Justice and Mrs. Black: The Memoirs of Hugo L. Black and Elizabeth Black*, as well as cross references in books, articles, and theses, was reviewed.

Fifth Circuit Judicial Conference Address (May 29, 1970).
Fifth Circuit Judicial Conference Address (May 7, 1971).
The James Madison Lecture: "The Bill of Rights," New York University Law School (Feb. 17, 1960), 35 N.Y.U. L. Rev. 865-81 (1960).
Memorial Address For Meiklejohn, St. Johns College, Annapolis, Md. (Jan. 26, 1965).
The Miami Bar Association Address (Feb. 19, 1968).
"The Part Southerners Played in Writing the Constitution and the Bill of Rights," Birmingham, Ala. (May 3, 1968).
Speeches and Articles by Mr. Justice Hugo L. Black, 10 Am. U.L. Rev. 116-19 (1961).
Tuscaloosa Speech (July 19, 1968).
University of Georgia Commencement Address at the Dedication of the New Building, Athens, Ga. (Nov. 18, 1967).
World Peace Through Law Conference Speech (July 11, 1967).

K. *Manuscripts*[9]

U.S. Libr. of Congress, Manuscript Division, *The Justice Hugo L. Black Papers* (Wash. 1972).
A. Wigdor, *The Personal Papers of Supreme Court Justices, A Descriptive Guide*, 47 (Garland).

IV. Supreme Court Opinions[10]

A. *Majority Opinions*

Arkansas Fuel Oil Co. v. Louisiana ex rel. Muslow, 304 U.S. 197 (1938). The Court was not required to determine the constitution-

---

9. Research Sources: In 1972, the Black family gave a 117,000 item collection of Justice Black's papers to the Library of Congress. These papers covered every aspect of Justice Black's public career.

10. Research Sources: Both Lexis and Westlaw were researched to identify opinions written by Justice Black. The computer-generated lists of citations were compared with published lists contained in Patricia Evans' *Supreme Court of the United States 1780-1980: An Index to Opinions Arranged by Justice* and in Elizabeth Black's *Mr. Justice and Mrs. Black: The Memoirs of Hugo L. Black and Elizabeth Black*. Although the vast majority of opinions appeared on all four lists, a few did not. After all references were examined and those opinions clearly categorized on their face were arranged, the remaining opinions were arranged by using phraseology from the body of the opinion itself as a guide. Where the face of an opinion indicated that Justice Black "joined" another justice, that wording was taken to mean the opinion was not in Black's own words, and the opinion was not included. How-

ality of a Louisiana statute where enforcement of the statute would not deprive appellant of any constitutional rights. The statute provided that a purchaser of oil, such as appellant, could extinguish his indebtedness for the oil by paying one, such as appellee, who sold it under a lease from the last record owner where the owner held pursuant to a recorded instrument sufficient to pass title in Louisiana and no notice of a title dispute had been given. Since the owner here had such title and there was no indication that it was or would be disputed, appellant could pay appellee without fear of subsequently having to pay someone else. Enforcement of the statute thus did not threaten appellant with an unconstitutional taking of its property.

Bates Manufacturing Co. v. United States, 303 U.S. 567 (1938). As a result of the Tucker Act, 24 Stat. 505-06, which recognized that substantial rights of claimants are to be governed alike whether suit is brought in district court or the Court of Claims, the statute of limitations applicable under the Revenue Act of 1926 applies alike to suits in either court.

Brotherhood of Locomotive Engineers v. Chicago, Rock Island & Pacific Railroad, 382 U.S. 423 (1966). State statutes requiring that train crews be comprised of certain personnel not preempted by a federal statute relating to binding arbitration with respect to disputes over firemen and full-crew questions on railroads or awards made thereunder.

Brotherhood of Locomotive Firemen & Enginemen v. Chicago, Rock Island & Pacific Railroad, 393 U.S. 129 (1968). The Arkansas "full-crew" laws, title 73, sections 720 and 726 to 729 of the Arkansas Code, which required that a minimum number of employees be designated to serve as part of a train crew under certain circumstances, did not violate the Equal Protection Clause by

---

ever, those opinions that identify Justice Black "jointly" with another justice have been included.

A category called "Statements Concurring and Dissenting in Part" contains those cases in which Justice Black felt it necessary to differentiate his position from that of either the majority or minority by making a brief comment, often referring to his own reasoning in an earlier decision to support his position. Statements issued "jointly" are not considered Black's own words and have been excluded.

discriminating against the railroad industry and did not violate the Due Process Clause by being unduly oppressive.

Brotherhood of Railroad Trainmen v. Virginia ex rel. Virginia State Bar, 377 U.S. 1 (1964). An injunction by a Virginia state court, which prevented the Brotherhood of Railroad Trainmen from advising injured members to seek legal advice and recommending specific attorneys, violated the Brotherhood's First and Fourteenth Amendment rights of freedom of speech, petition, and assembly.

Chippewa Indians v. United States, 305 U.S. 479 (1939). The appropriate date for valuation of timber appraised under the Act of May 23, 1908, is the date of the Act when the taking of the property occurred. The Act converted certain Chippewa woodlands into a national forest as of that date, depriving the Chippewa of their beneficial interest therein and effecting a taking for which compenstion was required. The Chippewas' other claim against the government, for alleged wrongful appropriation of other lands, could not be resolved in the Court of Claims. That court's jurisdiction over Chippewa claims pursuant to the Act of January 14, 1889, did not encompass land not on Chippewa reservations as of that date.

City of New York v. New York, New Haven & Hartford Railroad, 344 U.S. 293 (1953). In a bankruptcy reorganization of a railroad under the Bankruptcy Act, section 77, ch. 204, 47 Stat. 1474, as amended ch. 77, 44 Stat. 911, a city was not given "reasonable notice" when it was served notice of the order to file by publication rather than by service of process. Knowledge by the city that the reorganization was taking place in the court also did not constitute "reasonable notice."

Confederated Bands of Ute Indians v. United States, 330 U.S. 169 (1947). Land given to the Ute Indians by executive order of November 22, 1875, did not convey title to the land, but only preserved use of the land. Even though a treaty is to be construed as carrying out the obligations in the fair understanding of the Indians, Presidential authority may not be created.

County of Mahnomen v. United States, 319 U.S. 474 (1943). Land held in trust for Indians was exempt from state taxation until the enactment of the Clap Amendments of 1906 and 1907, but this taxation could be challenged by demonstrating that the Indians did not consent to it.

Detroit & Toledo Shore Line Railroad v. United Transportation Union, 396 U.S. 142 (1969). In a dispute and a threatened strike between the railroad and the union concerning the railroad's change in "outlying work assignments," the railroad must make reasonable efforts to settle the dispute and could not, under the Railway Labor Act, affect the assignments and change the status quo while mediation proceedings were in process.

Estate of Spiegel v. Commissioner, 335 U.S. 701 (1949). Where trustor made no provision for distribution of corpus or accumulated income of a trust and trustor outlived all beneficiaries, the corpus reverted back to the trustor under Illinois law and became part of the taxable estate.

Federal Trade Commission v. Raladam Co., 316 U.S. 149 (1942). Where findings and proof were insufficient to enforce a cease and desist order of the Federal Trade Commission, reasons for the insufficiency were not controlling in later proceedings where such findings and proof were found to be a sufficient basis for the order.

Federal Trade Commission v. Standard Education Society, 302 U.S. 112 (1937). Findings of unfair trade practices by the Federal Trade Commission are conclusive if supported by evidence.

Foster v. United States, 303 U.S. 118 (1938). Because of the clear congressional intent to tax post-1913 corporate earnings, the courts must not allow the use of bookkeeping terms and accounting practices to devitalize valid tax laws.

Harris v. Avery Brundage Co., 305 U.S. 160 (1938). Parties having only a procedural right to require issues to be tried in a plenary suit may waive that right by consenting to summary trial in bankruptcy. In the absence of a substantial adverse claim, the bankruptcy court acquires jurisdiction both to determine controversies relating to an escrow fund and to compel surrender of the fund.

Helvering v. Winmill, 305 U.S. 79 (1938). Since Treasury regulations and interpretations applicable to unamended or substantially reenacted statutes are deemed to have received congressional approval and have the effect of law, the addition of section 23(r) of the Revenue Act of 1932 did not change the existing interpretation that brokers' commissions should be treated as a part of the cost of the securities purchased rather than as a current business expense.

Hines v. Lowrey, 305 U.S. 85 (1938). Section 500 of the World War Veterans Act, as amended, ch. 320, 43 Stat. 628 (1924), which limits the fee of any attorney or agent to ten dollars for services performed in prosecuting veterans' war risk insurance claims, is a valid exercise of congressional power.

Illinois ex rel. McCollum v. Board of Education, 333 U.S. 203 (1948). A local Illinois board of education agreement providing "release time" to students for elective attendance at religious instruction classes taught by outside instructors within the school building violated the First and Fourteenth Amendments as an invalid use of public school premises.

Inter-Island Steam Navigation Co. v. Hawaii, 305 U.S. 306 (1938). Because an act of Congress will not be deemed to supersede a territorial law unless the intention that it do so is clear, the imposition of a tax upon a common carrier under the Hawaii Utilities Act of 1913 violated neither the Fifth Amendment nor the Commerce Clause of the Federal Constitution.

Johnson v. Zerbst, 304 U.S. 458 (1938). In habeas corpus proceedings a prisoner may raise the issue of whether the assistance of counsel at trial was intelligently and competently waived, but the prisoner bears the burden of proof.

Laurens Federal Savings & Loan Association v. South Carolina Tax Commission, 365 U.S. 517 (1961). The state tax on documentary notes executed by a federal savings and loan association located within the state violated section 13 of the Federal Home Loan Bank Act of 1932, 12 U.S.C.]] 1433, which exempted the bank from state taxation. Also, section 13 was neither implicitly nor expressly repealed by section 5 of the Home Owners' Loan Act of 1933, 12 U.S.C. § 1464(h), which prohibited states from imposing discriminatory taxes on federal savings and loan associations.

Levers v. Anderson, 326 U.S. 219 (1945). Where district supervisor of the Alcohol Tax Unit of the Bureau of Internal Revenue annulled a permit to operate a wholesale liquor business under the Federal Alcohol Administration Act, 27 U.S.C. §§ 201-212, and the act authorized the applicant to appeal to the Circuit Court of Appeals, it was not necessary to exhaust all other permissible regulatory remedies before seeking judicial review.

Leyra v. Denno, 347 U.S. 556 (1954). The coerced nature of the defendant's first confession was part of a continuous process and so close to subsequent confessions as to control the character of the others and make them all inconsistent with the Due Process Clause of the Constitution.

Libby, McNeill & Libby v. United States, 340 U.S. 71 (1950). The United States was not liable under war risk insurance for damages sustained by a vessel due to the inexperience of the helmsman, even though the vessel was involved in warlike operations.

Lincoln Federal Labor Union v. Northwestern Iron & Metal Co., 335 U.S. 525 (1949). A North Carolina statute and Nebraska constitutional amendment prohibiting laws for or against unions were found not to violate the constitutional rights of freedom of speech, assembly, and petition guaranteed by the First and Fourteenth Amendments to the Constitution, but were found to fall within the power of the states to legislate against injurious practices in their internal commercial and busi-ness affairs so long as the laws did not run afoul of either a specific federal constitutional prohibition or a valid federal law.

Lloyd A. Fry Roofing Co. v. Wood, 344 U.S. 157 (1952). An action by the Arkansas Public Service Commission requiring owners of leased trucks to obtain a permit for transporting products was not unduly burdensome on interstate commerce absent attachment of burdensome conditions to the grant of such permits.

Lober v. United States, 346 U.S. 335 (1953). Trust property was properly included in settlor's gross estate for estate tax purposes because settlor could accumulate and reinvest the income until his children reached twenty-one and could hold the principal until the beneficiary reached twenty-five or until any time settlor saw fit.

Louisiana v. United States, 380 U.S. 145 (1965). A Louisiana interpretation test requiring voter registrants to read and to interpret any section of the federal or state constitution was discriminatorily applied by registrars who, in using their power to prevent Negroes from voting, violated the Fourteenth and Fifteenth Amendments to the United States Constitution and 42 U.S.C. § 1971(a).

Lusthaus v. Commissioner, 327 U.S. 293 (1946). All profits from a husband-wife partnership were taxable to the owner-husband, who retained full control of the management of the business. Wife was not a genuine partner, since she paid for her undivided half interest in the business by a check drawn on funds that husband had donated to wife and by notes that were to be paid from profits to be ascribed to the wife under a partnership agreement.

Lyon v. Mutual Benefit Health & Accident Association, 305 U.S. 484 (1939). Consistent with the requirements of the Conformity Act, the district court did not deprive the defendant of any constitutional right when it followed an Arkansas procedural rule governing the effect of a request for a peremptory instruction.

Macauley v. Waterman Steamship Corp., 327 U.S. 540 (1946). When Congress has delegated to an administrative agency the power to determine the scope of an act, all available administrative remedies provided for in the act must first be exhausted before resort is made to the courts.

McConnell, In re, 370 U.S. 230 (1962). Counsel's stated intention to prove economic injury over a directly contrary instruction by the judge was not of such a nature as to support holding counsel in contempt under 18 U.S.C. § 401, which requires that there be misbehavior to the extent of actually obstructing the judge in the performance of his judicial duty.

McCrone v. United States, 307 U.S. 61 (1939). Contempt of court is considered civil when the punishment is wholly remedial, serves only the purposes of the complainant, and is not intended to deter offenses against the public.

McCullough v. Kammerer Corp., 331 U.S. 96 (1947). A holding of patent infringement is considered "final" for purposes of appeal under the 1927 amendment to section 129 of the Judicial Code, even though the ordered accounting has not been made.

McGee v. International Life Insurance Co., 355 U.S. 220 (1957). A California statute extending jurisdiction over a corporation to its principal place of business in Texas did not violate due process, since the suit was based on a contract which had a substantial connection with California.

MacGregor v. Westinghouse Electric & Manufacturing Co., 329 U.S. 402 (1947). In a license agreement in which a covenant to pay royalties is not severable from the covenant to sell at fixed prices, the entire license agreement is invalid; thus, the licensee under the invalid agreement may attack the validity of the patent despite a covenant not to do so.

McNair v. Knott, 302 U.S. 369 (1937). Congress' creation, through the National Bank Enabling Amendment of June 15, 1930, of a mechanism for validating existing ultra vires pledges was a valid exercise of congressional power.

Madruga v. Superior Court of California, 346 U.S. 556 (1954). The savings clause of the 1948 revision of the Judicial Code, 23 U.S.C. § 1333, established federal admiralty court jurisdiction as concurrent with that of state courts in in personam proceedings, but federal courts have exclusive jurisdiction of in rem proceedings.

Mandel Brothers Inc. v. Wallace, 335 U.S. 291 (1948). A patent is invalid as lacking in invention when it merely adds a cosmetic use to publicly available knowledge.

Marine Cooks & Stewards, AFL v. Panama Steamship Co., 362 U.S. 365 (1960). Since the intent of the Norris-LaGuardia Act, 29 U.S.C. §§ 101-115, was to remove the power to grant injunctions in labor disputes from the jurisdiction of federal courts, an enlargement of jurisdiction would not be justified on grounds that the action to be enjoined amounted to an unlawful interference with foreign commerce because it interfered with the internal economy of a vessel registered under the flag of a friendly foreign power.

Marsh v. Alabama, 326 U.S. 501 (1946). A company town that was allowed to replicate functions and activities normally belonging to a city was subject to the limitations of the First and Fourteenth

Amendments and could not prevent an individual from distributing religious literature on company property, under the Alabama criminal trespass statute, Ala. Code tit. 14, § 426.

Marsh v. Buck, 313 U.S. 406 (1941). Where a state law contains a severability clause declaring that the unconstitutionality of a part of the law shall not affect the remaining sections thereof, federal courts will follow state law and will not enjoin enforcement of the statute absent a showing of exceptional circumstances, specific threats, or irreparable injury.

Martin v. City of Struthers, 319 U.S. 141 (1943). An ordinance prohibiting distributors of religious literature from delivering door to door handbills violated the First and Fourteenth Amendments to the Constitution by extending prohibitions further than was necessary for the protection of the community and by preventing the free flow of information.

Maryland & Virginia Milk Producers Association v. United States, 362 U.S. 458 (1960). The Association violated the Clayton Antitrust, Sherman Antitrust, and Capper-Volstead Acts by monopolizing interstate trade and commerce and conspiring to eliminate competition by buying all the assets of a competitor. The Association was not immune from the provisions of the Sherman Antitrust Act because it acted alone.

Mathis v. United States, 391 U.S. 1 (1968). Miranda warnings about self-incrimination and right to counsel are applicable to non-criminal tax investigations because such investigations may eventually lead to the instigation of criminal proceedings. That the subject of the investigation is incarcerated on unrelated charges at the time of the investigation is of no consequence.

Maty v. Grasselli Chemical Co., 303 U.S. 197 (1938). Since the importance of proper pleading is primarily its effectiveness as a means of reaching a just judgment, an amendment of a cause under New Jersey law that substantially alleged the same wrong as the original complaint after the period of limitations had run did not state a new cause of action barred by limitations.

Michael, In re, 326 U.S. 224 (1945). A false statement under oath may be grounds for a charge of perjury but is not a cause for a charge of contempt absent the additional element of obstruction of the court in the performance of its duty.

Milcor Steel Co. v. George A. Fuller Co., 316 U.S. 143 (1942). A disclaimer filed under Rev. 3d statute § 4917 (1946), may only narrow the scope of the patent and may not add a new element that was not recited in the original.

Milk Wagon Drivers' Union, Local 753 v. Lake Valley Farm Products, Inc., 311 U.S. 91 (1940). The plain mandate of the Norris-LaGuardia Act, 29 U.S.C.. §§ 101-115, is that federal courts do not have jurisdiction in areas of labor disputes, and as a result, allegations of violations of the Sherman Antitrust Act, 15 U.S.C. §§ 1-7, may not support bringing the action into federal court.

Millinery Creators' Guild, Inc. v. Federal Trade Commission, 312 U.S. 469 (1941). A plan by the Guild to combat "style piracy" by inducing retailers not to purchase from other manufacturers hats that were piracies of designs registered with the association was found to be a restraint of trade, a hindrance to competition, and a monopoly. Thus, the Guild was properly ordered to cease and desist.

Mills v. Alabama, 384 U.S. 214 (1966). A state statute providing criminal penalties for individuals who publish political comments on the day of an election urging people to vote a certain way was held unconstitu-tional as violating the First and Fourteenth Amendments.

Mine Safety Appliances Co. v. Forrestal, 326 U.S. 371 (1945). The proper avenue for an aggrieved contractor to seek redress is a trial de novo in the Tax Court as provided under the Renegotiation of War Contracts Act. Lack of consent by the government as a necessary party is required to support bringing an action in any other court.

Moore v. Illinois Central Railroad, 312 U.S. 630 (1941). Federal courts are bound to apply the latest interpretation of a state statute rendered by the state's highest court where such an interpretation exists. They can only depart from the interpretation when it is reconsidered by the state's highest court or the statute is amended by the state legislature. Thus, the Court of Appeals for the Fifth Circuit was bound by the Mississippi Supreme Court's determination that petitioner's suit was not time-barred, and it erred in departing from that determination. Respondent's other claim that petitioner's suit was barred because he had not exhausted his administrative remedies under the Railway Labor Act, 45 U.S.C. §§ 151-164, 181-188, was without merit because the Act makes no such requirement.

Murchison, In re, 349 U.S. 133 (1955). The trial of a defendant for contempt by a judge who had acted as "judge-grand jury" in the proceedings that prompted the contempt charge was a violation of the Due Process Clause of the Constitution.

Nash v. Florida Industrial Commission, 389 U.S. 235 (1967). The application of the Florida Unemployment Compensation Law by the Florida Industrial Commission to withhold unemployment compensation from a person who filed a dispute with the National Labor Relations Board violated the Supremacy Clause of the Constitution by imposing a financial burden on the former employee and frust-rating enforcement of the National Labor Relations Act.

National Labor Relations Board v. Falk Corporation, 308 U.S. 453 (1940). The National Labor Relations Act vests power in the National Labor Relations Board to determine the method to be used for electing a bargaining unit. The courts have no power of review or modification until an order predicated upon the result of an election is issued by the Board.

National Labor Relations Board v. Waterman Steamship Corp., 309 U.S. 206 (1940). The findings of the National Labor Relations Board shall be conclusive under 29 U.S.C. § 151, and the courts may not interfere in the Board's exclusive jurisdiction where its conclusions are supported by evidence.

National Lead Co. v. Commissioner, 352 U.S. 313 (1957). The War Production Board has the power, under I.R.C. § 124, to certify for amortization only part of a private manufacturer's expansion as "necessary in the national defense."

National Metropolitan Bank v. United States, 323 U.S. 454 (1945). In the absence of congressional action, federal courts determine the rules governing commercial paper issued by the federal government. Thus, the government may recover payment for checks drawn by a bank against the government, even though the checks were fraudulently drawn and endorsed by a government employee prior to payment and even though the government should have discovered the fraud.

New Hampshire Fire Insurance Co. v. Scanlon, 362 U.S. 404 (1960). A surety for a contractor had a right to federal judicial determination of its claim to the government's payment to the contractor in a plenary proceeding, since the surety had been required to complete the contract under a performance bond.

New York ex rel. Ray v. Martin, 326 U.S. 496 (1946). A New York state court could exercise its jurisdiction to prosecute a non-Indian for the murder of another non-Indian, notwithstanding the facts that the offense was committed on the Allegany Indian Reservation within the borders of the state, that 18 U.S.C. §§ 451 and 452 give the United States exclusive jurisdiction over crimes committed within the United States, and that 25 U.S.C. § 217 extends the jurisdiction to "Indian country."

North Carolina v. United States, 325 U.S. 507 (1945). A lower intrastate commerce passenger rail rate does not necessarily mean that the lower rate is discriminatory and prohibited by section 13(4) of the Interstate Commerce Act, 49 U.S.C, § 11501(e)(1)(B), and the Interstate Commerce Commission has power to raise those rates only if necessary to prevent injury to interstate commerce and to insure that the intrastate commerce is producing earnings adequate to satisfy maintenance and operating costs.

Northern Pacific Railway v. United States, 356 U.S. 1 (1958). "Preferential routing" clauses in leases or grants of land owned by the railroad, which required that products obtained by use of that land must be shipped on the owner railway lines, violated the Sherman Antitrust Act, 15 U.S.C. §§ 1 and 4, as amended, as an unreasonable restraint of trade.

Oklahoma Tax Commission v. United States, 319 U.S. 598 (1943). The Oklahoma inheritance tax is applicable to members of the Five Civilized Tribes, and all personal and real property is subject to that tax except land that has been exempted by Congress from direct state taxation.

Oliver, In re, 333 U.S. 257 (1948). A contempt charge and sentence of sixty days in jail imposed by a one-man grand jury in a secret proceeding is violative of due process guaranteed by the Fourteenth Amendment.

Order of Railroad Telegraphers v. Chicago & North Western Railway, 362 U.S. 330 (1960). District court could not enjoin railway workers from striking in protest of the railway company's failure to negotiate possible loss of jobs involved in the consolidation and abolition of rail stations. Since this case involved a "labor dispute" within the meaning of the Norris-LaGuardia Act, 29 U.S.C. § 104, and the Railway Labor Act, 45 U.S.C. § 152, the matter was required to be heard by the National Railroad Adjustment Board.

Order of Railway Conductors v. Pitney, 326 U.S. 561 (1946). The order by the district court during bankruptcy proceedings requiring replacement of "road conductors" with "yard conductors" was proper as long as it was construed as binding on the trustee but not binding on bargaining agents in later reaching agreements through the National Railroad Adjustment Board pursuant to the Railway Labor Act, 45 U.S.C. §§ 151-164, 181-188.

Order of Railway Conductors v. Southern Railway, 339 U.S. 255 (1950). A state court does not have the power to interpret or to adjudicate disputes involving a collective bargaining agreement drawn by the National Railroad Adjustment Board under the Railway Labor Act, 45 U.S.C. §§ 151-164, 181-188.

Orozco v. Texas, 394 U.S. 324 (1969). Use of admissions made by defendant in response to police questioning in his bedroom violated the defendant's Fifth Amendment rights, since he was under arrest and had not been informed of his rights under *Miranda v. Arizona*, 384 U.S. 436 (1966), at the time of the admission.

Palmer v. Ashe, 342 U.S. 134 (1951). Prior to dismissing a habeas corpus proceeding, the state court should have examined the petition, answer, and trial record to determine whether the defendant was entitled to offer evidence to prove, after almost eighteen years of serving two five-to-fifteen year sentences for armed robbery and attempt, that he believed that the charge was breaking and entering, that he had not been represented by counsel, and that he had not been told of his right to counsel.

Palmer v. Thompson, 403 U.S. 217 (1971). Closing public swimming pools rather than operating them under a desegregation order did not violate Negroes' rights to equal protection under the Constitution, since the city was under no affirmative duty to operate them, even though one of the pools subsequently was used as a private club open only to whites and another pool was owned and operated by a predominantly black state college.

Parker v. Fleming, 329 U.S. 531 (1947). Tenants evicted by their landlords after the Price Administrator had ordered issuance of eviction certificates were "subject" to the order under the Emergency Price Control Act of 1942, 50 U.S.C. Appendix § 923(a), and were entitled to judicial review of the Administrator's dismissal of their protest.

Parker v. Motor Boat Sales, Inc., 314 U.S. 244 (1941). The finding by the Deputy Commissioner under the Longshoremen's and Harbor Workers' Compensation Act, 33 U.S.C. § 919, that an employee hired as a janitor was acting within the scope of his employment when riding in a motorboat as a "lookout" with the acquiesence of his supervisor should have been accepted by the United States Circuit Court of Appeals.

Paterno v. Lyons, 334 U.S. 314 (1948). Conviction of the defendant for attempted grand larceny in the second degree after a guilty plea under an indictment for receiving stolen goods did not violate the defendant's due process rights under the Constitution.

Patterson v. Lamb, 329 U.S. 539 (1947). Issuance of a certificate of "discharge from a Draft" rather than an "honorable discharge" was proper when petitioner had been inducted but had not been fully processed before the selective service draft was cancelled, and the type of certificate to be issued was solely in the discretion of the War Department.

Patton v. Mississippi, 332 U.S. 463 (1947). The indictment and subsequent conviction of a Negro by all-white grand and petit juries violated the Equal Protection Clause of the Constitution where there had been a systematic, purposeful administrative exclusion of Negroes from jury duty.

Pearlman v. Reliance Insurance Co., 371 U.S. 132 (1962). A surety's right to subrogation (to be paid from a reimbursement fund withheld by the government under the terms of a government contract but turned over to the trustee in bankruptcy) is above the rights of general creditors.

Pennsylvania ex rel. Herman v. Claudy, 350 U.S. 116 (1956). Denial of a hearing of a habeas corpus petition of the defendant concerning his conviction eight years before violated the Due Process Clause of the Constitution, since defendant's petition made serious charges about matters not in the trial record, *i.e.*, that he had been coerced into confessing and that he had not had benefit of counsel.

Pennsylvania Railroad v. United States, 363 U.S. 202 (1960). In an action by the Pennsylvania Railroad in the Court of Claims to recover money from the government, the court suspended proceedings to have the Interstate Commerce Commission pass on the reasonableness of rates, and the court was required to suspend its proceedings further so that the Commission's order could be judicially reviewed by the district court.

Pennsylvania Water & Power Co. v. Federal Power Commission, 343 U.S. 414 (1952). The Pennsylvania Water and Power Company was subject to regulation under part two of the Federal Power Act, 16 U.S.C. §§ 791a-828c, even though the company was a licensee under part one of the Act. Consequently, the Federal Power Commission's rate reduction orders were proper, even though they constituted, in effect, private contractual agreements that would be disallowed under anti-trust laws or under Pennsylvania law.

Perez v. Ledesma, 401 U.S. 82 (1971). An order by a three-judge court to suppress evidence and to direct the return of illegally seized evidence, when the court had proper jurisdiction to rule on only the constitutionality of an ordinance, was an improper interference with a pending state criminal proceeding.

Perkins v. Lukens Steel Co., 310 U.S. 113 (1940). Bidders on public contracts have no standing to restrain the Secretary of Labor from enforcing the Secretary's determination of minimum wage in the locality in which the goods are manufactured, and the courts have no power to interfere with the performance of ordinary duties of an executive department.

Perkins v. Standard Oil Co., 395 U.S. 642 (1969). In an action by plaintiff against Standard Oil under the Clayton Antitrust Act, 15

U.S.C. §§ 12-27, 29 U.S.C. §§ 52-53, as amended by the Robinson-Patman Act, 15 U.S.C. §§ 13(a)-(b) & 21, for price discrimination, alleging that plaintiff was charged more for gasoline than his competitor, all losses could be considered in awarding a verdict to plaintiff, not only those losses proximately caused by the discrimination.

Perma Life Mufflers, Inc. v. International Parts Corp., 392 U.S. 134 (1968). In private antitrust litigation by a subsidiary against the parent corporation under the Sherman Antitrust Act, 15 U.S.C. §§ 1-7, and the Clayton Antitrust Act, 15 U.S.C. § 12-27, 29 U.S.C. §§ 52-53, as amended by the Robinson-Patman Act, 15 U.S.C. §§ 13(a)-(b) & 21, it is not a defense that the subsidiary was equally at fault in the violations.

Phyle v. Duffy, 334 U.S. 431 (1948). Defendant adjudged insane by judicial proceedings but then declared to be sane by the Superindendent of the State Hospital for the Insane, was not denied due process of law and could not obtain relief by petition of habeas corpus to the United States Supreme Court, since the defendant had not sought the proper remedy of mandamus to compel the warden to seek a judicial determination of sanity.

Pierre v. Louisiana, 306 U.S. 354 (1939). A conviction of a Negro for the murder of a white man upon an indictment by a grand jury composed of a venire from which Negroes had been intentionally and systematically excluded was void as a violation of the equal protection guaranteed by the Fourteenth Amendment. Affirmance by the Louisiana Supreme Court of the trial court's denial of a motion to quash the indictment was improper.

Plumbers Union, Local 298 v. County of Door, 359 U.S. 354 (1959). Labor disputes ordinarily proper for disposition by the National Labor Relations Board under the National Labor Relations Act, 15 U.S.C. §§ 151-169, are not exempt from the Board's jurisdiction merely because one of the parties is a county. Although political subdivisions are specifically excluded from the Act's definition of "employer" and are thereby not subject to many of its provisions, they are considered "persons" thereunder, and their disputes, when otherwise appropriate, must go to the Board.

Pointer v. Texas, 380 U.S. 400 (1965). The use at trial of the transcript of testimony given at a preliminary hearing where defendant had no counsel, was not informed of his right to counsel, and did not cross-examine the witness, was a denial of the defendant's right to confront the witnesses against him as guaranteed in the Sixth Amendment, made applicable to the states through the Fourteenth Amendment.

Pope & Talbot, Inc. v. Hawn, 346 U.S. 406 (1953). A carpenter, injured while working on a vessel in navigable waters inside the state of Pennsylvania, was entitled to have his claim determined by the admiralty rule of comparative negligence rather than the Pennsylvania rule of contributory negligence.

Porter v. Dicken, 328 U.S. 252 (1946). The provision in the Emergency Price Control Act of 1942, ch. 26, 56 Stat. 23, allowing the Administrator to seek injunctions "in the appropriate court," does not violate 28 U.S.C. § 379, prohibiting a federal court from staying state court proceedings, but it is an "implied amendment" to that statute.

Porter v. Lee, 328 U.S. 246 (1946). In a proceeding to prevent eviction of tenant, the state court had jurisdiction under state law to enjoin an act that violated the Emergency Price Control Act of 1942, ch. 26, 56 Stat. 23, but this jurisdiction was not concurrent jurisdiction with noncriminal enforcement proceedings contemplated by the Act.

Preston v. United States, 376 U.S. 364 (1964). In a prosecution for conspiracy to rob a federally insured bank, evidence obtained from the car of the defendants after their arrest for vagrancy and after the car had been towed was inadmissible because it was too remote in time and place to be incidental to arrest and reasonable under the Fourth Amendment.

Public Service Commission v. Brashear Freight Lines, Inc., 312 U.S. 621 (1941). In an action to enjoin officials from enforcing an allegedly unconstitutional Missouri Bus and Truck Law, a three-judge federal district court enjoined state officials where the officials had counterclaimed for assessment of damages, and the later dismissal by the district court of the injunction and counterclaim without prejudice was improper without an assessment of damages.

Purcell v. United States, 315 U.S. 381 (1942). The Interstate Commerce Commission may abandon a railway and not relocate it where the lines are included within the limits of a government flood control reservoir. The interests of those served by the system and the costs of relocation may be balanced, even though the costs would be paid by the goverment and not a private carrier.

Query v. United States, 316 U.S. 486 (1942). Action to enjoin enforcement of state tax on goods sold at an Army post exchange was properly brought before a three-judge federal district court and appeal then is to the Supreme Court. However, where appeal was taken to the U.S. Circuit Court in error and time for proper appeal had lapsed, a fresh decree by the district court was required before appeal to the Supreme Court could be taken.

Radio Corp. of America v. United States, 341 U.S. 412 (1951). The Federal Communications Commission order promulgating standards for color transmission, which allowed the Columbia Broadcasting Systems method to the exclusion of other methods, was within the power of the Commission under the Communications Act, ch. 652, 48 Stat. 1064, and it was based on substantial evidence. Courts should not overrule an administrative decision merely because they disagree with its wisdom.

Brotherhood of Railroad Trainmen v. Virginia ex rel. Virginia State Bar, 377 U.S. 1 (1964). An injunction issued by a Virginia state court preventing the Brotherhood of Railroad Trainmen from advising injured members to seek legal advice and recommending specific attorneys violated the Brotherhood's First and Fourteenth Amendment rights of freedom of speech, petition, and assembly.

Railroad Transfer Service v. Chicago, 386 U.S. 351 (1967). Petitioner's challenge to a Chicago ordinance regulating several aspects of the conduct of its business was not brought prematurely. Petitioner's payment of license fees into court and its operation under the city's reluctant sufferance did not make the action premature, since the controversy between the litigants had been alive for more than a decade and the city had continued to extend its regulation of petitioner's business while this suit was pending. Upon consideration of the merits, the Court declared the ordinance, which imposed stringent regulations on carriers transporting passengers between Chicago's two rail terminals, to be preempted by the Interstate Commerce Act.

Rainwater v. United States, 356 U.S. 590 (1958). The Commodity Credit Corporation was established to carry out the federal farm program and thus is a part of the government of the United States for purposes of the False Claims Act of 1878, ch. 67, 12 Stat. 698. It is true that the criminal provisions of the Act also provide the test of civil liability under the Act, that Congress explicitly amended only the criminal provisions in 1918 to prohibit false claims against corporations in which the United States is a shareholder, and that incorporations of one section of an act into another by reference normally do not include subsequent amendments to the incorporated section. That does not mean, however, that no civil liability attaches for false claims against such corporations, since such liability has always existed.

Rayonier Inc. v. United States, 352 U.S. 315 (1957). Liability of the United States Forest Service for allowing a fire to be started on government land and failing to excercise due care in extinguishing it may exist under the Federal Tort Claims Act, ch. 646, 62 Stat. 929 (1948) (codified as amended in scattered sections of 28 U.S.C.), if the applicable state law would impose liability upon private persons or corporations under similar circumstances.

Reconstruction Finance Corp. v. Beaver County, 328 U.S. 204 (1946). Notwithstanding section 10 of the Reconstruction Finance Corporation Act, ch. 8, 47 Stat. 5, 9, ch. 290, 55 Stat. 248, which prohibited taxation by state or local laws of the personal property of the Corporation, Pennsylvania properly taxed machinery that was heavy and was attached by nuts and screws, even though the Corporation had specified by contract with the lessee of the property that the machinery would remain personalty.

Reed v. The Yaka, 373 U.S. 410 (1963). Where a vessel was under "bareboat charter" arrangement, and there was no underlying personal liability for the unseaworthiness of the vessel, an injured worker could rely upon the liability of the charterer as shipowner to bring an action in rem against the vessel. Section 5 of the Longshoremen's and Harbor Workers' Compensation Act, 33 U.S.C. §§

901-950, which provides that only compensatory damages may be received from an employee, must be liberally construed to avoid harsh results for longshoremen.

Reilly v. Pinkus, 338 U.S. 269 (1949). The Postmaster's order enjoining defendant's use of the mails to advertise his weight reduction plan was improper. Although sufficient evidence was adduced at the hearing to support the Postmaster's finding that defendant's advertisements were fraudulent, defendant was improperly barred from using certain authoritative medical books in his cross-examination of the prosecution's medical witnesses. The conduct of an administrative hearing is left largely to the discretion of the agency, but where a defendant faces charges as serious as fraud, he must be given a reasonable opportunity to cross-examine witnesses on the vital issue of his intent to deceive. The presiding officer's subsequent examination of the books and his conclusion that defendant could not have believed on the basis of information in the books that his plan would work as well as his advertisements claimed was no substitute for their use in cross-examination.

Reynolds v. Cochran, 365 U.S. 525 (1961). Habeas corpus petition should not have been denied by the Florida Supreme Court, since defendant was entitled to a hearing on his claim of denial of due process where the trial judge had refused a continuance of proceedings until defendant's counsel arrived.

Rice v. Olson, 324 U.S. 786 (1945). Habeas corpus petition of Indian defendant who had entered a plea of guilty to a burglary charge without benefit of counsel or notice of his right to have counsel was improperly dismissed for lack of merit and without a hearing. The dismissal was improper because petitioner had shown a prima facie lack of due process where there were questions about effective waiver of his right to counsel and about state court jurisdiction over a crime that might have been committed on an Indian Reservation.

Roberts v. United States, 320 U.S. 264 (1943). Where a trial court imposed a two year sentence but suspended the sentence and placed the defendant on probation conditioned on payment of a fine, the court could not, after later revocation of probation, impose a greater sentence than was originally given.

Robinette v. Helvering, 318 U.S. 183 (1943). The reversionary interest in an irrevocable trust is a taxable gift. This is true even though the reversionary interest is subject to estate tax and cannot be deducted in computing gift tax because its value cannot be readily determined due to complex factors such as whether the donee or donor will marry and have children reaching age 21.

Robinson v. Florida, 378 U.S. 153 (1964). The conviction of appellants, a group of eighteen Negroes and Caucasians, for trespass when they refused to leave a restaurant which would not serve Negroes violated the Fourteenth Amendment. The promulgation by Florida Board of Health of regulations requiring separate restaurant lavatory facilities for the races and the publication by the state of a food and drink services manual reiterating that requirement constituted state action that encouraged the restaurant's racial policy to such an extent that appellants' convictions for trespass denied them their right to equal protection under the law. The Court specifically refused to reach the broader issue of whether the Fourteenth Amendment would forbid such arrests and convictions where state action has nothing to do with the establishment's racial policy.

Robinson v. United States, 324 U.S. 282 (1945). The provision in the Federal Kidnapping Act, ch. 271 47 Stat. 326, ch. 301, 48 Stat. 781 (1934), that the "death sentence shall not be imposed if the person has been liberated unharmed" means that the death sentence will not be imposed when the victim is liberated uninjured, and the provision does not require for imposition of the death sentence that the injuries received be permanent or that they remain in existence until the time of sentence.

Rodgers v. United States, 332 U.S. 371 (1947). Penalties under the Agricultural Adjustment Act, 7 U.S.C. §§ 1281-1393, shall not bear interest for the period between the time the interest was due and the judgment date, because the purpose of imposing a penalty is not to raise revenue for the financial advantage of the government, but to deter farmers from exceeding their quotas.

Rosenberg v. Yee Chien Woo, 402 U.S. 49 (1971). Under the Immigra-tion and Nationality Act, 8 U.S.C. §§ 1101-1503, 18 U.S.C. §§ 1114, 1429 & 1546, 22 U.S.C. §§ 618 & 1446, aliens fleeing Communist countries may apply for conditional entry into the United States, and whether the alien had "firmly resettled" in another country is relevant to determining whether he should be granted asylum.

Samuels v. Mackell, 401 U.S. 66 (1971). Where the federal district court properly refused to enjoin petitioners' prosecution under a state anarchy statute, it should also have dismissed their prayer for declaratory relief without consideration of the merits. An injunction would have been improper because petitioners would not suffer any immediate and irreparable harm from a state criminal prosecution while their federal suit was pending. Since a declaratory judgment in this case, as in most cases, would have had the same effect as an injunction, the same equitable principles should have governed its disposition.

Sanford v. Kepner, 344 U.S. 13 (1952). In a proceeding in federal district court to review an adverse determination in an interference proceeding in which the Board of Interference Examiners of the Patent Office had denied priority of defendant's patent, the federal court could not proceed to determine the patentability of plaintiff's device.

Schacht v. United States, 398 U.S. 58 (1970). Title 10, section 772(f), United States Code, which permits the unauthorized wearing of a military uniform while one is portraying a member of the armed forces in a theatrical performance "if the portrayal does not tend to discredit that armed force," imposes an unconstitutional restraint upon the freedom of speech guaranteed by the First Amendment, and that part of the statute must be stricken.

Schulz v. Pennsylvania Railroad, 350 U.S. 523 (1956). In an action under the Jones Act, 46 U.S.C. § 688, for the death of a person employed by the railroad, a directed verdict for the defendant was not proper where there were inferences and questions of fact that were within the province of the jury to determine.

Schware v. Board of Bar Examiners, 353 U.S. 232 (1957). Due process under the Fourteenth Amendment was violated where an applicant to New Mexico's State Bar was refused admission to the practice of law based on evidence offered to show lack of good moral character—that applicant had been a past member of the Communist Party, that he had been arrested but released without formal charges being filed, and that he had used aliases fifteen years before for purposes that were not illegal.

Scull v. Virginia ex rel. Committee on Law Reform and Racial Activities, 359 U.S. 344 (1959). The Legislative Investigative Committee of the Virginia General Assembly violated the defendant's right to due process of law under the Constitution by questioning him without informing him how the questions were pertinent to the subject under inquiry and by failing to inform him that his refusal to answer would constitute a crime.

Seaboard Air Line Railroad v. Daniel, 333 U.S. 118 (1948). The Interstate Commerce Commission had the power under the Interstate Commerce Act to authorize Seaboard to take over a six-state rail line and operate in South Carolina without being subject to the state laws involved, and the state supreme court had jurisdiction to issue an order against the state attorney general enjoining enforcement of state laws and determining whether exemption from state law was a proper interpretation of the Interstate Commerce Commission's order.

Sears, Roebuck & Co. v. Stiffel Co., 376 U.S. 225 (1964). A state may not, by use of the state's unfair competition laws, circumvent the United States patent laws that deny a patent for want of invention. Without a patent the design falls into the public domain and may be copied by others.

Seymour v. Superintendent of Washington State Penitentiary, 368 U.S. 351 (1962). Petition of habeas corpus by an Indian convicted of attempted burglary should not have been denied where the crime was committed on land that was within the boundaries of an Indian reservation, where there were issues of types of land included within "Indian Country" under 18 U.S.C. §§ 1151 and

1153, and where issues of possible exclusive federal jurisdiction existed.

Shaughnessy v. Pedreiro, 349 U.S. 48 (1955). Judicial review of a deportation order of the District Director of Immigration and Naturalization was properly brought in federal district court, and the sections of the 1952 Immigration and Nationality Act, 8 U.S.C. §§ 101-1503, 18 U.S.C. §§ 1114, 1429 & 1546, 22 U.S.C. §§ 618 & 1446, make orders of the District Director final for the purposes of administrative action. These sections did not abrogate the power of the courts to review the action as provided in the Administrative Procedure Act, sections 10 and 12, ch. 324, 60 Stat. 243-44.

Shawkee Manufacturing Co. v. Hartford-Empire Co., 322 U.S. 271 (1944). Where a district court judgment validating a patent was fraudulently obtained and used to obtain a judgment in circuit court and the parties remained silent in response to charges of fraud, the judgment should have been set aside in circuit court when proof of fraud was subsequently obtained. The parties were free from obligations under the judgment, with possible damages due to be determined in district court proceedings.

Simonson v. Granquist, 369 U.S. 38 (1962). The United States could not recover a federal tax lien against the estate of a bankrupt under the Bankruptcy Act, 11 U.S.C. §§ 545 & 724(a), even though the liens were secured and perfected prior to bankruptcy.

Sinclair Refining Co. v. Atkinson, 370 U.S. 195 (1962). The Taft-Hartley Act, 29 U.S.C. § 185, did not impliedly repeal sections of the Norris-LaGuardia Act, 29 U.S.C. § 104, prohibiting federal courts from issuing injunctions in labor disputes, and courts will abide by the intent made clear by Congressional rejection of the repeal of the Act and subsequent legislation.

Slocum v. Delaware, Lackawanna & Western Railroad, 339 U.S. 239 (1950). A state court has no jurisdiction to issue a declaratory judgment in a dispute between two competing unions concerning the scope of prior agreements with a railroad, since exclusive jurisdiction under the Railway Labor Act rests with the National Railway Adjustment Board, 45 U.S.C. § 153.

Small Business Administration v. McClellan, 364 U.S. 446 (1960). The Small Business Administration did not forfeit its governmental priority in bankruptcy by agreeing to share with a bank the amount received in a bankruptcy proceeding, even though the assignment of the note to the Administration was not made until after the filing of the petition in bankruptcy.

Smith v. O'Grady, 312 U.S. 329 (1941). The affirmance by the Nebraska Supreme Court of a dismissal of a petition of habeas corpus was in error where the defendant alleged that he had been denied his right to due process of law under the Constitution. The trial court had not required the state to answer the petition and had not given the defendant a chance to prove his allegations.

Smith v. Shaughnessy, 318 U.S. 176 (1943). Grantor's gift of stocks to wife for her use for life with reversion to grantor if living, and if not, to whomever the wife shall appoint created a life interest subject to gift tax and a remainder interest that was complete for purposes of gift tax except for the value of grantor's reversionary interest.

Smith v. Texas, 311 U.S. 128 (1940). A Texas statute providing means for selecting grand juries was not in itself unfair, but it was applied so as to systematically exclude blacks; therefore, an indictment rendered by an all-white grand jury against a black man which resulted in his subsequent conviction was a denial of his right to equal protection under the Constitution.

Snyder v. Harris, 394 U.S. 332 (1969). The 1966 amendments to the Federal Rules of Civil Procedure did not expand the jurisdiction of the courts to allow aggregation of claims in order to meet the jurisidictional amount in a diversity action. To so modify the settled judicial interpretation of the term "matter in controversy" would run counter to congressional intent as expressed by legislation passed over the years, even though Congress has steadily increased the jurisdictional amount.

Solesbee v. Balkcom, 339 U.S. 9 (1950). A Georgia statute providing for a nonadversial review by the Governor of the sanity of a convicted murderer sentenced to execution did not violate the right to due process under the Constitution. The agency given the power to pass on insanity was given broad discretion that was not subject to appellate review.

Spreckels v. Commissioner, 315 U.S. 626 (1942). Commissions paid on security sales are not deductible but may be used to offset the selling price in determining capital gains under the Revenue Act of 1934. The Treasury regulation stating that the deductibility of commissions paid in selling securities "when such commissions are not an ordinary and necessary business expense" applies to those individuals who normally engage in the business of buying and selling securities and not to a trader who is working on his own.

Standard Dredging Corp. v. Murphy, 319 U.S. 306 (1943). Taxation of unemployment insurance by the state of New York did not violate the exclusive federal jurisdiction of admiralty cases granted by the Constitution, and exemption of officers and members of a crew of a vessel on navigable waters from unemployment tax under the Federal Unemployment Tax Act, 26 U.S.C. §§ 3301-3311, did not create an exemption from state unemployment tax.

Standard Oil Co. v. Johnson, 316 U.S. 481 (1942). Army post exchanges are deemed essential for the performance of governmental functions as an integral part of the War Department and are entitled to the same immunities under the Constitution and federal statutes; therefore, fuel sold to exchanges is not subject to state license tax where a state statute exempts from taxation fuel sold to the federal govenment.

Standard Oil Co. v. United States, 340 U.S. 54 (1950). Whether the collision of a steam tanker and a Navy minesweeper was covered under a war risk policy insuring the tanker against all consequences of warlike operations was a question of fact to be determined by the trial court by exploring the causal relationship between a warlike operation and a collision where both vessels were at fault.

State Tax Commission v. Van Cott, 306 U.S. 511 (1939). Salaries of employees or officials of federal instrumentalities are not immune from state taxation under the Constitution.

Steele v. General Mills, Inc., 329 U.S. 433 (1947). Action to recover the difference between minimum transportation rate charges set by the Interstate Commerce Commission and the lower amount agreed to by a carrier in an unwritten secret agreement between the carrier and General Mills was not barred by the Texas statute of limitations on unwritten contracts, and under Texas law the doctrines of neither estoppel nor *pari delicto* can be invoked.

Stern v. South Chester Tube Co., 390 U.S. 606 (1968). Federal district court, under jurisdiction allowed by the All Writs Act, 28 U.S.C. § 1651, could order a writ of mandamus to a private individual to inspect the records of a Pennsylvania corporation, and such a mandamus is not within the meaning of cases holding that a mandamus can issue in a federal case only in order to grant some other form of relief.

Stewart v. United States, 366 U.S. 1 (1961). In a murder trial, cross-examination of a defendant that revealed that the defendant had failed to take the stand in previous trials for the same murder was not harmless, but was prejudicial; a mistrial thus should have been declared.

Still v. Norfolk & Western Railway, 368 U.S. 35 (1961). An employee could recover under the Federal Employers' Liability Act, 45 U.S.C. §§ 51-60, for injuries received during the course of his employment even though he used false and fraudulent representations about his physical condition, which may have contributed to his injury, in order to obtain employment.

Stirone v. United States, 361 U.S. 212 (1960). Instruction to the jury that defendant concrete mixing company could be convicted of extortion in interstate commerce under the Hobbs Act for either the importation of sand or the shipping of concrete for incorporation in a steel mill was prejudicial error, since defendant had been indicted on only the importation of sand.

Superior Bath House Co. v. McCarroll, 312 U.S. 176 (1941). The Act of Congress of 1891 giving the state of Arkansas the right to tax "personal property of all structures and other property in private ownership on the Hot Springs Reservation" allowed taxation on net income from a bath house located on property leased from the government. The Act was not to be construed as consenting to only *ad valorem* taxes on tangible property, since the privilege of use is "only one of the bundle of privileges that make up 'property' or 'ownership.' "

Surowitz v. Hilton Hotels Corp., 383 U.S. 363 (1966). In a derivative stockholder's action where the petitioner was an immigrant with little or no formal education and little knowledge of the English language and did not fully understand the complaint, but where the petitoner's son-in-law had carefully investigated the complaint and explained it to her and had filed an affidavit along with petitioner's counsel, the complaint should not have been dismissed. The purpose of the new federal rules is to see that bona fide complaints are carried to adjudication through fair trials.

Takahashi v. Fish & Game Commission, 334 U.S. 410 (1948). A state statute that, because of "special public interest," denied fishing licenses to Japanese aliens who were ineligible for citizenship under federal law was in violation of the Equal Protection Clause of the Constitution. The fact that the United States may regulate immigration and naturalization using race and color classifications does not permit a state to use these same classifications to prevent admitted aliens from earning a living in the same way as inhabitants.

Talley v. Calfornia, 362 U.S. 60 (1960). A city ordinance proscribing the distribution of handbills anywhere, under any circumstances, unless they bear the names and addresses of the persons who prepared, distributed, or sponsored them was an abridgment by the state of California of the freedoms of speech and press guaranteed to the states by the Constitution through the Fourteenth Amendment.

Testa v. Katt, 330 U.S. 386 (1947). The Federal Constitution and statutes passed pursuant to it are the supreme law of the land, and a state court with adequate jurisdiction may not refuse to enforce a statute of the federal govenment because it deems the statute to be penal in nature.

Texas v. New Jersey, 379 U.S. 674 (1965). The jurisdiction to escheat debt lies in the state of the debtor's last known address as found in the creditor's books, and in the absence of such address or escheat law, jurisdiction lies in the state of the debtor's corporate domicile, with the possibility of later escheat to the former state.

Thomas v. Hempt Brothers, 345 U.S. 19 (1953). Plaintiff, who operated a stone quarry that supplied stone used in manufacturing cement for building roadways and airport runways, was sufficiently involved in interstate commerce to have a recoverable cause of action under the Fair Labor Standards Act, 29 U.S.C. §§ 201-217.

Thompson v. City of Louisville, 362 U.S. 199 (1960). Conviction of the defendant under city loitering and disorderly conduct ordinances for walking around a store for thirty minutes and "shuffling his feet" in time to music while waiting for a bus was so devoid of evidence as to be a violation of due process under the Fourteenth Amendment.

Thompson v. Magnolia Petroleum Co., 309 U.S. 478 (1940). Trustee in Reorganization of a Railroad under Section 77 of the Bankruptcy Act, 11 U.S.C. § 107, properly asserted his rights to reduce fugitive oil underlying the railway to possession for sale and to keep the proceeds impounded for later distribution. The Bankruptcy Court must submit the question of title to state court for adjudication.

Tiller v. Atlantic Coast Line Railroad, 318 U.S. 54 (1943). The 1939 amendment to the Federal Employers' Liability Act, 45 U.S.C. §§ 51-60, abolished the common law doctrine of assumption of risk and substituted a standard of comparative negligence using common law standards of care. Where the evidence concerning negligence is in dispute, the question should be submitted to a jury for determination.

Tiller v. Atlantic Coast Line Railroad, 323 U.S. 574 (1945). In a wife's action for the death of her husband under the Federal Employers' Liability Act, 45 U.S.C. §§ 51-60, where he was killed at night by rail car being pushed backward with no lights, whether the lack of a backup light required by the Boiler Inspection Act was a proximate cause of death was a question for the jury. The instructions to the jury concerning unusual backup movements as a proximate cause of the death were not in error.

Timken Roller Bearing Co. v. United States, 341 U.S. 593 (1951). An arrangment among a company producing roller bearings and two foreign corporations to allocate trade territories and to fix prices was found to be in violation of the Sherman Antitrust Act, 15 U.S.C. §§ 1-7, and a claim of use of a trademark could not be used to avoid violation of the Act.

Torcaso v. Watkins, 367 U.S. 488 (1961). The refusal of a state to issue a notary commission because petitioner would not swear, as a test of office, to his belief in the existence of God was held unconstitutional as a violation of the Const. art. VI, which forbids use of a religious test as a qualification of an office of public trust, and of the First and Fourteenth Amendments, which give the right of freedom of religion to the states.

Toussie v. United States, 397 U.S. 112 (1970). Neither the statute requiring males between the ages of eighteen and twenty-six to register for the draft nor the regulation referring to "continuing duty" extended the statute of limitations on prosecution of criminal actions, and the statute began running five days after defendant's eighteenth birthday.

Transportation-Communication Employees Union v. Union Pacific Railroad, 385 U.S. 157 (1966). The Railroad Adjustment Board must extend its jurisdiction to settle disputes as to all parties where there are conflicting claims from different unions, and all parties must be present and not merely ready to participate.

Travelers Health Association v. Virginia ex rel. State Corporation Commission, 339 U.S. 643 (1950). Even though the order affected business activities outside the state of Virginia, the Virginia State Corporation Commission did not violate due process by issuing a cease and desist order against a Nebraska insurance association to enjoin it from soliciting business without a Virginia permit from Virginia residents unless it accepted service of process through the Nebraska Secretary of the Commonwealth.

Tucker v. Texas, 326 U.S. 517 (1946). A state statute making it an offense to distribute religious literature in a public housing village built to house workers on a national security project violated the defendant's right to freedom of religion and press as guaranteed by the Constitution.

Tulee v. Washington, 315 U.S. 681 (1942). The state of Washington could impose regulatory restrictions on time and manner of fishing by the Yakima Indians outside of the reservation just as it could impose restrictions on other citizens. However, a revenue-producing license was prohibited by the treaty between the United States and the Yakimas.

United Mine Workers, District 12 v. Illinois State Bar Association, 389 U.S. 217 (1967). The First and Fourteenth Amendments protect a labor union's right to hire an attorney on a salaried basis to assist its members in asserting their legal rights.

United States v. Acme Process Equipment Co., 385 U.S. 138 (1966). The government is entitled to cancel a contract where there was an arrangement, at the time or before the time the prime contract was awarded, to kick back money on a subcontract in violation of the Anti-Kickback Act, 41 U.S.C. § 54, even though the actual kickback did not take place until later.

United States v. Allen-Bradley Co., 352 U.S. 306 (1957). The War Production Board has authority to determine that only part of a manufacturer's expansion was essential to national interests such that the manufacturer was eligible for accelerated amortization.

United States v. Allied Oil Corp., 341 U.S. 1 (1951). The President of the United States had the power under the Constitution to issue Executive Orders 9841 and 9842, transferring the power to seek damages for prices charged above the ceiling price under the Emergency Price Control Act of 1942 from the Administrator of the Office of Price Administration to the United States Attorney General.

United States v. Atlantic Mutual Insurance Co., 343 U.S. 236 (1952). Where there is a "both to blame" clause, common carriers of cargo cannot stipulate to immunity from liability for damage to vessels for themselves or their agents under the Harter Act, 46 U.S.C. § 192, and the Carriage of Goods by Sea Act of 1936, 46 U.S.C. § 1304.

United States v. Atlantic Refining Co., 360 U.S. 19 (1959). Where a consent decree was agreed to and followed for many years allowing a payment of seven percent of valuation of pipeline property to be paid by oil companies as dividends to shipper-owners, the government's claim that dividends may be computed on the proportion of stock investment that the carrier bore to carrier's total invested capital, including debts owed to third persons, was rejected.

United States v. Baltimore & Ohio Railroad, 333 U.S. 169 (1948). Action enjoining enforcement of an order to carriers to cease and desist from refusing delivery to a packing plant because of exorbitant side rail rates was improper, since the packing plant's tracks were part of interstate commerce, and packing plant owners could not discriminate with high rates and restrain free exercise of commerce in violation of the Interstate Commerce Act.

United States v. Bethlehem Steel Corp., 315 U.S. 289 (1942). A contract between the United States Shipping Board Merchant Fleet Corporation and a shipbuilder, containing a clause awarding as profits one-half the difference in the cost estimate and the actual cost, was not invalid due to duress, since the U.S. Government could, under article I of the Constitution, compel the shipbuilder to manufacture ships in time of war.

United States v. Braverman, 373 U.S. 405 (1963). The Elkins Act, 49 U.S.C. § 41, makes it an offense for a person to solicit a rebate from a common carrier, regardless of who benefits from the rebate.

United States v. California, 332 U.S. 19 (1947). Where the United States claims title to land underlying the coastal waters in a three mile band along the shoreline of California, the United States govenment has superior title under article III of the Constitution, and the power of the government to assert title is binding upon the United States Supreme Court.

United States v. California Eastern Line, Inc., 348 U.S. 351 (1955). Section 1141 of Title 26, United States Code, gives a federal court of appeals the jurisdiction to hear appeals of Tax Court decisions on renegotiation orders, but the scope of this review is narrowed by the Renegotiation Act, 50 U.S.C. §1191, which provides that Tax Court determinations of excess profits are not reviewable.

United States v. Capital Transit Co., 325 U.S. 357 (1945). Where passengers were transported between their homes in the District of Columbia and their places of work at government agencies in Virginia, transportation by buses and streetcars was the equivalent of interstate commerce subject to regulation by the Interstate Commerce Commission, even though the trip was made in two segments, one of which was wholly within the District of Columbia.

United States v. Chicago Heights Trucking Co., 310 U.S. 344 (1940). Lower rates charged for less than truck-load shipments to forwarders was unjust discrimination and amounted to an illegal "rebate," in violation of the Federal Motor Carrier Act, 49 Stat. 543. It was within the power of the Interstate Commerce Commission to cancel the lower rates.

United States v. City & County of San Francisco, 310 U.S. 16 (1940). The sale by the City and County of San Francisco of electric power to Pacific Gas and Electric Company for resale to consumers violated the Raker Act of 1913, which provided that the land which produced the power was granted to San Francisco so that power could be sold directly to consumers at a low cost; selling or letting the power to another was prohibited.

United States v. City of Detroit, 355 U.S. 466 (1958). A state tax on government-owned, tax-exempt property leased by a for-profit corporation, where lessee may deduct the amount of taxes paid from rental payments, was not unconstitutional as a levy on government property, nor did it discriminate against the users of such property.

United States v. Coleman, 390 U.S. 599 (1968). The discovery of quartzite on land owned by the government did not qualify respondent for a patent under 30 U.S.C. § 22, which allows transfer of title to the discoverer of valuable deposits of minerals, because quartzite could not be marketed at a profit, or under 30 U.S.C. § 161, which allows transfer of title for land "chiefly valuable for building stone," because quartzite is a common variety of stone excluded under the language of 30 U.S.C. § 161.

United States v. Commodities Trading Corp., 339 U.S. 121 (1950). Just compensation paid to an investor for black pepper during World War II under the Emergency Price Control Act, 50 U.S.C. § 901, was rightfully set as the ceiling price fixed by the government, even though the investor originally purchased the pepper at a price greater than the ceiling price, and retention value was not to be treated as a separate and essential factor.

United States v. Commodore Park, Inc., 324 U.S. 386 (1945). Where the United States Government, under its power to regulate commerce, dredged the bay to improve navigation, the deposit of dredged materials in adjoining water, blocking its navigability, bore a substantial relation to commerce or navigiation, and the government was not liable to a riparian landowner for the loss of value of his land resulting from the deposit.

United States v. Cumberland Public Service Co., 338 U.S. 451 (1950). Capital gains tax could not be charged to a corporation upon liquidation and distribution of assets to shareholders and the subsequent sale of properties by the shareholders, notwithstanding that the corporation's motive may have been to reduce corporate taxation.

United States v. Demko, 385 U.S. 149 (1966). Workmen's compensation remedy under 18 U.S.C. § 4126 is exclusive to a prisoner injured while performing maintenance work at a federal prison, and he may not seek additional damages under the Federal Tort Claims Act.

United States v. Employing Lathers Association, 347 U.S. 198 (1954). Where a substantial quantity of lathing material used in local Chicago jobs was produced in other states and the combination of lathing contractors and union members had achieved almost complete control over the lathing business locally, and where there were certain restrictions over hiring and standards, there was sufficient evidence to show a substantial suppression of competition. The complaint, which alleged violations of section 1 of the Sherman Antitrust Act, 15 U.S.C. § 1, should not have been dismissed.

United States v. Employing Plasters Association, 347 U.S. 186 (1954). Dismissal for failure to state a cause of action under the Sherman Antitrust Act, 15 U.S.C. §§ 1-7, was improper where the government brought an action against a local contractors' association, a local labor union, and a union's president. Every element necessary was present to state a cause of action alleging that there were local restraints affecting interstate commerce, and additional evidentiary facts could have been sought under the Federal Rules of Civil Procedure.

United States v. Florida, 363 U.S. 121 (1960). Under the Submerged Lands Act, 43 U.S.C. §§ 1301-1315, which set as the boundaries of the Gulf states the boundaries established at the time of admission to the Union or as approved by Congress, the boundaries of the state of Florida were established as extending three leagues into the Gulf of Mexico, as stated in the Florida Constitution of 1868, which was approved by Congress upon the state's readmission to the Union after the Civil War.

United States v. Frankfort Distilleries, Inc., 324 U.S. 293 (1945). A conspiracy by producers, wholesalers, and retailers to fix, through contracts and boycotts, artifically high prices on liquor shipped into the state was a restraint on interstate commerce in violation of the Sherman Antitrust Act, 15 U.S.C. §§ 1-7, even though the Twenty-first Amendment to the Constitution gave regulatory power to the states over alcoholic beverages and the action of the defendants affected intrastate trade

United States v. Glenn L. Martin Co., 308 U.S. 62 (1939). A War Department contract with a manufacturer to pay a price that would be increased by the amount of any taxes that subsequently might be imposed by Congress upon goods supplied did not cover social security taxes, as this tax did not constitute a tax "on" the goods.

United States v. Hendler, 303 U.S. 564 (1938). A gain resulting from assumption of a debt by another corporation in a corporate reorganization was not exempt from taxation under section 112 of the Revenue Act of 1928 because the gain was not distributed as required for exemption under that section.

United States v. Hougham, 364 U.S. 310 (1960). The lower court was in error when it held that there had been an irrevocable election of remedies and that the government was unable to recover under an amended complaint where the government filed a complaint under section 26(1) of the Federal Property and Administrative Services Act of 1949. Acceptance of partial payment of the judgement after appeal, but before judgment on appeal, did not work to give accord and satisfaction of the entire claim.

United States v. Howard P. Foley Co., 329 U.S. 64 (1946). The government could not be held liable for delay of a construction contract to install lighting when it did not relinquish runways on time where there was no warranty in the contract that the government would make the runways available promptly and there were provisions that indicated that some delays were anticipated.

United States v. Interstate Commerce Commission, 337 U.S. 426 (1949). The Interstate Commerce Act, 49 U.S.C. § 1, which provides that a person may seek damages either with the Interstate Commerce Commission or in U.S. District Court, does not remove a Commission order from judicial review, and the statutory provision making the government a defendant in the review of an order does not prevent the government from challenging the order.

United States v. Jackson, 302 U.S. 628 (1938). Section 17 of the Economy Act, 48 Stat. 11, does not repeal by implication automatic insurance granted by section 401 of the War Risk Insurance Act, 46 U.S.C. §§ 1281-1294, since a law is not to be construed as impliedly repealing a prior law unless there is no other reasonable construction.

United States v. Jacobs, 306 U.S. 363 (1939). The tax levied on a joint tenancy at the death of one tenant does not act retroactively in violation of due process guaranteed by the Fifth Amendment when the tenancy had been created prior to the enactment of the § 302 of the 1924 Revenue Act. The section of the act that excludes that portion of the tenancy previously held by the decedent and survivor jointly does not apply where survivor received property for less than adequate consideration.

United States v. Johnson, 327 U.S. 106 (1946). An appeal from denial of a new trial on the ground of newly discovered evidence under Rule II(3) of the Criminal Appeals Rules, where the newly discovered evidence was that government's chief witness had testified falsely, does not present a reviewable issue of law when there is evidence to support the trial court's findings.

United States v. King, 395 U.S. 1 (1969). The Court of Claims has only the jurisdiction expressly given to it by the Court of Claims

Act, 28 U.C.C. § 1255, to give monetary relief, and it could not issue a declaratory judgement to have the defendant's military records changed to show his discharge was due to disability, since the government had not expressly waived its sovereign immunity to suit.

United States v. Korpan, 354 U.S. 271 (1957). The purpose of 26 U.S.C. § 4461 was to place a special occupational tax on all slot machines. A pinball machine for which free games were recorded and cash was paid for games won was a slot machine within the meaning of the statute and was appropriately taxed.

United States v. Laudani, 320 U.S. 543 (1944). A foreman who induced workers on a public works project to surrender part of their wages in order to keep their jobs was liable under the Kickback Racket Act, 41 U.S.C. §§ 51-54, and although he was not an employer under wording of the act, Congress intended the broad language of the act to impose liability on a foreman with power to hire and dismiss employees.

United States v. Lem Hoy, 330 U.S. 724 (1947). Section 5 of the Farm Labor Supply Appropriation Act, 50 U.S.C. § 1355, does not immunize farm labor contractors from prosecution under the Immigration Act for attempting to "induce or invite rewards" to aliens to circumvent the immigration law regarding farm laborers.

United States v. Lepowitch, 318 U.S. 702 (1943). Section 76 of Title 18, United States Code, prohibits impersonation of a Federal Bureau of Investigation officer with intent to defraud in order to find out the whereabouts of an individual. In this case, the impersonation did not deprive the defrauded individual of anything of "value," but was used merely to convince another to follow a course he would not have pursued but for the fraud.

United States v. Lewis, 340 U.S. 590 (1951). Even though the employee was required in a later year to return a portion of a bonus to the company, the employee was not entitled to a refund of a portion of taxes paid on the bonus, since he had used the full amount unconditionally as his own under a claim of right.

United States v. Lindsay, 346 U.S. 568 (1954). A 1952 claim by the government against a supplier for a 1945 delivery of defective wool was barred by the six year statute of limitations defined in the

Commodity Credit Corporation Charter Act, 15 U.S.C. § 714, since Congress must have intended, by lack of evidence to the contrary, that the right of action accrue at the time of delivery and not at the time of passage of the Act.

United States v. Louisiana, 389 U.S. 155 (1967). Under the Submerged Lands Act, 43 U.S.C. §§ 1301-1315, states are granted the boundaries, up to three marine miles from the shoreline extending into the sea, as they existed at the time of the state's admission to the Union, and jetties constructed outside the three mile limit belong to the federal government and are not considered shoreline for the purposes of the Act.

United States v. Lovett, 328 U.S. 303 (1946). Section 304 of the Urgent Deficiency Appropriation Act of 1943, 72 Stat. 108, cut off appropriations for payments to certain named government employees who had been deemed "subversive" by the House Un-American Activities Committee, and, as such, it acted as a bill of attainder, in violation of the Constitution.

United States v. McClure, 305 U.S. 472 (1939). Section 305 of the World War Veterans Act, 7 Stat. 158, providing that a lapsed insurance war risk policy could be revived where compensation is due a veteran, should be construed separately from section 301, which provides that all yearly renewable term insurance shall cease on July 29, 1929, except when death or total permanent disability shall have occurred. Where petitioner's compensation, due in December, 1929, upon permanent disability, was sufficient to pay intervening premiums, his insurance should have been revived.

United States v. McGowan, 302 U.S. 535 (1938). The Reno Indian Colony, purchased by the federal government for underprivileged Indians, was "Indian Country" within the meaning of 25 U.S.C. § 243, which provides that vehicles used to transport intoxicating liquors into Indian country may be forfeited.

United States v. McNinch, 356 U.S. 595 (1958). Submission of false applications for credit insurance to the FHA is an action "against the government" for the purposes of the False Claims Act, 31 U.S.C. §§ 3729-3731, since the FHA is an agency of the federal government, but an application for credit insurance is not a "claim" within the meaning of the False Claims Act.

United States v. Midstate Horticultural Co., 306 U.S. 161 (1939). An action under the Elkins Act, 49 U.S.C. §§ 41-43, for unlawful concessions or rebates may be brought in any state through which the goods are transported under the continuing offense doctrine; however, where transportation through eastern Pennsylvania was lawful but continued unlawfully through other states, an action could not be brought in eastern Pennsylvania.

United States v. Mississippi, 380 U.S. 128 (1965). The United States could bring an action against state registrars of Mississippi. There was a claim upon which relief could be granted under 42 U.S.C. § 1971 where the complaint alleged, and the United States stood ready to present evidence, of a legal and administrative history of discrimination against the Negro franchise.

United States v. Montgomery County Board of Education, 395 U.S. 225 (1969). A district court order for desegregation of Montgomery County schools, requiring every faculty of twelve or less to have at least one minority member and every faculty of twelve or more to have at least one minority member for every six, was not objectionable merely because it contained fixed mathematical ratios.

United States v. Moorman, 338 U.S. 457 (1950). A government contract is not reviewable by the Court of Claims and is binding on the parties where a clause in the contract provides that disputes about whether work falls outside the contract are to be settled by the Secretary of War or his representative.

United States v. Nielson, 349 U.S. 129 (1955). A tugboat owner could not collect damages resulting from the action of an employee who had gone aboard the steamboat, even though the contract to move the steamboat provided that the employee would become the servant of the steamboat with respect to the giving of orders to any tugs.

United States v. 93.970 Acres of Land, 360 U.S. 328 (1959). State law of election of remedies was inapplicable where the federal government leased an airfield to a private company with the provision that the government could revoke the lease, and the government started condemnation proceedings to gain immediate possession when lessee refused to give up the lease.

United States v. Ogilvie Hardware Co., 330 U.S. 709 (1947). The 1942 Amendment to the Revenue Act of 1936, 7 U.S.C. §§ 610-617, was designed to give a complete or partial refund of taxes paid on payments of undistributed profits taxes for tax years in which a company had accumulated a deficit, but the company was prohibited by law from distributing dividends. The use of the terms "deficit" and "accumulated earnings and profits" were not to be construed in usual tax terminology in light of the special purpose of the amendment.

United States v. Oregon, 366 U.S. 643 (1961). Property of incompetent veteran who died while in a veterans' hospital vested in the federal government under 38 U.S.C. § 17 rather than escheating to the state of Oregon, and the requirement of a contract was satisfied by the presumption of a contract between the veteran and the hospital. This devolution of property did not violate the Tenth Amendment provision leaving devolution of property to the states.

United States v. Pabst Brewing Co., 384 U.S. 546 (1966). The government's showing that the merger of Pabst and Blatz Brewing Companies, forming the tenth largest brewery, substantially lessened competition in a tri-state area was enough to prove a violation of section 7 of the Clayton Act, 15 U.S.C. § 18, as amended by the Celler-Kefauver Act, which requires that a lessening of competition in any section of the country be shown.

United States v. Patryas, 303 U.S. 341 (1938). The government could not contest a war risk insurance policy reinstated under the War Risk Insurance Act, even though the the total permanent disability was determined to have been established at a date prior to the reinstatement.

United States v. Pennsylvania Railroad, 323 U.S. 612 (1945). The Interstate Commerce Commission's order that water carriers pay rail carriers $1.00 per day for the use of rail cars was within the power of the Commission to regulate interstate transportation, even though part of the interstate transportation took place outside of the territorial waters of the United States.

United States v. Petrillo, 332 U.S. 1 (1947). The Communications Act of 1934, 15 U.S.C. § 21, which prohibits a federal broadcast licensee from employing persons in excess of the number needed for actual services is not unconstitutionally vague and does not abridge the freedom of speech when applied to an individual's placement of a picket line in front of the place of business of a licensee.

United States v. Plesha, 352 U.S. 202 (1957). The Soldiers' and Sailors' Civil Relief Act of 1940, 50 U.S.C. § 540, provided that a soldier with a commercial life insurance policy could elect to have the government later pay back premiums, the soldier could pick up the payments one year after the individual was no longer in service, and the government was not due to be reimbursed for those premium payments if a soldier allowed the policy to lapse.

United States v. Pyne, 313 U.S. 127 (1941). Attorney's fees properly incurred by an administrator of an estate as financier or invester in administering the estate were not deductible as business expenses, since they were not expenses incurred in "carrying on a trade or business."

United States v. Ragen, 314 U.S. 513 (1942). Statute providing a criminal penalty for income tax evasion was not so vague as to be unconstitutional, and the question of evasion may be left to the jury for a determination of the reasonableness of compensation as a deductible commission, rather than a non-deductible dividend.

United States v. Raynor, 302 U.S. 540. (1938). In construing a penal statute such as Section 150 of the Criminal Code, no rule of construction requires that the narrowest meaning be given, but rather the words may be given their fair meaning according to evident Congressional intent.

United States v. Rice, 317 U.S. 61 (1942). A plumbing, heating, and electrical contractor was not allowed damages for delay where his notice to proceed was contingent upon a concurrent construction contract which allowed for delays.

United States v. Sampson, 371 U.S. 75 (1962). Conviction under 18 U.S.C. § 1341 for using the mail to execute a "fraudulent scheme" was proper, even though defendants had already defrauded victims and merely mailed an accepted application and letter in order to lull victims into thinking the services were being performed.

United States v. Seatrain Lines, Inc., 329 U.S. 424 (1947). The Interstate Commerce Commission was without power under part three of the Interstate Commerce Act to hold proceedings to order a cancellation of the original certificate of public convenience and to issue a new, more restrictive certificate.

United States v. South-Eastern Underwriters Association, 322 U.S. 533 (1944). Although Congress knew that states were regulating the insurance business, this knowledge did not show that Congress intended to exempt insurance companies from the Sherman Antitrust Act. Thus, conspiring to restrain interstate trade and commerce by fixing and maintaining arbitrary and noncompetitive rates was a violation of the Act.

United States v. Sponenbarger, 308 U.S. 256 (1939). The beginning of work under the Mississippi Flood Control Act of 1928, 33 U.S.C. § 702(a), which resulted in the construction of levees and plans to build a floodway that might flood the plaintiff's land, was not a taking of land by eminent domain resulting in damages to the plaintiff, since plaintiff had actually benefited by the absence of recurring floods.

United States v. Stevens, 302 U.S. 623 (1938). A contract following the language of the Act of June 25, 1910, between an ex-soldier and the National Home for Disabled Soldiers in Massachusetts, which provided that at the soldier's death all personal property unclaimed by legatees after five years vested in the Home and which contained no provision for notification of the heirs, was valid under Massachusetts law.

United States v. Sullivan, 332 U.S. 689 (1948). The intrastate purchase by a druggist of Sulfathoazole tablets and his subsequent transfer of these tablets, used in interstate commerce, from their properly labeled container to a container without proper directions for their use, was a violation, as a "misbranding" of a drug offered for resale, of section 301 of the Federal Food, Drug, and Cosmetic Act, 21 U.S.C. § 331.

United States v. Township of Muskegon, 355 U.S. 484 (1958). A state tax on the tax-exempt property used by a corporation involved in a for-profit business was not unconstitutional, even though the corporation was performing work for the federal government.

United States v. Union Central Life Insurance Co., 368 U.S. 291 (1961). The filing of a standard federal tax lien on "all property" of an individual in the federal district court, because the Michigan register of deeds would not accept a lien on property without a "description," was proper because Michigan was deemed not to have designated a state office for filing, since the descriptive requirement presented an obstacle to the enforcement of federal tax liens.

United States v. Von's Grocery Co., 384 U.S. 270 (1966). The merger of two of the largest grocery companies in Los Angeles was a violation of the Celler-Devauver Anti-merger Act, 15 U.S.C. § 18, which sought to prevent concentration of business in the hands of a few to the disadvantage of small businessmen. The court could consider in its determination the competitiveness of the market at the time of merger, and the court could also predict the effect of the merger on future competitive conditions.

United States v. Vuitch, 402 U.S. 62 (1971). A District of Columbia statute prohibiting abortion unless "necessary for the preservation of the mother's life or health" was not unconstitutionally void for vagueness. The burden was on the prosecution to prove that the abortion was not necessary for the preservation of the mother's health.

United States v. Wallace & Tiernan Co., 336 U.S. 793 (1949). Where a subpoena was properly served and documents were produced in a criminal trial, the subsequent dismissal of the indictment due to the improper makeup on the grand jury did not render the documents illegal in a later civil trial as fruits of an unreasonable search and seizure.

United States v. Wurts, 303 U.S. 414 (1938). The two year statute of limitations under the Revenue Act of 1928, 45 Stat. § 791, for the bringing of an action by the government to recover an erroneous tax refund begins to run at the time of the making of the payment of refund and not at the date of its assessment.

United States ex rel. Marcus v. Hess, 317 U.S. 537 (1943). An informer's action for fraud against the government should not be strictly construed so as to detract from the meaning of the criminal statute. An action on defendant's collusive bids on a P.W.A. project was properly brought under section 5438 of the Act of March 2, 1868, and did not violate the Fifth Amendment prohibition against double jeopardy.

United States ex rel. Ostrager v. New Orleans Chapter, Associated General Contractors, Inc., 317 U.S. 562 (1943). A private individual may bring an informer's action for fraud against the government. The Fifth Amendment's prohibition against double jeopardy does not apply where the liability in one action is penal and in the other, is remedial.

United States ex rel. Toth v. Quarles, 350 U.S. 11 (1955). An ex-serviceman may not be arrested and taken to Korea to face a court-martial for a murder committed while in the service, but must be afforded the safeguards afforded by a trial in our constitutional court system.

United States ex rel. Tennessee Valley Authority v. Welch, 327 U.S. 546 (1946). Congress delegated to the Tennessee Valley Authority the power to determine the type of taking permissible for public use under the Tennessee Valley Authority Act of 1933, 16 U.S.C. § 831, and an action under the Act should be broadly viewed as a whole and not broken into separate parts.

United States Trust Co. v. Helvering, 307 U.S. 57 (1939). A War Risk Insurance policy payable to a wife was properly included in decedent's estate for estate tax purposes, and section 22 of the World War Veterans's Act, 43 Stat. 607-13, which provides that the insurance shall be exempt from all taxation, did not prevent estate tax from attaching, since this is a tax on the transfer of property.

United Transportation Union v. State Bar of Michigan, 401 U.S. 576 (1971). A state court injunction prohibiting a union from recommending attorneys, providing transportation, and otherwise providing assistance in obtaining legal aid was unconstitutional as violating the First Amendment right of the union and its members to engage in collective activities and to gain access to the courts.

Upshaw v. United States, 335 U.S. 410 (1948). A confession made by defendant thirty hours after he was arrested on suspicion without a warrant and before he had been taken before a magistrate was inadmissible in defendant's grand larceny trial because the Federal Rules of Criminal Procedure, Rule 5, requiring that a defendant be brought before a magistrate without delay, was intended to prevent secret interrogation.

Vanderbilt v. Vanderbilt, 354 U.S. 416 (1957). A New York court could adjudicate a wife's support since the husband's property was located within the state, and the New York court need not recognize an *ex parte* divorce obtained in Nevada by husband, dissolving all obligations, where the Nevada court had no personal jurisdiction over the wife.

Vanston Bondholders Protective Committee v. Green, 329 U.S. 156 (1946). A bankruptcy court may balance the equities among creditors and between creditor and debtor, and may order the debtor not to pay interest on interest due on a mortgage as agreed by contract in order to protect the interests of smaller creditors.

Voeller v. Neilston Warehouse Co., 311 U.S. 531 (1941). A state statute requiring a corporation to pay a dissenting stockholder the fair market value he places on his shares if within six months the corporation does not make a counter offer, get an appraisal, or request stockholder to get an appraisal did not violate the Due Process Clause of the Fourteenth Amendment.

Wade v. Hunter, 336 U.S. 684 (1949). When a new court martial trial was convened after defendant's first trial was discontinued due to removal of the trial to a location where witnesses could not appear, the constitutional prohibition against double jeopardy was not violated by the new trial.

Waldron v. Moore-McCormack Lines, Inc., 386 U.S. 724 (1967). Unseaworthiness due to the lack of an adequate number of men on a work crew to perform a designated task in a safe and prudent manner is a cause of action that may be presented to the trier of fact.

Walker v. City of Hutchinson, 352 U.S. 112 (1956). Where landowner was a resident of the state and his name was known to the state, newspaper publication alone of condemnation proceedings against his property was insufficient to meet the standard set by the due process provisions of the Fourteenth Amendment.

Wallace Corp. v. National Labor Relations Board, 323 U.S. 248 (1944). The National Labor Relations Board has the power to order that a company cease and desist carrying out a contract with an independent union under a labor dispute agreement and to order reinstatement with back pay to employees who had been discharged where it found that the contract had been entered into with the intention to deny membership to employees who had previousely been members of another union.

Walling v. Nashville, Chattanooga & Saint Louis Railway, 330 U.S. 158 (1947). When an injunction was sought against two groups of employees, the injunction was properly denied as to one group where requirements of the Fair Labor Standards Act, 29 U.S.C. §§ 201-217, were being met and to the other group where the individuals in question were not employees under the meaning of the Act.

Walling v. Portland Terminal Co., 330 U.S. 148 (1947). Individuals who are accepted for training as yard brakemen are not "employees" within the meaning of the Fair Labor Standards Act, 29 U.S.C. §§ 201, since they cannot be compelled to become employees and they do no actual work until qualified at the end of the training period.

Walton v. Southern Package Corp., 320 U.S. 540 (1944). An individual who was employed by a company as a night watchman as required by the insurer of the company in order to qualify for reduced rates made a valuable contribution to production and was engaged in interstate commerce for the purposes of the Fair Labor Standards Act.

Warren Trading Post Co. v. Arizona Tax Commission, 380 U.S. 685 (1965). There is no room for a state to exercise its ability to tax the gross income of traders in an Indian Reservation, since Congress pre-empts the state when it exercises its power to regulate reservation trading in a comprehensive way.

Watson v. Buck, 313 U.S. 387 (1941). Where a statute contains a severability clause to preserve its constitutionality, a federal court may not determine that the intent of the legislature was that the legislation should be kept intact. A federal court may not enjoin enforcement of a state criminal statute without a showing of exceptional and irreparable injury.

Watson v. Employers Liability Assurance Corp., 348 U.S. 66 (1954). A Louisiana statute allowing direct action against an insurer was not unconstitutional as a violation of equal protection since it was applied equally to insurance companies from all states and did not violate the constitutional prohibition against freedom to contract, since the insurer agreed to allow a direct action in order to gain a certificate to do business in Louisiana.

Weiler v. United States, 323 U.S. 606 (1945). Failure to instruct a jury that a conviction of perjury requires that the falsity of a statement be established by the testimony of two witnesses, or in the alternative, by one witness and testimony of a corroborating circumstance, was not harmless error.

Wesberry v. Sanders, 376 U.S. 1 (1964). Congressional districting so that a Congressman in one district in Georgia represented two to three times the number of people represented by Congressmen in other districts was a violation of the constitutional requirement that, as nearly as possible, one man's vote should count as much as another man's vote based on population.

Western Union Telegraph Co. v. Pennsylvania, 368 U.S. 71 (1961). Pennsylvania could not render an escheat judgement over property consisting of undeliverable money orders of Western Union, whose principal place of business was in New York, since there was no assurance that another state could not claim the same debts.

White v. Texas, 310 U.S. 530 (1940). Evidence obtained by taking defendant out of jail and into the woods on several successive nights, whipping him, and then reducing his confession to writing was a denial of due process as guaranteed by the Constitution.

Wilburn Boat Co. v. Fireman's Fund Insurance Co., 348 U.S. 310 (1955). Failure of an insurance company to pay the amount due resulting from a boat company's breach of contract is an admiralty matter within the jurisdiction of federal courts. Since there is no federal law governing regulation of marine insurance, Texas state law would apply, limiting the effects of a breach of contract.

Wilkerson v. McCarthy, 336 U.S. 53 (1949). In an action under the Federal Employer's Liability Act, 15 U.S.C. §§ 51-60, where an employee slipped and fell off a greasy plank into a pit when chains had been erected around the pit, the court erroneously granted a motion by the railroad for a directed verdict, and the question of liability should have been submitted to the jury.

Williams v. Lee, 358 U.S. 217 (1959). Where the plaintiff was not an Indian, but was running a business on an Indian reservation, a state court had no power where the plaintiff brought an action against an Indian couple for debts owing the business because Congress has given Indians control over their own affairs, and this was a matter for the Indian tribal courts.

Williams v. New York, 337 U.S. 241 (1949). It was not a denial of due process for a judge, after the jury has delivered a sentence of life imprisonment for defendant, to change the sentence to death after consideration of additional information from the court's "Probation Department and through other sources," since judges have long been permitted wide discretion as to sources and types of information to assist them in sentencing.

Williams v. Rhodes, 393 U.S. 23 (1968). The Ohio election laws requiring signatures totaling fifteen percent of the last gubernatorial race for a new party to appear on the ballot and ten percent for an established party to change its position on the ballot violated the Equal Protection Clause of the Constitution as being too discriminatory. The Independent Party and its candidates must be permitted to be write-ins if they qualify by the statutory date.

Woods v. Nierstheimer, 328 U.S. 211 (1946). Dismissal of a habeas corpus petition was proper for failure to state a claim where the defendant alleged denial of due process under the Constitution, since the proper action under Illinios law was a statutory writ of *coram nobis*, and the state should act upon that action before a federal court intervenes.

Wright v. Logan, 315 U.S. 139 (1942). Where a farmer, on the last day allowed by statute, sought to redeem property that had been foreclosed and sold in bankruptcy, his rights should not have been conditioned on the diligence with which he acted to receive an extension on the payment of his debts under the Bankruptcy Act.

Wright v. Rockefeller, 376 U.S. 52 (1964). Dismissal of a complaint alleging that congressional districts had been drawn upon racially operative lines was proper where there was disputed evidence and the trier of fact could have determined that the evidence of discrimination was insufficient.

Young v. Higbee Co., 324 U.S. 204 (1945). An action to compel an accounting by two preferred stockholders was proper where stockholders originally brought an action against a corporation on behalf of all preferred stockholders, but later sold their shares for more than they were worth in settlement of the dispute.

Younger v. Harris, 401 U.S. 37 (1971). Without a showing of great, immediate, and irreparable injury, the possible unconstitutionality of a state statute on its face does not justify the federal intervention through an injunction to prevent enforcement of the statute, and there must be a threat to a federal right that could not be eliminated by defense against a single criminal prosecution.

Youngstown Sheet & Tube Co. v. Sawyer, 343 U.S. 579 (1952). The President was without authority to issue Executive Order 10340, directing the Secretary of Commerce to take control of the steel mills threatening to strike during time of war. Congress alone has lawmaking power to take such private property, and the steel industry is not subject to presidential or military control.

Zerbst v. Kidwell, 304 U.S. 359 (1938). A prisoner who has been sentenced to a federal penal institution for an offense committed while he was on parole from a federal prison may be required to serve the unexpired part of his first sentence after the expiration of his second.

B. *Dissenting Opinions*

Abbate v. United States, 359 U.S. 187, 201 (1959) (Warren, C.J., and Douglas, J., concur).
Ackermann v. United States, 340 U.S. 193, 202 (1950) (Frankfurter and Douglas, JJ., concur).
Adamson v. California, 332 U.S. 46, 68 (1947).
Adler v. Board of Education, 342 U.S. 485, 496 (1952).
Alabama v. Texas, 347 U.S. 272, 277 (1954).
Algoma Plywood & Veneer Co. v. Wisconsin Employment Relations Board, 336 U.S. 301, 315 (1949) (Douglas, J., joins).
Allen v. State Board of Elections, 393 U.S. 544, 595 (1969).

Amalgamated Food Employees Union Local 590 v. Logan Valley Plaza, Inc., 391 U.S. 308, 327 (1968).

American Committee for Protection of Foreign Born v. Subversive Activities Control Board, 380 U.S. 503, 511 (1965).

American Communications Association v. Douds, 339 U.S. 382, 445 (1950).

American Trucking Associations, Inc. v. United States, 344 U.S. 298, 327 (1953) (Douglas, J., concurs).

Anastaplo, In re, 366 U.S. 82, 97 (1961) (Warren, C.J., and Douglas and Brennan, JJ., concur).

Anonymous Nos. 6 & 7 v. Baker, 360 U.S. 287, 298 (1959) (Warren, C.J., and Douglas and Brennan, JJ., concur).

Aro Manufacturing Co. v. Convertible Top Co., 377 U.S. 476, 515 (1964) (Warren, C.J., and Douglas and Clark, JJ., join).

Ashcraft v. United States, 361 U.S. 925, 925 (1959) (Douglas, J., joins).

Baltimore Contractors, Inc. v. Bodinger, 348 U.S. 176, 185 (1955) (Douglas, J., concurs).

Bank of America National Trust & Savings Association v. Parnell, 352 U.S. 29, 35 (1956) (Douglas, J., joins).

Barenblatt v. United States, 360 U.S. 109, 134 (1959) (Warren, C.J., and Douglas, J., concur).

Barskey v. Board of Regents, 347 U.S. 442, 456 (1954) (Douglas, J., concurs).

Bartkus v. Illinois, 359 U.S. 121, 150 (1959) (Warren, C.J., and Douglas, J., concur).

Beaufort Concrete Co. v. Atlantic States Construction Co., 384 U.S. 1004, 1004 (1966).

Beauharnais v. Illinois, 343 U.S. 250, 267 (1952) (Douglas, J., concurs).

Beck v. Washington, 369 U.S. 541, 558 (1962) (Warren, C.J., concurs).

Bell v. Maryland, 378 U.S. 226, 318 (1964) (Harlan and White, JJ., join).

Berger v. New York, 388 U.S. 41, 70 (1967).

Berman v. United States, 378 U.S. 530, 530 (1964) (Warren, C.J., and Douglas and Goldberg, JJ., join).

Berra v. United States, 351 U.S. 131, 135 (1956) (Douglas, J., joins).

Bertman v. J.A. Kirsch Co., 377 U.S. 995, 995 (1964) (Douglas and Goldberg, JJ., join).

Betts v. Brady, 316 U.S. 455, 474 (1942) (Douglas and Murphy, JJ., concur).

Bihn v. United States, 328 U.S. 633, 639 (1946).

Bivens v. Six Unknown Named Agents of Federal Bureau of Narcotics, 403 U.S. 388, 427 (1971).

Board of Education v. Allen, 392 U.S. 236, 250 (1968).

Boddie v. Connecticut, 401 U.S. 371, 389 (1971).

Bogardus v. Commissioner, 302 U.S. 34, 44 (1937) (Brandeis, Stone, and Cardozo, JJ., join).

Bollenbach v. United States, 326 U.S. 607, 615 (1946).

Boone v. Lightner, 319 U.S. 561, 576 (1943).

Bouie v. Columbia, 378 U.S. 347, 363 (1964) (Harlan and White, JJ., join).

Boys Markets, Inc. v. Retail Clerks Union, Local 770, 398 U.S. 235, 255 (1970).

Braden v. United States, 365 U.S. 431, 438 (1961) (Warren, C.J., and Douglas, J., concur).

Brady v. Southern Railway, 320 U.S. 476, 484 (1943).

Brannan v. Stark, 342 U.S. 451, 466 (1952) (Reed and Douglas, JJ., concur).

Braswell v. Florida, 400 U.S. 873, 873 (1970) (Douglas and Brennan, JJ., join).

Breard v. Alexandria, 341 U.S. 622, 649 (1951) (Douglas, J., joins).

Brown v. Allen, 344 U.S. 443, 548 (1953) (Douglas, J., concurs).

Brown v. Louisiana, 383 U.S. 131, 151 (1966) (Clark, Harlan, and Stewart, JJ., join).

Brown v. United States, 356 U.S. 148, 157 (1958) (Warren, C.J., and Douglas, J., concur).

Bumper v. North Carolina, 391 U.S. 543, 554 (1968).

Byrne v. Karalexis, 396 U.S. 976, 982 (1969).

Cahill v. New York, New Haven & Hartford Railroad, 351 U.S. 183, 184 (1956) (Warren, C.J., and Douglas and Clark, JJ., join).

California v. Byers, 402 U.S. 424, 459 (1971) (Douglas and Brennan, JJ., join).

Cameron v. Johnson, 381 U.S. 741, 742 (1965) (Harlan and Stewart, JJ., join).

Campbell v. Hussey, 368 U.S. 297, 302 (1961) (Frankfurter and Harlan, JJ., join).

Carey v. Westinghouse Electric Corp., 375 U.S. 261, 273 (1964) (Clark, J., joins).

Carlson v. Landon, 342 U.S. 524, 547 (1952).

Carpenters & Joiners Union v. Ritter's Cafe, 315 U.S. 722, 729 (1942) (Douglas and Murphy, JJ., concur).

Central States Electric Co. v. Muscatine, 324 U.S. 138, 146 (1945).

Chandler v. Judicial Council of the Tenth Circuit, 398 U.S. 74, 141 (1970) (Douglas, J., joins).

Chandler v. Judicial Council of the Tenth Circuit, 382 U.S. 1003, 1004 (1966) (Douglas, J., joins).

Chicago & Eastern Illinois Railroad v. United States, 375 U.S. 150, 150 (1963) (Douglas, J., joins).

Chicago, Rock Island & Pacific Railroad v. Stude, 346 U.S. 574, 582 (1954).

C.J. Hendry Co. v. Moore, 318 U.S. 133, 154 (1943).

Clay v. Sun Insurance Office, 363 U.S. 207, 213 (1960) (Warren, C.J., and Douglas, J., join).

Cohen v. Hurley, 366 U.S. 117, 131 (1961) (Warren, C.J., and Douglas, J., concur).

Colegrove v. Green, 328 U.S. 549, 566 (1946).

Colonnade Catering Corp. v. United States, 397 U.S. 72, 79 (1970) (Burger, C.J., and Stewart, J., join).

Colorado National Bank v. Commissioner, 305 U.S. 23, 27 (1938).

Commercial Molasses Corp. v. New York Tank Barge Corp., 314 U.S. 104, 114 (1941).

Commissioner v. Stern, 357 U.S. 39, 47 (1958) (Burger, C.J., and Whittaker, J., join).

Communist Party v. Subversive Activities Control Board, 367 U.S. 1, 137 (1961).

Connecticut General Life Insurance Co. v. Johnson, 303 U.S. 77, 83 (1938).

Connor v. Johnson, 402 U.S. 690, 693 (1971) (Burger, C.J., and Harlan, J., join).

Crane v. Cedar Rapids & Iowa City Railway, 395 U.S. 164, 167 (1969) (Warren, C.J., and Douglas, J., join).

Crown Cork & Seal Co. v. Ferdinand Gutmann Co., 304 U.S. 159, 168 (1938).

Daniel v. Paul, 395 U.S. 298, 309 (1969).

Davis v. Mississippi, 394 U.S. 721, 729 (1969).
Dean Milk Co. v. Madison, 340 U.S. 349, 357 (1951) (Douglas and Minton, JJ., concur).
DeBacker v. Brainard, 396 U.S. 28, 33 (1969).
Deitrick v. Standard Surety & Casualty Co., 303 U.S. 471, 481 (1938).
Dennis v. United States, 341 U.S. 494, 579 (1951).
Dennis v. United States, 339 U.S. 162, 175 (1950).
Denver & Rio Grande Western Railroad v. Brotherhood of Railroad Trainmen, 387 U.S. 556, 564 (1967) (Douglas and Fortas, JJ., join).
Department of Revenue v. James B. Beam Distilling Co., 377 U.S. 341, 346 (1964) (Goldberg, J., joins).
Detenber v. American Universal Insurance Co., 389 U.S. 987, 987 (1967).
De Zon v. American President Lines, 318 U.S. 660, 672 (1943).
Dickinson v. Petroleum Conversion Corp., 338 U.S. 507, 516 (1950).
Dyke v. Taylor Implement Manufacturing Co., 391 U.S. 216, 223 (1968) (Douglas, J., joins).
Edelman v. California, 344 U.S. 357, 362 (1953) (Douglas, J., concurs).
Eilers v. Hercules, Inc., 403 U.S. 937, 937 (1971) (Douglas, J., joins).
El Paso v. Simmons, 379 U.S. 497, 517 (1965).
Evans v. Newton, 382 U.S. 296, 312 (1966).
Exhibit Supply Co. v. Ace Patents Corp., 315 U.S. 126, 137 (1942) (Douglas, J., concurs).
Federal Power Commission v. Panhandle Eastern Pipe Line Co., 337 U.S. 498, 516 (1949) (Douglas and Rutledge, JJ., concur).
Federal Power Commission v. Tuscarora Indian Nation, 362 U.S. 99, 124 (1960) (Warren, C.J., and Douglas, J., join).
Federal Trade Commission v. Minneapolis-Honeywell Regulator Co., 344 U.S. 206, 213 (1952).
Feiner v. New York, 340 U.S. 315, 321 (1951).
Felber v. Association of the Bar, 386 U.S. 1005, 1005 (1967) (Douglas, J., joins).
Feldman v. United States, 322 U.S. 487, 494 (1944).
Felter v. Southern Pacific Co., 359 U.S. 326, 338 (1959) (Frankfurter and Douglas, JJ., concur).

First National Bank v. Cities Service Co., 391 U.S. 253, 299 (1968) (Warren, C.J., and Brennan, J., join).

Fishgold v. Sullivan Drydock Corp., 328 U.S. 275, 291 (1946).

Flemming v. Nestor, 363 U.S. 603, 621 (1960).

Ford Motor Co. v. United States, 335 U.S. 303, 322 (1948).

Foster v. California, 394 U.S. 440, 444 (1969).

Foster v. Illinois, 332 U.S. 134, 139 (1947) (Douglas, Murphy, and Rutledge, JJ., join).

Francis v. Southern Pacific Co., 333 U.S. 445, 451 (1948) (Murphy and Rutledge, JJ., join).

Frank v. United States, 395 U.S. 147, 159 (1969) (Douglas, J., joins).

F.W. Woolworth Co. v. Contemporary Arts, Inc., 344 U.S. 228, 234 (1952) (Frankfurter, J., concurs).

Gallegos v. Nebraska, 342 U.S. 55, 73 (1951) (Douglas, J., joins).

Galloway v. United States, 319 U.S. 372, 396 (1943) (Douglas and Murphy, JJ., concur).

Galvan v. Press, 347 U.S. 522, 532 (1954) (Douglas, J., concurs).

Garner v. Board of Public Works, 341 U.S. 716, 730 (1951).

General Talking Pictures Corp. v. Western Electric Co., 304 U.S. 175, 183 (1938).

General Talking Pictures Corp. v. Western Electric Co., 305 U.S. 124, 128 (1938).

Gibbs v. Buck, 307 U.S. 66, 79 (1939).

Ginzburg v. Goldwater, 396 U.S. 1049, 1049 (1970) (Douglas, J., joins).

Ginzburg v. United States, 383 U.S. 463, 476 (1966).

Goldberg v. Kelly, 397 U.S. 254, 271 (1970).

Goodyear Tire & Rubber Co. v. Ray-O-Vac Co., 321 U.S. 275, 279 (1944).

Graver Tank & Manufacturing Co. v. Linde Air Products Co., 339 U.S. 605, 612 (1950) (Douglas, J., concurs).

Green v. United States, 356 U.S. 165, 193 (1958) (Warren, C.J., and Douglas, J., concur).

Green v. United States, 365 U.S. 301, 307 (1961) (Warren, C.J., and Douglas and Brennan, JJ., concur).

Griggs v. Allegheny County, 369 U.S. 84, 90 (1962) (Frankfurter, J., concurs).

Griswold v. Connecticut, 381 U.S. 479, 507 (1965) (Stewart, J., joins).

Groban, In re, 352 U.S. 330, 337 (1957) (Warren, C.J., and Douglas and Brennan, JJ., join).
Groppi v. Wisconsin, 400 U.S. 505, 515 (1971).
Gulf Oil Corp. v. Gilbert, 330 U.S. 501, 512 (1947).
Gwin, White & Prince v. Henneford, 305 U.S. 434, 442 (1939).
Halliday v. United States, 394 U.S. 831, 835 (1969) (Douglas, J., joins).
Hamm v. Rock Hill, 379 U.S. 306, 318 (1964).
Hanson v. Denckla, 357 U.S. 235, 256 (1958) (Burton and Brennan, JJ., join).
Harper v. Virginia Board of Elections, 383 U.S. 663, 670 (1966).
Harris v. Nelson, 394 U.S. 286, 301 (1969).
Harrison v. United States, 392 U.S. 219, 226 (1968).
Heiser v. Woodruff, 327 U.S. 726, 740 (1946) (Douglas, J., joins).
Helvering v. Sabine Transportation Co., 318 U.S. 306, 312 (1943) (Douglas and Murphy, JJ., concur).
Henry v. Mississippi, 379 U.S. 443, 453 (1965).
Herb v. Pitcairn, 324 U.S. 117, 128 (1945).
Hill v. United States, 368 U.S. 424, 430 (1962) (Warren, C.J., and Douglas and Brennan, JJ., concur).
Hooven & Allison Co. v. Evatt, 324 U.S. 652, 686 (1945).
H.P. Hood & Sons v. Du Mond, 336 U.S. 525, 545 (1949).
Hostetter v. Idlewild Bon Voyage Liquor Corp., 377 U.S. 324, 334 (1964) (Goldberg, J., joins).
Hunter v. Erickson, 393 U.S. 385, 396 (1969).
Hysler v. Florida, 315 U.S. 411, 423 (1942) (Douglas and Murphy, JJ., concur).
Illinois Central Railroad v. Norfolk & Western Railway, 385 U.S. 57, 75 (1966).
Immigration & Naturalization Service v. Stanisic, 395 U.S. 62, 80 (1969) (Douglas and Marshall, JJ., join).
Indiana ex rel. Anderson v. Brand, 303 U.S. 95, 109 (1938).
International Association of Machinists v. Street, 367 U.S. 740, 780 (1961).
International Longshoremen's & Warehousemen's Union, Local 37 v. Boyd, 347 U.S. 222, 224 (1954) (Douglas, J., concurs).
International Shoe Co. v. Washington, 326 U.S. 301, 322 (1945).
Interstate Commerce Commission v. Inland Waterways Corp., 319 U.S. 671, 692 (1943).

Irvine v. California, 347 U.S. 128, 139 (1954) (Douglas, J., concurs).

Isserman v. Ethics Committee of Essex County Bar Association, 345 U.S. 927, 927 (1953) (Douglas, J., joins).

Italia Societa per Azioni di Navigazione v. Oregon Stevedoring Co., 376 U.S. 315, 325 (1964) (Warren, C.J., and Douglas, J., join).

Jay v. Boyd, 351 U.S. 345, 362 (1956).

Johansen v. United States, 343 U.S. 427, 441 (1952) (Vinson, C.J., and Douglas and Minton, JJ., concur).

Johnson v. Eisentrager, 339 U.S. 763, 791 (1950) (Douglas and Burton, JJ., concur).

Jones v. Opelika, 316 U.S. 584, 623 (1942) (Douglas and Murphy, JJ., join).

Katz v. United States, 389 U.S. 347, 364 (1967).

Kaufman v. United States, 394 U.S. 217, 231 (1969).

Kelley v. Everglades Drainage District, 319 U.S. 415, 422 (1943).

Kern-Limerick, Inc. v. Scurlock, 347 U.S. 110, 123 (1954) (Warren, C.J., and Douglas, J., concur).

Kesler v. Department of Public Safety, 369 U.S. 153, 182 (1962) (Douglas, J., concurs).

Killian v. United States, 368 U.S. 231, 258 (1961).

Kinsella v. Krueger, 351 U.S. 470, 485 (1956) (Warren, C.J., and Douglas, J., join).

Knapp v. Schweitzer, 357 U.S. 371, 382 (1958) (Douglas, J., joins).

Koehring Co. v. Hyde Construction Co., 382 U.S. 362, 365 (1966) (Douglas, J., joins).

Konigsberg v. State Bar of California, 366 U.S. 36, 56 (1961) (Warren, C.J., and Douglas, J., concur).

Kordel v. United States, 335 U.S. 345, 352 (1948) (Frankfurter, Murphy, and Jackson, JJ., concur).

Koster v. (American) Lumbermens Mutual Casualty Co., 330 U.S. 518, 532 (1947).

Kovacs v. Cooper, 336 U.S. 77, 98 (1949) (Douglas and Rutledge JJ., concur).

Lance v. Plummer, 384 U.S. 929, 929 (1966).

Lathrop v. Donohue, 367 U.S. 820, 865 (1961).

Law Students Civil Rights Research Council v. Wadmond, 401 U.S. 154, 174 (1971) (Douglas, J., joins).

Lee v. Florida, 392 U.S. 378, 387 (1968).

Lehigh Valley Cooperative Farmers, Inc. v. United States, 370 U.S. 76, 100 (1962).

Lehmann v. United States ex rel. Carson, 353 U.S. 685, 690 (1957) (Douglas, J., concurs).

Levine v. United States, 362 U.S. 610, 620 (1960) (Warren, C.J., and Douglas, J., join).

Lewis v. Martin, 397 U.S. 552, 560 (1970) (Burger, C.J., joins).

Lewis v. United States, 348 U.S. 419, 423 (1955) (Douglas, J., joins).

Link v. Wabash Railroad, 370 U.S. 626, 636 (1962) (Warren, C.J., concurs).

Linkletter v. Walker, 381 U.S. 618, 640 (1965) (Douglas, J., joins).

Linn v. United Plant Guard Workers, Local 114, 383 U.S. 53, 67 (1966).

Lisenba v. California, 314 U.S. 219, 241 (1941) (Douglas, J., concurs).

Lopinson v. Pennsylvania, 392 U.S. 647, 648 (1968).

Ludecke v. Watkins, 335 U.S. 160, 173 (1948) (Douglas, Murphy, and Rutledge, JJ., join).

M. Kraus & Bros. v. United States, 327 U.S. 614, 629 (1946).

McCarroll v. Dixie Greyhound Lines, 309 U.S. 176, 183 (1940) (Frankfurter and Douglas, JJ., join).

McCart v. Indianapolis Water Co., 302 U.S. 419, 423 (1938).

McDonald v. Commissioner, 323 U.S. 57, 65 (1944).

Madseir v. Kinsella, 343 U.S. 341, 371 (1952).

Magnolia Petroleum Co. v. Hunt, 320 U.S. 430, 450 (1943).

Mancusi v. DeForte, 392 U.S. 364, 372 (1968) (Stewart, J., joins).

Marcello v. Bonds, 349 U.S. 302, 315 (1955) (Frankfurter, J., joins).

Marshall v. Pletz, 317 U.S. 383, 391 (1943) (Douglas and Murphy, JJ., concur).

Maryland Casualty Co. v. Cushing, 347 U.S. 409, 427 (1954) (Warren, C.J., and Douglas and Minton, JJ., concur).

Maxwell v. Bishop, 398 U.S. 262, 267 (1970).

Michel v. Louisiana, 350 U.S. 91, 102 (1955) (Warren, C.J., and Douglas, J., concur).

Milk Wagon Drivers Union of Chicago, Local 753 v. Meadowmoor Dairies, 312 U.S. 287, 299 (1941).

Minnesota Mining & Manufacturing Co. v. New Jersey Wood Finishing Co., 381 U.S. 311, 324 (1965).

Mishawaka Rubber & Woolen Manufacturing v. S.S. Kresge Co., 316 U.S. 203, 208 (1942) (Douglas and Murphy, JJ., concur).

Mishkin v. New York, 383 U.S. 502, 515 (1966).

Moore v. Chesapeake & Ohio Railway, 340 U.S. 573, 578 (1951) (Douglas, J., concurs).

Morey v. Doud, 354 U.S. 457, 470 (1957).

Morgantown v. Royal Insurance Co., 337 U.S. 254, 261 (1949) (Rutledge, J., concurs).

Morris v. Florida, 393 U.S. 850, 850 (1968) (Douglas, J., joins).

Mosser v. Darrow, 341 U.S. 267, 275 (1951).

Mulcahey v. Catalanotte, 353 U.S. 692, 694 (1957); dissenting opinion reported at *Lehmann v. United States ex rel. Carson*, 353 U.S. 685, 690 (1957) (Douglas, J., concurs).

Muschany v. United States, 324 U.S. 49, 69 (1945).

Named Individual Members of the San Antonio Conservation Society v. Texas Highway Department, 400 U.S. 968, 968 (1970) (Douglas and Brennan, JJ., join).

Namet v. United States, 373 U.S. 179, 191 (1963) (Douglas, J., joins).

Nash v. United States, 398 U.S. 1, 5 (1970) (Stewart, J., joins).

National Board of Young Men's Christian Association v. United States, 395 U.S. 85, 99 (1969) (Douglas, J., joins).

National Equipment Rental v. Szukhent, 375 U.S. 311, 318 (1964).

National Labor Relations Board v. Allis-Chalmers Manufacturing Co., 388 U.S. 175, 199 (1967) (Douglas, Harlan, and Stewart, JJ., join).

National Labor Relations Board v. Columbian Enameling & Stamping Co., 306 U.S. 292, 300 (1939).

National Labor Relations Board v. Indiana & Michigan Electric Co., 318 U.S. 9, 30 (1943) (Douglas and Murphy, JJ., concur).

National Labor Relations Board v. Rockaway News Supply Co., 345 U.S. 71, 81 (1953) (Douglas and Minton, JJ., concur).

National Union of Marine Cooks & Stewards v. Arnold, 348 U.S. 37, 45 (1954) (Douglas, J., concurs).

Neely v. Martin K. Eby Construction Co., 386 U.S. 317, 330 (1967).

Nelson v. Los Angeles County, 362 U.S. 1, 9 (1960) (Douglas, J., joins).

New Haven Inclusion Cases, 399 U.S. 392, 495 (1970) (Harlan, J., joins).

New Jersey Realty Title Insurance Co. v. Division of Tax Appeals, 338 U.S. 665, 676 (1950).

New York Life Insurance Co. v. Gamer, 303 U.S. 161, 172 (1938).

Nilva v. United States, 352 U.S. 385, 396 (1957) (Warren, C.J., and Douglas and Brennan, JJ., join).

Norfolk & Western Railway v. Missouri State Tax Commission, 390 U.S. 317, 330 (1968).

N.V. Handelsbureau La Mola v. Kennedy, 370 U.S. 940, 940 (1962).

Oil Workers Union v. Missouri, 361 U.S. 363, 371 (1960) (Warren, C.J., and Brennan, J., join).

Order of United Commercial Travelers of America v. Wolfe, 331 U.S. 586, 625 (1947) (Douglas, Murphy, and Rutledge, JJ., join).

Orloff v. Willoughby, 345 U.S. 83, 95 (1953) (Frankfurter and Douglas, JJ., concur).

Pennsylvania Railroad v. Day, 360 U.S. 548, 554 (1959) (Warren, C.J., and Douglas, J., concur).

Perkins v. Matthews, 400 U.S. 379, 401 (1971).

Pittsburgh Towing Co. v. Mississippi Valley Barge Line Co., 385 U.S. 32, 33 (1966).

Polk Co. v. Glover, 305 U.S. 5, 10 (1938).

Poulos v. New Hampshire, 345 U.S. 395, 421 (1953).

Priebe & Sons v. United States, 332 U.S. 407, 414 (1947) (Murphy, J., joins).

Prima Paint Corp. v. Flood & Conklin Manufacturing Co., 388 U.S. 395, 407 (1967) (Douglas and Stewart, JJ., join).

Public Utilities Commission v. United Fuel Gas Co., 317 U.S. 456, 470 (1943) (Douglas and Murphy, JJ., concur).

Radio Officers' Union v. National Labor Relations Board, 347 U.S. 17, 57 (1954) (Douglas, J., joins).

Ramspeck v. Federal Trial Examiners Conference, 345 U.S. 128, 143 (1953) (Frankfurter and Douglas, JJ., concur).

Recznik v. City of Lorain, 393 U.S. 166, 170 (1968) (Harlan, J., joins).

Rederi A/B v. Cunard Steamship Co., 389 U.S. 852, 852 (1967) (Douglas, J., joins).

Reeves v. Pacific Far East Lines, Inc., 396 U.S. 908, 908 (1969) (Brennan, J., joins).

Regan v. New York, 349 U.S. 58, 66 (1955) (Douglas, J., concurs).

Reid v. Covert, 351 U.S. 487, 492 (1956); dissenting opinion reported at *Kinsella v. Krueger*, 351 U.S. 470, 485 (1956) (Warren, C.J., and Douglas, J., join).

Reina v. United States, 364 U.S. 507, 515 (1960) (Warren, C.J., concurs).

Remington v. United States, 343 U.S. 907, 907 (1952) (Douglas, J., concurs).

Republic Steel Corp. v. Maddox, 379 U.S. 650, 659 (1965).

Republic Steel Corp. v. National Labor Relations Board, 311 U.S. 7, 13 (1940) (Douglas, J., joins).

Rice v. Sioux City Memorial Park Cemetery, 349 U.S. 70, 80 (1955) (Warren, C.J., and Douglas, J., join).

Richfield Oil Corp. v. State Board of Equalization, 329 U.S. 69, 86 (1946).

Rodicker v. Illinois Central Railroad, 400 U.S. 1012, 1012 (1971) (Douglas and Brennan, JJ., join).

Rogers v. Bellei, 401 U.S. 815, 836 (1971) (Douglas and Marshall, JJ., join).

Rogers v. United States, 340 U.S. 367, 375 (1951) (Frankfurter and Douglas, JJ., concur).

Romero v. International Terminal Operating Co., 358 U.S. 354, 388 (1959).

Rosado v. Wyman, 397 U.S. 397, 430 (1970) (Burger, C.J., joins).

Rosenberg v. United States, 346 U.S. 273, 296 (1953).

Royal Indemnity Co. v. United States, 313 U.S. 289, 297 (1941).

Rutkin v. United States, 343 U.S. 130, 139 (1952) (Reed, Frankfurter, and Douglas, JJ., concur).

Ryan Stevedoring Co. v. Pan-Atlantic Steamship Corp., 350 U.S. 124, 135 (1956) (Warren, C.J., and Douglas and Clark, JJ., concur).

Sacher v. United States, 343 U.S. 1, 14 (1952).

St. Regis Paper Co. v. United States, 368 U.S. 208, 227 (1961) (Whittaker and Stewart, JJ., concur).

Santana v. United States, 385 U.S. 848, 848 (1966).

Scales v. United States, 367 U.S. 203, 259 (1961).

Schmerber v. California, 384 U.S. 757, 773 (1966) (Douglas, J., joins).

Scofield v. National Labor Relations Board, 394 U.S. 423, 436 (1969).

Securities & Exchange Commission v. Chenery Corp., 318 U.S. 80, 95 (1943) (Reed and Murphy, JJ., concur).
Security Sewage Equipment Co. v. Woodle, 396 U.S. 907, 907 (1969).
Shapiro v. Doe, 396 U.S. 488, 488 (1970) (Douglas, J., joins).
Shaughnessy v. United States ex rel. Accardi, 349 U.S. 280, 284 (1955) (Frankfurter, J., joins).
Shaughnessy v. United States ex rel. Mezei, 345 U.S. 206, 216 (1953) (Douglas, J., concurs).
Shotwell Manufacturing Co. v. United States, 371 U.S. 341, 367 (1963) (Warren, C.J., and Douglas, J., concur).
Shub v. Simpson, 340 U.S. 861, 862 (1950) (Warren, C.J., and Douglas, J., join).
Sigler v. Parker, 396 U.S. 482, 484 (1970) (Burger, C.J., joins).
Simmons v. Union News Co., 382 U.S. 884, 884 (1965) (Warren, C.J., joins).
Smith v. Evening News Association, 371 U.S. 195, 201 (1962).
Sniadach v. Family Finance Corp., 395 U.S. 337, 344 (1969).
Southern Pacific Co. v. Arizona, 325 U.S. 761, 784 (1945).
Southern Railway v. Jackson, 375 U.S. 837, 837 (1963) (Douglas, J., joins).
Spinelli v. United States, 393 U.S. 410, 429 (1969).
Standard Industries, Inc. v. Tigrett Industries, Inc., 397 U.S. 586, 586 (1970) (Douglas, J., joins).
State Board of Insurance v. Todd Shipyards Corp., 370 U.S. 451, 458 (1962).
Stein v. New York, 346 U.S. 156, 197 (1953).
Stewart v. Southern Railway, 315 U.S. 283, 287 (1942).
Stovall v. Denno, 388 U.S. 293, 303 (1967).
Street v. New York, 394 U.S. 576, 609 (1969).
Summers, In re, 325 U.S. 561, 573 (1945).
Sutphen Estates, Inc. v. United States, 342 U.S. 19, 23 (1951).
Teague v. Regional Commissioner of Customers, Region II, 394 U.S. 977, 977 (1969) (Douglas, J., joins).
Teamsters Local v. Lucas Flour Co., 369 U.S. 95, 106 (1962).
Temple v. United States, 386 U.S. 961, 961 (1967) (Douglas, J., joins).
Thomas Paper Stock Co. v. Porter, 328 U.S. 50, 56 (1946).
Thompson v. Lawson, 347 U.S. 334, 337 (1954) (Douglas and Minton, JJ., concur).

Time, Inc. v. Bon Air Hotel, Inc., 393 U.S. 859, 859 (1968) (Douglas, J., concurs).
T.I.M.E. Inc. v. United States, 359 U.S. 464, 480 (1959) (Warren, C.J., and Douglas and Clark, JJ., join).
Tinker v. Des Moines Independent Community School District, 393 U.S. 503, 515 (1969).
Turner v. United States, 396 U.S. 398, 425 (1970) (Douglas, J., joins).
Union Joint Stock Land Bank v. Byerly, 310 U.S. 1, 11 (1940) (Douglas and Murphy, JJ., concur).
United Public Workers v. Mitchell, 330 U.S. 75, 105 (1947).
United States v. Alpers, 338 U.S. 680, 685 (1950) (Frankfurter and Jackson, JJ., concur).
United States v. Barnett, 376 U.S. 681, 724 (1964) (Douglas, J., joins).
United States v. Brown, 348 U.S. 110, 113 (1954) (Reed and Minton, JJ., join).
United States v. Bryan, 339 U.S. 323, 346 (1950) (Frankfurter, J., concurs).
United States v. California, 381 U.S. 139, 178 (1965) (Douglas, J., joins).
United States v. Causby, 328 U.S. 256, 268 (1946).
United States v. Champlin Refining Co., 341 U.S. 290, 302 (1951).
United States v. Cooper Corp., 312 U.S. 600, 615 (1941).
United States v. Dixon, 347 U.S. 381, 386 (1954) (Douglas, Jackson, and Minton, JJ., concur).
United States v. Embassy Restaurant, 359 U.S. 29, 35 (1959) (Warren, C.J., and Douglas, J., concur).
United States v. Fleischman, 339 U.S. 349, 365 (1950) (Frankfurter, J., concurs).
United States v. Gainey, 380 U.S. 63, 74 (1965).
United States v. Hood, 343 U.S. 148, 152 (1952) (Reed, Douglas, and Minton, JJ., concur).
United States v. Interstate Commerce Commission, 352 U.S. 158, 176 (1956) (Warren, C.J., concurs).
United States v. Kahriger, 345 U.S. 22, 36 (1953) (Douglas, J., concurs).
United States v. Louisiana (Louisiana Boundary Case), 394 U.S. 11, 78 (1969) (Douglas, J., joins).

United States v. Louisiana (Texas Boundary Case), 394 U.S. 1, 6 (1969).

United States v. National Dairy Products Corp., 372 U.S. 29, 37 (1963) (Stewart and Goldberg, JJ., join).

United States v. Rabinowitz, 339 U.S. 56, 66 (1950).

United States v. Reidel, 402 U.S. 351, 357 (1971); dissenting opinion reported at *United States v. Thirty-Seven (37) Photographs*, 402 U.S. 363, 379 (1971) (Douglas, J., joins).

United States v. Shotwell Manufacturing Co., 355 U.S. 233, 246 (1957) (Warren, C.J., and Douglas, J., concur).

United States v. Spector, 343 U.S. 169, 173 (1952).

United States v. Speers, 382 U.S. 266, 278 (1965).

United States v. Thirty-Seven (37) Photographs, 402 U.S. 363, 379 (1971) (Douglas, J., joins).

United States v. Welden, 377 U.S. 95, 107 (1964) (Douglas, J., joins).

United States v. Yazell, 382 U.S. 341, 359 (1966) (Douglas and White, JJ., join).

United States v. Yellow Cab Co., 338 U.S. 338, 342 (1949) (Reed, J., concurs).

United States Gypsum Co. v. National Gypsum Co., 352 U.S. 457, 477 (1957) (Warren, C.J., and Douglas, J., join).

Uphaus v. Wyman, 364 U.S. 388, 389 (1960) (Warren, C.J., and Douglas, J., concur).

Vaca v. Sipes, 386 U.S. 171, 203 (1967).

Vale v. Louisiana, 399 U.S. 30, 36 (1970) (Burger, C.J., joins).

Veterans of the Abraham Lincoln Brigade v. Subversive Activities Control Board, 380 U.S. 513, 514 (1965); dissenting opinion reported at *American Committee for Protection of Foreign Born v. Subversive Activities Control Board*, 380 U.S. 503, 511 (1965).

Viereck v. United States, 318 U.S. 236, 249 (1943) (Douglas, J., concurs).

Virginia Petroleum Jobbers Association v. Federal Power Commission, 368 U.S. 940, 940 (1961) (Douglas, J., concurs).

Wade v. Wilson, 396 U.S. 282, 287 (1970).

Warner v. Kewanee Machinery & Conveyor Co., 398 U.S. 906, 906 (1970) (Douglas, J., joins).

Washingtonian Publishing Co. v. Pearson, 306 U.S. 30, 42 (1939).

Whiteley v. Warden, 401 U.S. 560, 570 (1971) (Burger, J., joins).

Whitney National Bank v. Bank of New Orleans & Trust Co., 379 U.S. 411, 432 (1965).
Wilkinson v. United States, 365 U.S. 399, 415 (1961) (Warren, C.J., and Douglas, J., concur).
Willard Dairy Corp. v. National Dairy Products Corp., 373 U.S. 934, 934 (1963).
Williams v. Jacksonville Terminal Co., 315 U.S. 386, 410 (1942) (Douglas and Murphy, JJ., concur).
Williams v. North Carolina, 325 U.S. 226, 261 (1945).
Williams Manufacturing Co. v. United Shoe Machinery Co., 316 U.S. 364, 371 (1942) (Douglas and Murphy, JJ., concur).
Winship, In re, 397 U.S. 358, 377 (1970).
Wisconsin v. Constantineau, 400 U.S. 433, 443 (1971) (Blackmun, J., joins).
Witherspoon v. Illinois, 391 U.S. 510, 532 (1968) (Harlan and White, JJ., join).
Wood v. Lovett, 313 U.S. 362, 372 (1941).
Wyman v. Rothstein, 398 U.S. 275, 277 (1970) (Burger, J., joins).
Zemel v. Rusk, 381 U.S. 1, 20 (1965).
Zorach v. Clauson, 343 U.S. 306, 315 (1952).
Zuber v. Allen, 396 U.S. 168, 197 (1969) (White, J., joins).

C. Concurring Opinions

Adickes v. S.H. Kress & Co., 398 U.S. 144, 175 (1970).
Aptheker v. Secretary of State, 378 U.S. 500, 517 (1964).
Armstrong v. Armstrong, 350 U.S. 568, 575 (1956) (Warren, C.J., and Douglas and Clark, JJ., join).
Aro Manufacturing Co. v. Convertible Top Replacement Co., 365 U.S. 336, 346 (1961).
Ashe v. Swenson, 397 U.S. 436, 447 (1970).
Associated Press v. Walker, 388 U.S. 130, 170 (1967) (Douglas, J., joins).
Baldwin v. New York, 399 U.S. 66, 74 (1970) (Douglas, J., joins).
Barr v. Matteo, 360 U.S. 564, 576 (1959).
Bates v. Little Rock, 361 U.S. 516, 527 (1960) (Douglas, J., concurs).
Board of County Commissioners v. United States, 308 U.S. 343, 353 (1939).
Brandenburg v. Ohio, 395 U.S. 444, 449 (1969).

Carnley v. Cochran, 369 U.S. 506, 517 (1962).

Carter v. Jury Commission, 396 U.S. 320, 341 (1970).

Carter v. Virginia, 321 U.S. 131, 138 (1944).

Central Railroad Company v. Pennsylvania, 370 U.S. 607, 618 (1962).

Chandler v. Wise, 307 U.S. 474, 478 (1939) (Douglas, J., joins).

Coleman v. Alabama, 399 U.S. 1, 11 (1970).

Coleman v. Miller, 307 U.S. 433, 456 (1939) (Roberts, Frankfurter, and Douglas, JJ., join).

Cox v. Louisiana, 379 U.S. 536, 558 (1965); concurring opinion reported at *Cox v. Louisiana*, 379 U.S. 559, 575 (1965).

Dandridge v. Williams, 397 U.S. 471, 489 (1970) (Burger, C.J., joins).

Duncan v. Louisiana, 391 U.S. 145, 162 (1968) (Douglas, J., joins).

Durfee v. Duke, 375 U.S. 106, 116 (1963).

Epperson v. Arkansas, 393 U.S. 97, 109 (1968).

Federal Power Commission v. Hope Natural Gas Co., 320 U.S. 591, 619 (1944) (Murphy, J., joins).

Federal Power Commission v. Natural Gas Pipeline Co., 315 U.S. 575, 599 (1942) (Douglas and Murphy, JJ., join).

First Unitarian Church v. Los Angeles County, 357 U.S. 545, 547 (1958); concurring opinion reported at *Speiser v. Randall*, 357 U.S. 513, 529 (1958) (Douglas, J., joins).

Garrison v. Louisiana, 379 U.S. 64, 79 (1964) (Douglas, J., joins).

Gault, In re, 387 U.S. 1, 59 (1967).

Gibson v. Florida Legislative Investigation Committee, 372 U.S. 539, 558 (1963).

Graver Tank & Manufacturing Co. v. Linde Air Products Co., 336 U.S. 271, 280 (1949) (Douglas, J., joins).

Gregory v. Chicago, 394 U.S. 111, 113 (1969) (Douglas, J., joins).

Grunewald v. United States, 353 U.S. 391, 425 (1957) (Warren, C.J., and Douglas and Brennan, JJ., join).

Heart of Atlanta Motel v. United States, 379 U.S. 241, 268 (1964).

Helvering v. Gerhardt, 304 U.S. 405, 424 (1938).

Hoyt v. Florida, 368 U.S. 57, 69 (1961) (Warren, C.J., and Douglas, J., join).

Jacobellis v. Ohio, 378 U.S. 184, 196 (1964) (Douglas, J., joins).

Jenkins v. McKeithen, 395 U.S. 411, 432 (1969).

Joint Anti-Fascist Refugee Committee v. McGrath, 341 U.S. 123, 142 (1951).

Katzenbach v. McClung, 379 U.S. 294, 305 (1964); concurring opinion reported at *Heart of Atlanta Motel v. United States*, 379 U.S. 241, 268 (1964).
Keegan v. United States, 325 U.S. 478, 495 (1945).
Kingsley International Pictures Corp. v. Regents of the University of the State of New York, 360 U.S. 684, 690 (1959).
Knauer v. United States, 328 U.S. 654, 674 (1946).
Leary v. United States, 395 U.S. 6, 55 (1969).
Lee v. Washington, 390 U.S. 333, 334 (1968) (Harlan and Stewart, JJ., join).
McCarthy v. United States, 394 U.S. 459, 477 (1969).
Maggio v. Zeitz, 333 U.S. 56, 78 (1948) (Rutledge, J., concurs).
Mapp v. Ohio, 367 U.S. 643, 661 (1961).
Marcus v. Search Warrant of Property, 367 U.S. 717, 738 (1961) (Douglas, J., joins).
Mercoid Corp. v. Mid-Continent Investment Co., 320 U.S. 661, 672 (1944).
Michigan National Bank v. Robertson, 372 U.S. 591, 594 (1963) (Douglas, J., joins).
Morgan v. Virginia, 328 U.S. 373, 386 (1946).
Moseley v. Electronic & Missile Facilities, 374 U.S. 167, 172 (1963) (Warren, C.J., joins).
National Labor Relations Board v. Fruit & Vegetable Packers & Warehousemen, 377 U.S. 58, 76 (1964).
National Labor Relations Board v. Wyman-Gordon Co., 394 U.S. 759, 769 (1969) (Brennan and Marshall, JJ., join).
New York Times Co. v. Sullivan, 376 U.S. 254, 293 (1964) (Douglas, J., joins).
New York Times Co. v. United States, 403 U.S. 713, 714 (1971) (Douglas, J., joins).
Nishikawa v. Dulles, 356 U.S. 129, 138 (1958) (Douglas, J., joins).
Northwest Airlines Inc. v. Minnesota, 322 U.S. 292, 301 (1944).
Noto v. United States, 367 U.S. 290, 300 (1961).
One 1958 Plymouth Sedan v. Pennsylvania, 380 U.S. 693, 703 (1965).
Oyama v. California, 332 U.S. 633, 647 (1948) (Douglas, J., joins).
Parker v. North Carolina, 397 U.S. 790, 799 (1970).
Peters v. Hobby, 349 U.S. 331, 349 (1955).
Peters v. New York, 392 U.S. 40, 79 (1968).

Polish National Alliance v. National Labor Relations Board, 322 U.S. 643, 651 (1944).
Powell v. Texas, 392 U.S. 514, 537 (1968) (Harlan, J., joins).
Pullman Co. v. Jenkins, 305 U.S. 534, 542 (1939).
A Quantity of Copies of Books v. Kansas, 378 U.S. 205, 213 (1964) (Douglas, J., concurs).
Rochin v. California, 342 U.S. 165, 174 (1952).
Rosenbloom v. Metromedia, Inc., 403 U.S. 29, 57 (1971).
Sawyer, In re, 360 U.S. 622, 646 (1959).
Simons v. Miami Beach First National Bank, 381 U.S. 81, 88 (1965) (Douglas, J., joins).
Smith v. California, 361 U.S. 147, 155 (1959).
Smyth v. United States, 302 U.S. 329, 364 (1937).
Speiser v. Randall, 357 U.S. 513, 529 (1958) (Douglas, J., joins).
Stanley v. Georgia, 394 U.S. 557, 568 (1969).
Taglianetti v. United States, 394 U.S. 316, 318 (1969).
Tenney v. Brandhove, 341 U.S. 367, 379 (1951).
Thorpe v. Housing Authority, 393 U.S. 268, 284 (1969).
Time, Inc. v. Hill, 385 U.S. 374, 398 (1967) (Douglas, J., joins).
Tot v. United States, 319 U.S. 463, 473 (1943) (Douglas, J., joins).
Trop v. Dulles, 356 U.S. 86, 104 (1958) (Douglas, J., joins).
United Gas Public Service Co. v. Texas, 303 U.S. 123, 146 (1938).
Unites States v. Alcea Band of Tillamooks, 329 U.S. 40, 54 (1946).
United States v. Bess, 357 U.S. 51, 59 (1958) (Warren, C.J., and Whittaker, J., join).
United States v. Five Gambling Devices, 346 U.S. 441, 452 (1953) (Douglas, J., joins).
United States v. Harris, 403 U.S. 573, 585 (1971).
United States v. Minker, 350 U.S. 179, 190 (1956).
United States v. Public Utilities Commission, 345 U.S. 295, 318 (1953).
United States v. Williams, 341 U.S. 70, 85 (1951).
Utah Fuel Co. v. National Bituminous Coal Commission, 306 U.S. 56, 62 (1939).
West Virginia State Board of Education v. Barnette, 319 U.S. 624, 643 (1943) (Douglas, J., joins).
Wieman v. Updegraff, 344 U.S. 183, 192 (1952).
Will v. United States, 389 U.S. 90, 107 (1967).
Willingham v. Morgan, 395 U.S. 402, 410 (1969).
Wolf v. Colorado, 338 U.S. 25, 39 (1949).

Z.& F. Assets Realization Corp. v. Hull, 311 U.S. 470, 490 (1941).

D. Statements Concurring and Dissenting in Part

Burlington Truck Lines v. United States, 371 U.S. 156, 174 (1962).
Citizens to Preserve Overton Park v. Volpe, 401 U.S. 402, 421 (1971) (Brennan, J., joins).
Coates v. City of Cincinnati, 402 U.S. 611, 616 (1971).
Commissioner v. Duberstein, 363 U.S. 278, 293 (1960).
Coolidge v. New Hampshire, 403 U.S. 443, 493 (1971).
Cox v. Louisiana, 379 U.S. 559, 575 (1965).
Curtis Publishing Co. v. Butts, 388 U.S. 130, 170 (1967).
Dennis v. United States, 384 U.S. 855, 875 (1966) (Douglas, J., joins).
England v. Medical Examiners, 375 U.S. 411, 437 (1964).
Federal Power Commission v. Interstate Natural Gas Co., 336 U.S. 577, 595 (1949).
Gilbert v. California, 388 U.S. 263, 277 (1967).
Jackson v. Denno, 378 U.S. 368, 401 (1964) (Clark, J., joins).
James v. United States, 366 U.S. 213, 222 (1961) (Douglas, J., joins).
Lear, Inc. v. Adkins, 395 U.S. 653, 676 (1969) (Warren, C.J., and Douglas, J., join).
McGautha v. California, 402 U.S. 183, 225 (1971).
Meltzer v. Buck Lecraw & Co., 402 U.S. 954, 954 (1971).
Mills v. Electric Auto-Lite Co., 396 U.S. 375, 397 (1970).
Monitor Patriot Co. v. Roy, 401 U.S. 265, 277 (1971) (Douglas, J., joins).
North Carolina v. Pearce, 395 U.S. 711, 737 (1969).
Ocala Star-Banner Co. v. Damron, 401 U.S. 295, 301 (1971); opinion reported at *Monitor Patriot Co. v. Roy*, 401 U.S. 265, 277 (1971) (Douglas, J., joins).
Polizzi v. Cowles Magazines, Inc., 345 U.S. 663, 667 (1953) (Jackson, J., joins).
Public Utilities Commission v. Pollak, 343 U.S. 451, 466 (1952).
Rosenblatt v. Baer, 383 U.S. 75, 94 (1966) (Douglas, J., joins).
Schlagenhauf v. Holder, 379 U.S. 104, 122 (1964) (Clark, J., joins).
Sibron v. New York, 392 U.S. 40, 79 (1968).
Simmons v. United States, 390 U.S. 377, 395 (1968).
Simpson v. Union Oil Co., 396 U.S. 13, 15 (1969).

South Carolina v. Katzenbach, 383 U.S. 301, 355 (1966).
Time, Inc. v. Pape, 401 U.S. 279, 292 (1971); opinion reported at *Monitor Patriot Co. v. Roy*, 401 U.S. 265, 277 (1971) (Douglas, J., joins).
United States v. Louisiana, 363 U.S. 1, 85 (1960).
United States v. United Mine Workers, 330 U.S. 258, 328 (1947) (Douglas, J., joins).
United States v. Wade, 388 U.S. 218, 243 (1967).
Williams v. Florida, 399 U.S. 78, 106 (1970) (Douglas, J., joins).
Yates v. United States, 354 U.S. 298, 339 (1957) (Douglas, J., joins).

E. Statements In Dissent

Adams v. Washington, 403 U.S. 947, 947 (1971).
Adams Newark Theater Co. v. Newark, 354 U.S. 931, 931 (1957).
Adirondack Transit Lines, Inc. v. Hudson Transit Lines, Inc., 338 U.S. 802, 802 (1949).
Akins v. Texas, 325 U.S. 398, 407 (1945).
Albertson v. Millard, 345 U.S. 242, 245 (1953).
Alderman v. United States, 394 U.S. 165, 187 (1969).
Allen Calculators, Inc. v. National Cash Register Co., 322 U.S. 137, 143 (1944).
Alton v. Alton, No. 531, 347 U.S. 610, 611 (1954).
American Civil Liberties Union v. Chicago, 348 U.S. 979, 979 (1955).
American Oil Co. v. Neill, 380 U.S. 451, 459 (1965).
American Trucking Associations v. Atchison, Topeka & Santa Fe Railway, 387 U.S. 397, 422 (1967).
Anastaplo, In re, 348 U.S. 946, 946 (1955).
Anderson v. Jordan, 343 U.S. 912, 912 (1952).
Anderson v. Louisiana, 403 U.S. 949, 949 (1971).
Angelet v. Fay, 381 U.S. 654, 656 (1965).
Asbury Hospital v. Cass County, 326 U.S. 207, 216 (1945).
Ashland Coal & Ice Co. v. United States, 325 U.S. 840, 840 (1945).
Associated Food Retailers of Greater Chicago v. Jewel Tea Co., 381 U.S. 761, 761 (1965).
Atkins v. Atkins, 326 U.S. 683, 683 (1945).
Atkinson v. North Carolina, 403 U.S. 948, 948 (1971).
Balistrieri v. United States, 395 U.S. 710, 710 (1969).

Barr v. Matteo, 355 U.S. 171, 178 (1957).
Beltowski v. Tahash, 381 U.S. 948, 948 (1965).
Benz v. New York State Thruway Authority, 369 U.S. 147, 148 (1962).
Berman v. Fay, 381 U.S. 955, 955 (1965).
Blackmar v. Guerre, 342 U.S. 512, 516 (1952).
Blow v. North Carolina, 379 U.S. 684, 686 (1965).
Boles v. Stevenson, 379 U.S. 43, 46 (1964).
Bounds v. Crawford, 393 U.S. 76, 76 (1968).
Briggs v. Elliott, 342 U.S. 350, 352 (1952).
Brotherhood of Locomotive Engineers v. Louisville & Nashville Railroad, 373 U.S. 33, 42 (1963).
Bruner v. United States, 343 U.S. 112, 117 (1952).
Bruns, Nordeman & Co. v. American National Bank & Trust Co., 393 U.S. 855, 855 (1968).
Buck v. Gallagher, 307 U.S. 95, 104 (1939).
California v. Hurst, 381 U.S. 760, 760 (1965).
California State Automobile Association Inter-Insurance Bureau v. Maloney, 341 U.S. 105, 111 (1951).
Callen v. Pennsylvania Railroad, 332 U.S. 625, 631 (1948).
Capital Service, Inc. v. National Labor Relations Board, 347 U.S. 501, 506 (1954).
Carney v. Lavallee, 381 U.S. 955, 955 (1965).
Carter v. General American Life Insurance Co., 323 U.S. 676, 676 (1944).
Catanzaro v. New York, 378 U.S. 573, 573 (1964).
Chemical Tank Lines, Inc. v. Holstine, 393 U.S. 78, 78 (1968).
Chicago, Milwaukee, St. Paul & Pacific Railroad v. Acme Fast Freight, Inc., 336 U.S. 465, 489 (1949).
Childs v. North Carolina, 403 U.S. 948, 948 (1971).
Cities Service Gas Co. v. Peerless Oil & Gas Co., 340 U.S. 179, 189 (1950).
Ciucci v. Illinois, 356 U.S. 571, 575 (1958).
Clark v. Gabriel, 393 U.S. 256, 259 (1968).
Clark v. Paul Gray, Inc., 306 U.S. 583, 600 (1939).
Clark v. Smith, 403 U.S. 946, 946 (1971).
Cleveland v. United States, 329 U.S. 14, 20 (1946).
Colegrove v. Barrett, 330 U.S. 804, 804 (1947).
Collett, Ex Parte, 337 U.S. 55, 72 (1949).
The Colony, Inc. v. Commissioner, 357 U.S. 28, 38 (1958).

Commissioner v. Cooper, 381 U.S. 274, 274 (1965).
Commissioner v. Korell, 339 U.S. 619, 628 (1950).
Conner v. Simler, 367 U.S. 486, 486 (1961).
Cook v. United States, 392 U.S. 646, 646 (1968).
Cosmopolitan Shipping Co. v. McAllister, 337 U.S. 783, 801 (1949).
County Board of Arlington County v. State Milk Commission, 346 U.S. 932, 932 (1954).
Crawford v. Bannan, 381 U.S. 955, 955 (1965).
Daniel v. Goliday, 398 U.S. 73, 73 (1970).
Davis v. Board of Regents, 348 U.S. 934, 934 (1955).
Davis v. Board of School Commissioners, 400 U.S. 804, 804 (1970).
Dayton Rubber Co. v. Cordovan Associates, Inc., 364 U.S. 299, 299 (1960).
DeGregory v. Attorney General, 368 U.S. 19, 19 (1961).
Del Hoyo v. New York, 378 U.S. 570, 570 (1964).
Department of Alcoholic Beverage Control v. Ammex Warehouse Co. of San Ysidro, Inc., 378 U.S. 124, 124 (1964).
Desper v. Starved Rock Ferry Co., 342 U.S. 187, 192 (1952).
Donaducy v. Pennsylvania, 349 U.S. 913, 913 (1955).
Drews v. Maryland, 378 U.S. 547, 547 (1964).
Eastman v. Fay, 381 U.S. 954, 954 (1965).
Eckenrode v. Pennsylvania Railroad, 335 U.S. 329, 330 (1948).
Elder v. Brannan, 341 U.S. 277, 289 (1951).
Ellis v. Dixon, 349 U.S. 458, 464 (1955).
Esso Standard Oil Co. v. Evans, 345 U.S. 495, 501 (1953).
Etchieson v. Texas, 378 U.S. 589, 589 (1964).
Fannon v. United States, 394 U.S. 457, 457 (1969).
Federal Communications Commission v. RCA Communications, 346 U.S. 86, 98 (1953).
Federal Crop Insurance Corp. v. Merrill, 332 U.S. 380, 386 (1947).
Federal Power Commission v. Wisconsin, 346 U.S. 935, 935 (1954).
Fink v. Shepard Steamship Co., 337 U.S. 810, 816 (1949).
Fischer, In re, 391 U.S. 600, 600 (1968).
Fowler v. Wilkinson, 353 U.S. 583, 585 (1957).
Fox v. North Carolina, 378 U.S. 587, 589 (1964).
Fred Fisher Music Co. v. M. Witmark & Sons, 318 U.S. 643, 659 (1943).
Freeman v. Hewit, 329 U.S. 249, 259 (1946).
Fuller v. Alaska, 393 U.S. 80, 81 (1968).

Gaston County, North Carolina v. United States, 395 U.S. 285, 297 (1969).
General Electric Co. v. Local Union 191, International Union of Electrical, Radio & Machine Workers, 398 U.S. 436, 436 (1970).
General Motors Corp. v. District of Columbia, 380 U.S. 553, 562 (1965).
Gilbert v. United States, 370 U.S. 650, 659 (1962).
Giordano v. United States, 394 U.S. 310, 313 (1969).
Graham v. Pennsylvania Railroad, 381 U.S. 904, 904 (1965).
Hackney v. Machado, 397 U.S. 593, 593 (1970).
Haines v. Southern Pacific Co., 393 U.S. 860, 860 (1968).
Hammerstein v. Superior Court, 341 U.S. 491, 493 (1951).
Hanauer v. Elkins, 358 U.S. 643, 643 (1959).
Harris v. New York, 401 U.S. 222, 226 (1971).
Harris v. Texas, 378 U.S. 572, 572 (1964).
Harris v. Texas, 403 U.S. 947, 947 (1971).
Harris v. United States, 359 U.S. 19, 24 (1959).
Hass v. New York, 338 U.S. 803, 803 (1949).
Heiser v. Woodruff, 327 U.S. 726, 740 (1946).
Heisey v. Alameda, 352 U.S. 921, 921 (1956).
Helvering v. Credit Alliance Corp., 316 U.S. 107, 113 (1942).
Henderson v. Pryor, 394 U.S. 969, 969 (1969).
Hobson v. Board of Elections, 402 U.S. 988, 988 (1971).
Hoffa v. United States, 387 U.S. 231, 234 (1967).
Holt v. Alleghany Corp., 384 U.S. 28, 28 (1966).
Hopper v. Louisiana, 392 U.S. 658, 658 (1968).
Hortencio v. Whitehead, 402 U.S. 966, 966 (1971).
Houston Insulation Contractors Association v. National Labor Relations Board, 386 U.S. 664, 669 (1967).
Hunt v. Connecticut, 392 U.S. 304, 304 (1968).
Hunter v. Tennessee, 403 U.S. 711, 712 (1971).
Hunter v. Texas Electric Railway, 332 U.S. 827, 827 (1947).
Indiana Department of State Revenue v. Nebeker, 348 U.S. 933, 933 (1955).
Indiana ex rel. Valentine v. Marker, 303 U.S. 628, 628 (1938).
International Brotherhood of Teamsters v. Denver Milk Producers, Inc., 334 U.S. 809, 809 (1948).
International Brotherhood of Teamsters v. Hanke, 339 U.S. 470, 481 (1950).

International Union, United Automobile, Aircraft & Agricultural Implement Workers of America v. Anderson, 351 U.S. 959, 959 (1956).
Interstate Circuit v. United States, 304 U.S. 55, 58 (1938).
Interstate Commerce Commission v. New York Central Railroad, 342 U.S. 890, 890 (1951).
Jackson v. Department of Public Welfare, 397 U.S. 589, 589 (1970).
Jackson v. Taylor, 353 U.S. 569, 585 (1957).
Jenkins v. Delaware, 395 U.S. 213, 222 (1969).
Johnson v. Bennett, 393 U.S. 253, 255 (1968).
Johnson v. New Jersey, 384 U.S. 719, 736 (1966).
Johnson v. United States, 333 U.S. 10, 17 (1948).
Jones v. Louisiana, 392 U.S. 302, 302 (1968).
Joseph v. Carter & Weekes Stevedoring Co., 330 U.S. 422, 434 (1947).
Karadzole v. Artukovic, 355 U.S. 393, 393 (1958).
Katchen v. Landy, 382 U.S. 323, 340 (1966).
Kelly v. Kosuga, 358 U.S. 516, 521 (1959).
Kennedy v. Silas Mason Co., 334 U.S. 249, 257 (1948).
Kennedy v. Walker, 337 U.S. 901, 901 (1949).
Kenosha Motor Coach Lines, Inc. v. Public Service Commission, 338 U.S. 805, 805 (1949).
Kerotest Manufacturing Co. v. C-O-Two Fire Equipment Co., 342 U.S. 180, 186 (1952).
Kilpatrick v. Texas & Pacific Railway, 337 U.S. 75, 78 (1949).
King v. United States, 344 U.S. 254, 276 (1952).
King v. United States, 379 U.S. 329, 340 (1964).
Kirk v. Wyoming, 389 U.S. 53, 53 (1967).
Klapprott v. United States, 336 U.S. 942, 942 (1949).
Koehler v. United States, 342 U.S. 852, 852 (1951).
Kolod v. United States, 390 U.S. 136, 138 (1968).
L'Hommedieu v. Board of Regents, 342 U.S. 951, 951 (1952).
Lampton v. Bonin, 397 U.S. 663, 663 (1970).
Lathan v. New York, 378 U.S. 566, 566 (1964).
Lisker v. Kelley, 401 U.S. 928, 928 (1971).
United Association of Journeymen Plumbers v. Graham, 345 U.S. 192, 201 (1953).
Lone Star Gas Co. v. Texas, 304 U.S. 224, 242 (1938).
Lopez v. Texas, 378 U.S. 567, 567 (1964).

Luckenbach Steamship Co. v. United States, 364 U.S. 280, 280 (1960).
Lykes v. United States, 343 U.S. 118, 127 (1952).
Lynch v. Maryland, 393 U.S. 915, 915 (1968).
Maass v. Higgins, 312 U.S. 443, 449 (1941).
McAllister Lighterage Line, Inc. v. United States, 327 U.S. 655, 661 (1946).
McDaniel v. Barresi, 400 U.S. 804, 804 (1970).
McDaniel v. North Carolina, 392 U.S. 665, 665 (1968).
McGowan v. Maryland, 366 U.S. 420, 429 (1961).
McGrath v. Kristensen, 340 U.S. 162, 189 (1950).
McIlvaine v. Louisiana, 379 U.S. 10, 10 (1964).
McKenzie v. Irving Trust Co., 323 U.S. 365, 372 (1945).
McKinney v. Missouri-Kansas-Texas Railroad, 357 U.S. 265, 274 (1958).
McKinnie v. Tennessee, 380 U.S. 449, 449 (1965).
McMahon v. United States, 342 U.S. 25, 28 (1951).
McNerlin v. Denno, 378 U.S. 575, 575 (1964).
Marshall v. United States, 360 U.S. 310, 313 (1959).
Martone v. Morgan, 393 U.S. 12, 12 (1968).
Memphis Steam Laundry Cleaner, Inc. v. Stone, 342 U.S. 389, 395 (1952).
Meredith v. Winter Haven, 320 U.S. 228, 238 (1943).
Metlakatla Indian Community, Annette Island Reserve v. Egan, 363 U.S. 555, 563 (1960).
Mitchell v. Charleston, 378 U.S. 551, 551 (1964).
Montgomery v. Burns, 394 U.S. 848, 848 (1969).
Mooney v. Smith, 305 U.S. 598, 598 (1938).
Morales v. New York, 396 U.S. 102, 106 (1969).
Morgan v. United States, 304 U.S. 1, 26 (1938).
Motorlease Corp. v. United States, 383 U.S. 573, 573 (1966).
Mrkonjic-Ruzic v. United States, 394 U.S. 454, 454 (1969).
Murphey v. Reed, 335 U.S. 865, 865 (1948).
Murphy v. United States, 369 U.S. 402, 402 (1962).
Muschette v. United States, 378 U.S. 569, 569 (1964).
Muth v. Aetna Oil Co., 342 U.S. 844, 844 (1951).
Named Individual Members of the San Antonio Conservation Society v. Texas Highway Department, 400 U.S. 961, 961 (1970).
National Labor Relations Board v. Milk Drivers & Dairy Employees Local Unions Nos. 338 and 680, 357 U.S. 345, 345 (1958).

National Labor Relations Board v. Sands Manufacturing Co., 306 U.S. 332, 346 (1939).
Neuberger v. Commissioner, 311 U.S. 83, 91 (1940).
New Orleans v. Barthe, 376 U.S. 189, 189 (1964).
New York v. Illinois, 313 U.S. 547, 547 (1941).
New York v. United States, 342 U.S. 882, 882 (1951).
New York, New Haven & Hartford Railroad v. Henagan, 364 U.S. 441, 442 (1960).
Nippert v. Richmond, 327 U.S. 416, 435 (1946).
Nostrand v. Little, 368 U.S. 436, 438 (1962).
Oister v. Pennsylvania, 378 U.S. 568, 568 (1964).
Oklahoma v. United States Civil Service Commission, 330 U.S. 127, 146 (1947).
On Lee v. United States, 343 U.S. 747, 758 (1952).
Osman v. Douds, 339 U.S. 846, 847 (1950).
Overton v. New York, 393 U.S. 85, 85 (1968).
Owen v. Arizona, 378 U.S. 574, 574 (1964).
Patterson v. United States, 359 U.S. 495, 497 (1959).
Pea v. United States, 378 U.S. 571, 571 (1964).
Phillips v. California, 386 U.S. 212, 212 (1967).
Phillips Petroleum Co. v. Oklahoma, 340 U.S. 190, 192 (1950).
Phillips Petroleum Co. v. Wisconsin, 346 U.S. 934, 934 (1954).
Piccirillo v. New York, 400 U.S. 548, 549 (1971).
Poe v. Ullman, 367 U.S. 497, 509 (1961).
Pope v. United States, 392 U.S. 651, 651 (1968).
Ray v. Seaboard Air Line Railroad, 393 U.S. 859, 859 (1968).
Redwine v. Georgia Railroad & Banking Co., 344 U.S. 925, 926 (1953).
Reserve Life Insurance Co. v. Bowers, 380 U.S. 258, 258 (1965).
Reynolds v. Atlantic Coast Line Railroad, 336 U.S. 207, 209 (1949).
Rice v. Rice, 336 U.S. 674, 676 (1949).
Richard S. v. New York, 397 U.S. 597, 597 (1970).
Riss & Company, Inc. v. United States, 320 U.S. 709, 710 (1943).
Roberts v. United States, 389 U.S. 18, 19 (1967).
Robinson v. Johnson, 394 U.S. 847, 847 (1969).
Robinson v. Tennessee, 392 U.S. 666, 666 (1968).
Rogers v. Quan, 357 U.S. 193, 196 (1958).
Rohr Aircraft Corp. v. San Diego, 362 U.S. 628, 636 (1960).
Rollerson v. United States, 394 U.S. 575, 575 (1969).

Rosenberg v. Denno, 346 U.S. 271, 271 (1953).
Rosenberg v. United States, 346 U.S. 322, 322 (1953).
Sabbath v. United States, 391 U.S. 585, 591 (1968).
Santana v. Texas, 397 U.S. 596, 596 (1970).
Secretary of Agriculture v. Central Roig Refining Co., 338 U.S. 604, 620 (1950).
Secretary of Agriculture v. United States, 347 U.S. 645, 655 (1954).
Securities & Exchange Commission v. National Securities, Inc., 393 U.S. 453, 469 (1969).
Senk v. Pennsylvania, 378 U.S. 562, 562 (1964).
Serio v. United States, 392 U.S. 305, 305 (1968).
Sheppard v. Maxwell, 384 U.S. 333, 363 (1966).
Sims v. Georgia, 385 U.S. 538, 544 (1967).
Smith v. Arizona, 389 U.S. 10, 10 (1967).
Southwestern Sugar & Molasses Co. v. River Terminals Corp., 360 U.S. 411, 422 (1959).
Spector Motor Service, Inc. v. McLaughlin, 323 U.S. 101, 106 (1944).
Spence v. North Carolina, 392 U.S. 649, 650 (1968).
Stafford v. Michigan, 402 U.S. 968, 968 (1971).
Stamler v. Willis, 393 U.S. 217, 217 (1968).
Standard Oil Co. v. Peck, 342 U.S. 382, 385 (1952).
Stark v. Wickard, 321 U.S. 288, 311 (1944).
Stembridge v. Georgia, 343 U.S. 541, 548 (1952).
Sterrett v. Grubb, 400 U.S. 922, 922 (1970).
Sugden v. United States, 351 U.S. 916, 916 (1956).
Sutton v. Leib, 342 U.S. 402, 412 (1952).
Swann v. Charlotte-Mecklenburg Board of Education, 399 U.S. 926, 926 (1970).
Swann v. Charlotte-Mecklenburg Board of Education, 400 U.S. 802, 802 (1970).
Taggart v. Weinacker's, Inc., 397 U.S. 223, 226 (1970).
Tak Shan Fong v. United States, 359 U.S. 102, 107 (1959).
Tampa Electric Co. v. Nashville Coal Co., 365 U.S. 320, 335 (1961).
Tehan v. United States ex rel. Shott, 382 U.S. 406, 419 (1966).
Tennessee v. United States, 346 U.S. 891, 891 (1953).
Texas v. Florida, 306 U.S. 398, 435 (1939).
Texas v. United States, 384 U.S. 155, 155 (1966).

Theatre Enterprises, Inc. v. Paramount Film Distributing Corp., 346 U.S. 537, 544 (1954).

Thibaut v. Car & General Insurance Corp., 332 U.S. 828, 828 (1947).

Thomas v. Arizona, 356 U.S. 390, 404 (1958).

Thomas v. Virginia, 364 U.S. 443, 443 (1960).

Tillman v. United States, 395 U.S. 830, 830 (1969).

Tooahnippah v. Hickel, 397 U.S. 598, 610 (1970).

Traffic Telephone Workers' Federation v. Driscoll, 332 U.S. 833, 833 (1947).

Transparent-Wrap Machine Corp. v. Stokes & Smith Co., 329 U.S. 637, 648 (1947).

Treichler v. Wisconsin, 338 U.S. 251, 257 (1949).

Two Guys From Harrison-Allentown, Inc. v. McGinley, 366 U.S. 582, 592 (1961).

Union National Bank v. Lamb, 337 U.S. 38, 45 (1949).

United States v. Aetna Casualty & Surety Co., 338 U.S. 366, 383 (1949).

United States v. Beacon Brass Co., 344 U.S. 43, 47 (1952).

United States v. Benedict, 338 U.S. 692, 699 (1950).

United States v. Brown, 333 U.S. 18, 27 (1948).

United States v. Burnison, 339 U.S. 87, 95 (1950).

United States v. Di Re, 332 U.S. 581, 595 (1948).

United States v. Esnault-Pelterie, 303 U.S. 26, 32 (1938).

United States v. Gilmore, 372 U.S. 39, 52 (1963).

United States v. Grainger, 346 U.S. 235, 248 (1953).

United States v. Mitchell, 322 U.S. 65, 71 (1944).

United States v. Munsingwear, Inc., 340 U.S. 36, 41 (1950).

United States v. Nunnally Investment Co., 316 U.S. 258, 265 (1942).

United States v. Oklahoma Gas & Electric Co., 318 U.S. 206, 218 (1943).

United States v. Oregon State Medical Society, 343 U.S. 326, 340 (1952).

United States v. Patrick, 372 U.S. 53, 57 (1963).

United States v. Reidel, 402 U.S. 351, 357 (1971).

United States v. Reynolds, 345 U.S. 1, 12 (1953).

United States v. Robinson, 361 U.S. 220, 230 (1960).

United States v. Rock Island Motor Transit Co., 340 U.S. 419, 449 (1951).

United States v. Shannon, 342 U.S. 288, 294 (1952).
United States v. Shimer, 367 U.S. 374, 388 (1961).
United States v. Silk, 331 U.S. 704, 719 (1947).
United States v. Standard Rice Co., 323 U.S. 106, 111 (1944).
United States v. Swift & Co., 318 U.S. 442, 446 (1943).
United States v. Texas & Pacific Motor Transport Co., 340 U.S. 450, 461 (1951).
United States v. Urbuteit, 335 U.S. 355, 358 (1948).
United States v. Wayne Pump Co., 317 U.S. 200, 210 (1942).
United States v. Williams, 341 U.S. 58, 69 (1951).
United States v. Yellow Cab Co., 340 U.S. 543, 557 (1951).
United States ex rel. Touchy v. Ragen, 340 U.S. 462, 470 (1951).
United States Gypsum Co. v. Glander, 337 U.S. 951, 951 (1949).
Uphaus v. Wyman, 360 U.S. 72, 108 (1959).
Wade v. Yeager, 392 U.S. 661, 661 (1968).
Walder v. United States, 347 U.S. 62, 66 (1954).
Walker v. Georgia, 381 U.S. 355, 355 (1965).
Wallis v. Pan American Petroleum Corp., 384 U.S. 63, 72 (1966).
Weade v. Dichmann, Wright & Pugh, Inc., 337 U.S. 801, 809 (1949).
West Point Wholesale Grocery Co. v. City of Opelika, Alabama, 354 U.S. 390, 392 (1957).
Wheat v. Washington, 392 U.S. 652, 652 (1968).
Wheeler v. Montgomery, 397 U.S. 280, 282 (1970).
White v. Evansville American Legion Home Association, 393 U.S. 859, 859 (1968).
White v. Howard, 347 U.S. 910, 910 (1954).
Whyy, Inc. v. Burrough of Glassboro, 393 U.S. 117, 121 (1968).
Williams v. North Carolina, 378 U.S. 548, 548 (1964).
Williams v. United States, 341 U.S. 97, 104 (1951).
Wilson v. Louisiana, 341 U.S. 901, 901 (1951).
Witmer v. United States, 348 U.S. 375, 384 (1955).
Womble v. United States, 324 U.S. 830, 830 (1945).
Wood v. United States, 389 U.S. 20, 21 (1967).
Yates v. United States, 355 U.S. 66, 76 (1957).
Yonkers v. United States, 321 U.S. 745, 745 (1944).
Youngdahl v. Rainfair, Inc., 355 U.S. 131, 140 (1957).
Zim Israel Navigation Co. v. Tarabocchia, 401 U.S. 930, 930 (1971).
Zimmerman v. Maryland, 336 U.S. 901, 901 (1949).

F. Statements In Concurrence

Albertson v. Subversive Activities Control Board, 382 U.S. 70, 82 (1965).
Aquilino v. United States, 363 U.S. 509, 521 (1960).
Bailey v. Patterson, 368 U.S. 346, 347 (1961).
Bob-Lo Excursion Co. v. Michigan, 333 U.S. 28, 43 (1948).
A Book Named "John Cleland's Memoirs of a Woman of Pleasure" v. Attorney General, 383 U.S. 413, 421 (1966).
Boulden v. Holman, 394 U.S. 478, 485 (1969).
Braunfeld v. Brown, 366 U.S. 599, 600 (1961).
Brotherhood of Railway & Steamship Clerks v. Allen, 373 U.S. 113, 124 (1963).
Building Service Employees International Union, Local 262 v. Gazzam, 339 U.S. 532, 541 (1950).
Cardinale v. Louisiana, 394 U.S. 437, 439 (1969).
Chandler v. Wise, 307 U.S. 474, 478 (1939).
Charleston Federal Savings & Loan Association v. Alderson, 324 U.S. 182, 192 (1945).
Cichos v. Indiana, 385 U.S. 76, 80 (1966).
Cipriano v. Houma, 395 U.S. 701, 707 (1969).
Commissioner v. Culbertson, 337 U.S. 733, 748 (1949).
Cramp v. Board of Public Instruction, 368 U.S. 278, 288 (1961).
Desist v. United States, 394 U.S. 244, 254 (1969).
Gallagher v. Crown Kosher Super Market of Massachusetts, Inc., 366 U.S. 617, 618 (1961).
Gibbs v. Burke, 337 U.S. 773, 782 (1949).
Gojack v. United States, 384 U.S. 702, 717 (1966).
Greenbelt Cooperative Publishing Association v. Bresler, 398 U.S. 6, 24 (1970).
Hamilton v. Alabama, 376 U.S. 650, 650 (1964).
Harris v. South Carolina, 338 U.S. 68, 71 (1949).
Henry v. Collins, 380 U.S. 356, 358 (1965).
Henry v. Mississippi, 388 U.S. 901, 901 (1967).
Hess v. United States, 361 U.S. 314, 321 (1960).
Howard v. Lyons, 360 U.S. 593, 598 (1959).
Hughes v. Superior Court, 339 U.S. 460, 469 (1950).
Kaiser v. New York, 394 U.S. 280, 283 (1969).
Kedroff v. Saint Nicholas Cathedral of the Russian Orthodox Church, 344 U.S. 94, 126 (1952).
Kennedy v. Mendoza-Martinez, 372 U.S. 144, 186 (1963).

Lee Art Theatre, Inc. v. Virginia, 392 U.S. 636, 637 (1968).
Lustig v. United States, 338 U.S. 74, 80 (1949).
McMann v. Richardson, 397 U.S. 759, 775 (1970).
Marakar v. United States, 370 U.S. 723, 723 (1962).
Morford v. United States, 339 U.S. 258, 259 (1950).
Murphy v. Waterfront Commission, 378 U.S. 52, 80 (1964).
On Lee v. United States, 343 U.S. 924, 924 (1952).
Petty v. Tennessee-Missouri Bridge Commission, 359 U.S. 275, 283 (1959).
Pope v. Atlantic Coast Line Railroad, 345 U.S. 379, 387 (1953).
St. Amant v. Thompson, 390 U.S. 727, 733 (1968).
Schneider v. Smith, 390 U.S. 17, 27 (1968).
Shenandoah Valley Broadcasting v. American Society of Composers, 375 U.S. 39, 41 (1963).
Slochower v. Board of Higher Education, 350 U.S. 551, 559 (1956).
Smith v. Hooey, 393 U.S. 374, 383 (1969).
Teitel Film Corp. v. Cusack, 390 U.S. 139, 142 (1968).
Turner v. Pennsylvania, 338 U.S. 62, 66 (1949).
United States v. Bess, 357 U.S. 51, 59 (1958).
United States v. Continental National Bank & Trust Co., 305 U.S. 398, 409 (1939).
United States v. Romano, 382 U.S. 136, 144 (1965).
United States Bulk Carriers, Inc. v. Arguelles, 400 U.S. 351, 358 (1971).
Universal Oil Products Co. v. Root Refining Co., 328 U.S. 575, 581 (1946).
Waller v. Florida, 397 U.S. 387, 395 (1970).
Watts v. Indiana, 338 U.S. 49, 55 (1949).

G. *Statements Concurring in Part*

Adam v. Saenger, 303 U.S. 59, 68 (1938).
Alabama Power Co. v. Ickes, 302 U.S. 464, 485 (1938).
American Power & Light Co. v. Securities & Exchange Commission, 325 U.S. 385, 393 (1945).
American Toll Bridge Co. v. Railroad Commission, 307 U.S. 486, 496 (1939).
American Trucking Associations v. United States, 326 U.S. 77, 87 (1945).
Askew v. Hargrave, 401 U.S. 476, 479 (1971).

Associated Press v. Walker, 389 U.S. 28, 28 (1967).
Avery v. Georgia, 345 U.S. 559, 563 (1953).
Bantam Books, Inc. v. Sullivan, 372 U.S. 58, 72 (1963).
Baxstrom v. Herold, 383 U.S. 107, 115 (1966).
Beckley Newspapers Corp. v. Hanks, 389 U.S. 81, 85 (1969).
Beecher v. Alabama, 389 U.S. 35, 38 (1967).
Bell v. Burson, 402 U.S. 535, 543 (1971).
Blount v. Rizzi, 400 U.S. 410, 422 (1971).
Brady v. United States, 397 U.S. 742, 758 (1970).
Braniff Airways, Inc. v. Nebraska State Board of Equalization & Assessment, 347 U.S. 590, 602 (1954).
Brooks v. Florida, 389 U.S. 413, 415 (1967).
Brotherhood of Railway & Steamship Clerks v. Association for the Benefit of Noncontract Employees, 380 U.S. 650, 671 (1965).
Bruton v. United States, 391 U.S. 123, 137 (1968).
Bryan v. United States, 338 U.S. 552, 560 (1950).
Butler v. Michigan, 352 U.S. 380, 384 (1957).
Callanan Road Improvement Co. v. United States, 345 U.S. 507, 513 (1953).
Carolene Products Co. v. United States, 323 U.S. 18, 32 (1944).
Carroll v. President & Commissioners of Princess Anne, 393 U.S. 175, 185 (1969).
Carter v. West Feliciana School Board, 396 U.S. 290, 293 (1970).
Castaldi v. United States, 384 U.S. 886, 886 (1966).
Chapman v. United States, 365 U.S. 610, 618 (1961).
Charles Dowd Box Co. v. Courtney, 368 U.S. 502, 514 (1962).
City of Phoenix v. Kolodziejski, 399 U.S. 204, 215 (1970).
Clewis v. Texas, 386 U.S. 707, 712 (1967).
Collier v. United States, 384 U.S. 59, 62 (1966).
Colombo v. New York, 400 U.S. 16, 16 (1970).
Communist Party, U.S.A. v. Catherwood, 367 U.S. 389, 395 (1961).
Davis v. North Carolina, 384 U.S. 737, 753 (1966).
Denver Union Stock Yard Co. v. United States, 304 U.S. 470, 485 (1938).
Dibella v. United States, 369 U.S. 121, 133 (1962).
Dixie Ohio Express Co. v. State Revenue Commission, 306 U.S. 72, 79 (1939).
Duke Power Co. v. Greenwood County, 302 U.S. 485, 490 (1938).
Faulkner v. Gibbs, 338 U.S. 267, 268 (1949).

Federal Land Bank v. Board of County Commissioners, 368 U.S. 146, 156 (1961).
Federal Trade Commission v. Henry Broch & Co., 368 U.S. 360, 368 (1962).
Federal Trade Commission v. Ruberoid Co., 343 U.S. 470, 480 (1952).
Ferguson v. Moore-McCormack Lines, Inc., 352 U.S. 521, 564 (1957).
Fogarty v. United States, 340 U.S. 8, 14 (1950).
Ford Motor Co. v. Beauchamp, 308 U.S. 331, 337 (1939).
Gange Lumber Co. v. Rowley, 326 U.S. 295, 308 (1945).
Gardner v. Broderick, 392 U.S. 273, 279 (1968).
Gardner v. California, 393 U.S. 367, 371 (1969).
Georgia v. Evans, 316 U.S. 159, 163 (1942).
Gillette v. United States, 401 U.S. 437, 463 (1971).
Gojack v. United States, 384 U.S. 702, 717 (1966).
Great Northern Railway v. Leionidas, 305 U.S. 1, 3 (1938).
Hanna v. Plumer, 380 U.S. 460, 474 (1965).
Henry v. United States, 361 U.S. 98, 104 (1959).
Hill v. California, 401 U.S. 797, 806 (1971).
International Harvester Credit Corp. v. Goodrich, 350 U.S. 537, 548 (1956).
Interstate Circuit, Inc. v. City of Dallas, 391 U.S. 53, 53 (1968).
Jenness v. Fortson, 403 U.S. 431, 442 (1971).
John Kelley Co. v. Commissioner, 326 U.S. 521, 530 (1946).
Jones v. State Board of Education ex rel. Tennessee, 397 U.S. 31, 32 (1970).
Kennedy v. Mendoza-Martinez, 372 U.S. 144, 186 (1963).
Kotteakos v. United States, 328 U.S. 750, 777 (1946).
Kunz v. New York, 340 U.S. 290, 295 (1951).
Local 761, International Union of Electrical Workers v. National Labor Relations Board, 366 U.S. 667, 682 (1961).
McDonald v. United States, 335 U.S. 451, 456 (1948).
Machibroda v. United States, 368 U.S. 487, 496 (1962).
Manual Enterprises, Inc. v. Day, 370 U.S. 478, 495 (1962).
Mayberry v. Pennsylvania, 400 U.S. 455, 466 (1971).
Mayo v. United States, 319 U.S. 441, 448 (1943).
Memphis Natural Gas Co. v. Stone, 335 U.S. 80, 96 (1948).
Mercantile National Bank v. Langdeau, 371 U.S. 555, 567 (1963).
Minor v. United States, 396 U.S. 87, 98 (1969).

Mitchell v. Donovan, 398 U.S. 427, 432 (1970).
Moon v. Maryland, 398 U.S. 319, 321 (1970).
Moser v. United States, 341 U.S. 41, 47 (1951).
Musser v. Utah, 333 U.S. 95, 98 (1948).
National Labor Relations Board v. Reliance Fuel Oil Corp., 371 U.S. 224, 227 (1963).
National Labor Relations Board v. Strong, 393 U.S. 357, 362 (1969).
National Labor Relations Board v. United Steelworkers, 357 U.S. 357, 365 (1958).
Niemotko v. Maryland, 340 U.S. 268, 273 (1951).
North Carolina v. Alford, 400 U.S. 25, 39 (1970).
Noyd v. Bond, 395 U.S. 683, 699 (1969).
Offutt v. United States, 348 U.S. 11, 18 (1954).
Perkins v. Benguet Consolidated Mining Co., 342 U.S. 437, 449 (1952).
Pinto v. Pierce, 389 U.S. 31, 33 (1967).
Price v. Moss, 374 U.S. 103, 103 (1963).
Procunier v. Atchley, 400 U.S. 446, 454 (1971).
Prudential Insurance Co. v. Benjamin, 328 U.S. 408, 440 (1946).
Railroad Commission v. Pacific Gas & Electric Co., 302 U.S. 388, 401 (1938).
Rescue Army v. Municipal Court, 331 U.S. 549, 585 (1947).
Roberts v. Russell, 392 U.S. 293, 295 (1968).
Sage Stores Co. v. Kansas ex rel. Mitchell, 323 U.S. 32, 36 (1944).
Sanks v. Georgia, 401 U.S. 144, 153 (1971).
Schwartz v. Texas, 344 U.S. 199, 204 (1952).
Shields v. Utah Idaho Central Railroad, 305 U.S. 177, 187 (1938).
Shillitani v. United States, 384 U.S. 364, 372 (1966).
Shipley v. California, 395 U.S. 818, 820 (1969).
Shuttlesworth v. Birmingham, 394 U.S. 147, 159 (1969).
Simmons v. United States, 348 U.S. 397, 406 (1955).
Sinclair & Carroll Co. v. Interchemical Corp., 325 U.S. 327, 335 (1945).
Slochower v. Board of Higher Education, 350 U.S. 551, 559 (1956).
Southern Pacific Co. v. Gallagher, 306 U.S. 167, 181 (1939).
Steele v. Louisville & Nashville Railroad, 323 U.S. 192, 208 (1944).
Stefanelli v. Minard, 342 U.S. 117, 124 (1951).
Swain v. Alabama, 380 U.S. 202, 228 (1965).
Taggart v. New York, 392 U.S. 667, 667 (1968).

Tate v. Short, 401 U.S. 395, 401 (1971).
Terry v. Ohio, 392 U.S. 1, 31 (1968).
Texas Gas Transmission Corp. v. Shell Oil Co., 363 U.S. 263, 277 (1960).
Thompson v. United States, 400 U.S. 17, 17 (1970).
Tom We Shung v. Brownell, 346 U.S. 906, 906 (1953).
Toomer v. Witsell, 334 U.S. 385, 407 (1948).
Uniformed Sanitation Men Association v. Commissioner of Sanitation, 392 U.S. 280, 285 (1968).
United States v. Carolene Products Co., 304 U.S. 144, 155 (1938).
United States v. County of Allegheny, 322 U.S. 174, 192 (1944).
United States v. Gerlach Live Stock Co., 339 U.S. 725, 756 (1950).
United States v. Great Northern Railway, 343 U.S. 562, 578 (1952).
United States v. Hancock Truck Lines, Inc., 324 U.S. 774, 780 (1945).
United States v. Hayman, 342 U.S. 205, 224 (1952).
United States v. Jorn, 400 U.S. 470, 488 (1971).
United States v. Klamath & Moadoc Tribes of Indians, 304 U.S. 119, 126 (1938).
United States v. Price, 383 U.S. 787, 807 (1966).
United States v. Rock Royal Co-Operative, Inc., 307 U.S. 533, 582 (1939).
United States v. Rompel, 326 U.S. 367, 370 (1945).
United States v. Sisson, 399 U.S. 267, 308 (1970).
United States v. United States Coin & Currency, Inc., 401 U.S. 715, 724 (1971).
United States v. White, 401 U.S. 745, 754 (1971).
United States v. Yellow Cab Co., 332 U.S. 218, 234 (1947).
Universal Camera Corp. v. National Labor Relations Board, 340 U.S. 474, 497 (1951).
Van Dusen v. Barrack, 376 U.S. 612, 646 (1964).
Von Cleef v. New Jersey, 395 U.S. 814, 816 (1969).
Warden v. Hayden, 387 U.S. 294, 310 (1967).
Weber v. Anheuser-Busch, Inc., 348 U.S. 468, 482 (1955).
West Virginia ex rel. Dyer v. Sims, 341 U.S. 22, 32 (1951).
Wetzel v. Ohio, 371 U.S. 62, 66 (1962).
Williams v. Oklahoma City, 395 U.S. 458, 460 (1969).
Williams v. United States, 401 U.S. 646, 660 (1971).

H. *Statements Dissenting in Part*

Barr v. Columbia, 578 U.S. 146, 151 (1964) (Harlan and White, JJ., join).
Colombo v. New York, 400 U.S. 16, 16 (1970).
Great Northern Railway v. Leonidas, 305 U.S. 1, 3 (1938).
Hartford-Empire Co. v. United States, 323 U.S. 386, 435 (1945).
Mercantile National Bank v. Langdeau, 371 U.S. 555, 567 (1963).
Minor v. United States, 396 U.S. 87, 98 (1969).
Tom We Shung v. Brownell, 346 U.S. 906, 906 (1953).
United States v. Jorn, 400 U.S. 470, 488 (1971).
United States v. United States Gypsum Co., 340 U.S. 76, 95 (1950).

I. *Opinions As Circuit Justice*

Alexander v. Holmes County Board of Education, 396 U.S. 1218, 90 S. Ct. 14, 24 L. Ed. 2d 41 (1969).
Arrow Transportation Co. v. Southern Railway, 83 S. Ct. 1, 9 L. Ed. 2d 36 (1962).
Arrow Transportation Co. v. Southern Railway, 83 S. Ct. 3, 9 L. Ed. 2d 40 (1962).
Atlantic Coast Line Railroad v. Brotherhood of Locomotive Engineers, 396 U.S. 1201, 90 S. Ct. 9, 24 L. Ed. 2d 23 (1969).
Board of School Commissioners v. Davis, 84 S. Ct. 10, 11 L. Ed. 2d 26 (1963).
Corpus Christi School District v. Cisneros, 404 U.S. 1211, 90 S. Ct. 9, 30 L. Ed. 2d 15 (1971).
Davis v. Adams, 400 U.S. 1203, 91 S. Ct. 1, 27 L. Ed. 2d 20 (1970).
Edgar v. United States, 404 U.S. 1206, 92 S. Ct. 8, 30 L. Ed. 2d 10 (1971).
Fowler v. Adams, 400 U.S. 1205, 91 S. Ct. 2, 27 L. Ed. 2d 10 (1970).
Heart of Atlanta Motel, Inc. v. United States, 85 S. Ct. 1, 13 L. Ed. 2d 12 (1964).
Karr v. Schmidt, 401 U.S. 1201, 91 S. Ct. 592, 27 L. Ed. 2d 797 (1971).
Katzenbach v. McClung, 85 S. Ct. 6, 13 L. Ed. 2d 15 (1964).
King v. Smith, 88 S. Ct. 842, 19 L. Ed. 2d 971 (1968).
Mahan v. Howell, 404 U.S. 1201, 92 S. Ct. 1, 30 L. Ed. 2d 5 (1971).
Marcello v. United States, 400 U.S. 1208, 91 S. Ct. 7, 27 L. Ed. 2d 26 (1970).

Matthews v. Little, 396 U.S. 1223, 90 S. Ct. 17, 24 L. Ed. 2d 45 (1969).
Meredith v. Fair, 83 S. Ct. 10, 9 L. Ed. 2d 43 (1962).
National Labor Relations Board v. Getman, 404 U.S. 1204, 92 S. Ct. 7, 30 L. Ed. 2d 8 (1971).
Oden v. Brittain, 396 U.S. 1210, 90 S. Ct. 4, 24 L. Ed. 2d 32 (1969).
Owen v. Kennedy, 84 S. Ct. 12, 11 L. Ed. 2d 18 (1963).
Sellers v. United States, 89 S. Ct. 36, 21 L. Ed. 2d 64 (1968).

INDEX